SOMALIA

SOMALIA
A STATE IN SEARCH OF EXCEPTIONAL LEADERSHIP

DR. ABDURAHMAN ABDULLAHI "BAADIYOW"

LOOH
PRESS
1446/2024
Leicester, England
Mogadishu, Somalia

LOOH PRESS LTD.
Copyright © Dr. Abdurahman Abdullahi "Baadiyow" 2024
First Edition, First Print October 2024

PRINTED & DISTRIBUTED BY
Looh Press Ltd.
56 Lethbridge Close
Leicester, LE1 2EB
England. UK
www.LoohPress.com
LoohPress@gmail.com

CONTACT AUTHOR:
abdurahmanba@yahoo.com

A catalogue record for this book is available from the British Library.
British Library Cataloguing-in-Publication Data

COVER DESIGN & TYPESET
Kusmin (Looh Press)

ISBN
978-1-912411-85-6.   (Hardback)
978-1-912411-86-3.   (Paperback)

CONTENTS

DEDICATION

I dedicate this book to my father, Moalim Abdullahi, who instilled in me invaluable reading and writing skills, taught me the Quran, and inspired me to excel in all my endeavors. I also extend my deepest gratitude to my beloved and caring mother, Zainab Afrah Shador, whose unconditional love and support have been my guiding light. Both of my parents have passed away, and I pray that Allah grants them mercy. This book is also dedicated to my wife, Muhubo Haji Iman, whose unwavering support and extraordinary patience have been a cornerstone of our lives. Her remarkable strength and dedication in raising our seven children while I was often preoccupied with reconciliation, Islamic activism, building educational institutions, and state-building activities in Somalia are truly admirable.

I owe immense gratitude to my children for their unwavering support, love, and understanding. They have been a constant source of inspiration and motivation throughout my struggles in the difficult decades of the Somali Civil War. They endured significant stress during my prolonged absences while I was occupied with the recovering Somali state since 1992.

I extend this dedication to my grandchildren and their future descendants, hoping they will find time to read these pages and draw wisdom and inspiration from them.

Finally, I dedicate this book to generations of Somali academics, students, and political elites. I earnestly hope they will strive to transform the toxic political culture that perpetually destroys our state into ethics and integrity, leading to good governance and a brighter future for our country. I am optimistic that this generation will correct the misguided paths previously taken in our country's state-building efforts by breaking free from the outdated and ineffective practices that led to the collapse of our state after 30 years. We have the potential to pave the way for a more stable and prosperous future. Be an exceptional leader or support one, but never be a bystander!

*S*OMALIA: A State in Search of Exceptional Leadership is a masterful examination of leadership paradigms and state-building in one of Africa's most complex political landscapes. This comprehensive work offers unprecedented insights into Somalia's governance challenges whilst presenting a thorough analysis of the exemplary leaders who have shaped its political trajectory.

The significance of this volume lies in its methodological rigour and innovative approach to understanding Somalia's political evolution. Through six meticulously crafted chapters, the author presents a compelling narrative that bridges theoretical frameworks with practical governance challenges, whilst offering fresh perspectives on leadership in post-colonial African states.

The opening chapter provides theoretical foundation, examining Somalia's governance challenges through multiple lenses. It brings together theories of state failure and collapse with an analysis of leadership paradigms, including valuable insights into Islamic perspectives on leadership. The chapter's examination of Somalia's experiences with both majoritarian democratic rule (1956-1969) and authoritarian governance (1969-1991) provides crucial context for understanding contemporary challenges.

Chapters two through four present intimate portraits of three exceptional leaders who defined Somalia's early independence era. The author's analysis of Abdullahi Isse Mohamud's tenure as the first Prime Minister (1956-1960) offers valuable insights into the formation of Somalia's political culture during the crucial transition from colonial administration to independence. The examination of

President Adan Abdulle Osman's leadership (1960-1967) presents a model of exceptional governance rarely seen in post-colonial Africa, whilst the study of Prime Minister Abdirazak H. Hussein's reformist agenda (1964-1967) demonstrates the potential for transformative leadership in challenging contexts.

The fifth chapter provides a critical analysis of what the author identifies as the core obstacle in Somali state-building: elite political culture. This section offers a sophisticated examination of how various elite groups—traditional clan elders, Islamic scholars, non-Islamist and Islamist elites—have influenced Somalia's political landscape. The analysis of the historical evolution of elite political culture, particularly during the formative period (1956-1969) and subsequent years (1969-1991), provides crucial insights into contemporary governance challenges.

The final chapter presents a comprehensive approach to Somali state-building, offering practical solutions and frameworks for addressing contemporary challenges. The author's proposed Inclusive Reconciliation Framework and Stability Model for the Somali state represent significant contributions to the discourse on post-conflict reconstruction.

What distinguishes this work is its balanced approach to complex issues. The author deftly navigates sensitive political and cultural dynamics whilst maintaining scholarly objectivity. The analysis is enriched by extensive primary research, including previously unpublished documents and interviews with key political figures.

This volume makes several notable contributions to the field:
- It provides the first comprehensive analysis of leadership paradigms in Somalia's political development
- It offers detailed case studies of successful leadership models in the Somali context
- It presents a sophisticated theoretical framework for understanding elite political culture

- It proposes practical solutions for contemporary state-building challenges

The work will prove invaluable for various audiences:
- Scholars of African politics and leadership studies
- Policymakers engaged in state-building initiatives
- Development practitioners working in fragile states
- Students of international relations and political science
- Anyone interested in understanding leadership challenges in complex political environments

As publishers, we believe this work represents a significant contribution to our understanding of leadership and governance in post-colonial Africa. Its thorough research, innovative theoretical frameworks, and practical recommendations make it an essential reference for anyone interested in Somalia's political development or broader questions of leadership in challenging contexts.

Mohammed Abdullah Artan
Founder and Director of Looh Press

ACKNOWLEDGMENTS

With the grace of Allah, writing this book would not have been possible without the foundational works of several distinguished scholars and authors. I extend my heartfelt gratitude to Professor Abdi Samatar for his illuminating work, "Africa's First Democrats," which provided deep insights and context for my research on President Adan Abdulle Osman and Abdirizak Haji Hussein. I am also profoundly indebted to Mohamed Trunji for his two seminal works, "Somalia: The Untold History" and "Adan Abdulle Osman: His Life and Legacy," which have been indispensable resources, shedding light on the early years of Somalia's state-building. Additionally, the memoir of Abdirizak Haji Hussein, edited by Professor Abdisalam Salwe, played a crucial role in shaping the narrative and depth of this book. Their invaluable contributions to Somali studies have been a guiding light and an inspiration throughout my writing process. Finally, I express my gratitude to Mustafa Abdullahi Fairus, director of the Institute of Islamic Studies at Mogadishu University, who continuously encouraged this research and published the last chapters in the Journal of Somali Studies, a peer-reviewed journal issued by the Institute.

I would like to extend my gratitude to Ali Gabow Jinow, Director of the Unigate Group, whose financial support was crucial for the editing and refinement of this book. His belief in the project's vision provided a strong foundation for its development. This publication has been made possible through the generous contributions of the Hormud Foundation, the philanthropic arm of Somalia's leading telecommunications company, Hormud. Their commitment to community initiatives has been essential in facilitating the dissemination of knowledge and addressing the complexities of state-building in Somalia that this book seeks to explore.

I am also deeply thankful to my wife, Muhubo, and our seven children—Ahmed, Muna, Omar, Hassan, Ali, Khalid, and Yasser. Their unwavering encouragement and support have been a constant source of motivation throughout my academic journey. Their emotional backing and various contributions have been invaluable; without their help, this work would not have reached its final form..

Finally, I would like to extend my profound gratitude to Mohamed Artan, the esteemed publisher of Loohpress. His unwavering dedication and commitment to ensuring this book was published on schedule and in its highest quality form have been remarkable. Mohamed's meticulous attention to detail, professional expertise, and tireless effort have transformed this manuscript into a polished and refined work. His support and collaboration have been invaluable, and I sincerely appreciate his contribution to bringing this book to life. Thank you, Mohamed, for your exceptional work and dedication.

*T*his book commemorates my 70th anniversary, which will be on November 15, 2024. Born 33 days after the rise of the Somali flag on October 12, 1954, I have witnessed critical moments in Somalia's history, from its independence celebrations to its various political transformations. My early education occurred during the democratic period, followed by the era of military rule. I am proud to serve the Somali National Army and studied missile engineering in the former Soviet Union (1972-1977). During the challenging decade of the 1980s, I faced a moral crossroads and chose to desert the army while in the USA for training in 1986. In 1987, I migrated to Canada and pursued a PhD in modern Islamic history at McGill University's Islamic Institute. This academic journey was an opportunity to study Somali history, society, and politics and to develop a comprehensive perspective of Somali studies, which was critical of Somali historiography. This new comprehension led me to actively participate in the country's reconciliation and reconstruction efforts through civil society activism since I returned to my country in 1992. During this challenging decade of civil war, I was part of the civil society movement to restore social services such as education and health and challenge warlords to promote peace and reconciliation.

A pivotal moment in my journey was my involvement in the Somali conference held in Djibouti in 2000, where I played a crucial role in efforts to restore the Somali state. As a member of the Somali technical committee responsible for organizing the conference, I was tasked with overseeing the development of the charter within a 30-day timeframe. My commitment to reconciliation and peace continued through the tumultuous decade that followed. In 2012, disillusioned by the deficiencies in leadership, I decided to run for president to make a more direct contribution to saving my country. Over the past 12 years, I have dedicated myself to researching and understanding the challenges in Somalia's state-building process, focusing on the importance of effective leadership. Since then, I dedicated myself to reconciliation, being a senior adviser for Prime Minister Hassan Ali Kheyre and President Hassan Sheikh, believing that reconciliation is the first step in building a viable state in Somalia.

This book initially explores leadership challenges and subsequently examines the lives and legacies of three iconic figures: President Aden Abdullah Osman Daar, Prime Minister Abdullahi Issa Mohamud, and Prime Minister Abdirizak Haji Hussein. Despite numerous obstacles, these leaders adhered to the principles of the Somali Youth League (SYL), aiming to build a democratic state with equality for all citizens, upholding the rule of law, and pursuing good governance. Their biographies and political cultures are presented as models for current and future Somali leaders. The final chapters delve into the broader context of Somali elite political culture as the obstacle to restoring a viable Somali state. They offer an in-depth analysis of its shaping factors and a comprehensive approach to resolving the Somali crisis. By reflecting on the past and drawing lessons for the future, this book contributes to the ongoing discourse on leadership in Somalia, offering insights and inspiration for those dedicated to the country's recovery and development.

In addition to consulting main reference books, experts meticulously reviewed each chapter on the respective topics. Mohamed Issa Trunji reviewed chapters on President Aden and Prime Minister Abdullahi Isse. Professor Abdisalam Salwe, the editor of the "Abdirizak Political Memoir," revised the chapter on Prime Minister Abdirizak Haji Hussein. Professor Abdulkadir Osman reviewed the first chapter on the Leadership Challenge in Somalia. All these academicians reviewed the whole book, and their valuable comments were considered in the final version of the book.

The final two chapters, initially published in the annual Somali Studies journal by the Institute of Somali Studies (ISOS) at Mogadishu

University, were revisited and refined to ensure coherence with the rest of the book. By incorporating these experts' insights, this book offers a well-rounded and deeply informed perspective on the leadership challenges and political dynamics shaping Somalia. It is a collaborative effort, drawing on the collective wisdom and expertise of those dedicated to understanding and improving Somali society.

This book aims to inspire and guide the new generation of Somali leaders by highlighting their challenges and offering examples of exemplary leadership to emulate. It aims to critically examine the current political culture and warn against its pitfalls, urging future leaders to avoid replicating existing failures. Additionally, the book outlines a path forward for effective Somali state-building, offering insights and strategies to overcome obstacles and build a more stable and prosperous future for the nation. Through a blend of historical examples, practical advice, and visionary goals, this work seeks to empower and equip emerging leaders with the tools and wisdom necessary to navigate and resolve the complex issues confronting Somalia.

Dr. Abdurahman Baadiyow
July 25, 2024.

$\mathcal{T}$he body of scholarship addressing the challenges of Somali leadership and governance as primary obstacles to state-building still needs to be explored. This pioneering book blends Somali history, leadership dynamics, and political culture with the core elements of Somali society. By providing a comprehensive understanding of the historical and cultural context shaping Somali elite political culture, it examines the evolution of leadership styles and governance practices and their impact on the country's state-building path. The book identifies the root causes of the Somali political crisis through rigorous research and insightful analysis and proposes culturally informed, locally driven solutions, challenging conventional state-building approaches.

This book is groundbreaking as it deeply explores the political culture of three of Somalia's most eminent political figures: Aden Abdulla, the first President of the Somali Republic (1960-1967); Abdullahi Issa, the first Somali Prime Minister (1956-1960); and Abdirazak Haji Hussein, Prime Minister from 1964 to 1967. These leaders, who began their political journeys in the 1940s with the Somali Youth League (SYL), which led Somalia to independence, quickly rose to prominence despite their lack of experience and formal education. Their leadership successfully guided Somalia into an era of democracy, stability, and peace. The extraordinary leadership qualities of Aden Abdulla, Abdullahi Issa, and Abdirazak Haji Hussein were not fully appreciated until years after they left office, making it difficult for today's generation to comprehend Somalia's past high-caliber leadership.

This book is invaluable for scholars, policymakers, and anyone interested in Somali politics and governance. It fills a critical gap in Somali leadership and governance studies. It offers fresh perspectives on addressing these enduring issues, ultimately contributing to the broader discourse on state-building in post-conflict societies. I recommend that current and prospective politicians read this book and learn lessons from the three exceptional leaders, as their biographies are well illustrated in this book. Finally, I commend Dr. Abdurahman Baadiyow for his remarkable work in bringing this important book to light and offering tentative solutions for Somali state-building challenges.

Mohammed Issa Trunji
Author of History, and Politics
July 31, 2024.

PROF. FARAH FOREWORD

*P*rofessor Abdurahman Abdullahi (Baadiyow) examines Somali governance's historical and contemporary landscapes in a comprehensive study of Somali leadership. He critiques the persistent shadow of colonialism, the narratives within Somali studies, the elite political culture, and state-society relations, identifying them as the primary obstacles to Somali state-building. The book highlights the efforts of civic and democratic leaders, focusing on the biographies and political culture of three exemplary figures from the early years of independence: President Adan Abdulle, Prime Minister Abdirizak, and Prime Minister Abdullahi Isse. Baadiyow emphasizes the importance of personal integrity, the rule of law, and ethical leadership for societal cohesion through these biographies.

The book discusses the challenge of reconciling tradition with modernity in Somalia, noting that effective leadership has helped other societies overcome similar issues. Baadiyow analyzes the failure of the two systems employed in postcolonial Somalia, which collapsed: the majoritarian liberal democratic and parliamentary system in 1969 and the authoritarian military rule with a presidential system in 1991. He advocates rethinking indigenous governance models that blend traditional values with Islamic principles, modernity, and exceptional leadership to address Somali state-building challenges.

Offering a new direction and approach for building a stable Somali state, the book applies a comprehensive perspective and critical reconciliation framework. It is the first book written by a Somali scholar who witnessed and studied during the military regime and civil war period. A scholar who participated in recovering the Somali state through civil society activism and political engagement. The author shares his wealth of experience and field research analysis with his readers. Diagnosing the persistent instability of Somali state-building suggests practical solutions. This book is a valuable resource and a must-read for the new generation of Somali students, educators, and the political elite.

Professor Abdulkadir Osman Farah
Academic, Lecturer of Civil Society, & Politics
August 2, 2024.

$\mathcal{D}$r. Abdurahman Abdullahi (Baadiyow) has contributed significantly to understanding Somalia's history, politics, and society by offering a comprehensive critique of Somali historiography and presenting an alternative perspective. His work focuses on the leadership challenges faced by the nation and highlights three prominent leaders as exemplary models for current and future leadership. Dr. Baadiyow's scholarly work provides profound insights into the aspirations, political culture, and achievements of President Adan Abdulle, Prime Minister Abdirizak Haji Hussein, and Prime Minister Abdullahi Isse. Drawing on the influential academic contributions of Professor Abdi Samatar in "Africa's First Democrats" and Mohamed I. Trunji's historical works and biography of President Adan, and the political memoir of Abdirizak H. Hussein, this research examines the political leadership challenges faced by Somalia. He presents these leaders as models, critiques the political elite culture as an obstacle to building effective state institutions, and suggests comprehensive solutions for creating a sustainable Somali state.

Despite the exceptional leadership and visionary policies of Somalia's early leaders, the democratic process was abruptly halted when the country fell under a military dictatorship in 1969. This regime introduced a new political culture of authoritarianism and exclusion, dismantled democratic foundations, and adopted the alien ideology of socialism. These policies put the state at odds with its people, ultimately leading to its collapse in 1991. This culture, albeit in a more eroded form, remains intact among the current Somali political elite. Dr. Baadiyow's work is particularly noteworthy for addressing issues often overlooked in Somali studies literature. His research illuminates Somali leadership's historical and contemporary challenges and explores pathways for restoring effective governance. It is highly recommended reading for students of Somali history and politics.

Proffesspr Abdisalam Mohamed Issa-Salwe.
Academic, Lecturer, & Author
August 2, 2024

INTRODUCTION

SOMALIA:
A STATE IN SEARCH OF
EXCEPTIONAL LEADERSHIP

The collapse of the Somali nation-state in 1991, the prolonged civil war, and the challenges in re-establishing the state have been deeply perplexing. Early academic analyses proposed that Somalia was a unique case in Africa, with a population united by a common language, the religion of Islam, and a shared cultural heritage. These factors implied that the primary task for Somalia was merely the development of state institutions. David Laitin and Said Sheikh Samatar's book, "Somalia: A Nation in Search of a State," theorizes the assumption of the challenging task of establishing a state in Somalia.[1] Building upon their title, this book's thesis argues that establishing Somalia's state hinges on various factors, foremost among them being exceptional leadership. This type of leadership should potentially transform the country's fragmented political landscape and guide it toward effective state-building. It must unite diverse political elites and foster reconciliation and unity while establishing a shared vision for the nation's future. Moreover, such leadership must be adept at reunifying a breakaway Somaliland with the Somali Federal Republic through an **attractive** unification approach. This leadership should be capable of developing the nation's resources to drive economic growth and eliminate poverty. Furthermore, this leadership must lay the foundation for long-term stability and prosperity by strategically investing in critical sectors

---

1. David Laitin and Said Samatar, *Somalia: Nation in Search of a State* (Boulder Co: Westview Press, 1987).

and prioritizing sustainable development. Additionally, it should inspire a sense of national pride and cohesion, uniting the people behind common goals and a collective identity.

Somalia's quest for such leadership echoes across its land, rivers, mountains, regions, communities, and diaspora. The country cries out for visionary leaders capable of lifting the agonizing Somali people from despair and poverty and instilling new hope for their future. The call for exceptional leadership resounds far beyond politics and extends its reach into various facets of society. While political leadership undoubtedly holds significant sway, the demand for leadership expertise permeates every stratum of society. The call for exceptional leadership persists in societal structures, intellectual institutions, economic performances, organizations of Islamic call, mosque management, and traditional communities. Indeed, the contemporary condition of Somalia is marked by a pervasive crisis in leadership, where competent and visionary leadership are outshined by mediocrity, incompetent, and myopic leadership. This crisis knows no boundaries; it is ubiquitous and deeply entrenched in the whole gamut of society. Across diverse domains, the fabric of leadership appears messy and caught in disarray. The need for exceptional leadership has never been more pressing in Somalia's fast-changing regional dynamics and globalized world, grappling with the post-civil war recovery. Whether navigating global challenges and regional dynamics or addressing local concerns, exceptional leadership is the linchpin for progress and stability. Nonetheless, as political institutions falter and traditional culture erodes, leadership's essence is tested and redefined. Amidst this backdrop, the imperative remains to cultivate leaders who can inspire, innovate, and unite across divides. Only through a concerted effort to foster exceptional leadership can we hope to surmount the myriad challenges that confront our nation and forge a path toward a brighter future.

Somalia endured the influence of various colonial powers and superpower rivalry during the Cold War, leaving its postcolonial state with significant challenges. These challenges were further exacerbated by the contentious relations between the modern state and traditional ethos and the failure to develop a modus vivendi of mutual accommodation. Nonetheless, it is the responsibility of the Somali leadership to build a stable and functional state despite these external pressures. This task requires confronting complex geopolitical dynamics and overcoming hurdles in state-building. Effective governance, strategic diplomacy, and comprehensive policies are essential for achieving stability and promoting national development. Somali leaders must balance external interests with internal needs, such as addressing clan divisions, fostering economic growth, and establishing institutions capable of upholding the rule of law. They aim to create a sustainable foundation for the nation's future by focusing on these priorities.

Many African scholars orient their scholarship to blame colonialism and international actors and concurrently blame their society for ethnicity, clan division, economic depreciation, etc.[2] As a result of this blame game, political scientists were divided into two distinct camps: the Afro-centrists blaming colonialism and the Euro-centrists blaming African societies and their leadership.[3] The focus on leadership deficiency and blaming political elites is a rarity among African scholars. Without denying the negative role of colonial heritage, it is the responsibility of the African leaders to deal with the challenges. For example, Afrocentist Prof. Ali Mazrui described external actors' influence, blaming them for the collapse of the Somali state when he wrote, "Somalia has been a victim of both the Cold War and the end of the Cold War. During the Cold War, the strategic value of Somalis to the superpower was inflated. As a result, the two superpowers poured the armament into that little country. When the Cold War ended, the strategic value of Somalia plunged like the stock market

---

2. Freeman, C. (2010, June 20). "Colonialism is no longer an excuse for Africa's failure," SundayView. Retrieved from http://www.zimbabwesituation.com/june20_2010.html.
3. Jephias Mapuva and Freeman Chari, "Colonialism no Longer an Excuse for Africa's Failure," Journal of Sustainable Development in Africa 12, no. 5 (2010).

price on Wall Street at the start of the great depression."[4] Even though the role of external actors is significant, we should shift our focus to internal factors and recognize that leaders build and break nations. By acknowledging our role in the state's failures, we can review our mistakes and take practical steps to address our shortcomings. This approach aligns with the Islamic perspective of taking personal responsibility for our actions.[5] Therefore, the reconstruction of our nation demands exceptional leaders in contrast to the mediocratic, kleptocratic, authoritarian, and self-serving leaders frequently dominating our nation.

Somalia's desperate cry for exceptional leadership is rooted in its enduring struggle for stability and progress. Despite over six decades since gaining independence in 1960, Somalia has trapped most of its history in turmoil and instability. The scars of prolonged civil conflict and state collapse run deep, leaving the nation grappling with the aftermath of devastation and loss. Moreover, the pervasive influence of extremism, masquerading under the guise of Islam and clan allegiance, continues to sow seeds of discord and division among our people. The quest for unity among Somalia's diverse regions still needs to be fulfilled, hindered by historical grievances and the persistent specter of regional and internal rivalries. At the crossroads of strategic significance, Somalia finds itself entangled in geopolitical tensions that further exacerbate its challenges. Leaders who rise based on morality and competence rather than corruption or clan affiliation hold the potential to lead Somalia out of the abyss of disaster it has fallen into for decades. These exceptional leaders, guided by a vision of inclusivity, can navigate the complexities of Somalia's so-

---

4. *Mazrui, Ali A., "Crisis in Somalia from Tyranny to Anarchy," in Mending Rips in the Sky: Options for Somali Communities in the 21st Century*, eds. Adam and Ford, (Lawrenceville: The Red Sea Press, 1997), 5–12.

5. This concept agrees with the Islamic perspective of self-blaming instead of blaming others for your calamities. This is what the Quranic verse teaches us, explaining their defeat in the battle of Uhud. See Quran (3:165). "And do you, now that a calamity has befallen you after you had inflicted twice as much [on your foes], ask yourselves, "How has this come about?" Say: "It has come from your own selves." Verily, God has the power to will anything."

cio-political melee and forge a path toward lasting peace and prosperity. Somalia's cry for exceptional leadership is not merely a lamentation of its past agonies but a rallying call for a brighter future. It is a call to break free from the shackles of division and strife, embrace the principles of meritocracy and unity, and chart a new course toward a stable, prosperous, and united Somalia.

Indeed, nations are graced with towering figures whose influence permeates society in every facet of human existence, spanning the sprawling corridors of political power, the scholarly realms of academia, and the economic landscapes. These celebrities, elevated to the status of role models, stand as living embodiments of excellence and virtuous leadership within their specialized domains. Their examples serve as guiding lights, illuminating generations' paths. The impact of these paragons extends far beyond their mortal existence, transcending the boundaries of time itself. Their legacies, engraved in the annals of history, intertwine with the fabric of collective memory, shaping societal consciousness for generations. Through education and deliberate instruction, their stories are woven into the learning curriculum, ensuring that their invaluable contributions remain eternally ingrained in the minds of successive generations. Moreover, the reverence afforded to these luminaries extends beyond mere scholarly pursuits. Their names reverberate through the halls of museums, where artifacts and relics serve as tangible reminders of their indelible mark on human history. Their citations serve as authoritative references in many political and social contexts, profoundly influencing discourse and shaping narratives in various events and discussions. These leaders are memorialized and emulated, serving as role models for national unity.

The past is an ever-present part of our lives, shaping our identity and influencing our life journey. It provides a foundation for building our future, carrying experiences, lessons, and memories that guide our path. Moreover, history serves as a profound teacher, illuminating the triumphs and tribulations of the past, regardless of their moral valence or subjective preferences. It is a repository of lessons where the actions of both exemplary leaders and those who led their nations astray are chronicled for future generations. Historians often turn to the stories of illustrious figures whose virtuous deeds serve as beacons of guidance and emulation when they seek to inspire future generations. Equally crucial, however, is the candid examination of leaders whose misguided actions brought ruin to their people. Just as the Quran recounts the tales of prophets and their adversaries, historians must faithfully narrate the histories of leaders who led their nations astray, providing valuable insights into the consequences of hubris, injustice, and moral decay. In the Quranic narrative, the juxtaposition of Prophet Moses and Pharaoh reminds us of the eternal struggle between righteousness and tyranny. The repeated mention of Pharaoh's name 128 times alongside that of Prophet Moses underscores the magnitude of his defiance and the enduring significance of his legacy as a cautionary tale for humanity. Indeed, the Quranic narrative prominently features Pharaoh, highlighting his arrogance, oppression, and eventual downfall in the face of divine justice. The repeated mention of his name is a stark reminder of the perils of unchecked power and the inevitable consequences of transgression against the divine order.

In the annals of every nation's history, as taught in their educational curriculum, prominent figures whose leadership steered their countries through challenging times and towards prosperity are narrated. For example, in the United States, Abraham Lincoln, George Washington, and Franklin D. Roosevelt are studied for their significant contributions to the country's development. Across the Atlantic, the United Kingdom reveres Winston Churchill and Margaret Thatcher for their determined leadership during times of crisis. General de Gaulle's influence and resilience during World War II and beyond are highly regarded in France. Meanwhile, in Egypt, Gamal Abdel Nasser and Anwar Sadat are celebrated for their roles in modern history. Russia's history is marked by the complex legacies of Vladimir Lenin, Joseph Stalin, Mikhail Gorbachev, and Vladimir Putin, each shaping the country's trajectory in distinct ways. In Turkey, Mustafa Kemal Atatürk's leadership laid the foundation for the modern state, while Recep Tayyip Erdoğan's impact on contemporary Turkey is well recognized. In Malaysia, Dr. Mahathir bin Mohamad is known for his transformative economic policies, while Dr. Anwar Ibrahim is recognized for his economic reforms. In South Africa, Nelson Mandela's name is synonymous with the struggle against apartheid and his unifying leadership in the nation's early years of democracy. Ethiopia acknowledges Meles Zenawi for modernizing the country, while Rwanda's Paul Kagame is recognized for his leadership in rebuilding the nation after the genocide. These leaders' enduring legacies serve as touchstones for their nations' historical narratives and continue to inspire future generations.

Unfortunately, a few notable figures in Somali history are studied and remembered for their roles in fighting anti-colonial domination. Names such as Ahmed Gurey, Sayid Mohamed Abdullahi Hassan, Sheikh Hassan Barsane, Sheikh Bashir, Hawa Tako, and Mohamed Halane are among the most well-known figures in Somali history, renowned for their contributions to the nation's struggles and achievements. However, beyond these distinguished names, it is undoubtedly that hundreds of other national heroes have significantly impacted the country's history and may be characterized as unknown heroes. This is so because Somalia's historical consciousness and the recognition of its heroes are underdeveloped due to decades of conflict, instability, and the impact of colonial legacies. As a result, the achievements and sacrifices of these leaders may not be as widely recognized or celebrated as they could be. Thus, a pressing need exists for a deeper understanding and appreciation of historical awareness, particularly concerning the roles of prominent personalities in shaping the nation's political development.[6] Across Somali history, a diverse array of leaders has emerged, each leaving a distinct imprint on the nation's trajectory, regardless of whether they contributed to its construction or dissolution, promoting democracy or authoritarianism.

---

6. See the author's attempt to write the biography of seventeen prominent personalities. Abdurahman Abdullahi, *Making Sense of Somali History, vol. 2* (Adonis & Abbey, 2018).

Indeed, Somalia's historical narrative is woven with the threads of myriad individuals whose actions and decisions have reverberated throughout the nation's past and present. The contributions of these leaders have often been ignored or marginalized, outshone by the prevailing emphasis on clan affiliations and identities. This undue emphasis on clan attachment has obscured the roles played by prominent national leaders, diminishing their legacies and detracting from a comprehensive understanding of Somali history. As a result, the rich Somali political evolution and social development remain obscured, with the stories of these influential figures relegated to the periphery of national discourse. To truly comprehend Somali history and chart a path towards a more cohesive and inclusive national narrative, it is imperative to acknowledge and celebrate the contributions of individuals from all walks of life. By elevating the stories of historical leaders and recognizing their multifaceted legacies, Somalia can begin to forge a collective identity rooted in shared experiences and aspirations rather than divisive clan affiliations.

Throughout Somalia's modern history, countless individuals at all levels of society have selflessly dedicated their lives to serving their communities, guided by a sense of duty and faith. These silent heroes include everyday citizens, such as mothers, fathers, and local leaders, who have made significant contributions to their communities without seeking recognition. Their inspiring stories of perseverance and altruism deserve to be shared widely, yet the full scope of their impact cannot be captured in this limited space. In stark contrast, other individuals have wreaked havoc across the country, destroying lives and properties, erasing national archives, and undermining national unity. These detrimental figures have fueled clan conflicts and wars, often profiting from their roles as agents for foreign interests. Both the virtuous and the vicious are part of Somalia's history; one group represents the positive impact of selfless service, while the other serves as a cautionary tale of the devastation caused by greed and division. By acknowledging both the commendable deeds of the self and the destructive actions of the villains, Somalia can learn from its past and work towards building a more peaceful and prosperous future.

Since Somalia struggled for independence and the early formation of the Somali government in 1956 until the collapse of the national state in 1991, prominent political leaders have emerged, each leaving its mark on the nation's development and identity. From the vibrant struggle for self-determination to the tumultuous post-independence era, figures such as President Adan Abdulle Osman, Prime Minister Abdullahi Isse, Prime Minister Mohamed Ibrahim Egal, Prime Minister Abdirizak Haji Hussein, President Abdirashid Ali Sharmarke, and President General Mohamed Siyad Barre have played diverse and influential roles in shaping Somalia's political landscape and socio-economic development. Despite their diverse roles and legacies, these prominent leaders collectively embody the complexities and contradictions of Somalia's political evolution. Whether lauded or criticized, their contributions remain integral to the nation's history and identity.

After the collapse of the Somali state in 1991 and throughout the subsequent difficult decade of civil war, Somali history cannot be understood without mentioning the various roles played by a wide range of critical figures. Prominent among these are Interim President Ali Mahdi Mohmed, General Mohamed Farah Aideed, Mohamed Omar Jees, Abdurahman Tuur, Osman Atto, Mohamed Qanraye Afrah, Hassan Mohamed Nur (Shati-Gaduud), General Mohamed Abshir, Cabdullahi Yusuf, General Omar Haji Masale, Hussein Haji Bood, General Adan Gabyow, and numerous military officers who were deeply involved in the civil wars that ensued. These individuals rose to prominence due to their involvement in the Somali Civil War in different ways, becoming well-known figures whose biographies are intertwined with the broader narrative of Somali history. Their stories are a significant part of the country's past and remain subjects awaiting an objective recounting, free from emotional bias or partiality rooted in clan allegiance or personal preference. It is essential to present their contributions and decisions without favoritism or prejudice, acknowledging their impact on Somalia's history while recognizing the complexity of their motives and the context in which they operated. An unbiased examination of their lives and legacies will offer a clearer understanding of the civil war and its lasting effects on Somali society.

In addition to these well-known political figures, thousands of unacknowledged heroes played crucial roles in protecting and saving the lives of Somalis during the civil war. Their contributions, often at significant personal risk, were essential in preserving communities and offering humanitarian assistance amid conflict. Furthermore, the efforts of prominent non-state actors, including civil society organizations, business communities, media outlets, and dedicated individuals, should also be recognized as significant in shaping the course of Somali history during this era. These groups and individuals provided much-needed support and stability in the face of ongoing violence and helped lay the groundwork for Somalia's reconciliation, reconstruction, and development. Educators and health workers in Somalia provided invaluable services during the civil war, often at significant personal risk and without the protection of a state. Amidst the chaos and ongoing violence, they worked tirelessly to deliver essential education and healthcare to communities across the country. Educators facilitated learning and personal development and offered a sense of normalcy and hope to countless children and adults living through the conflict. Their efforts helped preserve Somali society's future generations and intellectual fabric, laying the foundation for educational and health institutions. They opened universities to educate and nurture a new generation of Somalis who can reconstruct state institutions. Any comprehensive rewriting of Somali history must consider the complex and multifaceted contributions of these lesser-known yet equally essential actors.

After the formation of the third republic at the Somali Peace and Reconciliation Conference in Djibouti in 2000, a new leadership emerged in Somalia. This period saw the rise of several prominent figures who played crucial roles in shaping the country's political landscape. The interim president, Abdiqasim Salad Hassan, and his Prime Minister, Dr. Ali Khalif Galayr, led the initial efforts to establish a functional governance structure in the country. In 2004, President-elect Abdullahi Yusuf Ahmed was chosen at the Somali conference in Kenya, marking a significant milestone in the country's political journey. He worked closely with his Prime Ministers, Ali Mohamed Ghedi and Nur Hassan Hussein, to navigate the governance challenges and catapult the government to Mogadishu. The Islamic Courts Union, led by figures such as Sheikh Sharif Sheikh Ahmed and Hassan Dahir Aways, played a pivotal role in the country's political dynamics and diminishing the role of the warlords. Sheikh Sharif later became the interim president in 2009 and worked alongside his prime ministers, Omar Abdirashid, Mohamed Abdullahi Farmajo, and Dr. Abdiweli Ali Gaas, to steer the country through a complex political environment.

The 2012 elections marked a turning point for Somalia. Hassan Sheikh Mohamud was elected president, and the world officially began recognizing Somalia as a legitimate state in 2013. His tenure saw the appointment of several key prime ministers, including Saaid Farah Sheikhdon, Abdiweli Sheikh Ahmed, and Omar Abdirashid Ali Sharmarke. The election of President Mohamed Abdullahi Farmajo in 2017 and his Prime Minister, Hassan Ali Kheyre, worked to implement reforms and drive development initiatives. The re-election of President Hassan Sheikh Mohamud in 2022 and his Prime Minister Hamza Abdi Aar continue their efforts in the state-building. The stories of these leaders, prime ministers, and other key figures are essential to understanding Somalia's recent history. Their efforts and challenges are integral to the ongoing narrative of Somalia's elite political culture and attempt to restore the Somali state. The shared trait among these Somali leaders is the elite political culture that persists within the ranks of political leaders.

Reflecting on the lives of inspiring individuals and harmful figures, it is crucial to recognize the complexities of human nature. Whether remembered for their commendable acts or notorious deeds, each possesses a blend of virtues and flaws. No absolute heroism or villainy exists, as everyone is shaped by their experiences, challenges, and choices. The key distinction is determined by how much their conduct and demeanor influence their actions. This perspective allows us to appreciate the lessons we can learn from the lives of others. This balanced view serves as a reminder of our shared humanity and the potential for both positive and negative impacts within each of us. However, this book presents a focused account of three leaders who played vital roles in shaping the Somali state as devoted members of the original principles of the Somali Youth League (SYL). Its scope is limited to those who held the country's highest offices, such as presidents and prime ministers renowned for their integrity and commitment to democratic principles. Focusing on these three leaders aims to revive the biographical narratives of role models who have significantly contributed to Somalia beyond simply recounting the tenures of those who ruled the country at various times.

The rise of exceptional leaders is challenging in Somalia, but it is possible due to the prevalent issues in the sociopolitical landscape. Politicized clannism often influences power dynamics and decision-making, limiting the scope for potential leaders to emerge from a broader range of backgrounds. The limited development of an associational culture outside of clan affiliations, such as political parties and strong civil society organizations, creates an environment where collaboration and diverse perspectives are not fully developed. Furthermore, the lack of robust institutions that identify, nurture, and mentor emerging leaders presents a barrier to cultivating exceptional leadership. As a result, the emergence of extraordinary leadership becomes largely a matter of chance and probability. Without deliberate support structures, outstanding leaders' selection and development depend on unpredictable circumstances in the Somali context.

This book, comprising six chapters, offers students of Somali history and politics a fresh perspective on history and politics through the biographies of exceptional Somali leaders. Central to this narrative are the lives and legacies of prominent political figures who serve as exemplars for current and future generations, illuminating paths toward principled leadership. At its core, this book seeks to unravel the toxic tendrils of contemporary political culture, revealing its damaging effects on governance, unity, and national cohesion. Through a comparative lens, it juxtaposes the prevailing political ethos with historical instances of leadership characterized by adherence to the rule of law, equality of citizens, democratic principles, and unwavering commitment to nationalistic ideals. Each chapter serves as a window into a distinct facet of this narrative, offering deep insights into the lives, challenges, and triumphs of exemplary statesmen who have left an enduring mark on the fabric of their respective nations. From their early beginnings to leadership moments, readers are invited to explore and discover the political history through visionary leadership. Moreover, the book goes beyond mere historical retelling, extracting timeless lessons and principles that can inform and inspire contemporary political discourse. In addition to presenting an exemplary leadership model, the book explores the prevailing elite political culture that poses significant challenges to state-building in Somalia. Beyond this analysis, the book provides a detailed roadmap for achieving comprehensive reconciliation and lasting stability in Somalia.

Moreover, this book limits its scope to delving into the lives and legacies of three exceptional leaders in Somalia: President Aden Abdulle Osman, Prime Minister Abdirizak Haji Hussein, and Abdullahi Isse Mohamoud. A fresh start in recovering the Somali state is not a severance from the past but a continuation that integrates our history. By acknowledging and understanding the exceptional leadership of the past, we can move forward with intention and clarity, using the wisdom we have gained to forge anew in search of outstanding leadership. Our past acts as a bridge that connects where we have been with where we are going, and in this way, a new beginning is intimately linked to our past experiences. These leaders share a historical trajectory highlighting their deep commitment to the nation and its people. Their life started with being orphans, acquiring elementary education and the habit of reading, followed by their involvement in the first nationalist youth organization, the Somali Youth Club (SYC), in 1944. Fascinatingly, these three leaders come from three distinct and geographically separated regions of Somalia, showcasing the diverse origins of the country's prominent figures. Specifically, these leaders hail from Banadir, Hiiraan, and Majeertenia, three of the six key regions in southern Somalia. Each leader's unique background and regional heritage have significantly influenced their leadership style and approach to governance, offering a blend of cultural nuances and insights into the complex dynamics of Somali society. Through their dedication to the SYL's mission, all three leaders quickly ascended the party ranks, taking on either chairman or secretary-general roles. Their legacies continue to inspire successive generations of Somali leaders and serve as a beacon for those striving for good governance and the betterment of the country.

The book is crafted in a unique academic paper format that enhances the reader's ability to engage with, comprehend, and make informed decisions about the subject matter. This format is meticulously designed to cater to novice readers and seasoned scholars, providing a structured and accessible approach to complex topics. Each chapter is built upon a consistent foundation, presenting background information that remains uniform throughout the book. This deliberate repetition ensures that critical concepts are continually reinforced, allowing readers to grasp the material more thoroughly. As a result, readers might notice overlapping and repetitive elements in the background information. However, this intentional design bolsters the reader's understanding, making the content more cohesive and accessible. Whether readers explore the book sequentially or delve into individual chapters, hopefully, they will find the material accessible and understandable, supported by a familiar and consistent framework.

Chapter One deals with the challenges of political leadership and aims to foster a profound comprehension of the critical role of leaders in the formation and progression of nations. It dispels the fallacious notion that external influences, poverty, societal schisms, or colonial legacies bear sole responsibility for a nation's fate, emphasizing instead the decisive impact of leadership. The book provides a concise yet comprehensive overview of leadership theories. Condensing key concepts and principles equips readers with the analytical tools necessary to assess and understand leadership dynamics within the Somali context and beyond. It examines the two systems, majoritarian democracy and Bigman authoritarian rule, and concludes that both have failed. In conclusion, the chapter suggests one aspect of the governance system and the nature of leadership, which are rooted in the Somali culture.

Chapter Two embarks on the biography and legacy of Abdulahi Isse Mohamud, a towering figure in Somali political history. As the longest-serving Secretary General of the Somali Youth League (SYL) and the inaugural Prime Minister during the Trusteeship period from 1956 to 1960, Abdullahi's impact reverberates through the annals of Somali governance. This chapter examines Abdullahi's formative years, tracing his rise within the ranks of SYL and his role in galvanizing the SYL struggle toward independence. His biography was interwoven with the SYL history and Italian administration under the UN Trusteeship. His tenure as Prime Minister during the critical juncture of Somalia's transition to sovereignty provides a compelling narrative of leadership in the face of daunting challenges. Furthermore, the chapter delves into Abdullahi's leadership style, political philosophy, and vision for a unified and prosperous Somalia. By contextualizing his achievements within the broader socio-political landscape of the time, readers gain a nuanced understanding of the complexities and triumphs of Somalia's nascent statehood.

Chapter Three delves into the fascinating biographical history of President Adan Abdulle Osman, the inaugural President of Somalia and the father of the nation. His presidency spanned seven years, from 1960 to 1967, marked by the nation's early strides toward nation-building. This chapter traces Adans's remarkable journey from his humble beginnings as an orphan to the pinnacle of political power. Through meticulous research and vivid narrative, readers are transported through the critical moments and formative experiences that shaped Adan's character and leadership style. As the first President of Somalia, Adan's tenure was characterized by bold initiatives to consolidate national identity, foster economic development, and navigate the complexities of regional and international relations. From his early activism in the struggle for independence to his tenure as President, Adan's life story is evidence of resilience, vision, and unwavering dedication to the rule of law. The chapter offers the presidents' political culture and the factors that shaped it. Moreover, it delves into his multiple oppositions, finally out-voting him in 1967. In conclusion, the chapter answers some critical views of the political culture of the president of not campaigning during the election of 1967, assuming that would have prevented rigging the election, assassinating President Abdirashid, and the military coup of 1969.

Chapter Four comprehensively explores of the remarkable life and legacy of Prime Minister Abdirizak Haji Hussein, a transformative leader renowned for his ambitious reform programs. Hussein's leadership left an indelible mark on Somali governance and society. This chapter traces Abdirizak's biography from his early years to his ascent to the highest echelons of political power. Readers gain insights into the formative experiences and driving forces that shaped Hussein's character and leadership philosophy through research and compelling narrative. As Prime Minister, Hussein spearheaded a series of bold and innovative reforms to modernize and revitalize Somalia's institutions and infrastructure. His initiatives encompassed a wide range of areas, including education, healthcare, agriculture, and economic development, with the aim to improve the quality of life for all Somalis. Furthermore, this chapter delves into Hussein's leadership style, highlighting his pragmatism, decisiveness, and commitment to progress. Despite facing numerous challenges and obstacles, Hussein remained steadfast in his pursual of positive change, earning admiration and respect from both domestic and international quarters.

Chapter Five traces the development of Somali elite political culture, which gradually eroded to reach a breaking point in 1991 with the state collapse. The culture includes the enduring legacy of clan traditions, Islamic heritage, the imprint of Italian colonial rule, the ethos shaped by periods of military governance, the scars left by civil conflict, and the ensuing struggle to establish stable governance structures. This chapter dissects the complex interplay of these elements, illuminating how they have interwoven over time to shape the attitudes, behaviors, and power dynamics within Somalia's political elite. The prevailing political counterculture within Somalia presents a significant barrier to the country's state-building efforts. It is characterized by deep-rooted practices, beliefs, and attitudes that oppose modern governance principles, the rule of law, equality of citizens, and national cohesion. By unraveling the layers of influence, readers gain a deeper appreciation for the multifaceted nature of Somali political culture and the challenges inherent in navigating its intricacies.

Chapter Six is the culmination of the author's extensive research toward fostering comprehensive reconciliation and establishing a robust and stable Somali state. Drawing upon a wealth of personal experiences, scholarly insights, and pragmatic observations, this chapter offers constructive suggestions on the path forward, advocating for an approach that embraces inclusivity and cultural sensitivity. At its core, this chapter advocates for a paradigm shift in how Somalia's state-building efforts are conceptualized and implemented. By fostering dialogue, understanding, and reconciliation, it is argued that a new framework can be forged that transcends historical divisions and fosters unity in diversity. Furthermore, this chapter offers practical recommendations for policymakers, stakeholders, and civil society actors. From promoting participatory governance structures to investing in social cohesion initiatives, the proposed strategies are designed to cultivate an environment conducive to peace, stability, and progress. Ultimately, this chapter serves as a call to action—a call to embrace a new vision for Somalia, one that is grounded in inclusivity, empathy, and resilience.

CHAPTER

1

LEADERSHIP AND GOVERNANCE CHALLENGES IN SOMALIA

"The best leader is one who serves his people."
Prophet Muhammad (peace be upon him)

"The greatest leader is not necessarily the one who does the greatest things. He is the one that gets the people to do the greatest things."
— **Ronald Reagan**, former President of the USA.

"I am not afraid of an army of lions led by a sheep; I am afraid of an army of sheep led by a lion."
— **Alexander the Great.**

*L*eadership is a complex and multifaceted concept that varies in interpretation among individuals and experts. It is a subject of ongoing debate, with contrasting viewpoints from diverse cultural and geographical perspectives. Beyond the challenge of defining leadership, many leadership styles and theories exist, further complicating the understanding of this concept. Some definitions focus on inherent traits, suggesting that leadership is innate and predetermined, while others emphasize the development of leadership through learned qualities within social, cultural, economic, and political contexts.[7] Leadership is vital in building or breaking states, organizations, companies, and institutions.[8] Exceptional leaders make a big difference in developing their nations and saving them from the abyss of deprivation and despair. They ignite motivation, inspire, offer guidance, and impart wisdom to others, facilitating their growth and improvement.[9] Such leaders craft a compelling vision and believe in their followers' goals and purposes. These leaders serve

---

7. Burns, James MacGregor. *Leadership* (New York: Harper & Row, 1978).
8. Robert I. Rotberg, "The Failure and Collapse of Nation-States: Breakdown, Prevention, and Repair," 24–26, accessed February 16, 2024, https://assets. press.princeton.edu/chapters/s7666.pdf. Also, Mandangu, E.T.C. "Leadership Can Build or Destroy a State," Social Sciences, Leadership, Nationalism, and State Building, accessed April 14, 2024, https://www.academia.edu/9854728/ Leadership_can_build_or_destroy_a_state.
9. Olatunbosun, T.O. "The Characteristics of Exceptional Leaders," accessed April 15, 2024. https://www.academia.edu/9381172/The_Characteristic_of_ Exceptional_Leaders. Also, Chaudhry, Rajive, *Quest for Exceptional Leadership: Mirage to Reality* (New Delhi: Response Books, 2011), 286.

as exemplars through their actions and behavior, catalyzing positive societal transformations. In contrast, poor leadership can lead to the downfall of entire nations. When leaders lack integrity, vision, and the ability to inspire and unite their citizens, their decisions can have disastrous consequences. Corrupt or incompetent leadership often leads to economic mismanagement, social unrest, and the erosion of public trust. Such leaders may prioritize personal gain over the nation's well-being, resulting in widespread poverty, inequality, and declining quality of life. In the worst cases, their actions can escalate to civil wars, causing immense suffering and long-lasting damage to the country's infrastructure and its people's morale. Somalia could be characterized as a nation that was failed by its leaders, descending to state collapse and a protracted civil war.

Political leadership in Somalia has been fraught with many challenges stemming from a complex interplay of historical, socio-political, and economic factors. At its inception, Somalia faced four main challenges: the colonial legacy, economic constraints, the Greater Somalia policy, and a shortage of trained human resources. Moreover, at the forefront of these challenges is the need for a better understanding of how to reconcile traditional society with the modern system of governance.[10] Instead, these leaders were persuaded to consider their clan culture flawed, while the Western governance model held merit and was worthy of emulation.[11] During the inaugural formation of the Somali government in 1956 and post-independence, the Somali

---

10. Ahmed Samatar, "The Curse of Allah: Civic Disempowerment and the Collapse of the Somali State," in *The Somali Challenge: From Catastrophe to Renewal?*, ed. Ahmed Samatar (Boulder, CO: Lynne Rienner, 1994), 138.
11. Grew, Robert, "Modernization and Its Discontents," accessed April 15, 2024. https://deepblue.lib.umich.edu/bitstream/handle/2027.42/67022/10.1177_000276427702100208.pdf;sequence=2. Also, Lerner, Daniel, *The Passing of Traditional Society: Modernizing the Middle East* (Glencoe, IL: Free Press), 1958. Also, Mazrui, Ali A. "From Social Darwinism to Current Theories of Modernization: A Tradition of Analysis," World Politics 21, no. 1 (October 1968): 69–83. Also, Tipps, Dean C. "Modernization Theory and the Comparative Study of Societies: A Critical Perspective," Comparative Studies in Society and History 15, no. 2 (March 1973): 199–226.

political elite ascended to power with scant formal education and minimal administrative experience.[12] The weakness of governance institutions further exacerbated the situation. This propensity marks frail governance structures and the political elites' widespread and poisonous political culture of corruption, inefficiency, and lack of accountability.[13] Certainly, amidst the fluidity of societal norms, some political leaders of unwavering resolve invariably existed, steadfastly anchored to their principles and cherished values.[14] This governance weakness has left Somalia vulnerable to exploitation by external actors and internal factions vying for power and resources.[15]

Moreover, economic constraints posed another significant hurdle to effective political leadership. Somalia inherited an economic situation from its former colonial powers, making it dependent on foreign aid and handouts from foreign countries.[16] After independence in 1960, economic development lagged and failed to correspond with the growing population influx to urban cities seeking employment. The economic expectations of the Somali people after the independence were very high, as expressed in a famous lyric like "Let us milk our she-camel Maandeeq." (*aan maalno hashayna maandeeq*).[17] However, their expectations were dashed because of the lack of employment and economic development.

---

12. Most politicians never attended formal school, and few had their education at the elementary level. See Mohammed Turunji, *Somalia: The Untold History (1941-1969)* (London: Looh Press, 2015), 269.
13. Abdullahi, Abdurahman, "Somali Elite Political Culture: Conceptions, Structures, and Historical Evolution," Somali Studies: A Peer-Reviewed Academic Journal for Somali Studies 5 (2020): 30–92.
14. Abdi Samatar, *Africa's First Democrats: Somalia's Adan A. Osman and Abdirizak H. Hussein* (Bloomington: Indiana University Press, 2016), 8.
15. Ayoob, Mohammed, "The Horn of Africa: Regional Conflict and Superpower Involvement." Canberra Papers on Strategy and Defence no. 18 (Australian National University, 1978), accessed April 15, 2024, https://openresearch-repository.anu.edu.au/handle/1885/220448.
16. Abdullahi, Abdurahman, *Making Sense of Somali History, Volume One* (London: Adonis & Abbey, 2017), 130.
17. Sahardid Mohamud Elmi penned this lyric and was sung on June 26, 1960, in Hargeisa, the Independence Day of Somaliland from British colonial rule.

Another significant challenge was the unresolved border issue with neighboring states and Somalia's pursuit of its Great Somalia policy. This policy aimed to unite all Somali-inhabited regions of the Horn of Africa under one state, which exacerbated regional tensions. The territorial disputes and Somalia's ambitions drew the attention of the superpowers, the United States and the Soviet Union, each seeking to expand their influence during the Cold War.[18] The resulting geopolitical rivalry led to the militarization of the Horn of Africa. The superpowers provided military support to different countries, further intensifying conflicts and destabilizing the region. The influx of weapons and military aid from both the USA and the Soviet Union not only fueled ongoing disputes but also created new flashpoints for conflict, making the Horn of Africa one of the most volatile regions during this period. While rooted in legitimate historical grievances and aspirations for national unity, conflict with the neighbors has complicated peace and security in the Horn of Africa and diverted attention and resources from domestic priorities.[19]

Moreover, the military regime's adoption of socialism curtailed freedom of expression, suppressed traditional cultural values, and introduced an authoritarian system of governance. It also destroyed economic initiatives and private sector contributions due to nationalized economic enterprises.[20] Furthermore, after the state collapsed in 1991, and during the civil war, the economy was inundated by years of conflict and instability, hindering efforts to provide essential services, generate revenue, and foster economic growth. In addition, the rise of political clannism presents yet another formidable challenge. Deeply ingrained in Somali society, clan-based politics used

---

18. Mohamed Ayoob, *The Horn of Africa: Regional Conflict and Superpower Involvement*, Canberra Papers on Strategy and Defence, no. 18 (Canberra: The Australian National University, 1978), 9-14.

19. Omar, Mohamed Omar, *The Road to Zero: Somalia's Self-Destruction* (London: Haan Associates, 1993), 45.

20. Laitin, David D, "The Political Economy of Military Rule in Somalia," The Journal of Modern African Studies 14, no. 3 (1976): 449–68. Also, Harold D. Nelson, ed., *Somalia: A Country Study* (Washington, DC: American University, 1982), 135–36.

by the political elites often overshadow national interests, leading to factionalism, polarization, and instability. Rather than working towards the common good, political elites prioritized self-serving interests by perpetuating divisions and impeding efforts to forge a unified national identity.

The geopolitical dynamics of the Cold War further complicated the burden of political leadership in Somalia. Situated in a strategically important region, Somalia became a battleground for competing superpowers seeking to advance their strategic interests during the Cold War era.[21] In essence, the leadership challenges in Somalia are multifaceted and deeply entrenched, which requires sustained efforts to address them. From the need for competent and visionary leadership to strengthening governance institutions, resolving economic distresses, mitigating clan-based politics, and navigating complex geopolitical realities, the path to a stable, prosperous Somalia remains troubled with obstacles. Amidst the tumultuous environment of Somalia's faltering state-building, some hope emerged from historically exceptional leaders who defied the odds. Despite grappling with the same limitations of formal education and experience as their political counterparts, these remarkable leaders stand out due to their unique political ethos and unwavering commitment to the betterment of their nation. These leaders have left indelible good examples of Somalia's politics, embodying positive cultural traits, determination, and a profound sense of duty to their people.[22]

This research explores challenges surrounding political leadership in Somalia. Beginning with a background to the topic, the research

---

21. The Somali coastline, about 3025 miles long, is the longest in mainland Africa and the Middle East. About 33,000 commercial ships pass through its territorial waters every year. These ships carry 26 percent of global oil trade and 14–15 percent of international trade, costing $1.8 trillion annually. Abdullahi, *Making Sense of Somali History*, 184, note 54. Also, Bell, J. Bowyer, *The Horn of Africa: Strategic Magnet in the Seventies* (New York: Crane, Russak, 1973).
22. Even though there were many decent unknown leaders, the prominent among them are President Adan Abdulle, Prime Minister Abdirizak, and the first prime minister, Abdullahi Isse.

contextualizes the difficulties inherent in Somali leadership. It also explores various leadership theories, highlighting their applicability within Somalia's unique socio-political landscape. Moreover, the research delves into the Islamic perspective on leadership, recognizing the significant influence of Islamic principles and values on Somali society. By analyzing the intersection of Islamic teachings with contemporary leadership practices, the research elucidates insights into the role of faith in potentially shaping leadership paradigms within the Somali context. Furthermore, a synopsis of the distinctive features characterizing leadership in Somali traditional society is presented. Finally, the book elucidates the multifaceted nature of Somali leadership, characterized by consensus decision-making and inclusive leadership, and the appropriate leadership model and governance system.

BACKGROUND SETTING

The inception of the modern state in Somalia can be traced back to 1956, when the first Somali government under the Italian administration and the UN trusteeship was established. This marked a significant milestone in Somalia's political evolution toward self-governance. This success was realized thirteen years after the Somali Youth Club (SYC) was established by thirteen young Somalis who aimed to forge an independent and unified Somalia in 1943.[23] The formation

---

23. The oldest among the Somali Youth League (SYL) founders in 1943 was Yassin Haji Osman, aged 26 years (1917–47). See I.M. Lewis, *A Modern History of Somalia: Nation and State in the Horn of Africa* (Boulder, CO: Westview Press, 1988), 121–29. Also, Christopher Barnes, "The Somali Youth League, Ethiopian Somalis, and the Greater Somalia Idea, c.1946–48," Journal of Eastern African Studies 1, no. 2 (2007): 287–305. Moreover, It seems that the number 13 occurs in many events in Somali history. Thirteen persons founded SYC, the first government was established after thirteen years (1956) establishing SYC (1943), the military took over after thirteen years in 1969 after thirteen years of the establishing first government. Moreover, the Manifesto leadership comprised thirteen persons, and the Somali government was recognized after thirteen years in 2013 after its establishment in 2000.

of the Somali state, unfamiliar to the Somalis, was coached and supported by Italian advisers and experts until 1960.[24]

After gaining independence in 1960, Somalia faced many challenges inherited from its colonial past, including weak institutions, the integration of former Somaliland and Southern Somalia, territorial disputes with neighboring countries, and economic underdevelopment. Colonial legacies, such as institutional structures and languages, often clashed with local customs and values. Despite initial optimism and idealism, disillusionment grew among the population as the state failed to meet expectations. This disappointment was fueled by the emergence of a self-serving and corrupt political elite disconnected from the needs of the people. The gap between promised prosperity and the harsh realities of inequality, economic stagnation, and social unrest widened, deepening the populace's dissatisfaction with the government.

In 1969, Somalia underwent a significant shift as the military seized power, promising efficiency and ending the corruption of civilian elites. Initially welcomed by the Somali people, the military junta soon exhibited oppressive tactics. Despite hopes for reform, the military regime failed to uphold democratic values, perpetuating repression.[25] Geopolitically, Somalia transitioned from Soviet to American support after the Somali-Ethiopian war in 1977–78, sparking internal factionalism and armed opposition. This shift

---

24. It was evident that none of the ministers had a formal education to manage the ministry. As a result, Italian administrator Anzilotti appointed Italian advisers and experts to each ministry. See the names of these advisers in Trunji, M.I., *Somalia: The Untold History (1941-1969)* (Looh Press, 2015), 269.

25. Detailed brutality of the Military regime is well documented in Mohammed Haji Ingiriis, *The Suicidal State in Somalia: The Rise and Fall of the Siad Barre Regime, 1969-1991* (Lanham, MD: UPA, 2016). Regarding the devastation of the northern regions, see "Somalia: The Government at War with Its Own People—Testimonies about the Killings and Conflict in the North," Africa Watch Report (January 1990), accessed April 15, 2024, https://www.sahistory.org.za/sites/default/files/filepercent20uploads percent20/africa_watch_somalia_a_government_at_war_with_ibook4you.pdf.

exacerbated existing divisions, leading to political instability and violence. Economic decline worsened in the 1980s, with imposed Structural Adjustment Programs (SAPs) causing widespread poverty and discontent. A structural adjustment is a set of economic reforms a country must adhere to secure a loan from the International Monetary Fund and the World Bank. As internal strife escalated, the state collapsed in 1991, plunging Somalia into lawlessness and anarchy.

The collapse of the military regime in 1991 marked a watershed moment in Somalia's history, thrusting the nation into political turmoil, civil war, and social disorder. The destruction of the state and the regime's downfall unleashed a wave of power struggles among the warlords. This period of tumult precipitated a prolonged era of instability characterized by political factionalism, reciprocal violence of the armed oppositions and the government, the failure of state institutions, and economic stress. After the state collapse, twelve reconciliations among the warlords were conducted for ten years with the help of the international community and regional states. Deep-seated divisions, external interventions, and the absence of a cohesive political consensus hindered reconciliation efforts and the restoration of shattered institutions.[26] Despite the slow progress in achieving peace and stability, Somalia faced persistent obstacles to instituting sustainable statehood and effective governance.

Since the re-establishment of the Somali state in 2000 at the Somali Conference in Djibouti, six regimes have alternated in ruling Somalia, each bringing their own vision and leadership skills.[27] However, the efforts to achieve stability and effective governance have been met with considerable challenges. Numerous difficulties have marked

---

26. A concise account of the events after the collapse of the state in 1991 and various reconciliations referred to
Abdurahman Abdullahi, *Making Sense of Somali History, vol. 2* (Adonis & Abbey, 2018), 31–46.
27. The presidents of these six regimes are Abdiqasim Salad, Abdullahi Yusuf, Sheikh Sheikh Ahmed, Hassan Sheikh Mohamud, Mohamed Abdullahi Farmajo, and Hassan Sheikh Mohamud.

the journey toward a stable and effective government in Somalia. Persistent internal conflicts, ranging from clan-based disputes to the ongoing threat posed by militant groups such as Al-Shabaab, have created an environment of insecurity. Political instability is another significant hurdle, with frequent power struggles between the federal member states and the central government. Corruption further complicates the situation, eroding public trust and siphoning off resources desperately needed for development and public services. External pressures, including regional geopolitical dynamics and international interventions, complicate a volatile scenario. These intertwined issues have significantly hindered Somalia's progress toward establishing a fully operational and cohesive state apparatus. The path to Somali state recovery is complex and arduous, demanding sustained and concerted efforts. Both internal reforms and robust international support are crucial to overcoming these obstacles. Somalia's multifaceted challenges demand exceptional leaders with strategic vision and problem-solving abilities. These leaders must inspire confidence and cooperation among various factions, promote unity, and drive the nation's development agenda forward. They must also be capable of effectively harnessing domestic and international resources. They should also prioritize transparency and accountability to combat corruption, ensuring that resources are used efficiently and equitably. Through such leadership, Somalia can hope to overcome its obstacles and achieve lasting stability and development.

THEORIES OF STATE FAILURE AND COLLAPSE

Scholars across diverse academic disciplines and perspectives have embarked on a quest to unravel the enigma surrounding the puzzling collapse of the Somali nation-state. At the heart of their inquiry lies the perplexing question: why did a Somali nation possessing all the essential ingredients for unity witness such a dramatic collapse? Indeed, Somalia presented a unique case study, as its population primarily comprises Somalis renowned for high homogeneity and adherence to the Islamic faith.[28] As such, the collapse of the Somali state defies conventional explanations, prompting scholars to delve into an array of historical, political, socio-economic, and cultural dimensions in the quest for answers. While the Somali people's homogeneity might suggest a natural recipe for unity, the reality exposed more complications.[29]

Research on state failure and collapse often explores the concept of state capacities within comparative political analysis.[30] Scholar Joel Migdal has developed a set of theories to examine the characteristics of weak and strong states and societies. Migdal posits that a state must grant a unified political status of citizenship to all individuals within its jurisdiction and maintain hegemonic control over society. Several factors are crucial for a state's survival, including the organizational capabilities of its leaders, population size, available material and human resources, and the broader international environment.[31] States can be classified into empirical and juridical States. The empirical States de facto have the authority and power to effectively govern a defined territory and its population. They can perform

28. Mapping and analysis of different perspectives explaining factors that contributed to the collapse of the Somali state; see Abdurahman Abdullahi, *Making Sense of Somali History, vol. 1* (Adonis & Abbey, 2017), 183–96.
29. "Either ethnic homogeneity or heterogeneity does not follow an absolute linear relationship with economic performance as there are prosperous, stable, and rich homogenous and heterogenous societies, as well as there are poor, chaotic and stagnated homogenous and heterogenous societies." This is the conclusion of Manuel Andres Sanchez Cardenas's "Ethnic and Cultural Homogeneity: An Obstacle for Development?" Northeastern University (Fall 2019), 18. As is evident, Somali homogeneity is not contributing to its unity due to the poisonous political elite culture developed during the colonial period, which defies the cultural and Islamic norms of the Somali people.
30. States may be classified by their status with the international system, economic capabilities, or their leadership. As such, they are classified as weak and powerful, radical and conservative, patron and client, modern and traditional, and developed and developing. See Kamrava, Mehran, *Understanding Comparative Politics: A Framework for Analysis* (Routledge, 1996), 72.
31. Joel S. Migdal, *Strong Societies and Weak States: State-Society Relations and State Capabilities in the Third World* (Princeton University Press, 1988), 21.

the essential functions of a state. On the other hand, Juridical States (de jure States) are legally recognized by other states but may lack the practical ability to perform state functions.[32] However, despite their shortcomings, other states cannot intervene in their affairs without their consent. A state's capability is assessed by its ability to "penetrate society, regulate social relationships, extract resources, and appropriate or use resources in determined ways."[33] Moreover, the state should be able to regulate social relationships by establishing and enforcing laws and norms. It should also be able to extract resources by collecting taxes and mobilizing economic resources. Finally, the state should appropriately allocate resources to achieve determined goals. Strong states excel in these areas, while weak states struggle to accomplish these goals. Comparative state capacities are evaluated based on these governance capabilities. A key state performance indicator is the effective delivery of "political goods." Migdal's framework helps classify and understand states' varying capacities, distinguishing between those that can effectively govern and those that cannot. Scholars can better assess the factors leading to state strength or collapse by analyzing these capabilities.

The fundamental "political goods" can be summarized as providing security and establishing and maintaining an effective judicial system to uphold law and order. The other goods deliver essential services such as healthcare, education, and environmental protection. Moreover, other political goods provide and maintain basic infrastructure, including roads, railways, airports, and seaports. States must also ensure the smooth functioning of commerce by managing currency and banking systems.[34] A state's effectiveness is

---

32. R.H. Jackson and C.G. Rosberg, "Sovereignty and Underdevelopment: Juridical Statehood in the African Crisis," The Journal of Modern African Studies, vol. 24, no. 1, 1986, 1–31.
33. Joel S. Migdal, Strong Societies and Weak States: State-Society Relations and State Capabilities in the Third World (Princeton: Princeton University Press, 1988), 4.
34. Robert I. Rotberg, State Failure and State Weakness in a Time of Terror (The World Peace Foundation: Brooking Institution Press, 2003), 2–4.

reflected in its capacity to deliver these hierarchical political goods. A strong state safeguards its citizens and provides essential services, infrastructure, and a stable economic environment, fostering a well-functioning society.

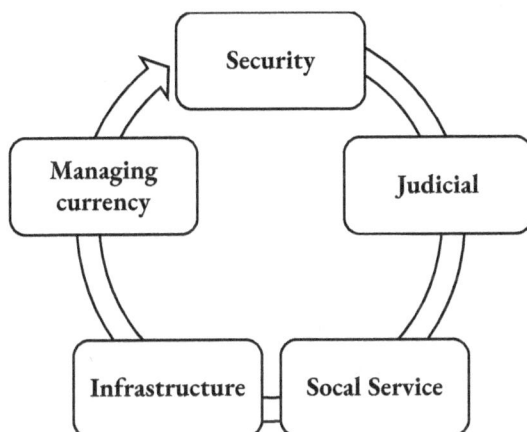

Fig 1. The five fundamental goods of the state

In developmental and security studies, states are evaluated along a continuum ranging from "strong," "weak," "failed," and "collapsed." Strong states are characterized by their ability to "control their territories and deliver a full range and a high quality of political goods to their citizens."[35] Key indicators of their high performance include "per capita GDP, the UNDP Human Development Index, Transparency International's Corruption Perceptions Index, and Freedom House's Freedom of the World Report".[36] Strong states also tend to show higher marks on the eight major characteristics of good governance, which are participatory, consensus-oriented, accountability, transparent, responsive, effective and efficient, equitable and inclusive, and following the rule of law. Good governance also assures that corruption is minimized, that the views of minorities are considered, and that the voices of the most vulnerable in society are

---

35. Robert I. Rotberg, *Nation-state failure: A recurrence Phenomenon?*, 3–5, retrieved from www.cia.gov/nic/PDF_GIF_2020_Support/ 2003_11_06_papers/panel2_nov6.pdf.
36. Ibid., 2

heard in decision-making. Moreover, good governance should also be responsive to society's present and future needs.

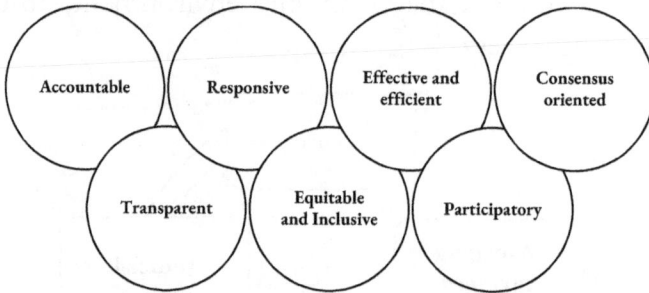

Fig 2. The 8 Elements of Good Governance

Weak states can be divided into two categories: those moving toward strength and those descending toward failure. The latter group faces objective challenges such as geographical, physical, and economic constraints and internal issues such as a lack of cohesion and ineffective leadership. These weak states struggle to resolve ethnic, religious, or linguistic tensions, leading to widespread conflict and a low capacity to provide essential political goods. As a result, physical infrastructure deteriorates, corruption escalates, and civil society faces repression. On the other hand, failed states exist at two extremes: they may either completely lose their ability to function or become excessively intrusive and oppressive. In the first scenario, the state fails to provide essential political goods, ceding control to warlords and other non-state actors. Institutions become dysfunctional, with a weak judiciary and unaccountable bureaucracy. Infrastructure crumbles, social services decline, and economic prospects plummet, leading to widespread discontent and economic instability.[37]

A collapsed state represents the end of state failure, characterized by the breakdown of political authority, law and order, and social

---

37. The new definitions and explanations contained in this paper are elaborated upon at much greater length in Robert I. Rotberg, "The Failure and Collapse of Nation-States: Breakdown, Prevention, and Repair," in Robert I. Rotberg (ed.), *Why States Fail: Causes and Consequences* (Princeton, 2004), 1–45.

cohesion. This collapse occurs gradually as the state loses legitima-cy and control over its territory. Communities realign along ethnic, kinship, and cultural lines, with armed clans often assuming control. Sub-state actors attempt to restore functionality, but full recovery requires significant external support. The progression from weakness to collapse is a gradual and cumulative process akin to degenerative diseases. While states may recover from weakness or failure with external assistance, complete collapse represents a breakdown of social and political order on an extensive scale.[38] Somalia is a country that degenerated from a weak to a failed and collapsed state in 1991.

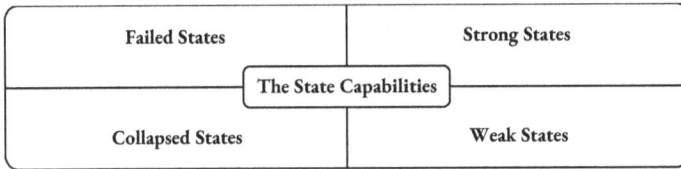

Failed States	Strong States
The State Capabilities	
Collapsed States	Weak States

Fig 3. Classification of the State Capabilities

The Sequential Stages of Somali State Collapse

The failure and eventual collapse of the Somali state were pro-tracted processes that unfolded from 1969 to 1991. This period was marked by political mismanagement, military defeats, economic hardship, and rising internal conflicts. Over two decades, these com-pounding issues eroded the state's ability to govern, culminating in its complete disintegration by 1991. The Somali state's failure and collapse can be understood by dividing the process into four distinct phases. Each phase encapsulates a series of critical events and dynamics that collectively led to the eventual disintegration of the central government. The first failure of the state began in 1969

---

38. Collapsed states could recover by returning to the status of failed if suffi-cient security is restored to rebuild the institutions and strengthen the legitima-cy of the resuscitated state. Lebanon did so thanks to Syrian security, Tajikistan because of Russia, and Sierra Leone because of British intervention. Somalia is in the process of recovery under the African Union Mission for Somalia (AMISOM). See Robert I. Rotberg, *Nation-state failure: A recurrence Phenom-enon?*.

when the election was marred by widespread allegations of fraud and manipulation, undermining public trust in the democratic process. Subsequently, the assassination of President Sharmarke on October 15, 1969, created a power vacuum and political instability. As a result, on October 21, 1969, Major General Siad Barre led a military coup, overthrowing the civilian government and marking the beginning of military rule. The second phase of the state's failure was the defeat in the war with Ethiopia (1977/78), severely affecting national pride, military, and public morale. Subsequently, a group of military officers attempted to overthrow Siad Barre's regime on April 9, 1978. However, the coup was swiftly suppressed, leading to the execution of 17 officers and the imprisonment of hundreds. As a result, the first armed opposition, the Somali Salvation Front (SSF), founded in 1978, was renamed the Somali Salvation Democratic Front (SSDF) in 1979, pioneering the emergence of organized armed resistance against Barre's government. The third phase was when the long-standing civil war peaked in 1988, and the cities of Hargeisa and Burco in the Northern regions (Somaliland) were leveled to the ground.[39] The populations of these cities were either killed or fled to Ethiopia and the nearby rural areas. Since then, the United Somali Congress (USC) and the Somali Patriotic Movement (SPM) were established afterward, weakening the government forces. The fourth and final phase of the complete collapse of the state culminated in the overthrow of Siad Barre's regime in January 1991. This event marked the complete disintegration of the central government, leading to a power vacuum and further fragmentation of the country. As evident in almost every decade, significant and tangible changes have occurred. These changes highlight a recurring pattern, with each ten years marking a distinct shift in various aspects of the situation. These decadal changes have consistently reshaped the Somali political landscape.

---

39. An African Watch Report, "Somalia: A Government at War with Its Own People: Testimonies about the Killings and Conflicts in the North," 1990.

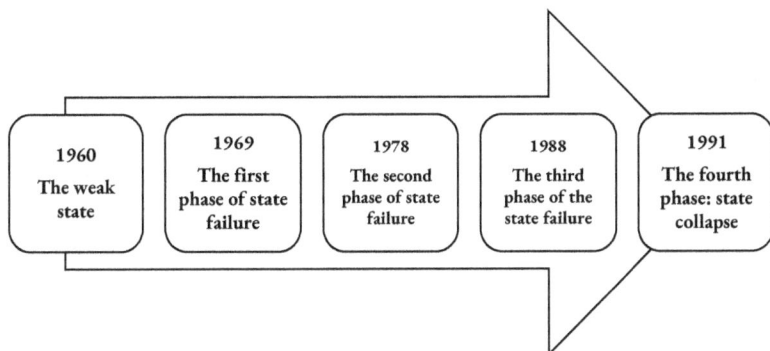

Fig 4. The four phases of state failure and collapse.

Understanding the collapse of states and the emergence of conflicts requires a nuanced analysis of long-term structural issues, factors that nurture and sustain conflict, and immediate triggers. By examining these layers, we can better grasp the complexity of intrastate conflicts and the diverse causes that underpin them. State collapse is invariably linked to conflict, which can be categorized into three main types: original causes, operational causes, and proximate efficient causes. Original Causes (Genesis) are deeply rooted conditions, the long-term, foundational issues that date back to the very formation of the society or state. They include historical grievances, structural inequalities, and deeply ingrained social divisions. Moreover, they include objective factors that create an environment ripe for conflict when combined with subjective factors such as leadership ambitions or ethnic tensions. The operational causes exacerbate and sustain conflict, deepening its likelihood and intensity. They often magnify the original causes, including economic hardships, political repression, and social injustice. The impact of operational causes is directly related to the severity and widespread nature of the original causes. The more significant and pervasive the original causes, the more potent the operational causes become. Proximate efficient causes are the trigger mechanisms, the immediate events or conditions that ignite conflict. They serve as catalysts for the outbreak of intrastate conflict and civil strife. Examples include political assassinations, economic crises, or sudden policy changes.

Perspectives on the Somali State Collapse

The collapse of the Somali state has been analyzed through various scholarly perspectives, each highlighting different contributing factors. Although scholars often focus on specific elements, they generally acknowledge a range of interconnected causes. The major themes identified in scholarly research on the collapse of the Somali state include:

1) *End of the Cold War and Withdrawal of Foreign Aid*: The end of the Cold War led to a significant reduction in foreign aid and support, which had been crucial for Somalia's economy and military. This withdrawal of international assistance left the state financially and politically vulnerable. The Cold War and the withdrawal of foreign assistance as the main factors of state collapse were the focus of several scholars, including Terrence Lyons, Walter S. Clarke, Robert Gosende, Ahmed Samatar, Ken Menkhaus, and John Prendergast.[40]

2) *Somali Irredentism and War with Ethiopia*: Somali Irredentism is rooted in the historical fact that the Somali-inhabited territories in the Horn of Africa were occupied and divided among four foreign powers during the European scramble for Africa. These powers were Italy, Britain, France, and the Ethiopian Empire. Encouraged by the Bevin Plan, Somali nationalists grasped the "Greater Somalia" concept, founded

---

40. Terrence Lyons and Ahmed Samatar, *Somalia: State Collapse, Multilateral Intervention, and Strategies for Political Reconstruction* (Washington: The Brooking Institution Occasional Paper, 1995), 1; Walter S. Clarke and Robert Gosende, "Somalia: Can a Collapsed State Reconstitute itself?" in Robert I. Rotberg (ed.), *State Failure and State Weakness in a Time of Terror* (Washington: Brooking Institution Press, 2000), 129–58; Ahmed Samatar, "The Curse of Allah: Civic Disembowelment and the collapse of the State in Somalia" in Ahmed Samatar (ed.), *The Somali Challenge: From Catastrophe to Renewal?* (Lynne Rienner Publishers, 1994), 117; Ken Menkhaus, "US Foreign Assistance Somalia: Phoenix from the Ashes?" Middle Eastern Policy, l, no. 5, 1997, 126; Ken Menkhaus and John Prendergast, "Governance and Economic Survival in Post-intervention Somalia" in CSIS Africa Note, no. 172 (May 1995).

on reunifying Somali populations in five different regions and represented by the Somali flag's five-pointed white stars. Somalia's efforts to unite all Somali-inhabited territories (irredentism) led to conflicts with neighboring Ethiopia, particularly the Ogaden War, which drained resources and destabilized the region.[41]

3) *Primordialism and Rampant Political Clannism*: Somalia is a nation of clans searching for a state, and the clan system can be used negatively or positively in nation-building. It can be used as a conflict tool or a peace and conflict resolution mechanism. Deep-rooted clan loyalties and rivalries (primordialism) played a significant role in the political landscape, leading to fragmented governance and frequent conflicts among clans vying for power. Proponents of this perspective are I.M. Lewis, Said Samatar, Anna Simons, and Okbazghi Yohannes.[42]

4) *Moral Corruption and Cultural Decay*: Widespread corruption and the erosion of cultural values weakened the state's moral and ethical foundations, contributing to ineffective governance and loss of public trust. Human history has evinced that when a society becomes morally corrupt, greed and selfishness prevail, the society becomes volatile, and inescapably, the nation slides toward collapse. The Islamic per-

---

41. John T. Fishel, *Civil Military Operations in the New World* (Praeger, 1997), 189; Joseph K. Nkaisserry, "The Ogaden War: An Analysis of Its Causes and Its Impact on Regional Peace and the Horn of Africa," USAWC Strategic Research Project, US Army War College Carlisle Barracks, Pennsylvania, 1997. Available from file:///C:/Users/Abdurahman/Downloads/ADA326941%20(1).pdf (accessed on February 2, 2017)

42. I.M. Lewis, *Blood, and Bone: The Call of Kinship in Somali Society* (Lawrenceville, Nj: Red Sea Press, 1994), 233; Said S. Samatar, "Unhappy Masses and the Challenges of Political Islam in the Horn of Africa," retrieved from www.wardheernews.com/March_05/05 (accessed on February 2, 2017); Okbhazghi Yohannes, *The United States and the Horn of Africa: An Analytical Study of Pattern and Process* (Westview Press, 1997), 225.

spective of the rise and fall of the states and civilizations may be summarized by injustice (*Zulm*) which creates discord (*Khilaf*), and the lack of a rectification mechanism to prevent evil and command goodness (*Al-amr bil al-ma'ruf wa nahyi ani al-munkar*), which produces personal and social moral degradation (*Fasad*).[43]

5) *Overextension of Resources*: The state's overextension in military spending and ambitious projects without sustainable economic planning led to financial strain and resource depletion. Ambassador Mohamed Osman was the only scholar who addressed the factor of the overextension of meager resources. He examined leadership policy guidelines towards Somali unity and respectfully criticized them on their prioritization plan of national goals. He sees overextension as reducing the state's capacity by undertaking too many tasks to be implemented too quickly.[44]

6) *Eclectic Factors*: Many scholars recognize that the collapse was due to a combination of various factors rather than a single cause. These include external influences, internal power struggles, economic challenges, and social dynamics. Proponents of this position include Bradbury, Geoge Kaly Kieth, Ida Rousseau Mukende, Ahmed Samatar, and Hussein Adam.[45]

---

43. There are many verses in the Qur'an and many Hadith Narrations regarding injustice. For instance, "We sent aforetime our apostles with Clear Signs and sent down with them the Book and the Balance (of right and wrong), that men may stand forth in justice." — Surah Al Hadid (57), Aayah 25. (Qist, Adl) Surah Al Nahl (16), Aayah 90 says: "God commands justice, the doing of good and liberality to kith and kin, and He forbids all shameful deeds, and injustice and rebellion: He instructs you that ye may receive admonition." Qudsi Hadith, "O My servant, I have forbidden injustice for Myself and forbade it also for you. So avoid being unjust to one another." [Muslim]
44. Mohamed Osman Omar, *The Road to Zero: Somalia's self-destruction* (HAAN associates, 1992), 45.
45. George Kaly Kieth and Ida Rousseau Mukenge, *Zones of Conflict in Africa: Theories and Cases* (Praeger, 2002), 124; Hussein M. Adam, "Somalia: Mili-

Most scholars tend to concentrate on secondary causes of the collapse based on their research objectives and specializations. Political scientists, for instance, emphasize the role of political clannism and governance failures; economists focus on economic mismanagement and resource overextension. Historians highlight historical griev- ances and colonial legacies. The collapse of the Somali state can be understood by categorizing the contributing factors into three his- torical periods, each highlighting different issues that progressively weakened the state.

1. *Original causes:* First, Somali society was fragmented into small, clan-based mini-states without a history of unified national institutions or collective leadership. Second, colonial powers divided Somali territory into five parts, notably granting Ethiopia a significant portion, creating lasting ter- ritorial disputes. Third, poor economic development and trained human resources to replace colonial bureaucracy hampered effective governance. These original causes set the stage for a weak and fragmented state at the time of indepen- dence in 1960.

2. *Operational Causes:* First, the new Somali state struggled with political instability, largely due to the legacy of colonial frag- mentation and ongoing clan rivalries before the establishment of the modern state. Second, persistent economic difficulties, including reliance on foreign aid and inadequate infrastruc- ture, further destabilized the state. Third, pursuing the Great Somalia policies, particularly the conflict with Ethiopia, drained resources and exacerbated internal divisions. The

tarism, Warlordism or Democracy?" Review of African Political Economy, 54 (1992): 11–26; Hussein M. Adan, "Somalia: A Terrible Beauty Being Born?" in I. William Zartman (ed.), *Collapsed States: The Disintegration and Restoration of Legitimate Authority* (London: Lynne Reinne, 1995), 69–89; David Rawson, "Dealing with Disintegration: US Assistance and Somali State" in *The Somali Challenge: From Catastrophe to Renewal?*, ed. Ahmed Samatar (London: Lyne Rienner Publisher, 1994), 147–78, 150.

Somali state's weaknesses became more pronounced during this period, leading to further decline.

3. *Proximate Causes:* First, the defeat of the Somali military in the Somali-Ethiopian war in 1977–78 weakened the state's military and economic position. Second, increased repression and the failure to address economic and social issues led to the emergence of armed opposition groups. Third, the combination of these factors culminated in the overthrow of Siad Barre's regime in 1991, leading to the complete disintegration of the central government and ensuing civil war.

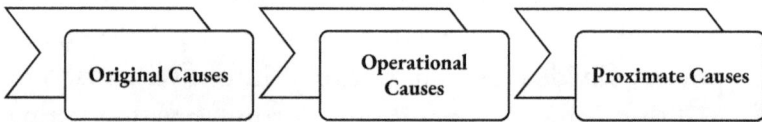

```
[ Original Causes ] > [ Operational Causes ] > [ Proximate Causes ]
```

Fig 5. Categorizing factors of the state collapse

In conclusion, the primary responsibility for the collapse of the Somali state rests squarely on the leadership within Somalia itself. The underlying causes of this collapse are predominantly internal, rooted in the destructive behaviors and ambitions of the country's elites. These leaders engaged in fierce competition for political power, fostering a toxic political culture characterized by despotism, rampant corruption, clannism, and a reliance on foreign patronage. As the state began to falter, the ruling regime and the leaders of armed opposition groups failed to take effective measures to prevent the impending collapse. Their inability to cooperate and find solutions exacerbated the situation, leading to the eventual disintegration of the state in 1991. The collapse of the Somali state marked a significant turning point in the nation's history. It signified not just the downfall of the post-colonial government but also the dissolution of the constructed national identity built since independence.

THE PARADIGM SHIFT OF SOMALI STATE-BUILDING IN 2000

The state-building paradigm has undergone three significant shifts in Somalia's recent history. The first occurred in 1969 when the country transitioned from a liberal democratic system to military rule and embraced socialist principles. The second pivotal shift occurred in 2000 when Somalia embraced clan power-sharing of the 4.5 formula and recognized Islam as a central guiding principle.[46] Two significant shifts occurred in 2000. The political elites, who had been claiming to eliminate clannism since the beginning of the liberation movement in 1943, accepted the clan factor. Also, the trend of the secularity of the state was reversed by accepting Islam as the ultimate reference of all laws. The third shift was adopting the Federal system in 2004 as part of the evolving Somali state reconfiguration in 2004. This move responded to perceived failures of inherited democratic systems and military rule, which could not provide stability or effectively integrate the diverse Somali society. By decentralizing power and incorporating traditional clan structures and Islamic principles into governance, proponents of this new approach argue for a more inclusive and locally grounded form of state-building.

However, the challenges culminated during the Somali Peace and Reconciliation conference in Djibouti in 2000 continued. The 4.5 formula, which allocated political representation based on clan identity, underscored how clan dynamics had permeated Somali governance structures focussed on for years. Amid the countless proposed solutions to the Somali crisis, Western experts championed liberal approaches to conflict resolution and state recovery. This approach emphasizes principles of democracy, human rights, and inclusive governance as essential pillars for rebuilding a collapsed state. However, in stark contrast to these Western perspectives, Islamists have advocated for a fundamentally different approach, asserting that the implemen-

---

46. During the Somali Peace and Reconciliation Conference in Djibouti in 2000, a clan-based quota was adopted, known as 4.5. The four stands for the equal quota of the four major clans: Digil & Mirifle Dir, Darood, and Hawiye, and the other half quota stands for the collection of other minority clans.

tation of Sharia law holds the key to resolving the Somali crisis and fostering unity among devout Muslims. Even though the concept is valid theoretically, nonetheless, Islamist scholars and those in power did not come up with specific programs, processes, approaches, consensus, and policies for implementing Sharia. It was confined mainly to rhetoric and advocacy.

The Impact of Islamists on Leadership and Governance

Central to the perspective of Islamists is the belief that adherence to Sharia law is an Islamic obligation and an acceptable solution to society. They argue that Sharia law provides a comprehensive framework for governance that encompasses aspects of justice, morality, and social welfare, thus offering a holistic approach to addressing the complex issues confronting Somali society. Implementing Sharia law is seen as a unifying approach that transcends clan divisions and fosters a collective identity among Muslims. Their narrative is that by grounding governance in Islamic principles, they contend that overcoming the fragmentation and discord plaguing Somali politics and society is possible. Moreover, they argue that Sharia law promotes values of compassion, solidarity, and mutual respect, essential for fostering harmony and cohesion among diverse clans.[47]

In theory, this argument is valid. Adopting Islam as the fundamental framework for conflict resolution is deeply entrenched in the annals of Islamic history, and it finds robust support from two primary sources: the Quran and the Prophetic tradition.[48] Neverthe-

---

47. There are many verses and prophetic traditions on this issue. However, the following verse provides a comprehensive understanding: "[And the believers, men, and women, are protecting friends one of another; they enjoin the right and forbid the wrong, and they establish worship, pay the poor dues, and obey Allah and His messenger. As for these, Allah will have mercy on them. Lo! Allah is Mighty, Wise]" (At-Tawbah 9:71).
48. The opening of Mecca after eight years of Muslim migration and continuous civil war serves as an example of transitional justice in Muslim history. The Prophet Muhammad applied a similar approach to current techniques, imple-

less, the practical application of these principles is far from straight-forward, as it necessitates a profound comprehension of procedural methodologies and approaches, coupled with dedication from a le-gitimate authority. Executing such a paradigm shift demanded me-ticulous navigation through complex socio-political situations and establishing mechanisms that ensure genuine adherence to Islamic values. Indeed, Islam provides distinctive solutions that differ from many of those claiming to advocate for its implementation. This delineation is crucial in discerning the authentic application of Islamic teachings from superficial assertions. Genuine adherence to Islam involves a comprehensive understanding and embodiment of its principles in both belief and action. In contrast, mere claims of advocating for the implementation of Sharia need sincerity to align with the true essence of Islamic values.[49] Therefore, it is imperative to differentiate between those who genuinely uphold Islam's teachings and those who merely espouse them superficially for various motives or agendas.

The Islamic Court Union's ascendancy in 2006 marked a critical moment in Somalia's recent history when various groups of Islamists and their supporters seized control of Mogadishu and surrounding areas, threatening the transitional government headquartered in Baidoa.[50] This challenge provoked Ethiopian military intervention to prevent the collapse of the transitional government they sponsored and propped.[51] This occurrence is a testament to the failure of the

---

menting general amnesty, prosecuting some individuals, pardoning others, and reforming oppressive institutions. This process fostered brotherhood, equality, and shared values and principles for all. See Abdurahman Abdullahi, *Recovering the Somali State: The Role of Islam, Islamism, and Transitional Justice* (London: Adonis & Abbey, 2018), 123–26.

49. Abdurahman Abdullahi, "Theorizing Islam and Islamists: Critical Concep-tions and Cultural Challenges," in *Theorizing Somali Society: Hope, Transfor-mation, and Development, vol. 1*, ed. Abdulkadir Osman Farah and Mohamed A. Eno (Authors Press, 2022), 122–50.

50. Cedric Barnes and Harun Hassan, "The Rise and Fall of Mogadishu's Islamic Courts," Journal of Eastern African Studies 1, no. 2 (2007): 151–60.

51. Zeray W. Yihdego, "Ethiopia's Military Action against the Union of Islamic

liberal narrative to establish stability and governance in Somalia, which paved the way for the Islamists to assert their influence. Amidst the escalating tensions and the armed Islamist resurgence, a significant development occurred in 2009 when reconciliation was held in Djibouti between the opposition by the Alliance of Re-liberation of Somalia (ARS) and the government. The ARS was a grand coalition party formed in Eritrea in September 2007 as the successor to the Islamic Courts Union (ICU) during the Ethiopian military occupation of Somalia. At this conference, a grand coalition government was formed between the two sides.[52] This marked a defining moment in Somali politics, as it brought together various factions, including both elements of the government and the opposition, in coalition with the Islamic Court Union.[53] Sheikh Sharif, a former leader of the Islamic Courts Union, was elected president, symbolizing a significant shift in power dynamics. However, the coalition government's formation was challenging. Despite Sheikh Sharif's assumption of the presidency, Al-Shabaab and Hizbul-Islam, militant groups associated with the Islamic Court Union, continued to wage a violent insurgency against the government headed by their former leader.[54] The two sides of the spectrum of the conflict were factions of the Islamic Courts Union and those claiming Islamism because of their different interpretation of Islam.

The two administrations of President Sheikh Sharif (2009-2012) and President Hassan Sheikh Mohamud (2012–2017), associated with Islamist groups, showed no difference from the previous

---

Courts and Others in Somalia: Some Legal Implications," International and Comparative Law Quarterly 56, no. 3 (July 2007): 666–76.
52. See a Copy of the Djibouti Agreement signed between the ARS and TFG. Available from https://peacemaker.un.org/sites/peacemaker.un.org/files/SO_080609_Agreement%20between%20the%20TFG%20and%20the%20ARS%20-%20Djibouti%20Agreement.pdf (Accessed on June 16, 2024).
53. Apuuli Phillip Kasaija, "The UN-led Djibouti Peace Process for Somalia, 2008–2009: Results and Problems," accessed August 24, 2010, 261–82.
54. Sheikh Sharif Sheikh Ahmed, elected president of Somalia in Djibouti in 2009, was the leader of the Islamic Courts Union, to which al-Shabaab belonged.

regimes despite their espousal of Islamic principles. The performance of these administrations in delivering good governance was below the expected level. President Sheikh Sharif and President Hassan Sheikh Mohamud's terms revealed broader debates surrounding the ability of Islamists to implement their rhetoric and Islamic values in real life. The two administrations grappled with the challenges of consolidating power amidst a volatile security debacle marked by the ongoing conflict with militant groups. Addressing deep-seated societal divisions and overcoming the legacy of conflict and instability also persisted. Against this backdrop, it is evident that the Somali elites' political culture has little difference, and their claimed ideological difference seems superficial and elusive.

From the Islamic perspective, there is a vital connection between ethical leadership and the stability of societies, highlighting the detrimental impact of non-ethical rulers. It urges significance on the quality of leadership and governance, advocating for honesty, integrity, and justice among those in positions of authority.[55] Many scholars addressed the interconnection between the welfare of the people and their leaders. For example, the Nigerian scholar Chinwe Achebe's question regarding Nigeria's troubles assumes significance as it is all about leadership. Achebe's inquiry critically examines the underlying factors hindering Nigeria's progress towards stability and development. He emphasized the role of political leadership in building or breaking states, stating, *"The trouble with Nigeria is simply and squarely the failure of Leadership."*[56] Moreover, prominent political scientist Noam Chomsky underscores that "Failed states are the outcome of ineffective leadership." Furthermore, he asserts that "a failed state serves as a tragic testament to governance failure."[57]

---

55. See the Allah's Messenger (□) said, "When honesty is lost, then wait for the Hour." It was asked, "How will honesty be lost, O Allah's Messenger (□)?" He said, "When authority is given to those who do not deserve it, then wait for the Hour."

56. Chinwe Achebe, The Trouble with Nigeria (Haiman Educational Publishers, 1983), 1.

57. "30 Best Failed States Quotes," in Noam Chomsky, *Failed States: The Crisis*

Furthermore, Robert I. Roberg, a researcher of state failure, bluntly concludes that

> It is that leadership errors across history have destroyed states for personal gain; in the contemporary era, leadership mistakes continue to erode fragile polities in Africa, Asia, and Oceania that already operate on the cusp of failure.[58]

A Note on the Application of Sharia.

Acknowledging the Somali complexities, this author embarked on a research project to critique prevailing perspectives in Somali studies. He delved into the state-society relations theory, founded on the fact that society provides crucial support for a state's effectiveness and that a state is critical to collective action in society. Moreover, Somali leadership was examined through the study of elite political culture. These two topics are used as units of analysis to explain the crisis of the Somali state.[59] Through analysis, it became evident that the Somali state institutions and its elites marginalized society by pursuing the European modernization approach, creating a conflict between modernity and tradition. This undertaking produced a state that conflicted with its society: Islam and clan structure and culture.

---

of Political Development in the Twenty-First Century, 2006 (accessed on June 25, 2024).

58. Robert I. Rotberg, "Failed States, Collapsed States, Weak States: Causes and Indicators," accessed on April 5, 2024, https://www.brookings.edu/wp-content/uploads/2016/07/statefailureandstateweaknessinatimeofterror_chapter.pdf, 22.

59. Joel Migdal, *State in Society: Studying How States and Societies Transform and Constitute Each Other* (New York: Cambridge University Press, 2001); Peter Evans, *Embedded Autonomy* (Princeton: Princeton University Press, 1995); Atul Kohli, "State, Society and Development," in Political Science: The State of the Discipline, ed. Ira Katznelson and Helen Milner (New York: Norton, 2002), 84–117. Abdullahi A. "Somali Elite Political Culture: Conceptions, Structures, and Historical Evolution," Somali Studies: A Peer-Reviewed Academic Journal for Somali Studies 5 (2020). Also, Abdullahi A. "Revisiting Somali Historiography: Critique and Idea of Comprehensive Perspective," Journal of Somali Studies: Research on Somalia and the Greater Horn of African Countries 5, no. 1–2.

Moreover, the outcome of the Somali elite political culture studies, contrasting secular liberal-minded elites and Islamists, concluded that meaningful distinctions should be based only on their achievements in good governance parameters.[60] Immersed in the evolving understanding of Somali elite political culture, this author crafted a comprehensive perspective on Somali reconciliation that hopefully sheds some light on the possibility of establishing a stable state.[61] Recognizing that the root cause of the collapse of the Somali state and the challenges of its reinstitution were tied to exceptional political leadership and appropriate state-society relations and institutions, the author delved into Somali history to identify leaders whose distinct elite cultures had made tangible differences in state-building. Somali political elites demonstrated a shared and commonly held similar political culture; whether they claimed democracy, dictatorship, or Islamists, the conclusive evidence was the failure to institute a viable Somali state over more than sixty-eight years, except for the early formative years, which also failed to sustain.

Thus, it is essential to note that the objectives and values outlined in Islam closely intersect with the principles upheld by non-Muslim nations in their pursuit of good governance.[62] The modern state's responsibilities align with a commitment to the rule of law, citizen equality, democratic processes in selecting political leadership, justice provision, economic opportunities, advancing infrastructure devel-

---

60. United Nations Economic and Social Commission for Asia and the Pacific, "What Is Good Governance?" accessed April 16, 2024, https://www.unescap. org/sites/default/files/good-governance.pdf.

61. Abdullahi "Baadiyow" A., "Theorizing Stability of the Somali State: In the Light of the Comprehensive Perspective of Somali Studies," Somali Studies: A Peer-Reviewed Academic Journal for Somali Studies 8 (2023): 11–55.

62. See Islamicity index Mehmet Ata Az, "European Values and Islam," in The Idea and Values of Europe: From Antigone to the Charter of Fundamental Rights, ed. Angelo Santagostino (Cambridge Scholars Publishing, 2020), 41–64. Also, Scheherazade S. Rehman and Hossein Askari, "How Islamic are Islamic Countries?" Global Economy Journal 10, no. 2 (2010): 1–40. Available from Islamicity-index.org/wp/latest-indices-2022/ (accessed on April 12, 2024).

opment, and ensuring robust social services.[63] Historically, states that have successfully delivered on these issues have flourished, and their populations live in peace and freedom, regardless of their religious affiliations. Consequently, the crux of the matter does not reside in mere rhetorical assertions invoking Islam and articulating empty references to the Quranic verses and prophetic traditions or adding a prefix of "Islamic" to the name of the state. Instead, the pivotal question revolves around the ability to translate their rhetoric into tangible, pragmatic solutions in line with the principles and values espoused by Islam. This demands a shift from mere ideological posturing to the pragmatic implementation of policies and practices that resonate with the essence of Islamic teachings, thereby fostering societal progress and harmony.

Effectively applying Sharia necessitates creating shared understanding and consensus on what it means to implement Sharia in the current modern state system and globalized world. This means cultivating a comprehensive approach rooted in a nuanced comprehension of three interconnected phases. Firstly, a profound understanding of Islam's foundational texts—the Quran and the prophetic tradition—alongside diverse interpretations offered by the past and present Sharia experts. This exploration unveils the essence of Islamic principles and reveals a spectrum of interpretations adaptable to various societal contexts. Secondly, a thorough grasp of the specificity of the society of the state becomes imperative, encompassing its customs, norms, economic dynamics, societal relations, and political conditions studied in the social science subjects. Briefly, this means "know Islam- and know the context." Recognizing the symbiotic relationship between Sharia and societal frameworks, practitioners must discern which societal customs align harmoniously with Sharia principles, facilitating their incorporation into legal practice. Thirdly, the practical implementation of Sharia mandates the establishment of requisite institutional frameworks, cultivating

---

63. Robert I. Rothberg, State and State Weakness in the Time of Terror (World Peace Foundation: Brookings Institution Press, 2003), 2–4. Also, Abdullahi A., *Making Sense of Somali History, vol. 1* (London: Adonis & Abey, 2019), 172.

trained human resources, and formulating the necessary procedural policies.[64] These mechanisms are essential for translating theoretical knowledge into tangible actions that uphold Sharia's integrity while fostering societal cohesion and progress. The application of sharia should not be limited to legal matters. I should encompass the whole body of the society and state by promoting ethical values and morality. Through attention to these three interwoven steps, Sharia can be applied judiciously, serving as a guiding beacon for ethical governance and societal flourishing.

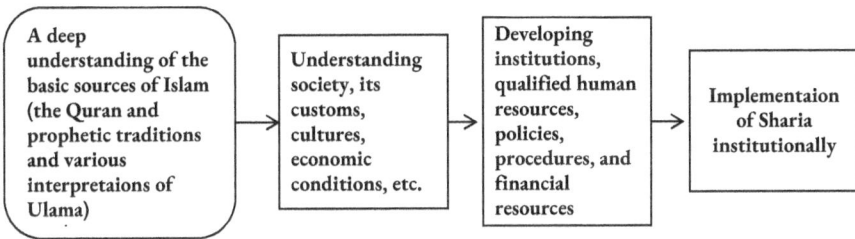

Fig. 6. The three necessary levels for the practical application of Sharia.

AN OVERVIEW OF THE THEORIES OF LEADERSHIP

Recognizing that leaders play a pivotal role in shaping the destiny of nations, Somalia faces significant state-building challenges that are intricately tied to its leadership. To delve into this discourse, providing an overview of various leadership theories is imperative. By exploring these diverse leadership theories, we can better understand the complex dynamics in Somalia's state-building efforts and leadership's critical role in navigating these challenges and fostering sustainable development.

Exploring leadership theories involves delving into various theories to elucidate why some leaders succeed while others falter. These theories serve as frameworks, offering guidelines and insights into the dynamics of effective leadership and the factors influenc-

---

64. Abdullahi A., "The Application of Sharia in Somalia," accessed April 17, 2024, https://www.scribd.com/document/15419600/The-application-of-Sharia-in-Somalia.

ing it. Broadly categorized, these theories can be classified into eight main categories: contingency theories, trait theories, behavioral theories, relationship theories, power theories, situational theories, participative theories, and transactional theories.[65] Contingency theories posit that effective leadership is contingent upon situational factors and contexts, suggesting that different situations require different leadership approaches.[66] On the other hand, trait theories focus on identifying innate characteristics and qualities predisposing individuals to effective leadership, emphasizing personal attributes such as intelligence, charisma, and integrity.[67] Moreover, behavioral theories examine leaders' behaviors and actions, suggesting that certain behaviors lead to more effective leadership outcomes.[68]

Furthermore, relationship theories emphasize the importance of interpersonal relationships and connections between leaders and followers, asserting that strong relationships contribute to effective leadership.[69] Additionally, power theories delve into the sources and

65. Kendra Chery, "The Major Leadership Theories: The Eight Major Theories of Leadership," accessed April 13, 2024, https://reachingnewheightsfoundation.com/rnhf-wp/wp-content/uploads/2016/12/8-Leadership-Theory.pdf.

66. B. Harney, "Contingency Theory," in *Encyclopedia of Human Resource Management*, ed. S. Johnstone and A. Wilkinson (Edward Elgar, 2023), 470. Also, Roya Ayman, Martin M. Chemers, and Fred Fiedler, "The Contingency Model of Leadership Effectiveness: Its Levels of Analysis," The Leadership Quarterly 6, no. 2 (1995): 147–67.

67. Rekha Kanodia and Arun Sacher, "Trait Theories of Leadership," International Journal of Science Technology and Management 5, no. 12 (2016), accessed April 12, 2024, http://www.ijstm.com/images/short_pdf/1480489811_537ijstm.pdf. Also, Yang Zhang, "Rethinking Trait Theory Analysis of the Impacts of Trait Level on Leadership," in ICEMCI 2022: AEBMR 231 (2023): 852–57.

68. Niam Sinno, "A Behavioral Approach to Understanding Leadership Effectiveness," master's thesis, Harvard Extension School, 2018. Also, Raveen Purohit, "Review on Study of Behavioral Approach to Leadership," International Journal of Scientific and Research Publications 11, no. 1 (2021).

69. A. L. Cunliffe and M. Eriksen, "Relational Leadership," Human Relations 64, no. 11 (2011): 1426–49. Also, R. Martin, "Relationship as a Core of Effective Leadership," Low Intensity Conflict & Law Enforcement 13, no. 1 (2013): 76.

dynamics of power within leadership contexts, exploring how leaders wield authority and influence over others. Situational theories propose that effective leadership is contingent upon a situation's specific circumstances and demands, advocating for adaptive leadership strategies.[70] Participative theories advocate for including followers in decision-making processes, positing that involving followers enhances commitment and engagement.[71] Transactional theories focus on exchanges between leaders and followers, emphasizing the role of rewards and incentives in motivating followers to achieve organizational goals.[72] Overall, these diverse leadership theories offer valuable insights into the nature of leadership, highlighting the complex interplay of individual characteristics, behaviors, relationships, and situational factors in shaping effective leadership outcomes.

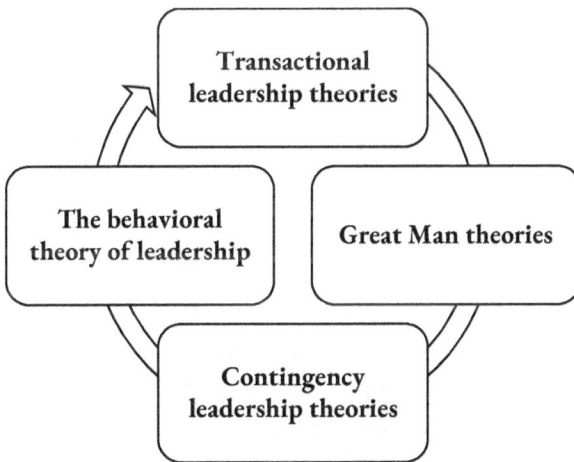

Fig 7. The four most crucial leadership theories.

---

70. D. Meier, "Situational Leadership Theory as a Foundation for a Blended Learning Framework," Journal of Education and Practice 7, no. 10 (2016), accessed from www.iiste.org.

71. Humaans, "Participative Leadership: Meaning and Best Practices," accessed April 13, 2024, https://humaans.io/hr-glossary/participative-leadership.

72. E. E. Jaqua, "Transactional Leadership," American Journal of Biomedical Science & Research 14, no. 5 (2021): 399–400.

The four main leadership theories:

Among many theories, four theories stand out as particularly significant: Great Man theories, Contingency theories, Behavioral theories, and Transactional theories.

Great Man Theory: Great Man theories assert that leaders possess inherent qualities that distinguish them from the general populace, suggesting that these traits are innate and cannot be fully developed through education or practice alone. This perspective contends that individuals with extraordinary abilities and a profound understanding of leadership drive historical change. According to the Great Man Theory, these exceptional individuals emerge as the primary architects of pivotal events and transformative movements throughout history. This view venerates these leaders' natural talents and innate characteristics, emphasizing their unique capacity to shape the course of human affairs.[73]

Contingency leadership theory proposes that the most effective leadership style varies depending on the circumstances and context. This theory suggests that there is no one-size-fits-all approach to leadership, and what works well in one situation may be less effective in another. Moreover, they argue that a leader's success in a particular type of organization or situation does not guarantee success in a different organizational context. Within the contingency theory framework, the effectiveness of a leader's actions is contingent upon various factors, such as the nature of the task, the characteristics of the followers, and the specific context in which leadership is exercised.[74]

---

73. "Great Man Theory," accessed from https://digitalcommons.imsa.edu/cgi/viewcontent.cgi?article=1013&context=core. Also, Bert Alan Spector, "Carlyle, Freud, and the Great Man Theory More Fully Considered," Volume 12, Issue 2 (2015), first published online on February 19, 2015.
74   Amghar, Abderrahim. "Revisiting the Contingency Theories of Leadership: Key Features, Meanings, and Lessons." 2022. Also, Vroom, Victor H., and Arthur G. Jago. "The Role of the Situation in Leadership." The American Psychologist 62, no. 1 (2007): 17–24. More, Cherry, K., Situational leadership theory (2018). Available at: https://www.Verywellmind.com/what-isthe-situ-

The behavioral theory of leadership rests on the notion that an individual's success is primarily shaped by their actions and behaviors, which marks a departure from the deterministic outlook of the Great Man theory. Contrary to the belief that leadership is an innate trait possessed by a select few, Behavioral theories assert that effective leadership skills can be acquired and developed over time, implying that leaders are made rather than born. Behavioral theory shifts the focus from inherent traits to observable actions and behaviors, suggesting that leadership effectiveness can be cultivated through deliberate practice and learning. Rather than fixating on leaders' mental, physical, or social attributes, these theories emphasize the importance of studying and understanding the behaviors that contribute to effective leadership. Leaders may need to adapt their behaviors based on the demands of different situations, tasks, and followers.[75]

Transactional leadership theory revolves around the concept that effective leadership is most successful when it operates within established systems and structures that emphasize exchanging rewards and punishments. Advocates of this theoretical framework propose that social systems function most efficiently when there is a clear and defined chain of command, where leaders wield authority and provide incentives for compliance while also implementing consequences for non-compliance. At the core of transactional theory is the idea that leadership is transactional, involving an exchange between leaders and followers. Leaders establish clear expectations, goals, and standards, offering rewards to individuals who meet or exceed these expectations while applying corrective measures or punishments to those who fall short. This transactional approach to leadership em-

ational–theory-of-leadership-2795321. Accessed on April 16, 2024. Furthermore, Shonhiwa, D.C., "An Examination of the Situational Leadership Approach: Strengths and Weaknesses," Crosscurrents: International Peer-Reviewed Journal on Humanities & Social Sciences, 2(2), 2016: 35–40.

75. Harrison, C. *Leadership Theory and Research* (Cham: Palgrave Macmillan, 2018). Also, Fleenor, J.W., *Trait Approach to Leadership. Encyclopedia of Industrial and Organizational Psychology* (Thousand Oaks, CA: Sage Publications), 830–832.

phasizes the importance of maintaining order, accountability, and adherence to established rules and procedures within organizational settings. Moreover, transactional theories highlight the significance of transactional leadership behaviors, such as monitoring performance, setting clear expectations, providing feedback, and administering rewards and punishments.[76]

Besides delving into leadership theories, exploring the fundamental traits often associated with effective leaders is imperative. These traits are foundational elements that contribute to a leader's ability to inspire, motivate, and guide others toward shared goals. The key traits commonly attributed to successful leaders are honesty, courage, a positive attitude, confidence, effective communication skills, and genuineness. Honesty is an essential trait of leadership. Effective leaders prioritize transparency and integrity in their actions and decisions. They establish trust among their team members by being truthful, straightforward, and ethical in their conduct. Moreover, effective leaders are courageous and resilient when facing challenges and uncertainties. They embrace change and take calculated risks, inspiring confidence and rallying their team members to overcome obstacles. Furthermore, effective leaders cultivate positive attitudes, optimism, and enthusiasm within their teams. They approach setbacks as opportunities for growth and maintain a hopeful outlook, even in challenging circumstances. In addition, effective leaders have self-confidence, a hallmark trait that enables leaders to make bold decisions and navigate complexities with assurance. Confident leaders inspire trust and credibility, empowering others to believe in their vision and abilities.

Effective leaders must be excellent communicators. Strong communication skills are essential for leaders to clearly articulate their vision, goals, and expectations. Effective communicators listen

---

76. Northouse, Peter G. *Leadership: Theories and Practices* (London: Sage), 2004. Also, Brymer, Emma, and Gray, Tom. "Effective Leadership: Transformational or Transactional?" Journal of Outdoor and Environmental Education 10 (2006): 13–19.

actively, convey information succinctly, and foster open dialogue, ensuring team members feel heard, valued, and understood.[77] Further, genuineness and authenticity are distinguishing traits of exceptional leaders who remain true to their values, beliefs, and principles. Genuine leaders build rapport and credibility by demonstrating sincerity, empathy, and a genuine concern for the well-being of their team members.[78] By embodying these traits, leaders cultivate a culture of trust, respect, and collaboration within their teams, laying the groundwork for collective success and organizational excellence. Moreover, these foundational qualities serve as guiding principles that enable leaders to navigate complex challenges, inspire innovation, and drive positive change in their spheres of influence.

> 1. *Genuineness to remain true to values, beliefs, and principles.*
> 2. *Honesty enables to prioritize transparency and integrity to establish trust.*
> 3. *Courage enables leaders to make bold decisions.*
> 4. *Positive attitude to cultivate optimism and enthusiasm*
> 5. *.Confidence enables leaders to make bold decisions with assurance*
> 6. *Effective communication articulate their vision, goals, and expectations.*

Fig.8. Fundamental Traits of an Effective Leader

Leadership Styles

Leadership styles can be categorized into several types: autocratic, democratic or participative, laissez-faire or free rein, and paternalistic.[79] In autocratic leadership, the leader holds all decision-making power and exercises control over the team without seeking input or feedback. The leader typically makes decisions unilaterally. Within

---

77. Luthra, Dr. (2015). "Effective Leadership is all about Communicating Effectively: Connecting Leadership and Communication," 5.3, 43–48.
78. Johnson, Hannah. "Authentic Leadership Theory: The State of Science on Honest Leaders." Missouri State University. Also, Shahin, Dr. Amany I. "Powerful Insights of Authentic Leadership." International Review of Management and Business Research Vol. 9, Issue 1, March 2020.
79. Cherry, Kendra. "Leadership Styles." Accessed April 16, 2024, from http://psychology.about.com/od/leadership/.

autocratic leadership, manipulative tactics may be employed, such as creating an illusion of follower's participation in decision-making while the autocrat retains full control over the outcome.[80] On the other hand, democratic or participative leadership encourages collaboration and participation from team members in decision-making processes. Leaders in this style solicit their team's input, ideas, and opinions, fostering a sense of inclusivity and empowerment. Moreover, laissez-faire or free-rein leadership involves minimal interference from the leader, allowing team members to operate autonomously with little direction or supervision.[81] While this approach can promote creativity and innovation, it may also lead to a lack of structure and accountability if not managed effectively. Lastly, paternalistic leadership adopts a paternalistic approach, acting as a caregiver or mentor to employees. While the leader may involve followers in decision-making to some extent, ultimate authority still rests with the leader. This style often emphasizes the well-being and welfare of the followers, but may also lead to dependency on the leader for direction and guidance.

- Paternalistic leadership
- Democratic leadership
- Laissez-Faire leadership
- Autocratic leadership

Fig.9. Leadership Styles

Leadership is a dynamic interaction between individuals, varying from person to person. It is concerned with what leaders think they do and how they meet followers' expectations.[82] Among the 19 char-

80. Jaafar, Syaiful Baharee, Noraihan Mamat Zambi, and Nor Fathimah Fathil. "Leadership Style: Is it Autocratic, Democratic, or Laissez-Faire?" ASEAN Journal of Management and Business Studies 3, no. 1 (2021): 1–7.
81. Ibid., 4.
82. Zarate, Rodrigo A, "What Followers Want from Their Leaders: An Analytical Perspective," December 2009, accessed on April 16, 2024, from https://www.researchgate.net/publication/262431070_What_Followers_Want_from_

acteristics of admired leaders measured worldwide from 1987 to 2017, these four scored the highest: honesty at 84 percent, competence at 66 percent, inspiration at 66 percent, and forward-looking at 62 percent.[83]

Honesty is the most valued trait in leaders, topping the list of leadership characteristics. People prioritize honesty in the leader-constituent relationship, as it forms the basis of trust. Whether in battle, the boardroom, or any other setting, individuals want trustworthy leaders who are truthful, ethical, and moral. Constituents often equate integrity and authenticity with honesty. Trust hinges on believing leaders possess authentic character and solid integrity, making honesty essential for inspiring confidence and followership.

Competence is vital because followers are unlikely to follow someone who lacks the necessary skills wholeheartedly. When leaders are perceived as incompetent, people reject the individual and their position. Leadership competence is demonstrated through a track record of accomplishing and achieving objectives, inspiring confidence in the leader's ability to effectively lead the state or organization. This confidence encourages followership and enhances the performance of followers who trust the leader's guidance.

Leaders must also inspire and exhibit enthusiasm, energy, and positivity toward the future. A leader's excitement and passion about future possibilities convey a stronger belief in those possibilities to others. People are more inclined to believe in a message when they sense that the speaker genuinely believes it. Conversely, lacking enthusiasm and energy can breed hopelessness and negativity among followers. Leaders who fail to inspire with words of encouragement, optimism, and excitement may struggle to motivate their teams to perform at their best.

Their_Leaders_An_Analytical_Perspectivas.
83. James Kouzes and Barry Posner, *The Leadership Challenges: How to Make Extraordinary Things Happen in Organization*, sixth edition (John Wily & Sons, 2017), 30.

Forward-looking leadership is one of the most desired leadership traits. People expect leaders to possess a sense of direction and concern for the state, institutions, and organization's future. This quality distinguishes leaders because it aligns with their ability to envision the future, a key aspect highlighted in personal-best leadership cases. Leaders are characterized by their focus on improving the future rather than maintaining the status quo.

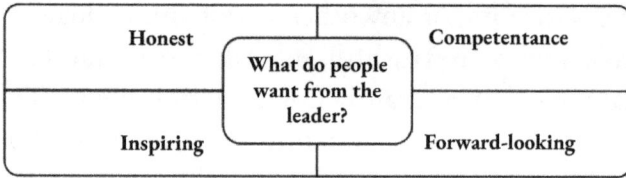

```
 ┌─────────────────────────────────────────────┐
 │  Honest        ┌──────────────┐  Competentance │
 │                │ What do people│               │
 │                │  want from the│               │
 │                │    leader?    │               │
 │  Inspiring     └──────────────┘  Forward-looking│
 └─────────────────────────────────────────────┘
```

Fig.10. People's expectations from their leaders

In conclusion, Honesty, competence, inspiration, and forward-thinking are the core qualities people seek in leaders, traits they would willingly follow. This set of qualities is known as source credibility, which is determined by perceived trustworthiness, expertise, and dynamism. For instance, several common expressions people use to express recognition of credibility are: they practice what they preach, they walk the talk, their actions align with their words, they back up their words with actions, they follow through on their commitments, they deliver on their promises, and they do as they say.

Islamic Perspective on Leadership

The current leadership in Somalia is ineffective and embroiled in a deep-seated crisis that extends beyond mere political incompetence. This crisis is a product of multiple factors, but the most important are deficient political leadership and a significant shortfall in intellectual guidance.[84] These dual deficiencies create a formidable lead-

---

84. Noam Chomsky, *The Responsibility of Intellectuals* (New York: The New Press, 2017). Also, Anna Yu. Karpova, "The Political Role of Intellectuals" (Tomsk Polytechnic University, June 2016), accessed April 15, 2024, from https://www.researchgate.net/. Also, Murad Wilfried Hofmann, "On the Role of Muslim Intellectuals," accessed April 16, 2024, from file:///C:/Downloads/

ership crisis that reverberates across all levels of society. The deficit in intellectual leadership has resulted in a need for more innovative thinking, critical discourse, and scholarly engagement. The absence of intellectual guidance has left societies adrift, unable to navigate the complex issues facing them with wisdom and insight.

The Somali people are Muslims, and the resurgence of Islamic revivalism has gained momentum since the 1960s. The influence of Islamic revivalism was evident in adopting a legal framework in 2000, solidifying Islam as the ultimate reference of all state laws.[85] Despite the visible presence of Islamic rituals, practices, and symbols throughout Somali society, the effective implementation of Islamic values still needs much improvement. Islamic-inspired leadership should draw authority from adherence to sacred texts, moral principles, and divine guidance, emphasizing ethical governance and spiritual integrity. However, the disparity between rhetoric and action underscores the complexities inherent in bridging the gap between religious ideals and practical governance.

The Quran is a profound guide, illustrating many qualities required from a leader through various verses. However, four primary leadership attributes—reliability, knowledge, strength, and trustworthiness—are derived from the stories of the prophets Yusuf and Musa. Prophet Yusuf's narrative emphasizes the necessity of reliability and knowledge, as he endured various trials with unwavering determination and relied on his wisdom to navigate adversity.[86]

---

ojsadmin,+AJISS+14-3-2+Reflections.pdf. Also, Abdolkarim Soroush, "The Responsibilities of the Muslim Intellectual in the 21st Century" (January 30, 2005), accessed April 15, 2024, from https://nawaat.org/2005/01/30/the-responsibilities-of-the-muslim-intellectual-in-the-21st-century/.

85. See Article Two of the Charter adopted in 2000 and the Provisional Somali Constitution of 2012. This article is as follows: 1.1. The official state religion is Islam. 2.2. The propagation of religions other than Islam is prohibited within the country. 2.3. All laws must adhere to the general principles and objectives of Sharia.

86. The verse from the Quran describes the conversation between the prophet Yusuf and the Egyptian king: Allah says: "Joseph proposed, "Put me in charge

Conversely, the account of Prophet Musa highlights the significance of strength and trustworthiness in leadership. Musa's character was described as robust and reliable, which earned him the responsibility of leading his people out of oppression and toward liberation.[87] Throughout the Quran, there is a consistent emphasis on the importance of resilience in confronting challenges, the pursuit of knowledge as a cornerstone for guidance, the cultivation of inner and outer strength to overcome obstacles, and the indispensable trait of being dependable and trustworthy in every endeavor. These teachings serve as timeless principles for aspiring leaders, guiding them toward a path of integrity, wisdom, and service to others.

The discourse surrounding the disparity between Muslim political leaders and their non-Muslim counterparts is a subject of considerable scrutiny. Many Muslim scholars engage with Islamic texts to elucidate the recommendations and guidance offered by the Quran and prophetic traditions regarding governance. However, the crux lies in the practical application of these teachings by political leaders within Muslim societies. Presently, many Muslim countries struggle with governance deficits, falling short of the ideals espoused by Islam. Instead of embodying justice, accountability, and equity principles, these nations often grapple with oppressive regimes, authoritarian rule, and quasi-democratic structures. Such realities starkly contrast with the essence of good governance that Islamic teachings demand.

Undeniably, democratic nations renowned for their adeptness in implementing robust governance frameworks have reaped the benefits of stability, economic prosperity, and comprehensive development across various sectors. These countries' adherence to principles such as justice, transparency, the rule of law, and equality mirrors

---

of the storehouses of the land, for I am truly reliable and adept." [Quran, 12:55].

87. After Prophet Musa left Egypt and arrived at Madaín and helped the daughters of prophet Shuaib, one of the daughters said to her father: "O my father, hire him. Indeed, the best one you can hire is the strong and the trustworthy." (Quran 28:26).

the ethical precepts advocated by Islam. The disparity lies in the values and the approaches taken to apply them. While democratic nations typically rely on empirical evidence and rational analysis to shape their governance structures, Muslims are encouraged to derive their society-related principles from the teachings enshrined in Islamic sacred texts and interpret them correctly and objectively. These texts offer moral guidance, emphasizing justice, accountability, and equitable treatment for all citizens. For Muslims, the challenge lies in bridging the gap between the ideals outlined in Islamic teachings and the practical realities of governance.

Over the years, various leadership theories have emerged from extensive investigation and research, ranging from the great man theory to contingency, behavioral, and transactional leadership theories. These theories have been studied and applied across diverse societies, irrespective of whether they are Muslim or non-Muslim. Similarly, the fundamental traits and leadership styles that define effective leaders remain consistent across cultures. The question is, what is the difference between the Islamic perspective and the secular perspective on leadership? One notable distinction in Islamic leadership philosophy is the demand for servant and pious leadership and ethical conduct, reiterated in numerous prophetic traditions and verses of the Quran.[88] In Islamic teachings, leadership is not merely about wielding authority or asserting dominance but rather about serving the community's needs and upholding high moral standards driven by Islamic values considering worldly and hereafter in mind.

The concept of servant leadership is deeply rooted in the teachings of Islam, where leaders are expected to prioritize the welfare of their constituents above their interests. Prophetic traditions highlight the exemplary behavior of the Prophet Muhammad (peace be upon

---

88. The Quran addresses all the parameters of good leadership. For instance, on honesty: "And do not cheat the people in their affairs" (6:152); on justice: "O you who have believed, be persistently standing firm for Allah, witnesses in justice" (4:135); and on responsibility: "And [they are] those who, when they spend, do so not excessively or sparingly but are ever, between that, [justly] moderate" (25:67).

him), who epitomized humility, compassion, and selflessness in his leadership approach. His actions serve as a model for Muslim leaders, emphasizing the importance of humility, empathy, and service to others. This concept is also rooted in all religious societies.[89] This concept has been highlighted as being practiced by the Prophet Muhammad (PBUH), who mentioned that "the leader of a people is their servant." Moreover, the Quran underscores the ethical responsibilities inherent in leadership roles, emphasizing the importance of justice, fairness, and integrity.[90] Leaders are called upon to uphold these values in their interactions with others, ensuring equity and accountability in governance and decision-making processes. By adhering to the principles of servant leadership and ethical conduct, Muslim leaders can cultivate trust, foster unity, and promote the well-being of their communities.

In wrapping up this point, it is imperative to distinguish between Islam, the sacred universal religion, and the deeds and actions of its followers, as these distinctions are frequently conflated. Islam finds its foundation in two primary sources: the Quran and the prophetic tradition, which serve as guiding principles for believers. However, the interpretation of Islam on some issues and its application can vary among individuals and communities of Muslims. The complexity arises from the amalgamation of societal cultures, western modernity, and Islamic teachings, often leading to confusion regarding the essence of pure Islam. Blending cultural practices with Islamic principles and values can obscure the fundamental principles of Islam, making it challenging to discern authentic teachings from cultural norms.

---

89. Robert K. Greenleaf, *On Becoming a Servant-Leader* (San Francisco: Jossey-Bass Publishers, 1996); Robert et al., *A Journey into the Nature of Legitimate Power & Greatness* (Mahwah, NJ: Paulist Press, 1977).

90. See the Quranic verse (4:135): "O ye who believe! Stand out firmly for justice, as witnesses to Allah, even as against yourselves, or your parents, or your kin, and whether it be (against) rich or poor, for Allah can best protect both. Follow not the lusts (of your hearts), lest ye swerve, and if ye distort (justice) or decline to do justice, verily Allah is well-acquainted with all that ye do."

Furthermore, governance performance in many modern Muslim states often deviates from Islamic teachings. Post-colonial influences, including colonial legislation, values, and traditional cultural practices, often supersede or dilute the application of Islamic principles in governance. This mixture of influences results in a hybrid system that may not fully align with Islam's ethical and moral objectives. Despite these challenges, Islam's core values and ethics remain the ultimate objectives for believers. These values, including justice, compassion, integrity, and equality, serve as guiding principles for Muslims in their personal and societal conduct. However, the gap between the ideal and the reality is often articulated, with Muslim societies lagging in fully embodying these values compared to others.

SOMALIA'S GOVERNANCE: EXPERIENCES FROM TWO SYSTEMS

Once a nation with great potential, Somalia has faced numerous challenges that have led to prolonged instability and fragmentation. Understanding what happened involves examining a complex interplay of historical, political, social, and economic factors. History is a vast laboratory where nations' experiments unfold, revealing invaluable lessons about what has succeeded and what has faltered in their historical evolution. It is a repository of human experiences, documenting the trials and triumphs. By studying history, societies gain insights into the factors that have shaped their destinies, enabling them to navigate the complexities of the present and chart a course for the future. In this laboratory of the past, the successes and failures of nations are exposed, offering profound insights into the mechanisms of progress and regression. By analyzing these historical patterns, societies can discern recurring themes and identify underlying principles contributing to societal advancement or decline. Moreover, history provides case studies, allowing societies to draw parallels between past events and contemporary challenges. By examining the strategies employed by previous generations to overcome adversity or achieve prosperity, nations can glean valuable lessons applicable to their contexts.

Accordingly, this research delves into two distinct periods of Somali history characterized by contrasting governance systems: periods marked by majoritarian democracy and those dominated by the rule of the "big man." By examining these contrasting periods of Somali history, we can gain insights into the diverse forms of governance that have shaped the country's trajectory and the socio-political factors that have influenced the balance of power between democratic ideals and authoritarian tendencies.

Majoritarian Democratic Rule 1956–1969

This historical analysis explores the events in Somalia during the SYL's dominant rule from 1956 until the military coup in 1969. As the ruling party, the SYL pursued a majoritarian approach to governance, which marginalized other political parties and ultimately led to their weakness and disappearance.[91] Instead of fostering a spirit of inclusivity and collaboration through coalition-building, the SYL absorbed leaders from opposing parties into its ranks in 1959, weakening opposition parties.[92] By monopolizing power and excluding dissenting voices, the SYL stifled political pluralism and hindered the development of a robust multi-party system. Rather than fostering healthy competition and debate, this approach consolidated power within a single party, limiting the avenues for alternative viewpoints. Furthermore, the absorption of opposition leaders into the SYL ranks undermined the integrity of those parties and eroded their capacity to function independently.

Furthermore, without any formidable external opposition to SYL, internal dissent within the SYL occurred with increasing regularity. The lack of significant external challenges allowed simmering tensions and disagreements within the party to surface, ultimately

---

91. Political parties disappeared finally when all MPs from political parties who participated in the 1969 election joined the SYL party, except the DAP of Abdirizak Haji Hussein.

92. For instance, in 1959, SYL offered membership to Abdulkadir Zoobe and Mohamed Abdinur Juje, the two prominent members of the Hiszbia Dastur Muataqil Party (HDMS).

resulting in internal strife. This internal discord grew so much that it precipitated the party's division into factions with differing ideologies or leadership preferences. The ruling party faced internal divisions, splintering parties such as the Great Somali League (GSL), the Somali National Congress (SNC), and the Democratic Action Party (DAP). These breakaway groups emerged because of dissatisfaction within the party. They were spearheaded by influential figures such as Haji Mohamed Hussein, Sheikh Ali Jimale, and Abdirizak Haji Hussein, who were stalwarts of the SYL Party. These dissenting groups sought to articulate alternative visions for the nation's future and challenge the hegemony of the dominant faction within the SYL.

The transformation of the ruling party SYL into a singular one-party reached its culmination when Mohamed Ibrahim Egal assumed leadership after joining the party in 1966. Egal's ascent to power marked a significant departure from the party's founding principles, as the party's ethos and values were discarded under his leadership. In 1969, the erosion of democratic processes reached a critical juncture when the president of the state, Abdirashid, was assassinated following extensively rigged elections—this tragic event catalyzed political upheaval, culminating in the military seizing control of the government. The SYL ruling party had failed to sustain itself after about 13 years and six months in power (February 1956–October 1969).

The Authoritarian Rule (1969–1991)

Somalia embarked on Bigman rule during the military regime led by General Mohamed Siyad Barre, who sought to institute a socialist regime and enact sweeping societal transformations. Under Barre's leadership, the government implemented policies aimed at rigidly centralizing power and imposing a top-down approach to governance, emphasizing state control over key sectors of the economy and society. The introduction of socialism and the pursuit of radical societal transformation exacerbated existing tensions between the state and society. The government's imposition of ideological tenets clashed with Islamic principles and societal norms, values, and cultural practices deeply ingrained within Somali society. Moreover, the policies enacted under Barre's regime violated citizens' rights, democratic principles, and freedom to preach Islam, further exacerbating the state-society conflict.

The introduction of secular family law sparked turmoil and clashes with the Ulama, resulting in the tragic execution of ten scholars and the incarceration of hundreds in 1975.[93] These repressive measures not only eroded the rule of law but also alienated large segments of the population, fueling resentment and resistance against the regime. Moreover, the imposition of socialist ideals clashed with the Islamic faith, which holds significant sway over Somali society. The government's attempts to secularize and undermine Islamic institutions sparked outrage among devout Muslims and intensified opposition to the regime. The state-society conflict that ensued laid bare the deep-seated tensions simmering beneath the surface of Somali society.

In 1976, the military regime solidified its grip on power by establishing a one-party system like a pre-military civilian regime. However, the imposition of one-party rule under socialism exacerbated existing social fissures and ignited a chain reaction of events that ultimately led to the regime's downfall. As a result, clan-based armed opposition groups emerged, challenging the ruling regime's legitimacy and seeking to assert their political and social interests. The emergence of clan-based armed oppositions signaled the fragmentation of Somali society along clan lines. In 1991, after twenty-one years of authoritarian rule, the military regime was ultimately toppled by clan-based armed opposition groups, marking the collapse of the state and plunging Somalia into a prolonged period of civil war and instability.

---

93. Abdullahi Abdullahi, "Women, Islamists, and the Military Regime in Somalia: The New Family Law and Its Implications," in *Milk and Peace, Drought and War: Somali Culture, Society and Politics*, ed. Markus Hoehne and Virginia Luling (London: Hurst, 2010), 137–60.

The historical trajectory of the Somali state serves as evidence of the shortcomings of the majoritarian political party system and the Bigman's rule. These governance models have proven ineffective and unsustainable, ultimately contributing to instability, conflict, and societal fragmentation. We must address the central question: what was the source of Somalia's state-building challenges? Was it due to the dominance of a majoritarian political party, SYL, or the concentration of power in the hands of a "Big man"? Are the problems embedded in the nation's leadership or governance system, or is there a complex interaction between the two? Moreover, we must consider how the system of governance interacts with society and its elite political culture. Does the governance framework exacerbate existing societal divisions, or does it provide opportunities for the concentration of power among a select group? Understanding the intricate relationship between Somalia's political system, leadership, and the broader society will be vital to identifying the root causes of the country's persistent instability.

However, despite the lessons of history, elements of the prevailing elite culture persist within the contemporary Somali political landscape, raising concerns about the potential for history to repeat itself. The entrenched political elite culture that characterized previous periods of Somali governance continues to influence the current political establishment. This political elite class, often comprising influential individuals wielding significant economic, social, and political power, tends to prioritize narrow self-interests over the broader needs of society. Moreover, the recurrence of familiar governance patterns among the current Somali political elite underscores the risk of repeating past mistakes. Despite the evident failures of majoritarianism and big-man rule, certain factions within the political establishment remain reluctant to embrace alternative approaches to governance. Indeed, as the adage goes, repeating the same process will undoubtedly produce the same result.

The Collapse of Democracy and Authoritarian Governance

Neither the majoritarian system nor the Bigman rule is inherently grounded in Somali traditional culture or Islamic principles. As such, it is imperative to delve into Somali tradition to seek a solution uniquely tailored to the Somali context and informed by indigenous values and beliefs. Drawing upon the rich Somali culture and heritage, we can uncover insights and approaches that offer a Somali-specific response to the state and government crisis. Somali tradition is characterized by consultation, consensus-building, and collective decision-making principles, which are deeply embedded in the fabric of society. Historically, Somali communities have relied on traditional forums such as the *Shir* (assembly) and the *Xeer* (customary law) to resolve disputes, address grievances, and make collective decisions.[94] These indigenous institutions embody the spirit of inclusivity and participatory governance, allowing all members of society to have a voice in matters that affect them. Furthermore, Islamic principles, which hold significant sway over Somali culture and identity, emphasize principles of justice, equality, and accountability in governance. The Quran and the teachings of the Prophet Muhammad (peace be upon him) provide a framework for ethical governance that prioritizes the community's welfare and upholds all individuals' rights.[95] Moreover, a Somali-specific solution would recognize the importance of building consensus and fostering unity among diverse communities, transcending clan divisions and political rivalries. It would draw upon the resilience and resourcefulness of the Somali people, harnessing their collective wisdom and ingenuity to chart a path toward a more stable, prosperous, and united nation.

---

94. Abdullahi Abdullahi, "Somali Elite Political Culture: Conceptions, Structures, and Historical Evolution," Somali Studies: A Peer-Reviewed Academic Journal for Somali Studies 5 (2020): 30–92, 59–60.

95. "Constitution of Medina," article 16, written by Prophet Muhammad in 622 CE, accessed April 19, 2024, from https://static1.squarespace.com/static/5097fe39e4b0c49016e4c58b/t/5c8153eeec212d7117477f8f/1551979503244/Constitution-Medina.pdf.

From the cultural perspective, the seminal work "Introduction to History" of Ibn Khaldun delves into the intricate dynamics of governance, mainly focusing on the psychology of nomadic societies. He astutely observes that political elites adhere to rules and norms in clan-based societies, each vying for leadership positions. This constant struggle for power and dominance, inherent in clan dynamics, often leads to instability and conflict within these societies. However, Ibn Khaldun posits that Islam's adoption as a guiding set of principles and values can unify within clan-based societies.[96] Islam, emphasizing justice, equality, and accountability, provides a framework for governance that transcends clan loyalties and fosters cohesion among diverse groups. Furthermore, Ibn Khaldun argues that Islam solves the inherent tensions and rivalries in clan-based societies by providing a shared moral code that governs interpersonal relations and societal interactions. By adhering to Islamic principles, political elites can mitigate the fractious nature of clan politics and work towards the community's common good.[97]

In a clan-based society, the pursuit of leadership is often motivated by economic incentives and the desire to enhance the prestige of one's clan. Individuals vie for leadership positions to wield political power, secure economic advantages, and elevate their clan's status within the social hierarchy. However, the existing political systems, whether characterized by a majoritarian political party or Bigman rule, tend to favor certain clans at the expense of others, perpetuating exclusion and marginalization.

Marginalized clans within Somali society frequently form alliances with external actors who seek to challenge the existing regime or support factions capable of exerting influence over Somali politics. This phenomenon is deeply intertwined with Ethiopia's historical involvement in supporting armed opposition groups within

---

96. Ibn Khaldun, *The Muqaddimah: An Introduction to History* (Princeton University Press, 1980), 302.
97. Ibid.

Somalia.[98] Ethiopia's backing of certain factions has played a pivotal role in shaping the political landscape of Somalia and exacerbating existing tensions among clans. The external support of marginalized clans reflects a strategic calculus aimed at advancing their political interests and redressing grievances stemming from exclusion and marginalization within the Somali political system. By aligning with external actors, these clans seek to bolster their political leverage and amplify their voices on the national stage. However, relying on external support to address internal grievances underscores the urgency of developing a new inclusive political system accommodating all Somali clans' diverse interests and aspirations. Such a system must be grounded in inclusivity, equity, and democratic governance, providing a platform for marginalized communities to participate meaningfully in the political process and contribute to decision-making processes.

THE QUEST FOR APPROPRIATE SYSTEM OF GOVERNANCE AND LEADERSHIP

For Somalia to achieve lasting stability and national unity, two interlinked reforms are required: establishing a governance system that respects its unique cultural and Islamic heritage and the emergence of exceptional leadership committed to these values. An appropriate governance system should be culturally inclusive and align with Islamic principles deeply rooted in Somali society. Moreover, exceptional leadership is crucial for the advancement and stability of any nation. Specifically, suppose this leadership must rebuild a collapsed state, a war-torn nation like Somalia. In that case, such leadership is characterized by individuals who are not only highly qualified and dedicated to societal values but also capable of implementing good

---

98. Somalia and Ethiopia supported armed opposition groups in each country. For example, Somalia supported EPLF and TPLF, while Ethiopia supported the Somali Salvation Democratic Front (SSDF), the Somali National Movement (SNM), and the Somali National Congress (SNC). See Abdullahi, Making Sense, vol. two, 20–21. Moreover, Ethiopia supported armed groups in opposition to the Somali government established in Djibouti in 2000.

governance parameters and effective socio-economic development policies.

A Note on a Proper System of Governance

Somalia, a nation with a rich history and a unified culture, has faced numerous challenges over the past decades, including state collapse, civil conflict, political instability, and social fragmentation. However, the pursuit of stability and national unity remains a central goal for Somali leaders and citizens. Achieving this vision requires a comprehensive approach that addresses political, economic, and social dimensions. Power-sharing based on a 4.5 clan quota succeeded in mitigating the conflict and enabling the establishment of the state in 2000. However, clan power-sharing based on the selection process failed to produce effective governance and lacked democratic credentials. It was a temporary measure for reconciliation and clan inclusivity in forming the national state institutions.[99] Developing a framework for national unity that preserves power-sharing involves creating a political system where diverse groups collaborate in governance, ensuring that all voices are heard and respected. This approach fosters stability, inclusiveness, and cooperation, all essential skills for nations with complex social, clan, or political landscapes. Could Somalia develop a democratic system where political parties, instead of clans, compete during elections and form a grand coalition government afterward? The concept of this system was proposed in 1956 and 1959 by Adan Abdulle, the parliament speaker.[100] By his wisdom, he realized that the majoritarian system does not contribute to the stability and inclusivity of the various political forces in the clannish societies. In such a system, all parties would be included in the coalition government in proportion to their representation in

99. Abdurahman Abdullahi, "Reflections on Somalia's Political Deadlock: The Need for a New Political Deal," accessed June 1, 2024. https://www.academia.edu/88431391/Reflections_on_Somalias_Political_Deadlock_The_Need_for_a_New_Political_Deal. Also, Abdurahman Abdullahi, "The Death of Arta Political Deal PDF," accessed June 1, 2024, https://www.academia.edu/87581583/The_death_of_Arta_Political_deal_pdf?uc-sb-sw=34087464.
100. Trunji, *Adan Abdulle*, 174.

parliament. The majoritarian party system had failed in Somalia, and as such, it should not be repeated. Alternatively, the majority party would lead the government, while others are part of the government following their parliamentary strength. This framework would involve several key elements.

During elections, various political parties should campaign and compete for seats in parliament. The constituency should be federal member states, and the election system should have proportional representation with a threshold of at least 5 percent of votes. This competitive phase is crucial for allowing the electorate to express their preferences and for ensuring that different political views are represented in the government. This system minimizes clan sensitivities and enables inclusivity. Whatever system of governance is adopted, presidential or parliamentary, after the election, the composition of the government should reflect the proportional representation of parties in parliament. This means that if a party wins 30 percent of the seats, it will hold approximately 30 percent of the positions in the coalition government. The majority party, which secures the most seats, would take the lead in forming the government. However, instead of governing alone or forming a coalition with just one or two other parties, it would work to include all parliamentary parties in the government preconditioned to a set of requirements. This inclusive approach aims to ensure broad representation and stability. In forming a government, the majority party should always consider clan inclusivity while balancing political party quotas in consultation with the coalition party leaders. By including all parties in the government, this system seeks to promote political stability and reduce the likelihood of conflict. It encourages cooperation and consensus-building among diverse political actors, which can be particularly important in a context like Somalia's, where historical divisions and ongoing challenges require inclusive governance. An inclusive coalition government can foster a sense of national unity and shared purpose. It sends a message that all political voices matter and that governance is a collective effort to serve all citizens' interests.

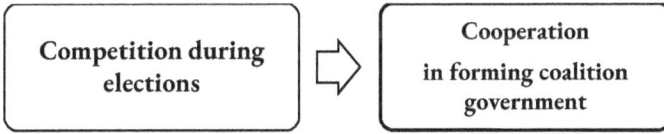

Fig 11. Process of Competing and Cooperation

What is the Most Suitable Model of Leadership?

This is the most relevant question of the time that begs an answer from academics, scholars, and policymakers. Determining the most suitable leadership model for Somalia necessitates aligning with its cultural ethos founded on consensus decision-making and active participation—a framework inherently resonant with Islamic principles. This requires adopting a new legal framework that ensures inclusivity-based political parties and the neutrality of the National President and federal member state presidents as the super elders of all clans, respectively. By embodying neutrality and impartiality, the presidents can transcend partisan divides and represent the collective interests of all Somalis, fostering a sense of unity and trust crucial for national progress and stability. As such, presidents must be above political squabbles and should be elected by the parliaments for one term of seven years. In this venue, President Adan considered seven years enough for the incumbent and a new person to lead the country. Few countries had adopted one term of seven years for the president. These countries are Armenia and Israel.[101]

These notes call for a more profound exploration and academic discourse to resolve persisting issues, particularly concerning adopting external systems that have proven unsustainable in Somalia. It is evident that simply importing foreign models without contextual adaptation has led to repeated failures in the Somali context. Therefore, a more nuanced and indigenous approach is needed to draw upon local knowledge, traditions, and values to develop sustainable solutions tailored to Somalia's unique circumstances. As

---

101. See the list of political term limits. Available from https://en.wikipedia.org/wiki/List_of_political_term_limits (accessed on June 1, 2024).

Martin Doornbos and John Markakis emphasized, "Somalia's special features require unorthodox and original thinking to develop appropriate institutional solutions."[102] Moreover, they recommended that "The Somalis must look into their own culture and political tradition for a solution to their problems."[103] By engaging in rigorous analysis and debate, scholars and policymakers can identify the root causes of these failures and devise innovative strategies that resonate with Somali realities.

Exceptional leadership should be defined by a history of integrity, a comprehensive national vision, and an unwavering commitment to upholding the law. The ideal leader must have experience as a reconciler and have the capability to govern a divided society effectively. This involves a deep understanding of such a community's unique dynamics and traditions and the ability to foster unity among its diverse groups. The leader must also implement policies that respect and preserve cultural heritage while promoting progress and development. Furthermore, the leader should demonstrate exceptional skills in building consensus and mediating conflicts, ensuring that principles of fairness and justice guide all decisions and actions. Their leadership should reflect a dedication to inclusivity, transparency, and the empowerment of all community members, enabling sustainable growth and harmony within society. Above all, exceptional leadership should have a track record of democratic values, decency, abiding by the law of the land, and respecting and promoting citizens' rights.

CONCLUSION

This research underscores that the core challenge of Somali state-building resides within its political leadership and system of governance. It provides a comprehensive overview of the Somali state's

---

102. Martin Doornbos and John Markakis, "What Went Wrong in Somalia?" In Mohamed Saleh and Lennard Wohlgemuth, *Crisis Management and Politics of Reconciliation in Somalia. Statements from Uppsala Forum*, 17–19 January 1994, 17
103. Ibid.

historical trajectory since 1956, examining the ebbs and flows of governance through various systems, including the majoritarian political party framework, Bigman rule, and periods characterized by Islamist governance. Through meticulous analysis, it becomes evident that they have yet to be able to address the underlying issues plaguing Somali state-building. Despite their differences, a common thread emerges in the Somali elite political culture of governance, which tends to prioritize narrow self-interests over the broader welfare of the nation. Considering this analysis, the research concludes that the recurrence of similar political cultures yields the same state failure. Without meaningful reforms that address the root causes of governance failures, Somalia risks perpetuating a cycle of instability. Therefore, it is imperative to break free from the constraints of past governance paradigms and chart a new course toward inclusive and accountable leadership. The research also provided a snapshot exploration of various theories of leadership and the diverse array of leadership styles. A nuanced analysis delves into the evolving conceptualizations of leadership, examining how different theoretical frameworks have shaped our understanding of effective leadership practices.

Drawing upon academic literature and empirical research, this research navigates through leadership theories, including, but not limited to, trait theory, behavioral theory, contingency theory, and transactional leadership theories. In addition, servant leadership is a type of leadership expected from a Muslim leader; this theory emphasizes the leader's commitment to serving the needs of others. Moreover, to delineate these theoretical frameworks, the research also examines the practical implications of different leadership styles, such as autocratic leadership, democratic leadership, transactional leadership, and paternalistic leadership.

The paper delves further into the Islamic and traditional perspectives on leadership. It underscores the disconnect between the majoritarian political party system, the Big Man rule, and the deeply ingrained values of Islam and the political culture of the Somali clan system. While these governance models have been prevalent over the past 64 years since the independence in 1960, this research argues that they are not inherently rooted in Islamic teachings or traditional Somali culture. From an Islamic perspective, leadership is characterized by principles of servant leadership and ethical conduct. The paper highlights the emphasis on humility, compassion, and stewardship in Islamic teachings, contrasting the often self-serving and authoritarian tendencies observed in Somali leadership styles. Furthermore, the research emphasizes the need for a leadership approach tailored to Somalia's cultural context. Traditional cultural norms and Islamic principles significantly shape governance structures and leadership behaviors in a clan-based society. The research advocates for a hybridized approach that draws from the rich Somali tradition, Islamic ethics, and modern state experiences. This hybridized approach to leadership entails synthesizing traditional cultural practices, such as consensus-building and communal decision-making, with the modern state-building approaches and principles of justice, equality, and accountability espoused in Islamic teachings and constitutions of the modern states. By integrating these diverse elements, Somalia can develop a political system and cultivate political elites better aligned with its people's needs and aspirations.

In conclusion, the research offers a critical analysis of the two predominant systems of governance in Somalia: the majoritarian democratic system and the authoritarian military regime. Building on these critiques, the research provides innovative suggestions to improve Somalia's governance system. It advocates for a more inclusive and representative political framework that ensures all political parties compete during the elections and cooperate in forming the government by building a grand coalition government. Additionally, the research proposes specific preconditions for leadership recruitment to ensure that leaders are impartial, qualified, and committed to democratic principles, the unity of the nation, and the welfare of the people.

2

ABDULLAHI ISSE MOHAMUD: HIS LIFE, LEGACY, AND POLITICAL CULTURE

Abdullahi Isse exhibited remarkable courage and dignity as he delivered a crucial message on behalf of the Somali Youth League (SYL) to the UN General Assembly in 1949. In his address, he strongly criticized the UN for its decision to place Somalia under Italian administration through a UN trusteeship, which he and many others viewed as a betrayal of Somali aspirations for self-governance and independence. He was widely regarded as a polite and calm politician known for his unwavering dedication to the nationalist principles of the SYL. He was devoted to serving his country as a Secretary General of SYL, Prime Minister, Minister, and Diplomat, embodying continuously the rule of law, citizens' rights, and ideals of democracy.

—**Mohamed Trunji,** The author and expert on Somali history from 1941–1969.

It appears that two political tendencies emerged within the party [SY] ... The first tendency has deep civic and nationalist roots.... The key personality among the civics were Adan Abdulle Osman, Abdirizak haji Hussein, and Abdullahi Isse Mohamoud. The second tendency was toward sectarianism and opportunism.

— **Abdi Samatar,** Africa's First Democrats, 85.

Abdullahi Isse's most significant achievement as the Somali Youth League's special envoy at the UN for four years was convincing the Haitian Ambassador to oppose the Bevin-Sforza plan to place Somalia under an indefinite Italian administration. Despite major powers supporting Italy's return, Abdullahi's advocacy secured a 10-year limit on the trusteeship and created a UN Advisory Committee.

— Dr. Abdurahman Baadiyow.

*A*bdullahi Isse Mohamud (1921–1988) stands matchless in his continued leadership in the early years of the national liberation of Somalia and his continuous devotion to SYL principles and values. This dedication has remained steadfast since his membership in the Somali Youth Club (SYC) in 1944 in Beledweyne (Hirshabelle state of Somalia). Alongside his colleagues in the Beledweyne SYC branch, Adan Abdulle Osman (1908–2007) and Sheikh Ali Jimale (1905–1979), Abdullahi is one of the few leaders who shaped the course of Somali history. After developing SYC into a full-fledged party of the Somali Youth League (SYL) in 1947, he was elected the party's Deputy Secretary General. He succeeded the respected Yassin Haji Osman, one of the founders of SYC and its first Secretary General, who passed away the same year in Jowhar.[104] From 1947 to 1956, Abdullahi held the position of Secretary General of the SYL for nearly a decade, steering the organization through turbulent times with his steadfast resolve and determination. His leadership was instrumental in galvanizing support for Somali independence and rallying the SYL towards a common goal of self-determination. He tirelessly advocated for the unification of all Somalis under four powers (Italy, Britain, France, and Ethiopia). His relentless pursuit of Somali unity and independence cemented his legacy as one of the towering figures in the annals of Somali nationalism. Moreover,

---

104. I.M. Lewis, *A Pastoral Democracy: A Study of Pastoralism and Politics Among the Northern Somali of the Horn of Africa* (LIT Verlag and Münster, 1999), 304; Abdurahman Abdullahi, *Making Sense of Somali History, Volume Two* (Adonis and Abbey, 2018), 84.

his relentless spirit for the liberation struggles inspired generations during the national movement era for freedom and independence.

Abdullahi Isse made history in 1956 as the inaugural Somali Prime Minister during the Italian administration under the UN trusteeship.[105] He navigated through this complex political environment, where the emergence of political clannism began to exert its influence and bring out its clout. Despite the SYL advocating for a non-clannish governance system, the first practical test of its principle could have been more promising, as some senior party members allegedly succumbed to nepotism and favoritism.[106] Establishing a merit-based political system clashed with entrenched clan allegiances, gradually eroding the SYL's founding principles. The idealistic elimination of clannism faulted the first experiment of the Somali state, as Mohamed Trunji expressed: "Abdullahi Isse and his SYL party fellow lived long enough to realize how unrealistic it was to expect to root out tribalism."[107] Moreover, the government and party dealt with the increasing influence of the leftist tendency of some politicians who stirred tensions between the Italians and the SYL party and government, which resulted in the expulsion of the party's chairman, Haji Mohamed Hussein.[108] As Abdullahi Isse grappled with the new system of governance, the tensions between political ideals and clan affiliations underscored the formidable task of steering Somalia toward a unified and inclusive future.

---

105. Paolo Tripodi, *The Colonial Legacy in Somalia: Rome and Mogadishu: From Colonial Administration to Operation Restore Hope* (London: Macmillan Press, 1999); Robert L. Hess, *Italian Colonialism in Somalia* (Chicago: The University of Chicago Press, 1966); Mohamed Trunji, *Somalia: The Untold History (1941-1969)*, 2nd ed. (Looh Press, 2020), 266; Abdi Samatar, Africa's First Democrats: Somalia's Adan A. Osman and Abdirizak H. Hussein (Indiana University Press, 2016), 66.

106. Samatar, *Africa's First Democrats*, 62–63.

107. Trunji, *The Untold History*, second edition, 25.

108. Samatar, *Africa's First Democrats*, 64; Trunji, *The Untold History*, 300–301.

After independence, Abdullahi was appointed as Somalia's foreign minister in the government led by Prime Minister Abdirashid Ali Sharmarke (1960–64). His appointment was part of a spirit of national unity and building a grand coalition that included the most prominent political figures in the government.[109] Abdullahi's tenure as Foreign Minister saw him serve as Somalia's emissary to international arenas, representing the nation in international forums. Armed with a commitment to advancing Somalia's interests on the global stage, he engaged diplomatically to secure support for the realization of Somali peoples' self-determination and territorial integrity. In these gatherings, Abdullahi articulated Somalia's stance on various issues ranging from sovereignty and territorial disputes with Ethiopia, Kenya, and France to regional stability and economic development. His presence underscored Somalia's emergence as a sovereign nation with a distinct voice in shaping the course of African and international affairs. He also held various ministerial portfolios in all civilian governments until it was toppled by the military coup in 1969.

Abdullahi's biography intertwines with the SYL, a pioneer party in Somalia's quest for independence. His biography mirrors his generation's aspirations, struggles, and triumphs. In the turbulent years following World War II, Somalia was controlled by different colonial powers. Abdullahi, being the Secretary General of SYL, lent his voice to the SYL's advocacy for self-determination on national and international platforms. His impassioned pleas resonated in many forums, rallying support for Somalia's independence in the aftermath of World War II. Notably, Abdullahi played a pivotal role in shaping the discourse surrounding Somalia's fate. Abdullahi Isse was among the SYL delegation at the UN commission hearing in 1948.[110] He was dispatched to the UN as the envoy of SYL in 1948, and the Somali diaspora in New York supported him financially.[111] The Four Power

---

109. Ibid., 384–5.
110. Helen Chapin Metz, ed., *Somalia: A Country Study* (Washington: GPO for the Library of Congress, 1992), 27.
111. A total of 120 Somalis lived in New York financially supported Abdullahi

Conferences, where the fate of the former Italian colonies was deliberated. Through his adept diplomacy, he advocated for Somalia's sovereignty. These efforts culminated in adopting a compromise resolution at the United Nations General Assembly, entrusting Somalia to the Italian administration under the UN trusteeship for ten years.[112] During this period, Italy was not a member of the UN, and this decision was made against the wishes of the SYL, which demanded a collective four-power trusteeship or at least one of the four powers. Still, three favorable conditions for Somalia were attached to Italy's return: the UN trusteeship, a limited term of ten years, and the UN Advisory Council.[113]

There is a significant gap in the history of Abdullahi's valuable contributions to the national struggle for independence, which necessitates further scholarly investigation. The literature documenting his struggle for Somali independence is very limited. Delving into his legacy and political culture is imperative in revitalizing Somali national identity and fostering state-building efforts. His leadership model during the embryonic stages of Somalia's quest for sovereignty profoundly shaped the nation's course of history. As Somalia grapples with nation-building and restoring a cohesive national identity since the total collapse of the state in 1991, exploring Abdullahi's legacy, life history, and contributions becomes increasingly essential. Thus, this Chapter fills the historical lacuna by piecing together available information and through interviews with those living persons who knew Abdullahi Isse.[114]

Isse. Abdulkadir Qurabe, Jama Aburas, Ismael Ahmed anjeer, Haji Sitten Yusuf, and two other men. Abdirizak Haji Hussein, *My Role in the Foundation of the Somali Nation-State: A Political Memoir*, ed. Abdisalam Ise-Salwe (Trenton, NJ: The Red Sea Press, 2017), 103–104.
112. Samatar, *Africa's First democrats*, 48; Trunji, *The Untold History*, 157–8.
113. Samatar, ibid.
114. Ali Hashi Dhoore, Salad Osman Roble, and Ambassador Abdisalam Dhabancad I interviewed in May and June 2024 in Mogadishu and via telephone.

This chapter delves into Abdullahi's political culture and the factors that shaped his worldview, tracing his life from childhood to his significant role in shaping Somali politics and diplomacy. It examines Abdullahi's early upbringing, providing insight into the influences and experiences that shaped his early culture. Central to Abdullahi's narrative is his involvement in the liberation movement through his affiliation with the SYC in 1944 and the SYL party. His tenure as the Secretary-General of the SYL is of particular significance. The Chapter further explores Abdullahi's ascent to the position of the first Prime Minister of Somalia from 1956 to 1960. Moreover, his tenure in the Ministry of Foreign Affairs (1960–1964) is studied, shedding light on his diplomatic insight and contributions to Somalia's international relations agenda. Finally, the Chapter delves into Abdullahi's role in the various ministerial portfolios until the military took over in 1969. Lastly, the research examines Abdullahi's final chapter of public service as a diplomat in Scandinavian states (1974–1988), offering an understanding of his diplomatic work.

A CONCISE BIOGRAPHY OF ABDULLAHI ISSE

Abdullahi Isse was born in 1921 in Afgoye, about 30 km south of Mogadishu, where his mother lived.[115] His father, Mohamud Bidar, a respected elder of his sub-clan, died before Abdullahi was born from malaria, and his mother, Marrero Dini Ahmed, raised him as an orphan. The father hails from the port city of Hobia and belongs to a Habar-Gidir/Saad subclan, and his mother hails from Abudwaaq town and belongs to the Mareehan clan/Reer Dini.[116] His birth date coincides with the end of the Darwish movement led

---

115. Salah Mohamed Ali, *Huddur & the History of Southern Somalia* (Nahda Bookshop Publisher, 2005), 487–488; Abdulahi et al. Souare, eds., *Somalia at the Crossroads: Challenges and Perspectives in Reconstituting a Failed State* (Adonis & Abbey 2007), 10; Jama Mohamed Ghalīb, *The Cost of Dictatorship: The Somali Experience* (L. Barber Press, 1995), 41.
116. Mohamed Ingriis, "A Brief Biographic Lecture on Abdullahi Isse," YouTube video, accessed 4 April 2024, https://youtu.be/vwcukLSEaD0.

by Mohamed Abdulle Hassan.[117] The convergence of the two dates could signify Allah's predestination for the continuation of the anti-colonial Somali struggle through different means and the advent of new flag-bearers of the movement. Abdullahi had one half-brother through his mother and was the father of two daughters and one son. His mother lived with him until she died while he was an ambassador in Sweden. Although Abdullahi's lineage traces back to his Habar-Gidir/Saád sub-clan ancestors in Galmudug, his upbringing in urban centers (Afgoye, Mogadishu, and Merca) within the Banadir region has endowed him with different cultural attributes. He was famous for his reserved attitude, humbleness, civility, mild temperament, and respect, which contrasted with the prevailing nomadic culture associated with most politicians.[118] Affectionately known as "Bidaar," his father's nickname, he began his education by attending an Italian primary school in Mogadishu, where he learned the Italian language and, in parallel, enrolled in Qur'anic school. Teaching children the Quran in early childhood is a common culture in Somalia as the initial phase of traditional Islamic education.[119]

In October 1922, the Fascists, led by Benito Mussolini, seized power in Italy, ushering in a new era of aggressive ultra-nationalism and imperial ambition. Mussolini's regime was determined to expand Italy's influence and prestige on the global stage, with one of its central aims being the creation of La Grande Somalia. To realize this vision, the Italian government appointed Cesare Maria De Vecchi as the Governor of Italian Somaliland. Arriving on December 15,

---

117. Abdisalam Issa-Salwe, "The Failure of The Daraawiish State: The Clash Between Somali Clanship and State System" (paper presented at the 5th International Congress of Somali Studies, December 1993); Abdi Sheik Abdi, *Divine Madness: Mohammed Abdulle Hassan (1856–1920)* (London: Zed Books Ltd., 1993).

118. Since Abdullahi's family hailed from the Mudug region, known for war-like people, his manners were influenced by urban Banadir culture of mild manners and civility.

119. Salah Mohamed, *Huddur & the History of Southern Somalia*, 487–488. Jama Mohamed Ghalīb, *The Cost of Dictatorship: The Somali Experience* (L. Barber Press, 1995), 41.

1923, De Vecchi was tasked with implementing Mussolini's colonial policies. He extended direct Italian rule over the northeastern sultanates (Hobia and Majeerteen).[120] During the fascist period, Somalis were granted access to only a restricted education to the elementary level, underscoring the oppressive policies and limitations imposed on their intellectual development.[121] Even as the storm clouds gathered in preparation for World War II, Abdullahi Issa remained occupied in his school.[122] At 18 years old, he was given a job as a postal clerk in the port city of Merca from 1939 to 1941. Afterward, he returned to Mogadishu and worked in the Department of Economic Affairs during the last months of Italian rule in Somalia. The winds of change swept across the Horn of Africa with the British military occupation of Italian Somalia in April 1941 during World War II, bringing all Somali territory except Djibouti under British administration. In the upheaval that followed, Abdullahi was relieved from his official duties. Abdullahi got a job in Bulaburte as a post office clerk. Then, he ventured into the restaurant business in Beledweyne. Thus, the new chapter in his eventful life began, marked by entrepreneurial spirit.[123]

Abdullahi Isse joined the Somali Youth Club (SYC) during the British Military Administration of Somalia in 1944, at the same time as Adan Abdulle Osman and Sheikh Ali Jimale afterward.[124] Epitomizing the aspirations of a new generation of Somali leaders, Abdullahi embodied cultural qualities that defined this era: youth-

120. "The Majeerteen Sultanates," accessed July 1, 2024, http://www.mudugonline.com/MajertainSaltanates/Sultanate.htm
121. Sylvia Pankhurst, *Ex-Italian Somaliland* (London: Watts, 1951), 121; Robert Hess, *Italian Colonialism* (Chicago: University of Chicago Press, 1966), 169–170.
122. Smith Hempstone, *The New Africa* (London: Faber and Fabe, 1961), 145.
123. Ibid.
124. Abdullahi Isse and Adan Abdulle joined SYC simultaneously, carrying two consecutive numbers, 129 and 130, respectively. Samatar, Africa's First Democrats, 27 (Samatar made a mistake by writing 29 and 30). Mohamed Trunji, *President Adan Abdulla*, 2023, 39. I have interviewed Trunji and ensured that the member number is correct.

fulness, intellect, a propensity for self-education, unyielding confidence, and stubborn determination. At twenty-six, he was elected a member of the Central Committee and the Secretary-General, shouldering the responsibility of steering the SYL toward its lofty goals after the death of Yassin Haji Osman, one of the founders of SYC and its Secretary General in 1947. His impact transcended national boundaries as he embarked on diplomatic missions to Paris and New York, representing the SYL and advocating for the inherent rights of the Somali people to self-determination and independence.[125] His tenure as SYL envoy to the United Nations Trusteeship Council from 1948 to 1954 showcased his diplomatic finesse and firm commitment to advancing Somalia's cause on the global stage.

Abdullahi made history in 1956 as the inaugural Somali Prime Minister during the Italian administration under the UN trusteeship.[126] His appointment marked a significant milestone in Somali political evolution because of the outcome of the nation's first parliamentary elections. SYL emerged as the majority party in these elections, gaining 43 seats out of 60 contested seats.[127] This means that SYL received 333,820 votes cast of 608,361 votes (54.9 percent), while the remaining parties collectively gained 274,541 votes, equivalent to (45.1 percent), nonetheless dispersed, yielding only 17 seats.[128] This SYL victory compelled Italian administrator Enrico Anzilotti to accommodate the party with whom the Italian administration previously had a tense relationship. This new era, however, posed a formidable challenge as it intersected the traditional societal culture of clan solidarity with modern political institutions based on citizenship and the rule of law.

Abdullahi Isse was re-elected as MP in 1959 from Beledwayne, and his tenure as Premier of Somalia was reaffirmed. He assumed

---

125. Samatar, *Africa's First Democrats*, 46–47.
126. Trunji, *The Untold History*, 266.
127. Trunji, *The Untold History*, 264.
128. Parties that gained seats were SYL (43), HDMS (13), SDU (3), and Marehan party (1). See Samatar, 59.

multifaceted challenges and responsibilities alongside his premiership, such as facing the opposition of senior SYL members opposing
his pragmatic clan-balanced, alleged low capacity, and enlarged
Council of Ministers.[129] Under his leadership, the inaugural interim
Somali constitution was developed.[130] This foundational document
remained provisional until it was ratified in the 1961 referendum.
With Somalia's independence in July 1960, Abdullahi Isse was
appointed Foreign Minister, benefiting from his ample experience.[131]
His diplomatic endeavors took him far. He represented Somalia at
prestigious international forums such as the United Nations (UN),
the Organization of African Unity (OAU), and the Non-Aligned
Movement. After the 1964 war with Ethiopia, Abdullahi Isse led the
Somali delegation to Khartoum, where talks between Somalia and
Ethiopia were conducted under the auspices of the Organization of
African Unity.[132]

After the conclusion of the general election in March 1964,
Abdullahi Isse returned to the National Assembly as a representative
from Beledweyne. He joined subsequent governments as Minister
of Health, Labor, and Veterinary (Abdirizak government) and
Minister of Industry and Commerce (Egal government) until the
military coup of 1969. However, the political landscape of Somalia
underwent seismic shifts with the rise of the Supreme Revolutionary
Council (SRC), which seized power and was detained among other
prominent politicians released after three years in 1973. The military
government appointed prominent politicians as ambassadors, and
Abdullahi Isse was appointed Somalia's Ambassador to the Scan-

---

129. Trunji, *The Untold History*, 339.
130. Paoli Contini, *The Somali Republic: An Experiment in Legal Integration*
(London: F. Cass & Company, 1969).
131. Saadia Touval, *Somali Nationalism: International Politics and the Drive
for Unity in the Horn of Africa* (Lincoln: iUniverse, 1999), 113.
132. The Somali forces and the Ethiopian forces were incomparable. Somalia
had 5,000 soldiers and 5,000 police forces, while Ethiopia had 75,000 well-
equipped and well-trained forces trained by the USA. Even though Somali forces did well in this war because of a train of war, which was the Somali populated
area. Abdirizak, *A Political Memoir*, 170.

dinavian countries (Norway, Sweden, and Denmark) in 1974.[133] At the inaugural congress of the Somali Revolutionary Youth Organization, held in Mogadishu on May 15, 1977, General Mohamed Siyad honored Abdullahi Isse with a prestigious Gold Medal for his outstanding contributions and dedication to the nation's cause.[134]

Abdullahi continued to represent Somalia with distinction on the international stage as an ambassador. In 1986, after a long and illustrious career in politics and diplomacy, Abdullahi chose to step down from public office. Retiring to Rome, he embraced a tranquil life.[135] The final chapter of Abdullahi's remarkable national contribution ended in March 1988 when he passed away in Rome. His mortal remains were transported to Mogadishu, where he was laid to rest at the National Cemetery next to President Abdirashid Ali Sharmarke. He was accorded a state funeral, and Abdullahi's family, friends, and SYL veterans, President Adan Abdulle, joined President Mohamed Siyad and government officials at the burial site.[136] Abdullahi's life journey is a witness to the profound respect he commanded from all who knew him. Throughout his life, he cultivated relationships based on mutual understanding and cooperation, avoiding creating adversaries. His focus was singularly directed towards serving his nation and government with utmost sincerity and devotion. Abdullahi mirrors President Adan Abdulle in their deliberate avoidance of creating adversaries, projecting good manners, and abiding by the rule of law. These two leaders' cultures are deeply committed to the SYL's fundamental principles and epitomize its core values, embodying ideals of unity, progress, and national pride. Their devotion to the SYL's principles was a guiding light, influenc-

133. Other prominent politicians appointed as ambassadors were Michael Mariano, ambassador to Zambia; Adan Isak, ambassador to Pakistan; and Mohamed Ibrahim Egal, Ambassador to India (1976-78).
134. Sald Osman Roble, the former Chairman of the Somali Revolutionary Youth Organization, was present during the ceremony of offering Abdullahi Isse the Gold Medal. I interviewed him in Mogadishu on June 3, 2024.
135. Ali Hashi, a close relative, used to accompany him to Rome. I interviewed him in Mogadishu on June 3, 2024.
136. Trunji, *President Adan Abdulle*, 166.

ing their decision-making and policy implementation, transcending tribal and regional divides.

AN OVERVIEW AND ANALYSIS OF SYL'S HISTORY

The Somali people grappled with segmentation and a lack of political unity, rendering them vulnerable to colonization by European powers and the Ethiopian Empire in the nineteenth century. Italy, Britain, France, and Ethiopia seized Somali territories, triggering sporadic resistance led initially by the scholars of Islam— the Ulama.[137] However, this resistance gained momentum with the emergence of the Darwish movement under the leadership of Sayid Mohamed Abdulla Hassan, which lasted for two decades. The Fascist Governor of Italian Somaliland, Cesare Maria De Vecchi, undertook a military operation in 1923. He oversaw a brutal campaign referred to as "a war of pacification in Somalia," aimed at establishing direct Italian rule over all of Southern Somalia. One of the most egregious acts occurred in October 1926, when the Italian troops massacred approximately 100 people who had sought refuge in a mosque in the town of Merca.[138]

By 1927, initial anti-colonial Somali resistance had faltered with the Italian conquest of the Majeerteen kingdom in the current Puntland state of Somalia. Since then, traditional leaders found themselves either co-opted, integrated, or marginalized by colonial powers. The span of fifteen years, from 1927 to 1943, marked a period of "disorientation" for the Somali people.[139] Stripped of their traditional leadership, Somalis were often conscripted into conflicts such as the Italian-Ethiopian War and World War II, serving as fierce warriors and cannon fodder.[140] This era of adversity spurred the growth of the Somali national consciousness, and Somalis coalesced around

---

137. Abdullahi, *Making Sense of Somali History*, volume one, 90.
138. Tom Behan, *The Italian Resistance: Fascists, Guerrillas, and the Allies* (London: Pluto Press, 2009), 13.
139. Abdullahi, *Making Sense of Somali History*, 91
140. Ibid., 92

new nationalistic organizations. In Italian Somalia, conquered by Britain in 1941 during World War II, the Somali Youth Club (SYC) was founded. Transforming to a full-fledged party in 1947 under the new name, the Somali Youth League (SYL) represented a significant shift towards organized and concerted efforts to reclaim Somali independence and forge a unified national identity.

The SYC was established in Mogadishu by thirteen young Somalis on May 15, 1943, representing diverse backgrounds and professions. Among them were self-employed individuals, scholars of Islam, and the best-educated Somalis who were keenly aware of the shifting global dynamics during the tumultuous years of World War II. This founding group sought to mobilize Somali youth towards a common cause of liberation. The onset of World War II heralded a watershed moment in international affairs with the emergence of the Atlantic Charter. Crafted by US President Franklin D. Roosevelt and British Prime Minister Winston Churchill, the charter articulated principles of freedom, self-determination, and dismantling colonialism.[141] The Atlantic Charter represented hope for the colonized territories in Africa, Asia, and Latin America languishing under European dominion. The charter's principles were incorporated into the UN charter in 1945. The founders of the SYC seized upon the ideals espoused in the Atlantic Charter as inspiration for their aspirations of freedom from colonialism. Thus, establishing the SYC reflected the spirit of the time and heralded a new chapter in the Somali struggle for independence.

The socioeconomic backdrop of the Italian Fascist regime, the upheaval of World War II, and the anticipation of a new post-war order under the British Military Administration (BMA) catalyzed Somali political engagement. Britain captured southern Somalia in January 1941, whereas the capture of British Somaliland happened two months later.[142] The formation of SYC coincided with wartime

---

141. Ibid., 120.
142. Mohamed Issa-Salwe Abdisalam, *The Collapse of the Somali State: The Impact of the Colonial Legacy* (London: Haan Associates, 1996).

uncertainties and a population surge due to the influx of demobilized soldiers in the urban centers. The SYC increased in popularity and gained an estimated membership of 25,000 by 1946.[143] Membership in the club included private traders and young individuals from various monthly salaried occupations, such as government clerks, home servants, medical assistants, and members of the Somalia Gendarmerie. By 1947, around 60–80 percent of the Somalia Gendarmerie stationed in Mogadishu were club members.[144] This policy was against the traditional rule of excluding military personnel and bureaucracy from publicly joining political parties to safeguard their neutrality.[145] However, these exceptions were possible because SYC was considered a valuable ally of the British Military Administration (BMA). This partnership was forged in the aftermath of the rapid collapse of the Italian colonial forces in 1941 when the BMA found itself hastily established and lacking in experience in southern Somalia. The British authorities viewed the SYC favorably, albeit with one reservation: the club's oath of allegiance, which required members to eschew clan affiliation and identify solely as Somali, ran counter to the British preference for indirect rule through clan structures.[146]

In 1946, amidst discussions concerning the fate of former Italian colonies at the Paris Peace Conference, British Foreign Secretary Earnest Bevin proposed the concept of Greater Somalia under British rule conditioned with the acceptance of Ethiopia.[147]

---

143. Helen Chapin Metz, ed. *Somalia: A Country Study*, 26.
144. There was a significant discrepancy in the percentage of the SYL gendarmerie members. Some literature claims 60 percent, others 75 percent. Mohamed Mukhtar even gives 80 percent. Mohamed Mukhtar, Historical Dictionary of Somalia: African Historical Dictionary Series, No. 87, new ed. (The Scarecrow Press, 2003, 150). For 60 percent, see Abdullahi, *Making Sense of Somali History*, vol. one, 132.
145. Ibid., 125.
146. Cedric Barnes, "The Somali Youth League, Ethiopian Somalis and the Greater Somalia Idea, c.1946–48," Journal of Eastern African Studies 1, no. 2 (2007): 277–79, 280; Samatar, *Africa's First Democrats*, 40.
147. A detailed Bevin plan for Great Somalia, see Mohamed Osman Omar, *The*

However, Ethiopian Emperor Haile Selassie responded immediately with rejection. The Italian fascist government proclaimed the same idea in pursuing "le Garand Somalia" during its invasion of Ethiopia in 1935.[148] This notion aimed to improve the socio-economic conditions of Somali nomads while also serving British interests in East Africa. The idea had long circulated within colonial circles and found resonance among imperial strategists and idealistic colonial officers. The proposal envisioned unifying all Somali territories under British administration, preferably under United Nations Trusteeship.[149] However, this proposal faced immediate opposition from the United States, the Soviet Union, and France for different reasons. Ethiopia claimed Somali territory as part of their Empire's consistent expansionism into Somali territories to access the Indian Ocean and Red Sea. However, Ethiopia's efforts have been thwarted since the nineteenth century on three occasions. In 1905, Somali forces belonging to the Moobleen Osman clan defeated Ethiopian soldiers near Balad district, about 30 km north of Mogadishu.[150] Secondly, European colonial powers occupied coastal areas of Somalia, preventing Ethiopia's advancement to the direction of the ocean. Thirdly, after Italy's defeat in the Horn of Africa war, Ethiopia claimed historical ties to Somalia. Still, it failed to reclaim it as part of the Ethiopian Empire during discussions on the future of the former Italian colonies. The SYC, energized by Bevin's proposal, passionately championed the cause of Greater Somalia. Though not officially endorsing the idea,

---

Scramble in the Horn of Africa: History of Somalia (1827-1977), 500; Trunji, *President Adan Abdulle*, 40.

148. Over 40,000 Somali troops served in the war, primarily as combat units. They backed up the over 80,000 Italians serving alongside them at the start of the offensive. See Harold D. Nelson, *Somalia, a Country Study* (U.S. Government Printing Office, 1982, 24); Hamish Ion and Elizabeth Jane Errington, eds., *Great Powers and Little Wars: The Limits of Power* (Bloomsbury Academic, 1993), 179.

149. Samatar, *Africa's First Democrats*, 48.

150. Records on this war are not available and lack documentation. However, the clan named the day they finally defeated the Ethiopians as the Abyssinians' Monday, during which hundreds of young men died.

British authorities tacitly supported Somali efforts toward political organization for this purpose. The changing international discourse of self-determination spurred a reorganization within the SYC, prompting its transformation into the Somali Youth League (SYL) on April 1, 1947.[151] The SYL emerged as a disciplined and proactive political organization fueled by the sincere hope of achieving Greater Somalia.

Amidst the shifting political landscape that saw the evolution of the SYC into the formal political entity of the SYL, a significant figure in the SYC, Yasin Haji Osman, passed away. Yassin H. Osman, regarded as the mastermind behind the SYC's inception and the inaugural Secretary General of the SYL, left a void upon his early death in June 1947.[152] Abdullahi Isse was a friend of Yassin Haji Osman in Mogadishu and shared anti-colonial sentiment.[153] Three months before his death, Yassin recommended appointing Abdullahi Isse as SYL's secretary general.[154] However, stepping into his shoes with determination and resolve, Abdullahi Isse assumed the mantle of SYL Secretary-General in June 1947. As Abdullahi ascended to the leadership position within the SYL, he inherited not only the responsibilities of his predecessor but also the aspirations and dreams of a growing Somali nationalist movement. Charged with the task of guiding the SYL through a crucial juncture in Somali history, Abdullahi brought with him a commitment to the ideals of self-determination and national unity. In the annals of Somali political history, the passing of Yasin Haji Osman and the subsequent ascension of Abdullahi Isse to the helm of the SYL serves as a reminder of the resilience and determination of the Somali people.

---

151. The establishment date of SYL, where its name and new constitution were, was April 1, 1947. Some literature claiming this date to be 1946 is a mistake that requires correction. See the official announcement of SYL in the Somalia Courier as quoted by Trunji, *Untold History*, 15.
152. Ibid.,
153. Interview with Ali Hashi Dhoore, a friend and a relative of Abdullahi Isse. Mogadishu, April 15, 2024.
154. Ibid.

The SYL distinguished itself from other political parties through five key factors, fostering its strength. First, it garnered the backing of the British Military administration, strategically positioning itself as a proponent of anti-Italian political forces in Somalia.[155] Second, it was financially sustainable because it systematically collected membership fees from individuals across the Somalia region, including personnel affiliated with the British administration and gendarmerie.[156] Third, the SYL leadership boasted better education and expertise during its era, offering a distinct advantage in dealing with the complex issues of the national movement. Fourth, the party's ideology struck a chord with the people by championing the unification of all Somali people under the banner of a Great Somali state, tapping into deep-seated aspirations for national unity. Fifth, if necessary, the SYL maintained a Vanguard (*Horseed*) militia to defend the party, deal with the adversaries of the SYL, and undertake forceful actions against colonial powers as needed.[157]

The history of the SYL unfolds across three distinct phases, each encapsulating significant shifts in the party's trajectory and the broader political landscape of Somalia. The first phase, from its inception as a nationalist movement in 1943 to 1956, saw the SYL emerge as a formidable movement advocating for Somali independence and unity. During this period, the SYL galvanized widespread support among the Somali people, rallying behind the common goal of liberation from colonial rule and establishing a sovereign Somali state. Fervent activism, grassroots mobilization, an inclusive agenda, and an ardent commitment to the principles of self-determination characterized the party's early years. However, transitioning into the second phase, from 1956 to 1967, the SYL became the ruling

---

155. I.M. Lewis, *The Modern History of Somaliland, from Nation to State* (New York: Frederick A. Prager, 1965), 122.
156. British Military administrations allowed the best-educated police and civil servants to join the SYC, contrary to the policy of separating civil service from the political parties because they considered the SYC anti-Italian and progressive. Lewis, *The Modern History of Somaliland*, 122.
157. Truni, *The Untold History*, 17.

party following Somalia's attainment of independence. The party and its senior leaders found themselves confronted with a crucial test that directly challenged their professed rhetoric to reject clannism, advocate for the equality of all Somalis, and work towards the unification of the Somali people. However, this period witnessed the weakness of claimed principles and values, internal power struggles, the surge of political clannism, and challenges as the SYL grappled with the intricacies of governing a newly independent nation.

The third phase was marked by Prime Minister Mohamed Ibrahim Egal's tenure as the SYL leader, who joined the SYL in 1966. The SYL had lost its compass and drifted towards authoritarian tendencies. Egal's pursuit of a one-party system mirrored the trajectory of many post-independence African states. This shift towards authoritarianism underscored personal power-seeking motives and stirred dissent within the party ranks. I.M. Lewis characterized the Egal government as "official corruption and nepotism seemed to be flourishing on a scale hitherto unknown in the Republic, ...but there was little sign that either the [Prime Minister] or the President were unduly disturbed by their persistence."[158] However, the SYL's trajectory took an unexpected turn with the assassination of President Abdirashid Ali Sharmarke and the subsequent 1969 military coup. This event marked the demise of the nationalist party after twenty-two years of existence, symbolizing a profound turning point in Somali politics. The coup reshaped Somalia, plunging Somalia into a period of political turbulence and uncertainty that would reverberate for decades. The legacy of the SYL, once a beacon of Somali nationalism, now stood as a testament to the complexities and challenges of post-colonial statehood in Africa.

Since its inception, the SYL has demonstrated internal democracy through its annual congresses, the one-year term of the central committee, and the democratic election of party officeholders, including the chairman.[159] These institutional mechanisms were

---

158. Helen Chapin Metz, ed., *Somalia: A Country Study*, 4th edition, 1992, 45.
159. See the list of the central committee from Trunji, *President Adan Abdulle,*

pillars of the party's governance structure, fostering transparency and collective decision-making. While the annual rejuvenation of the central committee may appear to be a potential source of instability, conversely, it played a crucial role in unifying the party and ensuring its continuity. These congresses provided an opportunity for the emergence of fresh leadership equipped to navigate the evolving political environment. By embracing leadership turnover, SYL demonstrated its dedication to institutional resilience and adaptability in changing circumstances. From 1947 to 1960, the party elected seven chairmen and five secretary generals, showcasing a culture of dynamic leadership renewal. Abdullahi Isse served as Secretary General of SYL under three chairmen: Haji Mohamed Hussein (1947–1951), Haji Farah Ali Omar (1952), and Adan Abdulle Osman (1953–1956).[160] In 1960, the party further solidified its dedication to democratic governance by abolishing the chairman's position and retaining the secretary general. Over the subsequent eight years (1960–1968), four secretary generals were elected, highlighting a continued emphasis on leadership rotation and shared responsibility.[161] The absence of a dominant leader within the SYL fostered a more dynamic and inclusive political environment where no individual held an irreplaceable position of power. Instead, leadership transitions were guided by democratic processes and the collective will of the party's members.

Mohamed Trunji eloquently articulates the gradual decline of the SYL. He highlights the departure of numerous esteemed party figures, including former Chairman Haji Mohamed Hussein, Haji Farah Ali Omar, Abdirizak Haji Hussein, and Sheikh Ali Jimale, amid President Adan's stance of neutrality towards all factions. Trunji laments the hijacking of the party's once-proud nationalist ethos, describing the third phase of SYL, "The party lost its nationalistic zeal, values, and prestige, and reduced itself to a mafia-like organization in the hands of unscrupulous elements whose aim drive was the lust

---

199–209.
160. Ibid.
161. Ibid.

for power and greed for wealth." Further, "the party's nationalistic values were hijacked by factionalism and sectarian division with the party itself, a circumstance that unfortunately paved the way for the military to seize power."[162] This regrettable shift towards factionalism not only compromised the SYL's integrity but also paved the way for the destabilizing influence of military intervention.

The demise of the SYL following the military coup over twenty-two years ago is a significant historical phenomenon worthy of close examination. Initially, the party's downfall stemmed from a decline in its foundational ethos, marked by the dissolution of strict membership criteria and a lax attitude towards inclusion, allowing opportunistic individuals to infiltrate its ranks solely for personal gain. This gradual erosion of standards and values weakened the SYL from within. As stalwart party members departed one after another, disillusioned by its deviation from its original principles, a new breed of individuals gradually assumed control, disregarding the party's founding principles and policies. Consequently, the SYL underwent a stark transformation, rendering only its inaugural phase worthy of emulation and a model for the new generation. Despite numerous missteps during its governance from 1956 to 1967, the SYL's complete downfall was witnessed after 1967. The party was converted as a tool for exclusion, nepotism, and electoral malpractice, disregarding its guiding principles, policies, and long history of struggling to establish good governance practices.

In conclusion, throughout the twenty-two-year tenure of the SYL, Abdullahi Isse remained a consistent presence, being elected annually for a remarkable ten-year period. This continuity underscores the trust and confidence bestowed upon him by successive SYL central committees, which themselves changed every year over these ten years. Indeed, Abdullahi's history becomes intertwined with that of the SYL leading up to Somalia's independence in 1960. As either the SYL Secretary General or the first Prime Minister until 1960, Abdullahi Isse emerged as a central figure in the struggle for Somali

---

162. Trunji, *The Untold History*, 20.

79

independence. His dedication and leadership were instrumental in guiding the SYL through the tumultuous years preceding independence, navigating internal challenges and external pressures with resilience and determination. It is not an exaggeration to assert that Abdullahi's life path mirrors the SYL itself, epitomizing the party's journey from an early liberation movement to a beacon of hope for Somali independence. During his tenure as Secretary General and subsequent role as the first Prime Minister, various ministerial portfolios encapsulate the persistence of the aspirations and struggles of Abdullahi Isse.

THE ITALIAN ADMINISTRATION OF SOMALIA UNDER UN TRUSTEESHIP

Following the defeat of Fascist Italy in World War II, particularly in the Horn of Africa theatre in 1941, the British Military Administration assumed control over most Somali territories, except Djibouti, which remained under French control. The British administration dismantled much of the economic infrastructure established by Italy during the fascist era.[163] On the other hand, the British authorities promoted individual freedoms and encouraged the formation of political organizations that contrasted sharply with the restrictive policies of the previous Italian Fascist rule. The post-war period was marked by extensive and often contentious deliberations among the four major Allied powers—namely the United States, the Soviet Union, the United Kingdom, and France—regarding the fate of former Italian colonies. These debates were driven by differing geopolitical interests and visions for the future of these regions, leading to a protracted negotiation and decision-making process on the governance and sovereignty of the affected territories.

---

163. The destroyed projects include the Railway line connecting Mogadishu-Afgoye-Jowhar, the Afgoye bridge, and Salt production in the Hafun, Majayan, and Qandla mines. See Paolo Tripodi, *The Colonial Legacy in Somalia*, 45.

After years of disagreement about the future of former Somalia Italiano, the Haitian Ambassador defeated the Bevin-Sforza agreement, which proposed returning Somalia to Italy without UN trusteeship and time limits.[164] Abdullahi Isse called this agreement "Survival of colonialism of the worst type."[165] Britain changed its relations with SYL and aligned with Italy. Abdullahi Isse sent a cable to the SYL regarding Britain's role, saying that "Notorious imperialist Britain intends to suggest again the restoration of hated Italian rule in Somalia."[166] Instead, the proposal to return Somalia to Italy under UN trusteeship for ten years was approved.[167] Additionally, India and Pakistan proposed establishing three Advisory Councils of representatives from Egypt, the Philippines, and Colombia.[168] It was adopted by the U.N. Resolution 289 by the General Assembly in its 250th Meeting on November 21, 1949.[169] Mohamed Trunji, in his analysis of the trusteeship agreement, considers Somalia a unique case of trusteeship. First, it was the first instance where a defeated former colonial power (Italy), not a member of the United Nations, was entrusted with administering its former colony.[170] Second, setting a time limit of ten years for the administration was another uniqueness. Third, establishing a United Nations advisory council to oversee the administering authority further distinguished Somalia's trusteeship from other cases.[171]

---

164. Earnet Bevin was the foreign secretary of the UK during the post-war labor government of 1945–51, and Carlo Sforza was the foreign minister of Italy (1947–1951).
165. Trunji, *The Told History*, second edition, 146.
166. Ibid., 156.
167. Samatar, *Africa's First Democrats*, 48.
168. Ibid.
169. Mohamed Osman Omar, *The Road to Zero: Somalia's Self-Destruction* (Personal reminiscence. HAAN Associates, 1992), 14.
170. On 14 December 1955, Italy signed the United Nations Charter and became a member of the Organization. See Pietro Pastorelli, Italy's Accession to the United Nations Organization. Available from https://www.diplomatie.gouv.fr/IMG/pdf/ONU_pietro_pastorelli.pdf (accessed on July 1, 2024).
171 Trunji, *President Adan Abdulla*, 41.

On April 1, 1950, the Italian Trust Administration of Somalia (*Administrazione Fiduciaria Italiana della Somalia* "AFIS") began administering Somalia, deploying 6,500 troops under Giovanni Fornari. This was eight months before the Trusteeship Agreement's official signing, which took effect on November 2, 1950.[172] At the start of the mission, Giuseppe Brusasca, the undersecretary for foreign affairs, made Italy's intentions clear: "We were going back to demonstrate that we were able to inaugurate a new politics in Africa, not one of exploitation anymore, but of collaboration."[173]

The general conditions in Somalia were highly challenging. Out of a population of 1.242 million, only 20,000 people lived in stone houses. The literacy rate was a mere 0.6 percent, and there was only one doctor for every 60,000 people.[174] The UN summarized the objectives of creating independent Somalia in five main points: (1) creation and development of a regional government organization, (2) economic and financial development, (3) improvement of education, (4) social progress and welfare, and (5) the transfer of power from administration to local government.[175] Significant challenges and unrest marked his first three years. The early years of AFIS rule saw intense conflict with the Somali Youth League (SYL), as many SYL officials, previously influential under the British, were demoted, removed, or imprisoned by the Italians. This marginalization strategy led to widespread demonstrations, which the govern-

---

172. Paolo Tripodi, "Back to the Horn: Italian Administration and Somalia's Troubled Independence," The International Journal of African Historical Studies 32, no. 2–3 (1999): 359–380.

173. Angelo Del Boca, "The Myths, Suppressions, Denials, and Defaults of Italian Colonialism," in *A Place in the Sun: Africa in Italian Colonial Culture from Post-Unification to the Present*, ed. Patrizia Palumbo (Berkeley: University of California Press, 2003, 17–37).

174. Patrizia Palumbo, ed., *A Place in the Sun: Africa in Italian Colonial Culture from Post-Unification to the Present* (Berkeley: University of California Press, 2003, 30).

175. Reviglio della Veneria, M., "The United Nations, Italy and Somalia: A 'Sui Generis' Relation 1948-1969," MA thesis, Utrecht Universiteit, 2014, 31.

ment harshly repressed.[176] The Italian authority of the former fascist officers refused to cooperate with the SYL, fueling ongoing tensions and resistance and shaping a contentious political landscape during the trusteeship.[177]

To prepare Somalia for self-governance, the Italian administration established a Territorial Council to represent a broad spectrum of its societal interests in 1951. The Territorial Council consisted of 35 councilors, 28 of whom were Somalis; it was "a consultative and representative central body with responsibilities for all government activities, except foreign policy."[178] Adan Abdulle, the deputy chairman of the Territorial Council representing SYL, played a pivotal role in improving relations with the Italians. The first clear sign of this improved relationship emerged on May 15, 1953, during the tenth anniversary celebration of the Somali Youth League (SYL). On this significant occasion, Dr. Benerdelli, a political officeholder, delivered a welcoming speech that was warmly received, symbolizing a new era of cooperation.[179] However, despite these positive developments, Abdullahi Isse, the secretary general of SYL at the United Nations, maintained a steadfast hardline against Italy. This position starkly contrasted with other Somali political parties, which had expressed satisfaction with Somalia's progress during the initial three years of self-governance.[180] In a strategic move, the Italian Ambassador to the United Nations attempted to remove Abdullahi Isse from the United States, but this effort was unsuccessful.[181] Alternatively, the SYL decided to recall Abdullahi Isse to Somalia and replaced him with Abdirizak Haji Hussein as part of the new SYL policy of cooperating with AFIS.[182] However, the Italians, determined to delay his return until after the municipal elections scheduled for March

---

176. Tripodi, The colonial legacy in Somalia, 46.
177. Ibid., 57. *Angelo del Boca*, 30.
178. Tripodi, *The Colonial Legacy in Somalia*, 58.
179. Trunji, *Untold History*, 234.
180. Ibid, 235.
181. Ibid., 236.
182. Ibid., 236.

28, 1954, tried to entertain him in Rome during his journey back to Mogadishu. However, this plan also failed, allowing Abdullahi Isse to return to Somalia as intended.[183]

The first municipal elections were held throughout Somalia on March 28, 1954, marking a significant milestone in the territory's political development. The SYL emerged as the dominant political force, capturing 141 out of 281 contested seats and achieving a decisive victory that underscored its popularity and influence nation-wide.[184] This electoral success led to a notable shift in the relationship between the SYL and the Italian administration. Recognizing the SYL's widespread support and political clout, AFIS acknowledged the necessity of collaborating with the SYL to govern the territory effectively. This realization prompted the Italian administration to adopt a more cooperative and conciliatory approach towards the SYL. Conversely, the SYL understood the importance of maintaining a constructive relationship with AFIS and recognized that working alongside AFIS would strengthen its political position and enhance its ability to influence the transition towards self-governance and eventual independence.

On October 12, 1954, the Somali flag of sky color with the white star was raised alongside the tricolor Italian flag on the government offices. By then, significant strides had been made in Somalia's security sector and civil administration, and there was a noticeable trend towards Somali empowerment and participation. This shift in demographics within the civil administration reflected a delib-erate effort to decentralize power and promote local governance, aligning with broader aspirations for self-rule and independence. At the beginning of 1956, there were more than 5,000 officials, of whom 4,380 were Somalis and only 621 were Italians.[185] The social service sector also experienced significant advancements during this period, marked by notable improvements in education and training

---

183. Ibid., 237.
184. Samatar, *Africa's First Democrats*, 58.
185. P. Tripodi, *The Colonial Legacy in Somalia*, 75.

initiatives. While progress was evident in the social sphere, economic development remained a pressing concern, with efforts underway to bridge existing gaps and stimulate growth. Recognizing the importance of economic advancement, Italy provided crucial support to bolster the administration's budget, facilitating infrastructure projects and investment initiatives to foster economic prosperity. However, challenges persisted, particularly regarding unresolved border disputes with neighboring Ethiopia, which continued to pose a significant obstacle to regional stability and cooperation. Addressing this longstanding issue remained a priority for the Somali administration as it sought to safeguard national sovereignty and territorial integrity.

Abdullahi Isse was the SYL envoy to New York, where he lobbied for Somali self-determination and unity and against the Italian return to Somalia under any circumstances. He stayed there from 1948 to 1954, and Abdirashid was the acting Secretary General.[186] He was replaced by Abdirizak Haji Hussein as an expression of changed relations with Italy. Upon his arrival, he found that the ties between the SYL and the Italian administration had improved under Governor Anzelotti. This information was withheld from the public for fear of affecting SYL's reputation as an anti-Italian movement. Abdullahi Isse was dismayed by such cordial relations with Italy and stayed aloof from the party for a certain period, and Mohamud Yusuf Muro was appointed deputy secretary general.[187]

However, he emerged as a pivotal figure in Somali politics navigating issues related to social progress, economic aspirations, and diplomatic challenges. In the 1956 parliamentary election, Abdullahi Isse was elected from Mogadishu, receiving 7,158 votes, competing with Yusuf Igal and Osman Ahmed Roble, who received 382 and 882 votes, respectively.[188] Abdullahi Isse was then nominated as the first prime minister and entrusted with steering the nation through a

---

186. Abdirizak, *A Political Memoir*, 65
187. Trunji, *Untold History*, second edition, 249.
188. Ibid., 261.

period of transition and consolidation. After being appointed prime minister, he cemented his relationship with the Italians and worked closely with them, contrasting with his early hardline position.[189]

POLITICAL CULTURE OF ABDULLAHI ISSE MOHAMUD

History demonstrates that the advancement of any society hinges upon the actions of its political elite. Elite political culture refers to influential participants' beliefs, values, and habits within a political system. The prevailing political landscape in Somalia is primarily characterized by the dominance of clan-based politics, the commercialization of electoral processes, electoral fraud, and a heavy reliance on foreign support. However, amidst this prevalent culture, select individuals within the ruling elite stand as beacons of a contrasting ethos—one that champions good governance, upholds the rule of law, advocates for citizen equality, and vehemently opposes corruption. Among this distinguished group are figures like Abdullahi Isse, alongside President Adan Abdulle and Abdirizak H. Hussein. Together, these individuals embody a rare breed of leadership—one that transcends narrow clan affiliations and prioritizes the collective welfare of the nation.

Abdullahi's allegiance to the SYL throughout its twenty-two-year history is a testament to his steadfast commitment to the party's ideals despite challenges and disagreements. In a period marked by political upheaval and shifting allegiances, Abdullahi Isse remained resolute in his support for the SYL despite witnessing the departure or expulsion of many of his fellow party stalwarts. His loyalty to the SYL was not merely a matter of convenience but a profoundly ingrained principle rooted in his belief in the party's vision for Somalia. Even in moments of disagreement or dissatisfaction with the party's performance, Abdullahi Isse remained dedicated, recognizing the importance of maintaining unity and solidarity within the ranks. The following section explores the episodes that witness his

---

189. Ibid., 267.

continued political culture in his different roles within the party and the government.

Abdullahi's Political Culture as Secretary General of SYL (1947–1956)

Abdullahi's long-term tenure as secretary general demonstrated his trustworthiness in the SYL central committee and his commitment to the party's principles. He remained a steadfast leader throughout his decade-long tenure, navigating the party through turbulent times and ever-changing political landscapes. Despite continuous changes in the composition of the Central Committee, Abdullahi's leadership remained permanent, ensuring continuity and coherence in pursuing the SYL's objectives. The central committee underwent a series of transformations, culminating in seven reconfigurations in the first ten years. Throughout these ten years, 111 individuals joined the SYL central committee, which endorsed Abdullahi Isse.[190] These seven central committees testified to his trustworthiness and capacity to accomplish the program of SYL. His ability to work with successive committees underscores his reliability and effectiveness in advancing the party's objectives. Moreover, the dynamic nature of the SYL during Abdullahi's tenure is exemplified by the influx of forty-five new members into the central committee.[191] To illustrate Abdullahi's political culture, it is imperative to delve into episodes and events that vividly depict his demeanor, approach to diplomacy, and political inclinations. One such story is his role in lobbying for Somali self-determination and unity.

The arrival of the four power commissions in Somalia on January 3, 1948, marked the beginning of hearings aimed at gauging the preferences of the Somali people regarding the administration of their territory. The Somali Youth League (SYL), alarmed by the pro-

---

190. See the list of the central committee of SYL from its inception in 1947 to its end in 1969. Analyzing its members over ten years (1947–1956), 111 had been produced. Trunji, *Legacy*, 199–202.
191. These numbers were produced in analyzing the list of the central committees of SYL. Ibid.

ceedings, dispatched Abdullahi Isse to Paris to lobby against Italy's potential return to Somalia. Abdullahi remained in New York for five years (1948–1953) as SYL's envoy to the UN. He initially journeyed to the UK, where some SYL members warmly welcomed him.[192] Despite being denied a visa for Paris, Ali Nur, another SYL member, clandestinely sneaked him in, and despite being barred from addressing the commission, Abdullahi proceeded to New York.[193] At the United Nations, the final proposal of the Bevin-Sforza Plan was made, endorsing Italy to administer Somalia under a UN trusteeship without a fixed date. Abdullahi Isse related the Bevin-Spfoza and SYL project, leading the SYL to organize a massive demonstration on October 5, 1949. At least five people died, and 12 were injured.[194] The Ambassador of Haiti, Mr. Emile Saint-Lot, convinced by Abdullahi Isse, defied his country's instructions and defeated the Bevin-Sforza agreement.[195] He diverged from the stances held by other Latin American nations, renowned for backing Italy's reinstatement in its former African territories. Furthermore, India and Pakistan proposed the establishment of an advisory council comprising Egypt, the Philippines, and Colombia. During its fourth regular session on November 21, 1949, the UN General Assembly overwhelmingly adopted the resolution to place Somalia under Italian trusteeship.[196] Abdullahi remained in New York for almost two years

---

192. Samatar, Africa's First Democrat, 46.

193. Ibid.

194. This incident is called "Dhagaxtoor" in Somali history, and a massive monument was erected where the British forces confronted them. Abdirizak, *A Political Memoir*, 68–69.

195. Ambassador Emile Saint-Lot was decorated with the Order of Somali Star by the President of Somalia, Adan Abdulle, on August 26, 1961. He was also hired as an adviser to the Somali Embassy in New York. Mohamed Trunji, a Haitian diplomat who openly defied his government to support the Somali cause at the UN. November 23, 2022. Available from https://www.hiiraan.com/op4/2022/nov/188832/haitian_diplomat_who_openly_defied_his_government_to_support_the_somali_cause_at_the_un.aspx (accessed on April 3, 2024)

196. United Nations, *Draft Trusteeship Agreement for the Territory of Somaliland under Italian Administration: Special Report of the Trusteeship Council,*

(January 1948–November 21, 1949) before adopting the final UN decision. After that, he stayed in New York for three years until 1954, tirelessly submitting petitions to the UN and demonstrating loyalty to his party and devotion to the principles of liberating Somalia from colonialism. During his tenure as Secretary General, Abdullahi Isse showcased a distinctive political culture characterized by his dedication to fostering trust within the Somali Youth League's (SYL) central committee. His commitment to the principles of the SYL, particularly the importance of Somali unity, was evident in his actions and leadership style. Isse's belief in these ideals guided his approach to building cohesive and effective relationships within the organization, contributing to the success and longevity of the SYL's mission. His emphasis on trust and unity helped solidify his reputation as a leader who prioritized his country's and people's well-being.

Abdullahi's Political Culture as Prime Minister (1956–60)

Abdullahi Isse was summoned back to Somalia in 1953 following a rapprochement between SYL and the Italian Administrator in Somalia while he was persisting in anti-Italian SYL policy at the UN. He was succeeded by Abdirizak Haji Hussein, who embraced a new vision of cooperation with Italy. Upon his return, Abdullahi was disheartened by SYL's reconciliation with Italy and chose to distance himself from participation in the SYL central committee.[197] However, he was eventually persuaded and resumed his regular duties within the party. During his tenure in New York, Abdullahi immersed himself in world politics, achieved fluency in English, and sustained the trust of this party. Thus, in the deliberations to establish the inaugural government, all political factions collectively recommended Abdullahi Isse for the Italian administrator. One of his strong supporters was Adan Abdulle Osman, who abstained from the SYL proposal to designate Adan for the Prime Minister

---

General Assembly Official Records: Fifth Session, Supplement No. 10 (A/1294) (Lake Success, New York, 1950)
197. Samatar, *Africa's First Democrats*, 57.

position and instead endorsed Abdullahi Isse.[198] Bolstered by this widespread trust from the political spectrum, Enrico Anzilotti, the administrator, appointed Abdullahi Isse as the Prime Minister of the Somali government after SYL won the election of what Ahmed Kheyre called "Experimental Democracy."[199]

After he was appointed prime minister, he considered the unification of all Somali territory the priority of his government. As I.M. Lewis relates, Abdullahi Isse made the following statement in front of the parliament session:

> Abdullahi Isse explained his government's programme to the Somalia assembly has given first place to the unification of the Somali territories. The Somali he told the assembly from a single race, practice the same religion, and speak a single language. They inhabit a vast territory, which, in its turn, constitutes a well-defined geographic unit. All must know that the government of Somalia will strive its uttermost, with legal and peaceful means, which are its democratic prerogatives to attain this end: the union of Somalis until all Somalis form a single Great Somalia.[200]

Abdullahi Isse's leadership style can be best characterized as situational leadership, where he adapts his approach based on the specific circumstances and context. Situational leaders are known for their flexibility and ability to tailor their leadership strategies to fit the situation's needs. Analysing Abdullahi's early political culture as Somalia's inaugural Prime Minister in 1956 is driven by his situational leadership, which requires flexibility, pragmatism, and decisiveness when needed. Assuming the mantle of Prime Minister and guiding the Council of Ministers marked a profound shift for Abdullahi and

---

198. Abdirizak, *A Political Memoir*, 113.
199. Ahmed Ali M. Khayre, "Somalia: An Overview of the Historical and Current Situation," Social Science Research Network, 2016, 15. https://www.academia.edu/24800571/ (accessed April 30, 2024).
200. I.M. Lewis, *A Modern History of the Somali: Revised, Updated & Expanded*, 4th ed. (Ohio University Press, 2002), 161.

his cohorts. A notable distinction marked their journey: they were largely self-educated individuals navigating unfamiliar terrain in the realm of governance with limited economic resources.[201] Transitioning from idealistic national movements to the governance of clan-based societies presented a unique, unprecedented challenge of running a modern state administration. This transition demanded a delicate balance between their aspirational ideals and the pragmatic realities governing diverse and often fragmented communities. Initially, the inaugural Council of Ministers was handpicked from the ranks of SYL stalwarts, predominantly drawn from the Hawiye and Darood sub-clans, thereby marginalizing representation from other clans and political factions.[202] This exclusivity of representation raised concerns about inclusivity and equitable governance, prompting discussions on the need for broader representation to foster national unity and cohesion.

Even though Speaker of Parliament Adan Abdulle proposed an inclusive Cabinet with another political party, the SYL Central Committee refused. The HDMS accused the government of favoring nomadic people and marginalizing the farming population of the southern regions. Nevertheless, Abdullahi's astute political acumen became evident as he recognized the importance of addressing grievances and clan sentiments within the political landscape. Responding pragmatically to these concerns, he undertook a significant policy shift by forming the 15-member Council of Ministers in 1959. This time, emphasis was placed on achieving clan balance, with appointments drawn from the Hawiye, Darood, and Digil & Mirifle clans, reflecting a more inclusive and representative government.[203] Indeed,

---

201. Paolo Tripodi, "Back to the Horn," 369.
202. The government consisted of three ministers, including the Prime minister from Hawiye (2 Habar-gidir/sa'ad, one Hawadle), two ministers from Darood (Majeerteen), and one from Dir.
203. SYL members, mainly Darood members, were not satisfied with the new council ministers, which created a rift within SYL, which became a clan line between Hawiye and Darood. This row was resolved through traditional conflict resolution mechanisms, and the party was reunited again.

minority groups and women were not represented in the Council of Ministers. This omission underscored a critical lacuna in the government's composition, reflecting broader societal disparities in political participation and representation. The pragmatism of clan-based inclusivity angered some senior SYL members, who criticized the government for lacking capacity, large numbers, and clan balance.[204] The clan balancing and inclusivity formula became a permanent approach in Somali politics, although clannism was formally and rhetorically disdained. However, Abdullahi was firm in his position, and the central committee expelled these members from the party. Nonetheless, the situation was calmed through reconciliation and unity among the party.[205]

During this period, a notable phenomenon emerged: clans begged their members to represent them in parliament, reflecting the misunderstanding of modern state systems and politics and indicating the low education and capacity of the people in general. Moreover, the desire to assume ministerial positions seemed even more challenging, with reluctance among many approached individuals, primarily due to the perceived educational qualifications required for such roles. Furthermore, for those who did agree to join the Council of Ministers, their effectiveness was supported by the coaching of the Italian advisers directly reporting to the Italian administrator. They were replaced after a year by experts working and reporting to the Somali ministers.[206] A confidential report from the British Consulate General in Mogadishu in 1957 describes the capacities of the Somalis in running a modern state, stating:

> When the administrator decided to form a Somali government, it was with difficulty that six Somali members of the legislative assembly could be found sufficiently capable to

---

204. Samatar, *Africa's First Democrats*, 72. Trunji, *The Told History*, volume two, 339.
205. Abdirizak, *A Political Memoir*, 126–30.
206. Trunji, *The Untold History*, volume two, 269.

begin on the task of becoming minister, and if they resigned today, it would prove almost impossible to find another six.[207]

Moreover, the Abdullahi government confronted numerous challenges demanding decisive action rooted in legal frameworks or recourse to traditional conflict resolution mechanisms. Abdullahi demonstrated a remarkable degree of flexibility in navigating these complexities, often prioritizing the overarching goal of national unity above all else. When formal legal procedures seemed impractical or insufficient to address pressing issues, Abdullahi was willing to engage with traditional conflict resolution mechanisms.

For example, Abdullahi encountered repeated conflicts with his Interior Minister, Haji Muse Boqor, which required him to navigate delicate compromises and decisive actions. The first instance arose when Haji Muse Boqor appointed his cousin, Haji Muse Samatar, as the director of the central prison in Mogadishu without seeking approval from the Council of Ministers. Although the prime minister cautioned Haji Muse about this oversight, he refrained from reversing the appointment. The second conflict occurred when Haji Muse Boqor resisted cooperating with interim Prime Minister Sheikh Ali Jimale in countering the interference of Haji Mohamed Hussein, Chairman of the SYL, in government affairs while the Prime Minister was on a foreign trip. Haji Muse abstained from working in his Ministry and influenced the minister of finance, Salad Abdi Mohamud, belonging to the same clan. Responding decisively, the Prime Minister assumed control of the Interior and Finance Ministries. He immediately transferred to different regions those who supported Haji Muse Boqor, like the governor of Mogadishu. However, after reconciliation efforts, Haji Muse Boqor agreed to resume his duties, prompting the Prime Minister to reverse his orders, thereby diffusing the crisis.[208]

---

207. quoted by Trunji, Ibid.
208. Trunji, *The Untold History*, volume two, 332-4.

The third incident was when Haji Muse Boqor unilaterally reopened the GSL and Banadiria parties' offices in Mogadishu, which had been closed by government order due to allegations of violence and disturbing public order.[209] GSL was associated with Haji Mohamed Hussein, the former SYL chairman expelled from the party due to his leftist ideology. In response, the Prime Minister demanded Haji Boqor's resignation or threatened to resign himself, signaling a firm stance against compromising on matters of principle.[210] Another noteworthy incident occurred in 1959, following the formation of a large, clan-balanced Council of Ministers. Thirteen senior SYL members who opposed the government were expelled from the party, only to be reinstated later through a traditional conflict resolution mechanism. These incidents underscore Abdullahi's adeptness in navigating complex political dynamics and his willingness to compromise to maintain stability and unity. They also demonstrate his pragmatism in dealing with clan-based society and unwavering commitment to upholding the integrity of government institutions and principles, even in the face of internal challenges.

THE MAIN AGENDAS OF THE ABDULLAHI ISSE GOVERNMENT

One notable indicator of Abdullahi Isse's leadership is his adept handling of three key issues. The first is drafting the provisional constitution, which involves extensive consultation with legal experts, political stakeholders, and international advisors. The second is holding municipal and national elections in 1959. The third is the Great Somalia Project and the unification of the Trust Territory of Somalia (the southern part under Italian administration) with the British Somaliland Protectorate. In addition, state institutions should be built, and the capacity of public administrators and security apparatus should be enhanced under the mandate of the Italian administration under the UN trusteeship mandate.

---

209. Samatar, *Africa's First Democrats*, 67.
210. Ibid., 68.

Drafting the Provisional Constitution

Regarding developing a Provisional Somali Constitution, the Council of Ministers and leaders of the Legislative Assembly began drafting a constitution to be ready before Somalia's independence date. Two committees were established to achieve this project: a political committee led by the speaker Aden Abdulla Osman and PM Abdullahi Isse and a technical committee chaired by Professor Giuseppe Aurelio Costanzo. This technical committee included international experts from the United Nations and other countries. The committee used various existing constitutions as references, especially the Italian constitutional model, due to its influence on the legal system in Somalia, which Italy administrated under the UN trusteeship. The Legislative Assembly was then transformed into a Constituent Assembly to approve the constitution and handle legislative matters. With the recommendation of The UN Trusteeship, representatives from all existing political parties and essential social organizations were included in the Constituent Assembly for broader representation. Despite the government's initial hesitation, the proposal was accepted.[211] An important principle introduced by the Political Committee was the adoption of Islam as the primary source of state laws, giving the constitution a distinct Islamic character. Regarding the form of government, HDMS advocated for a federal system, and others like SYL and other parties advocated for a unitary system. When the pan-Somali conference was held in Mogadishu on April 16–23, 1960, an agreement was reached: "The two territories should be united on July 1, 1960. The new Republic would be a unitary, democratic, and parliamentary state, and the legislative body of the two territories would be merged into a national assembly."[212] The draft constitution was handed over to the Northern delegation for review by their legislative assembly, and their comments were incorporated into the Constitution.[213] The Constituent Assembly

---

211. Truni, *President Adan*, 68.
212. Poalo Contini, *The Somali Republic*, 8.
213. Articles 88 and 89 were proposed by the Somaliland assembly and were included in the constitution. See Samatar, *Africa's Democrats*, 83.

approved the draft constitution on June 21, 1960, just over two weeks before Somalia's independence on July 1, 1960.[214]

Democratic Elections

Fulfilling its mandate of democratization of the territory under its administration, Italian administrators ran the first municipal election in 1954, marking a significant milestone in local governance. The SYL emerged as the dominant political force, receiving 141 seats out of 281 councilors, fostering improved relations between the SYL and Italian administrators.[215] Notably, Enrico Anzilotti, an Italian administrator, played a vital role during this period of rapprochement. Although Anzilotti eventually had to leave Somalia in 1958, the Somali government widely acknowledged his contributions to establishing a peaceful and democratic environment.[216] 1956 marked a turning point with the initiation of "Somaliization," a process that aimed to replace all Italian government officials with Somali administrators. This shift created a legislative body with 70 seats, with ten reserved for ethnic minorities.[217] The SYL received 43 seats out of 70, which enabled the party to form the first Somali government under Prime Minister Abdullahi Isse. Although the assembly had complete authority over domestic affairs, the head of the Trust Administration retained absolute veto power. One of the significant developments was offering Somali women universal suffrage in the second municipal election of October 1958.[218] Moreover, on March 8, 1959, the government held and administered the second parlia-

---

214. Ibid. Truni, *President Adan*, 68.

215. Tripodi, Paolo, *Back to the Horn*.

216. In recognition of his efforts, he became the only Italian dignitary to receive the prestigious Somali Star, the nation's highest award, upon Somalia's independence in 1960. His legacy also lives on in Mogadishu, where a neighborhood was named Quartier Anzilotti in his honor. Mohamed Aden Sheikh, *Back to Mogadishu: Memoirs of a Somali Herder* (Barkin Publishing 2021), 60–61.

217. The ten seats were allocated to Italians, Pakistanis, Indians, and Arabs. See Abdurahman Abdullahi, *Making Sense of Somali History*, Volume One (Adonis & Abbey 2017), 136.

218. Abdullahi, *Making Sense of Somali History*, volume two, 196.

mentary elections. All political parties were wholly boycotted during this election at the beginning. Still, some parties broke this boycott, and only the Somali Independent Constitutional Party (SICP) and the Greater Somalia League (GSL) continued their boycott. The ruling SYL secured 83 of the 90 seats in the expanded Legislative Council.[219] The UN Advisory Council, the US Consul General, and 13 stalwart SYL members criticized the election process. However, the Italian administrator Marion DeStefano resolved the crisis for political consideration in support of the SYL victory.[220] Within SYL, the situation was resolved through Somalia's traditional conflict resolution methods, underscoring the enduring importance of indigenous practices in navigating political challenges. The Somali political elite lacked the maturity needed for a democratic political system and party structure. They consistently relied on traditional methods they had mastered and accepted to resolve crises.

The Great Somalia Agenda and Unification of South and North

Great Somalia was one of the priorities of SYL and the Abdullahi Isse government, as he expressed in his government program in 1956. Pursuing the agenda, he invited Somaliland dignitaries in September 1958, and a delegation from Somaliland traveled to Mogadishu to discuss the potential unification of the two regions.[221] Both sides concurred on the need to unify the divided parts of Somalia, reflecting the growing aspiration for national unity. The British Colonial Secretary supported the Somali people's wishes, indicating a step toward autonomy and self-governance. Additionally, the British Governor of the Somaliland Protectorate, Douglass Hall, visited Mogadishu and met with Somali Youth League (SYL) leaders and Prime Minister Abdullahi Isse. He expressed his government's endorsement of Somalia's unification.[222] This high-level engagement un-

---

219. Lewis, I.M. *A Modern History of the Somali: Revised,* 145.
220. Trunj, *The Untold History,* 399–444
221. Samatar, *Africa's First Democrats,* 81.
222. Ibid., 80

derscored the increasing support for the unification process from local and international entities. By November 1958, a delegation headed by Speaker Adan Abdulle Osman visited Hargeisa to gauge the local sentiment toward unification. They found strong support among the population, affirming the widespread desire for a united Somalia. This promising response further validated the unification efforts and indicated a shared vision of a united future for the Somali people.[223]

A delegation from Somaliland traveled to London to engage in high-level discussions about the future of their region with two observers from Southern Somalia.[224] During these talks, they finalized a momentous decision: setting the date for Somaliland's independence as June 26, 1960. A delegation led by the Speaker of Parliament of the Trust Territory, Adan Abdulle Osman, participated in the inaugural festivities of Somaliland's independence.[225] This historic milestone was established to align closely with the planned date for the independence of the Italian-administered part of Somalia, which was set for July 1, 1960.[226] This strategic timing was chosen to facilitate a seamless transition to the creation of the Somali Republic, uniting the two previously separate regions into a single sovereign nation. Upon achieving independence, the union of the two parts of Somalia marked the birth of the Somali Republic. This event was met with enthusiasm and high hopes for the nation's future. On July 1, Haji Bashir Ismael (1912–1984) was the interim speaker being the oldest among the PMs, and Adan Abdullahi was elected the interim president of Somalia. On July 26, Jama Abdullahi Ghalib was elected the speaker of the Parliament. Also, Abdirashid Ali Sharmarke was appointed Prime Minister on July 12, 1960. Indeed, Abdirashid was

223. Ibid.
224. Abdulkadir Zoppo and Mohamud Yusuf Muro represented SYL in the final negotiation of the Northern delegate with the British government that independence should be on June 26, 1960. Ibid., 83–84.
225. Ibid.
226. This date is two months late for the designated ten years of offering independence to Somalia when we count from the date Italy took over the Somali administration on the first of April 1950. It was also four months earlier when we signed the official trusteeship agreement on the second of November, 1950.

among the few educated individuals among the contenders for Prime Minister. He earned a scholarship and studied Political Science at the Sapienza University of Rome.[227]

Abdullahi's Political Culture (1960–1969)

Contrary to some expectations, Abdullahi Issa was not appointed Prime Minister of the newly independent Somali Republic in 1960. This was surprising given his extensive experience as the secretary general of the Somali Youth League (SYL) and his tenure as the first Prime Minister under the United Nations trusteeship of the Italian administration since 1956. SYL's principles emphasize not focusing on clan affiliation, which might have supported Issa's appointment. During his time in office in 1956, Abdullahi Issa gained valuable experience after forming a non-clan-based government.[228] Thus, he revised the composition of the government in 1959, aiming for the equitable representation of all main clans after the romantic view of the SYL demonstrated its inapplicability in the Somali clan-based society. This approach, however, drew criticism from some SYL stalwarts who lacked experience in governance but showed attachment to the SYL ideals. Given these factors, and mainly that Abdullahi Issa shared the same clan affiliation as President Adan Abdulle, appointing him as prime minister was deemed unwise to avoid potential accusations of nepotism or favoritism within the new government. There may also be other reasons besides clan factors that prevented Abdullahi Isse from being nominated as the prime minister.

Another valid question arose regarding why President Adan did not appoint Mohamed Ibrahim Egal, a prominent figure among

---

227. Europa Publications Limited, 970.
228. The Prime Minister did not consider the clan factor in forming the first council of ministers. His cabinet consisted of six ministers: three Hawiye, two Darood, and one dir. The Hawiye ministers were two from the Saád sub-clan of Habargidir (Abdullahi Isse and Haji Farah Ali) and Sheikh Ali Jimale (Hawadle). On the other hand, the two Darod ministers from the Majeerteen sub-clan (Haji Muse Boqor, Salad Abdi Mohamud). Dir, Mohamed Abdinor (Juje). Trunj, *The Untold History*, second edition, 266–69.

Somaliland politicians, as prime minister. Several reasons presented obstacles to his appointment. Firstly, Somalia operated under a parliamentary system, and Egal was not affiliated with the ruling SYL party. His lack of party membership posed challenges in working effectively with the existing government structure and political alliances. Secondly, Egal needed more experience in the Southern political landscape, as his political training and experience had primarily occurred in Somaliland. This could have made it more difficult for him to navigate the complexities of the broader national political environment. Thirdly, the elected speaker of the parliament belonged to his clan, a move that may have been orchestrated by those who aspired to prevent appointing Egal to the position of Prime Minister. These factors collectively contributed to the decision not to appoint Mohamed Ibrahim Egal as prime minister despite his leadership stature within Somaliland. It is evident that after he became experienced with the politics of the South, he was finally appointed to the position of Prime Minister in 1967.

In a strategic move, Prime Minister Abdirashid formed a coalition government and appointed Abdullahi Isse as foreign minister and Mohamed Ibrahim Egal as defense minister, Sheikh Jimale, Minister of Health and labor, and Abdirizak haji Hussein as Minister of the Interior in his first government. While Abdullahi's inclusion was done reluctantly, this decision allowed Abdirashid to bring together the two leading contenders for the position of prime minister, fostering a sense of collaboration and compromise. By offering prominent positions to these two influential figures, Abdirashid aimed to unite the government and create a national unity cabinet. This approach helped secure the support of different factions within the parliament and emphasized a commitment to inclusive governance and stability. The inclusion of Abdullahi Isse and Mohamed I. Egal in the government provided a strong foundation for navigating the early challenges of the newly independent Somali Republic. It demonstrated Abdirashid's dedication to fostering cooperation among diverse political perspectives.

From 1960 onward, Abdullahi Isse served in various ministerial positions across multiple governments, with only brief breaks in his tenure. Throughout these years, he earned a reputation as a pragmatic and principled politician, steadfastly loyal to the SYL party despite occasionally disagreeing with its decisions. For example, Abdullahi Isse, as a foreign minister, disagreed with the Prime Minister about severing relations with Britain because of the NFD case. However, he abided by the prime minister's direction.[229] Unlike some of his peers who left the party over disagreements, Abdullahi remained committed to SYL, demonstrating his dedication to the party's long-term vision. Another example of Abdullahi Isse, like his friend Sheikh Jimale, who had a problematic relationship working with Prime Minister Abdirashid. However, he always abided by the government's laws and policies. He refused when his group pressured him to refuse to travel to participate in the Tanganyika independence to embarrass the prime minister. As he related to President Adan, Abdullahi Isse said: "I resisted the pressure because I could not do that without first resigning from the government."[230] As foreign affairs Minister, Abdullahi Isse represented Somalia in the Khartoum talks between Somalia and Ethiopia after the border clash in 1964.[231] He was also admired for his integrity and strong moral character. He was known for his respectful demeanor, adherence to the law, and incorruptibility. His fair approach to governance made him a respected figure among his colleagues and the public. As a staunch advocate for Somali unity and development, Abdullahi Isse's efforts often focused on promoting cohesion and progress. His legacy is marked by his dedication to public service and his enduring commitment to the betterment of Somalia.

---

229. Abdirizak, *A Political Memoir*, 451.

230. Trunji quoted from the Diary of Adan Abdulle. See Trunji, The Untold History, second edition, 403.

231. The military balance was extensively tilted towards Ethiopia. Somalia had 5,000 soldiers and 5,000 police, and Ethiopia had 70,000 well-equipped forces trained by the USA. See Abdirizak, *A Political Memoir*, 170.

FACTORS THAT SHAPED HIS POLITICAL CULTURE

His early life as an orphan and upbringing under his mother's care significantly shaped his character and resilience. Abdullahi Isse's varied experiences, from working with the Italians to his ventures in business entrepreneurship, provided him with practical skills and insights into different facets of life. His long tenure as the secretary general of SYL offered him a deep understanding of governance and leadership, especially during the challenging transition from a movement to a ruling party. His exposure to American political culture and his four years in New York gave him a global perspective on democracy and diplomacy. In addition, his travels to the UK and France exposed him to European culture and political systems, further enriching his worldview. Through these experiences, he navigated complex political landscapes with adeptness and a nuanced approach. His passion for reading complemented his travels, providing him with knowledge and perspectives that deepened his understanding of the world and its intricacies.

His being an orphan and his mother's upbringing.

Abdullahi Isse's political outlook and values were profoundly shaped by his life story, which includes his challenging childhood as an orphan. Raised by his mother as a single parent, he developed a strong sense of resilience and an acute empathy for those confronting hardships. This upbringing molded his approach to political engagement, fostering a deep understanding of social issues and a commitment to championing the interests of marginalized and vulnerable populations. Isse's formative experiences gave him a unique perspective on governance, emphasizing the importance of compassion, inclusivity, and social justice. His early exposure to adversity instilled in him the drive to pursue policies that promote equality and support for those in need. As a result, his political career has been marked by a focus on creating equitable opportunities and fostering a society where everyone's voice is heard and respected.

His experience working with the Italians.

Abdullahi Isse's career journey included working as a clerk alongside Italians in Merca, an experience that provided him with valuable insights into European business practices and organizational structures. This early exposure to international work culture offered him a unique perspective on efficiency, professionalism, and the importance of adhering to structured processes. Later, Abdullahi Isse took on a role in the economic department in Mogadishu, where he further immersed himself in European work methods. This environment allowed him to understand different financial management and governance approaches, enriching his knowledge of global business and administrative practices. These experiences broadened Isse's horizons and equipped him with a versatile skill set, including cross-cultural communication and an appreciation for diverse viewpoints. His familiarity with European work culture also helped him navigate complex situations with an analytical mindset, paving the way for his later accomplishments in his professional and political endeavors.

His Business Entrepreneurship

After the British military administration assumed control of Somalia from the Italians in 1941, Abdullahi Isse experienced a significant career shift when he lost his job. This setback, however, marked the beginning of a new chapter for Isse as he ventured into entrepreneurship by establishing a restaurant business in the town of Beledweyne. In his new role, Abdullahi Isse quickly integrated himself into the local business community, forging connections with various individuals from diverse backgrounds. This network not only broadened his perspective on the economic and cultural landscape of Beledweyne but also deepened his understanding of the community's needs and aspirations. His restaurant became a hub for local meetings and dialogue, allowing Abdullahi Isse to build relationships with fellow entrepreneurs, traders, and community leaders. These interactions gave him valuable insights into the challenges and opportunities within the local economy, shaping his future endeavors. Abdullahi Isse's experience in Beledweyne highlighted his adaptabil-

SOMALIA: A STATE IN SEARCH OF EXCEPTIONAL LEADERSHIP

ity and resourcefulness, which would later play a crucial role in his professional and political pursuits.

In Beledweyne, Abdullahi Isse embarked on his political journey in 1944 when he joined the Somali Youth Club (SYC), a pivotal moment that marked the start of his involvement in the national movement for Somali independence. His decision to align himself with the SYC demonstrated his commitment to the cause and his desire to contribute to the broader struggle for self-determination. Abdullahi Isse's association with the SYC brought him into close collaboration with key figures in the Somali nationalist movement, including Adan Abdulle Osman and Sheikh Ali Jumale. These influential stalwarts were central to galvanizing support for Somali sovereignty and played significant roles in shaping the country's political landscape. As part of the SYC, Abdullahi Isse actively participated in the movement's activities and initiatives to unite Somalis across different regions and tribes. Through his engagement with the organization, he honed his leadership skills and developed a deeper understanding of the political dynamics in the quest for independence. Abdullahi Isse's involvement in the SYC laid the foundation for his future contributions to Somali politics, providing him with a platform to advocate for the interests of his community and the nation. This early experience solidified his place within the emerging political scene and established him as a prominent figure in the Somali liberation and governance struggle.

His long term as the Secretary General of SYL

Abdullahi Isse's political identity and values were profoundly shaped by his extensive tenure as the secretary-general of the Somali Youth League (SYL). During his time in this influential role, his life became closely intertwined with the party's core principles and values, which championed the equality of all citizens and the supremacy of the rule of law. The SYL's commitment to eradicating tribalism and fostering unity across Somalia resonated deeply with Abdullahi. He embraced the organization's ethos of promoting a cohesive national identity, transcending clan divisions, and advocating for harmony and cooperation among different groups. His dedication to this cause helped him gain respect and admiration from others for his inclusive approach. Abdullahi Isse's involvement with the SYL also instilled a strong sense of democratic values, emphasizing the importance of fair representation and participatory governance. His adherence to these principles guided his political decisions and actions, shaping him into a leader who valued transparency, accountability, and protecting individual rights. Abdullahi developed a reputation as a principled and dedicated statesman who prioritized the collective good over personal interests through his leadership role in the SYL. His steadfast commitment to the party's vision laid the groundwork for his later contributions to Somali politics, where he continued to champion democratic ideals and the welfare of his fellow citizens.

His four-year experience in New York (1948–1953)

Abdullahi Isse's international journey took him across Europe and eventually to New York, where he served as the Somali Youth League's envoy to the United Nations Trusteeship Council for about four years. In this role, he passionately advocated for the Somali people's self-determination and independence. He accused Italy of mismanaging and subjugating Somalia under its administration, bringing the plight of his nation to the attention of the international community. During his time in New York, Abdullahi expanded his global network, establishing vital international connections and relations. His interactions with career diplomats and exposure to the intricacies of international diplomacy enriched his understanding of civic culture and international governance. This experience deepened his appreciation for principles such as diplomacy, respect for diverse perspectives, and adherence to global protocols. His diplomatic endeavors aligned closely with the values he had raised within the Banadir region, known for its high standards of civility and modesty. Abdullahi's upbringing and international exposure gave him a nuanced perspective on global issues and a commitment to advocating for Somalia's rightful place on the world stage. As he navigated the complex world of international relations, Abdullahi's confidence and eloquence in representing Somalia's interests garnered respect from his peers. They solidified his reputation as a formidable advocate for his nation's independence. His experiences abroad shaped his approach to politics and diplomacy and reinforced his dedication to achieving self-determination and justice for the Somali people.

Managing the Difficult Transition Period of SYL

Abdullahi Isse played a crucial role in navigating the challenging transformation of the Somali Youth League (SYL) from a grassroots movement into the ruling party of the newly independent nation. This transition required adept leadership and strategic decision-making as the SYL shifted its focus from advocating for independence to governing a fledgling state. During this period, Abdullahi Isse faced the complexities of growing political clannism within the elite ranks of the SYL and the broader political landscape. This fragmentation posed a significant challenge to national unity and governance. Abdullahi Isse drew upon his deep understanding of traditional conflict resolution mechanisms to address these divisions. His reliance on these methods allowed him to mediate disputes and navigate crises within the government and society. As the prime minister of the nascent administration, Abdullahi Isse led a cabinet of ministers who often needed more experience and expertise, presenting additional obstacles to effective governance. Despite these challenges, he demonstrated remarkable resilience and adaptability. His tenure taught him the importance of compassion, pragmatism, and inclusive politics as vital tools for maintaining stability and fostering cooperation within the government. Abdullahi Isse's approach to leadership was characterized by his ability to balance competing interests and prioritize the nation's greater good. His emphasis on inclusivity and collaboration helped bridge divides and build a foundation for a more cohesive and stable government. Through his experiences, Abdullahi Isse emerged as a statesman who prioritized the long-term well-being of Somalia and its people, setting the stage for future leaders to follow in his footsteps.

His reading habits

Like President Adan and Abdirizak, Abdullahi Isse deeply appreciated reading and self-education. His dedication to continual learning sharpened his intellect and broadened his outlook on the world. This expanded perspective allowed him to rise above local political disputes and approach them with balance and a fair mind. His well-rounded approach empowered him to engage with challenges thoughtfully and insightfully, guiding him to address issues from a place of wisdom and understanding.

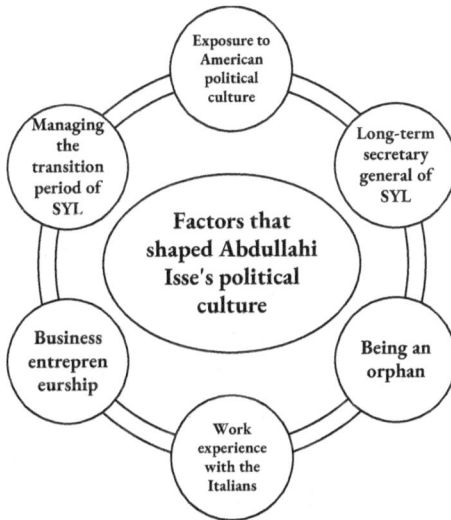

Fig. 12. Factors that shaped Abdullahi Isse's political culture

IMPORTANT EVENTS RELATED TO ABDULLAHI ISSE

The Politics of Presidential Age in the Provisional Constitution

One of the government's main tasks under Prime Minister Abdullahi Isse was drafting the provisional constitution of an independent Somalia. In the last three years of the trusteeship period, significant efforts were dedicated to preparing the Constitution for an independent Somali State. In September 1957, a Technical Committee of Experts was appointed to draft the preliminary Constitution, which consisted of 141 articles and was accompanied by a 316-page commentary. Subsequently, with the help of a constitutional law expert, the Minister for the Constitution prepared a revised and shorter draft of 64 articles. This revised draft was then thoroughly reviewed by a drafting Political Committee consisting of fifty Somali members. The Committee approved a new draft Constitution with 100 articles and submitted it to the Constituent Assembly, including the ninety Legislative Assembly Deputies and twenty additional Somali members.

The draft Constitution prepared by the government outlined three main eligibility requirements for presidential candidates in Somalia—that the candidate must be a descendant of a Somali family for at least two generations, a Muslim, and at least thirty-five years old. While the first two requirements were not contentious, the age requirement sparked significant debate in the Constituent Assembly in 1959. The Minister for the Constitution presented the draft text, initially including the 35-year age requirement. However, members of the Political Committee and Constituent Assembly had varying opinions. Some supported lowering the age limit to 30, while others advocated for 40 or higher, citing religious and maturity considerations. Ultimately, the Constituent Assembly set the minimum age at 45 years. They also included an additional requirement that the President must not be married to, or marry during their term, a woman who is not an original citizen of Somalia.

It was speculated that the age requirements in the Constitution were strategically linked to the anticipated candidates for the presidency of an independent Somalia. By 1960, several prominent figures were potential candidates for the highest office, each with varying ages that could influence their eligibility under different constitutional age requirements. For instance, Abdullahi Isse, born in 1921, would be 39 years old by 1960. If the age requirement were set at 35, he would be eligible, but his candidacy might be jeopardized if it were higher. Adan Abdulla, born in 1908, he would be 52 years old by 1960. He would comfortably meet even the most stringent age requirement, making him a strong candidate. Sheikh Ali Jimale, born in 1905, would be 55 years old by 1960. Like Adan Abdulla, he would easily surpass any age threshold, reinforcing his viability as a presidential contender. Abdirashid Ali Sharmarke, born in 1919, would be 41 years old by 1960. While he would be eligible under a 35-year requirement, a higher age limit, such as 45, would disqualify him from the race.

Given these potential candidates, the debate over the minimum age for the presidency took on significant political importance. Lowering the age limit would favor younger leaders like Abdullahi Isse and Abdirashid Ali Sharmarke, potentially aligning with a vision for a more youthful leadership. Conversely, raising the age limit would advantage older, established figures like Adan Abdulla and Sheikh Ali Jimale, who had extensive experience and could provide stability and continuity. Thus, the decision on the age requirement was not merely a matter of principle, but also a tactical move with far-reaching implications for the future leadership of Somalia.

Interestingly, the debate over the age requirement for the presidency was deeply intertwined with political allegiances and the anticipated candidates for the role. Those who advocated for a lower age limit tended to be supporters of Prime Minister Abdullahi Isse, who turned 39 in 1960. Conversely, supporters of Adan Abdulle Osman, 52 years old by 1960, championed a higher age limit. Some members, motivated by religious beliefs, proposed raising the presidential age requirement to 40–50 years. Notable proponents included Abdirashid Ali Sharmarke, Haji Moussa Samatar, and Dahir Nour Egal. Abdirashid Ali Sharmarke emphasized the head of State's significant powers and unifying role, arguing for higher age requirements than other constitutional positions. He noted that Islamic scholars consider 40 the "age of judgment," indicating maturity. However, Sharmarke felt that even 40 might be too young, asserting that older leaders would be less likely to pursue selfish interests over the nation's welfare. This gave their argument a religious color and cultural resonance, and Adan Abdulle was elected uncontested president in 1960.

Abdullahi Isse's Opposition to Adan Abdulle in 1961

I asked Mohamed Trunji, an expert historian of the period, about the opposition of Abdullahi Isse president Adan Abdulle Osman. I have paraphrased his reply here. Following the 1959 political elections, where the Somali Youth League (SYL) secured most parliamentary seats, the party experienced an internal split into two factions. "The two factions were largely split on a clan basis," reflecting deeper socio-political dynamics in anticipation of electing the future Head of State.[232] One faction was led by Abdullahi Issa, supported predominantly by members of the Hawiye clan. Key figures in this group included Haji Farah, Sheikh Ali Jimale, and Haji Barako. This faction strongly backed Sheikh Ali Jimale in the presidential election of June 1961, feeling that Adan Abdulle Osman had "abandoned" his Hawiye roots and interests. The other faction within the SYL was led by newly elected Darod MPs, including Abdirashid Ali Sharmarke, Abdirazak Haji Hussein, and Yassin Nour Hassan. This group supported Adan Abdulle Osman in the 1961 presidential election, highlighting the intra-party contest between the Hawiye and Darod members. The rivalry between these factions underscored the complex interplay of clan loyalties and political ambitions, influencing the SYL's strategies and alliances as they organized and competed for power within the nascent Somali state. Abdullahi Isse was part of this division, though he was not a hardliner and always stayed loyal to the SYL ideals. Thus, since his rivals supported Adan and his group opposed Adan's reelection, he joined his group in 1961.

CONCLUSION

The life and biography of Abdullahi Isse were deeply intertwined with the history of the Somali Youth League (SYL), marking him as a central figure during pivotal moments of the organization's journey. As the longest-serving secretary-general (1947–1956) during the movement's struggle for self-determination, Abdullahi Isse played a significant role in advocating for the unification of all Somalis

---

232. Interview with Mohamed Issa Trunji on June 4, 2024.

and strongly opposing the return of Italy to Somalia as the policy of SYL. During his tenure as secretary-general, Abdullahi Isse spent four years in New York, representing the SYL at the UN trusteeship. His mission was to further the SYL's aspirations on an international stage, negotiating and advocating for the rights and independence of the Somali people. His efforts contributed to a partial victory for the SYL when Italy returned to Somalia under a UN trusteeship, with the term-limited to ten years and sending the UN trusteeship committee. Abdullahi Isse's steadfast commitment and strategic diplomacy were instrumental in securing this compromise, a critical step toward achieving the broader goals of Somali self-determination and independence.

Abdullahi Isse's nomination as the first Prime Minister of Somalia in 1956 demonstrated the trust and respect he held among Somali political elites and his party of SYL. His appointment was pivotal in Somalia's history as it prepared for independence in 1960. The unanimous decision to appoint him reflected the political community's high regard for his leadership, diplomatic skills, and commitment to Somali unity and self-determination. As Prime Minister, Abdullahi Isse aimed to establish a stable political foundation for the new nation, leading the transitional government through this significant period. However, his tenure was marked by the challenges of transitioning from the Somali Youth League (SYL) as a movement to a ruling party. This transition exposed the contrast between SYL's ideals and the realities of operating within a deeply rooted clan-based society. Isse faced internal divisions within SYL as the party gained power, challenging its unity and foundational principles of nationalism and inclusivity. The SYL's exclusionary approach to other political parties also limited political pluralism and marginalized alternative voices. Abdullahi Isse's leadership involved balancing the ideals of unity and progress with the complex realities of a society influenced by clan allegiances. His nuanced approach and efforts to navigate these challenges were crucial to his leadership during this transformative period.

During Abdullahi Isse's four-year tenure as Prime Minister, he tackled three pivotal issues in shaping Somalia's future. His leadership was instrumental in drafting the provisional constitution, managing the 1959 elections, and overseeing the ambitious Great Somalia project to unify the Somaliland British Protectorate and Southern Somalia. Abdullahi Isse's tenure was marked by his ability to navigate these complex challenges while focusing on creating a stable, unified, and independent Somali state. His contributions during this period impacted the nation's trajectory and its quest for self-governance.

After Somalia gained independence, Abdullahi Isse dedicated himself to serving his nation by assuming leadership roles across multiple government ministries. He held key positions in three successive governments—those led by Abdirashid Ali Shermarke (1960–1964), Abdirizak Haji Hussein (1964–1967), and Mohamed Ibrahim Egal (1967–1969)—demonstrating his versatile expertise and commitment to his country's progress. Following the military coup in Somalia in 1969, Abdullahi Isse faced a significant turning point in his career and life. Along with many of his colleagues, he was detained by the new military regime, enduring imprisonment until 1973. After his release in 1973, Isse was appointed the Somali Ambassador to Scandinavian countries in 1974. Abdullahi Isse's tenure as ambassador lasted until 1986, marking more than a decade of dedicated service in the diplomatic arena. In 1986, Isse's diplomatic career ended, and he eventually moved to Rome, where he passed away in 1988. His death was a significant loss for Somalia, as he was a well-respected statesman who had devoted his life to his country's progress. In recognition of his service, the Somali government arranged an official burial in Mogadishu, his final resting place.

PRESIDENT ADAN ABDULLE OSMAN: A MODEL OF EXCEPTIONAL LEADERSHIP

During all my life, I have never said please elect me, not I will do it now, because the presidency is a post of trust and requires a great deal of responsibility. The election of the president of the Republic must be left to the decision of the members of the parliament who are solely responsible to elect a just man in the interest of the country and of the citizens. — Abdi Samatar quotes President Adan Abdulle Osman's saying in Africa's First Democrats: Somalia's Adan A. Osman and Abdirizak H. Hussein, 174). (Prime Minister Abdirizak Hajji Hussein, quoted by Mohamed Tunji, President Adan, 48)

Two essential qualities distinguished him [President Adan] from the rest of his fellow party members: firstly, he was above feuding factions within the ruling party, and secondly, he scorned the corrupt practice of buying voters, such as in the two presidential elections he contested in 1961 and again six years later. (Mohamed Isse Turunji, the author of "President Adan Abdulle: His Life and Legacy," xiii)

President Adan Abdulle Osman was the "first and only president who ruled a whole, sovereign, and democratic Somalia, reigned and finished his term with wisdom and diligence, handed over power peacefully, and lived and died in his homeland as an ordinary citizen, with dignity and honor. May his memory and legacy console and restore hope." (Dr. Hassan Kaynan, November 18, 2023)

*T*he significant role of leaders in building or breaking states is widely acknowledged. They utilize their attributes, positions, authority, and power to frame a vision and provide direction or contribute to governance deficits, internal conflicts, repression, and criminality.[233] Nations blessed with visionary, transformational, and virtuous leaders live peacefully and prosper. Conversely, nations governed by leaders without vision and integrity are entangled in crises, poverty, and perpetual conflicts. Allah's Messenger ﷺ said, "When honesty is lost, then wait for the Hour." It was asked, "How will honesty be lost, O Allah's Messenger ﷺ?" He said, "When authority is given to those who do not deserve it, then wait for the Hour." "Then wait for the hour" is generally interpreted as a warning of impending societal decay and turmoil or the end times (the Day of Judgment). In this renowned literary work, "The Trouble with Nigeria," the Nigerian scholar Chinua Achebe boldly asserts that Nigeria's fundamental challenge lies in its leadership deficit. He wrote: "The trouble with Nigeria is simply and squarely a failure of leadership. There is nothing basically wrong with the Nigerian land or climate or water or air or anything else. The Nigerian problem is the unwillingness or inability of its leaders to rise to the responsibility, to the challenge of personal example, which are the hallmarks of true leadership."[234] He contends that Nigeria harbors the potential

---

233. Robert I. Rotberg, "The Failure and Collapse of Nation-States: Breakdown, Prevention, and Repair," available from https://assets.press.princeton.edu/chapters/s7666.pdf (accessed February 16, 2024), 24-26.
234. Chinua Achebe, *The Trouble with Nigeria* (Heineman, 1984), 1.

to surmount its deep-rooted issues, including tribalism, lack of patriotism, social inequality, the pervasive culture of mediocrity, rampant indiscipline, and endemic corruption, provided capable and ethical leaders guide it. Achebe diagnosed the genuine sickness of all African states, including Somalia.

In post-independence Africa and Arab countries, to which Somalia belongs, a leadership tendency towards repression and treating states as personal possessions was generally observed.[235] Even so, a handful of laudable leaders, with President Adan A. Osman at the forefront, have established stable states despite formidable challenges.[236] Amid Somalia's reputation for military rule, state collapse, prolonged civil war, and persistent instability, it is essential to expose the democratic era of Somalia and its distinctive president, Adan A. Osman. Delving into the unique qualities that set him apart from his contemporaries is crucial to presenting him as a role model for the new generation of Somali political elites. As lucidly articulated by Mohamed Trunji, "Most of today's generation finds it incomprehensible that the Somali leaders of such high caliber existed in recent history."[237]

Adan Abdulle (1908–2007) emerged momentously during the struggle for Somali independence, exhibiting his early leadership

235. Jackson Robert and Karl Rosberg classified African leaders into Princes, Prophets, autocrats, and Tyrants. See Jackson Robert and Karl Rosberg, *Personal Rule in Black Africa* (University of California Press, 1982). See more on Marsha Prepstein Posusney and Michele Penner Angrist, eds., *Authoritarianism in the Middle East: Regimes and Resistance* (London: Lynne Rienner Publishers, 2005); Nicola et al., *In the Arab World* (London: Lynne Rienner Publishers, 2006); Nic Cheeseman and Jonathan Fisher, *Authoritarian Africa: Repression, Resistance, and the Power of Ideas* (Oxford: Oxford University Press, 2021).
236. Abdi Samatar criticized the complete generalization of all African leaders to be like princes, Prophets, autocrats, and tyrants, offering Somali leaders of the postcolonial period of 1960–1967 a different leadership model. See Abdi Samatar, *Africa's First Democrats: Somalia's Adan A. Osman and Abdirizak H. Hussein* (Bloomington: Indiana University Press, 2016), 8.
237. Mohamed Isse Turunji, *President Adan Abdulla: His Life & Legacy* (Looh Press, 2023), xiii.

qualities within the Somali Youth League Party (SYL).[238] His leadership ability was evident from the UN Trusteeship period (1950–1960), where he served as a member of the Territorial Council established in 1951, becoming its deputy chairman and the chairman of SYL (1953–56).[239] Central committees of SYL were elected every year. The following are the presidents of SYL from 1947–1960, after which the Chairmanship was abolished, and the secretary general of SYL was adopted. Haji Mohamed Hussein (1947–1950); Haji Farah Ali Omar (1952); Adan Abdulle Osman (1953–1956); Abdirizak Haji Hussein (1956); Haji Mohamed Hussein (1957); Adan Abdulle Osman (1958); Sheikh Isse Mohamed (1959). In 1960, SYL adopted the secretary general position only.[240] When SYL prevailed in the first parliamentary election in 1956, Adan was elected parliament speaker. During this period, his political shrewdness shone in dealing with the Italian administering authority, managing political polarization within SYL, reconciling clan-centric politicians, and dealing with left-wing tendencies.[241]

Introducing modern state governance and democratic elections to the Somali traditional society in the 1950s was a novel venture unfamiliar with Somalia's cultural context. As the political environment changed, politicized clan-based division emerged bluntly, even

---

238. Dr. Cedric Barnes, "The Somali Youth League, Ethiopian Somalis, and the Greater Somalia Idea, c.1946–48," Journal of Eastern African Studies 1, no. 2 (2007): 277–91.

239. Gilbert Ware, "Somalia: From Trust Territory to Nation, 1950-1960," Phylon 26, no. 2 (2nd Quarter, 1965): 173–85.

240. Following were the secretary generals of SYL: Sheikh Mohamud Mohamed Farah (1960–62); Yasin Nur Hassan (1963); Abdirizak Haji Hussein (1964-67); finally, in 1968, SYL adopted a party leader besides the secretary general. Mohamed Ibrahim Igal was elected party leader, and Ali Mohamed Hirabe was the secretary general.

241. While most politicians were aligned with the political norms of administering Italian authority, new individuals had appeared on the political scene expressing growing socialist ideologies. The most prominent among them was Haji Mohamed Hussein, the chairman of the SYL, who, after returning from Egypt, advocated Nasserism ideology. He was evicted from the SYL party in 1958.

among members of the SYL party.[242] As the parliament speaker and elected chairman of SYL in 1958–59, followed by his presidency of the Somali Republic in 1960 and six years in 1961, up to 1967, Adan Abdulle's decency played a vital role in instituting the Somali state. Under his leadership, the nation passed through difficult post-independence years, focusing on the unification of the Somaliland British Protectorate and Italian Somalia, the peaceful quest for the Greater Somalia project, the fostering of democracy, and the laying of a governance framework. Moreover, during President Adan's term, Somalia managed superpower rivalries in the Horn of Africa during the Cold War. Somalia actively engaged with various organizations to deal with that situation, such as joining the non-alignment movement in 1961, the Muslim World Congress in 1961, and the Organization of African Unity (OAU) in 1963.[243] Somalia hosted the Muslim World League's sixth conference in 1966 and recommended establishing the OIC.

President Adan Abdulle, often addressed as "the Father of the Nation," stood out as a symbol of Somali exceptional leadership and a pioneer of African democracy.[244] He earned extensive acclaim for his dedication to democratic principles, the rule of law, and political inclusivity. His distinct political culture positioned him apart from most Somali political elites entangled in political clannism, self-centeredness, and power-driven ambitions. His graceful assent of loss

---

242. Samatar, Abdi, *Africa's First Democrats*, 63–64.

243. Al-Ghamdi, Hassna. "Muslim World League: A Historical Look at Establishment, Goals and Projects." International Journal of Humanities and Social Science 11, no. 1 (January 2021). Somalia hosted the Congress' sixth conference in 1966. Bacik, Gokhan. "The Genesis, History, and Functioning of the Organization of Islamic Cooperation (OIC): A Formal-Institutional Analysis." Journal of Muslim Minority Affairs 31, no. 4 (December 2011): 594–614. Sesay, Amadu, *The African Union: Forward March or About Face-Turn?* (Uppsala: Universitetstryckeriet, 2008).

244. The second President of the Somali Republic, HE. Abdirashid Ali Sharmarke referred to President Adan Abdulle as the father of the nation in his Radio address on July 1, 1960, and the parliament gave the same title. Trunji, Mohamed Isse. President Adan Abdulle, p. xiii.

in the 1967 election and peaceful early power transfer to a democratically elected president engraved his name as the first African
president-democrat.[245] Unlike many African liberation movement
leaders, Adan Abdulle was not a political party founder but rose
democratically within the Somali Youth League. His distinct background as a locally educated set him apart from his contemporary
African leaders, mostly educated in European universities.[246] Despite
his limited education, Adan embraced democracy, rooted in Somali
cultural consensus-building. After concluding his term, ex-President
Adan Abdulle chose a path of non-involvement in active politics,
dedicating most of his time to his agricultural firm in Janale, a town
south of Mogadishu.

This research delves into President Adan Abdulle's political
culture compared to the broader Somali elite political culture.
Building mainly on the works of Professor Abdi Samatar and
Mohamed Isse Trunji, this Chapter focuses on a more nuanced understanding of President Adan's political culture.[247] It focuses on the
cultural subtleties ingrained in President Adan's approach, which
were essential in fostering and sustaining a democratic ethos and
inclusive politics throughout his term. Additionally, the Chapter
highlights factors that shaped his political culture and the motivations of his political opponents. The temporal nature of this democratic momentum showcases the subsequent challenges and shifts
in political culture following President Adan's departure from the
presidency. The President had interrupted his tranquil life in 1990,

---

245. The president transferred power from July 6 to June 30 to allow the new
president to preside over the celebrations of Independence Day, July 1.
246. While many African liberation leaders like Nkrumah, Nyerere, and
Kenyatta founded political parties instrumental in achieving independence and
education in Western countries, their political trajectory was toward authoritarianism. At the same time, Somalia took a different path under President Adan
Abdulle.
247. In his commendable work, Abdi Samatar combined the biographies of
Adan A. Abdulle and his PM Abdirizak, while Tunji focused on President
Adan. See Samatar, *Africa's First Democrats*, and Trunji, *President Adan Abdulle*.

when he led a Manifesto Group that sought to mediate the crisis by appealing to both the government and the armed opposition for dialogue and reconciliation. Moreover, the President spearheaded the first reconciliation conference in Djibouti in 1991. Finally, the Chapter offers a brief conclusion, finger-pointing that the evolution of the Somali elite political culture continues to reverberate through successive echelons, from the collapse of the military regime in 1991 to its resurgence in a more distressing form up to the present day.[248]

THE BRIEF BIOGRAPHY OF ADAN ABDULLE OSMAN

Born in 1908 in El-Qurun, situated in the Hiiraan region of the Hirshabelle Federal Member State, Adan Abdulle's early years were marked by adversity. He belongs to the Udeejeen Mudulood sub-clan.[249] As the sole child in the family, he faced the loss of his mother, Aurala Yusuf Dulad, within a month of his birth and his father at 18. Raised by his paternal grandmother, Hawa Herow, due to his mother's demise, Adan's father had been a devout member of the Darwish movement led by Sayid Mohamed. At age ten, Adan's father relocated the family from Hiiraan and settled among the Ogaden pastoralists, where he was employed as a camel herder. Tragically, he was struck by a lion, leaving him disabled and unable to continue herding. As a result, Adan and his father moved to Hudur town, and after a brief stay, they relocated to Baidoa again in 1921.[250] Adan's father established a Quranic school in Baidoa, while young Adan undertook various menial jobs, such as preparing tea and coffee and fetching water for military personnel stationed there. In 1923, Adan traveled to Mogadishu with his Italian employer, Lieutenant Stiffen, and gained exposure to new experiences. However, Adan

---

248. Abdullahi, Abdurahman. "Somali Elite Political Culture: Conceptions, Structures, and Historical Evolution," Somali Studies: A Peer-Reviewed Academic Journal for Somali Studies 5 (2020): 30–92.

249. Udeejeen is a branch of the Mudulood clan belonging to the Hawiye clan family.

250. Hudur is a town in the Bakol region, while Baidoa is the capital of the Bay region in the Southwest State of Somalia.

was highly motivated to enroll in school upon his return to Baidoa. Besides that, he served as a cook's assistant for his generous Italian teacher, Mr. Giuseppe Tusso, who was very encouraging and advised him to focus on mastering the Italian language and accountancy. His proficiency in the Italian language qualified him to become an interpreter, opening new avenues for personal and professional growth. Driven by a desire for further opportunities, he relocated again to Mogadishu, where he took on various jobs to sustain himself.

From 1925 to 1926, Aden's life took a significant turn as he was employed as a domestic helper in Janale, catering to the needs of various Italian settlers, most of whom embraced the fascist ideology.[251] During this period, Aden experienced the cruelty of Italian fascism and their forced labor and discriminatory policies. After suffering the loss of his father in Baidoa, he again relocated to Afgoye, where he got a job as a waiter in an Italian-owned restaurant. However, his life in Afgoye ends with suspicions about his relationship with the restaurant owner's daughter, Alfa.[252] As a result, Adan was deported to Wanlewayn; nonetheless, he moved to Baidoa, where he found employment with many Italians, including Commissioner Dominico Anda. He was selected to present a banquet for visiting Italian Crown Prince Umberto de Savoia in Baidoa, who later became the last king of Italy.[253] In 1928, Aden moved again to Mogadishu, enrolled in a nursing apprentice course and evening school, and completed up to the fifth year—the highest level permitted for Somalis. Aden's profound interest in reading books and newspapers fueled his intellectual curiosity, contributing significantly to his multifaceted growth and familiarity with global events.

---

251. Samatar, *Africa's First Democrats*, 26–29. Also, Trunji, *President Adan Abdulle*, 25–33.
252. During the fascist era, Somalis were not allowed to mix with Italians, implementing racial laws. Regardless, Adan used to practice his Italian language when talking to the children of the restaurant's owner, Mr. Cecchi. Samatar, *Africa's First Democrats*, 17.
253. Samatar, *Africa's First Democrats*, 18.

After securing a nursing job, Aden married Asha Elmi Matan, belonging to the Majeerteen clan family.[254] However, following Italy's defeat in 1941 and losing his job, Aden relocated to Beledweyne and immersed himself in commerce. In 1944, he joined the Somali Youth Club (SYC), the first nationalist youth movement, obtaining membership no. 130.[255] As the SYC evolved into the Somali Youth League (SYL) in 1947, Aden became the leader of the SYL chapter in Beledweyne. Continuing his dedication to the Party's values, policies, and various positions, Aden became a member of the Territorial Council in 1951 and its deputy chairman, and also Chairman of SYL in (1953–56), the parliament speaker in 1956, taking leadership of the SYL by 1958.[256] He became Somalia's first president after its independence in 1960, serving from 1960 to 1967.[257] After President Abdirashid was elected, Aden gracefully stepped down from the presidency. He actively participated in the parliament meetings as a permanent member.

The Council of Ministers recalled him as by his exceptional personal qualities, Adan Abdulle enhanced the luster, prestige, and dignity of high offices that he had been holding from time to time. The government expressed its highest

---

254. Ibid., 21.

255. Adan joined SYC and registered his friends Abdullahi Isse and Sheikh Ali Jimale, the two prominent members of SYL. Samatar, *Africa's First Democrats*, 27.

256. In this election, the contender was Sheikh Mohamud Ahmed "Kutubaxoor" from Adele district, who received 42 votes, while Adan received 44 votes. Adan was not satisfied with this simple majority. Insisting on resigning or having certain conditions be met, he finally accepted the chairmanship with a repeated vote of 66 votes.

257. Somalia became the fifth independent state of Africa in 1960 among the 17 African states: Cameron, Togo, Madagascar, and the Democratic Republic of Congo. Sheikh Ali Jimale was the presidential candidate competing with Adan Abdulle in the 1961 presidential election. In the final vote, Adan received 62, and Jimale received 59, which offered Adan an absolute majority with a tiny margin.

gratitude to the noble elder, wise leader, and respected President and wished him a long and healthy life.[258]

After two months of giving up his presidential position, he was elected as the deputy chairman of the World Muslim Congress. The president was very enthusiastic about the unity of the Muslim countries. His recommendation in the Mogadishu conference in 1966 established the Organization of Islamic Cooperation (OIC) in 1969.[259] After the military coup d'état in 1969, President Adan was detained with many civilian-era government officials (October 23, 1969–April 1, 1973).[260] Since his release from detention, he continued his work as a farmer in his firm in Janale.

However, with the country's outbreak of civil war, the ex-president led the Manifesto group, which consisted of about 114 prominent politicians, in 1990.[261] After signing a manifesto expressing concerns about the escalating violence and endorsing reconciliation, many of his fellow signatories were detained. After the regime collapsed in January 1991, President Adan led a reconciliation team, including former PMs Abdirizak and Egal, and other dignitaries to Djibouti to pave the way for restoring the Somali state through reconciling the armed factions. Since then, Adan lived at his firm until he died in Nairobi on June 8, 2007, at ninety-eight. The Somali Government declared twenty-one days of mourning and organized a national memorial service in Mogadishu, where he was buried in the family cemetery. In his honor, Mogadishu Airport was renamed Aden Adde International Airport.

Adan's biography portrays him as an orphaned and self-made individual who supported himself through diverse manual jobs, avoiding dependence on his clan or relatives. His passion and dedica-

---

258. Trunji, *President Adan Abdulle*, 134.
259. Ingiriis, Mohamed Haji. "The Making of the 1990 Manifesto: Somalia's Last Chance for State Survival." Northeast African Studies 12, no. 2 (2012): 63–94.
260. Trunji, *President Adan Abdulle*, 162.
261. Abdullahi, Abdurahman, *Making Sense of Somali History* (Adonis & Abbey, 2017), 24.

tion to education were complemented by the ingrained work ethic he experienced since his childhood. His commitment to goals, marked by self-reliance and confidence, extended to attributes such as decency, respect, lawfulness, non-power-hungriness, an anti-corruption stance, and adherence to democratic values.[262] These qualities shaped his successful leadership in the early years of Somalia's independence.

CONTEXT SETTING

Like many postcolonial nations, Somalia struggles with the imposition of the modern state system alongside the enduring traditional clan system and Islamic heritage. The political elites were caught up in the complexities of these two distinct systems, unable to create a smooth hybridization whereby modernity and tradition could coexist through cultural hybridization processes instead of clashing, producing what is termed multiple modernities.[263] Traditional societies are rooted in the customs and practices handed down through generations. In such societies, social structures often revolve around close-knit communities where familial ties and communal bonds are paramount. These societies tend to be ingrained with cultural rituals, customary practices, and oral traditions cultivated over time. The authority and governance within such societies usually stem from revered elders, tribal or clan leaders, and religious individuals who guide the community's shared values and collective wisdom.[264] Traditional societies may rely on informal systems of governance, where leadership is based on age, experience, or lineage.

---

262. Trunji, *President Adan Abdulle*, 28.
263. The developing nations have refuted the homogenizing and hegemonic assumptions of this Western program of modernity. They developed modern patterns depending on different cultures and belief systems. See Eisenstadt, S. N. "Multiple Modernities." Daedalus 129, no. 1 (2000): 1–29. Accessed February 18, 2024. http://www.jstor.org/stable/20027613.
264. Dasgupta, Rajashree. "Main Features of a Traditional Society." Available from https://www.govtgirlsekbalpur.com/Study_Materials/Geography/GEOG_PART_II_HONS_Main_Features_of_a_Traditional_Society.pdf. Accessed February 20, 2024.

Moreover, individuals often find their identity and purpose within the context of the collective, with clear roles and responsibilities. In the Somali context, the traditional elites comprise clan elders and Scholars of Islam who collaboratively oversee the governance of their clan, each entrusted with distinct roles and duties.[265] Furthermore, traditional societies rely mainly on subsistence agriculture, barter systems, or small-scale local trade. However, these traditions are changing with changes in communication and globalization.

On the other hand, the modern state system characterizes formal institutions, legal frameworks, and bureaucratic governance systems.[266] It introduces a more formalized and organized approach to governance, defined by territorial boundaries, citizenship, and authority that enforces laws and policies. It often involves the adoption of written constitutions, legal frameworks, and democratic institutions that aim to provide a structured and equitable system for diverse populations.[267] Economic systems are often characterized by complex economies driven by industrialization, globalization, and technological advancements. The modern state's economic framework is linked to global markets, financial institutions, and a complex division of labor. Moreover, the role of individuals within the modern state system emphasizes individual rights, personal freedoms, and opportunities for social mobility. Citizenship thus becomes a central concept, and individuals are seen as autonomous agents with rights and responsibilities protected by the state. Power structures in the modern state are typically codified and institutional-ized, with political leaders elected through democratic processes and

---

265. Abdurahman Abdullahi, *Tribalism, Nationalism, and Islam: The Crisis of Political Loyalty in Somalia* (Master's thesis, Islamic Institute, McGill University, 1992), 94.

266. de Oliveira, Márcio S B S. "Modernity and Modernization." Available from Modernità%20S.%20Eisenstadt%20Modernity%20and%20Moderniza-tion%20(1).pdf. Accessed on February 20, 2024.

267. Badie, Bertrand. *The Imported State: The Westernization of the Political Order* (Stanford, CA: Stanford University Press, 2000). Southall, Aidan. "State Formation in Africa." Annual Review of Anthropology 3, no. 1 (October 1974): 153–65.

accountable to the rule of law. The shift from traditional societies to modern state systems reflects a profound societal evolution, encompassing changes in governance, economic structures, individual roles, and power dynamics.

The most formidable dilemma faced by traditional societies' modern state systems lies in navigating the balance between preserving traditions and the necessity for adapting and accommodating new cultures stemming from modernity. Inherent in this challenge is determining whether to eliminate ingrained customs, traditions, and values to implant modern values, or to find ways to accommodate them within the newly adopted framework of the modern state. This predicament captures the broader dilemma of reconciling cultural heritage with the demands of modernity.[268] This task requires careful consideration, as the choices made in this regard can significantly influence the cohesion and resilience of the state system.[269] Regrettably, the Somali political elites opted for the policy of eradicating traditional norms and values, including the significant aspects of clan culture and the crucial role of Islam in shaping society.[270] This choice had profound consequences for state-society relations and provoked conflict, which caused the collapse of the state in 1991. The political culture of the Somali elite underwent a transformation characterized by a willingness to distance themselves from traditional norms and

---

268. Abdurahman Abdullahi and Ibrahim Farah, "Reconciling the State and Society: Reordering Islamic Work and Clan System," accessed April 4, 2024, http://www.scribd.com/doc/15327358/Reconciling-the-State-and-Society-in-Somalia.
269. Abdullahi, Abdurahman. "Theorizing Stability of the Somali State: In the Light of the Comprehensive Perspective of Somali Studies." Somali Studies: A Peer-Reviewed Academic Journal for Somali Studies 8 (2023): 11–55, 22.
270. See SYL Oath: "I swear by Almighty God that I will not take any action against any Somali. In trouble, I promise to help the Somali. I will become the brother of all other members. I will not reveal the name of my tribe. In matters of Mariage, I will not discriminate between the Somali tribes and Midgan, Yibirh, Yahar, and Tumal." See Abdi Samatar, 40. Mohamed Trunji observed the absence of highly discriminated groups of "Bantu descent" in the Oath. See Trunji, *Somalia: The Told History*, 17.

an eagerness to embrace modernity. They were oscillating between these contrasting ways of thinking and forces within this transitional sphere.

Many scholars have studied Somali culture and characterized the people of Somalia in various descriptions, highlighting a consistent trait over time. For instance, Richard Burton, a British explorer and intelligence officer who visited Northern Somalia in 1856, described the Somali clans as "a fierce and turbulent race of republicans."[271] On the other hand, other scholars have noted that the Somalis have "considerable independence of spirit."[272] Moreover, Said Samatar and David Laitin characterized the Somalis as "politically acephalous," meaning a society that lacks political leaders or hierarchies.[273] Moreover, Said Samatar and Davis Laitin articulated that Somali segmentation is a unique blend of centripetal forces, fostering strong kinship and cultural unity and centrifugal forces, creating intricate clan rivalries. Individuals prioritize political allegiance from their immediate family to the broader clan structure, leading to an integrated society where members view each other as kin. However, this cohesion is counteracted by clannish fission and factionalism, making political instability the norm in Somali culture.[274] The concept of these two scholars and followers of the anthropological school of Somali studies diminishes the role of other forms of culture stemming from a non-clan system. This dominant perspective of Somali studies accounts merely for the vertical relations of the clan system. It disregards the role of horizontal relationships through marriages and institutions such as Islamic, social, and political orga-

---

271. M.J. Fox criticized this quote as only about the Essa clan family; however, it was generalized to all Somalis. See See M.J. Fox, *The Roots of Somali Political Culture* (Boulder: Lynne Rienner Publishers, 2015), 34, footnote 19.
272. Ibid., 8.
273. Laitin, David, and Samatar, Samatar, *Somalia: Nation in Search of a State* (Boulder: Westview Press, 1987), 30.
274. Laitin and Samatar, *Somalia: Nation in Search*, 30–31.

nizations. This perspective was criticized for not providing a comprehensive picture of Somali culture.[275]

Indeed, it is crucial to highlight that the political instability mentioned by Laitin and Samatar has not led to complete chaos and the demise of the Somali people over the centuries. Despite the potential for internal conflict due to "clannish fission and factionalism," Somalis have a system of self-governance based on a customary legal system called Xeer, a hybrid of local customs and Islam. This legal system is a vital restraint in disputes and preventing endless internal fighting. Throughout Somali history, the combined influences of Xeer have mitigated conflicts by resolving issues through groups of clan elders and scholars of Islam.[276] Decisions in the clan system are made through clan gatherings, where all males can voice their opinions. Scholars of Islam are often consulted to legitimize collective decisions.

The core of the clan system is composed of Diya-paying units, resembling miniature states with defined territories, a robust legal system (Xeer), and governing councils of elders and scholars of Islam. These units, functioning as cohesive social structures bound by familial ties, establish well-structured legal frameworks within their territories to govern members' conduct. The council's traditional elders and scholars of Islam play a crucial role in decision-making, maintaining stability, adjudicating conflicts, and preserving cultural knowledge. These Diya-paying units are foundational building blocks that embody governance, legal order, and collective identity within the clan system. Before colonial intrusion in Somalia in the late nineteenth century, traditional governance was overseen only by two distinct elites: clan elders and scholars of Islam, and there was no superior authority above them. Clan elders handled worldly matters,

---

275. Abdullahi, Abdurahman. "Revisiting Somali Historiography: Critique and Idea of Comprehensive Perspective," Journal of Somali Studies: Research on Somalia and the Greater Horn of African Countries 5, no. 1–2 (2018), 48.
276. Abdullahi, Abdurahman. "Tribalism and Islam: Variations on the Basics of Somaliness." Proceedings of EASS/SSIA, Turku, Finland, 1998.

applying customary laws (Xeer), while Scholars of Islam managed religious affairs. This strategic division ensured a balanced approach to governance. Clan elders, organized in a hierarchical structure, managed everything from local dispute resolution to broader clan governance within a multi-tiered system, as conceptualized by I.M. Lewis. Traditional scholars of Islam in pre-colonial Somalia managed religious affairs, interpreting and spreading Islamic teachings for spiritual and moral guidance. These scholars, including Quranic instructors, jurisprudence experts, and Sufi masters, played unique roles in enriching Islamic knowledge and fostering spiritual growth within the community. This collaborative system, with clan elders handling worldly concerns and scholars of Islam overseeing religious matters, provided stability and coherence to the traditional Somali societal structure.[277] In essence, pre-colonial Somali society featured a dual elite system where clan elders and scholars of Islam worked together to maintain order, justice, and cultural/religious identity within the community.

The Somali peninsula witnessed the incursion of colonial powers at a time when the Somali people found themselves fragmented and debilitated. They had lost two pivotal central states, the Ajuran and Adal imamates, who had historically shielded them from external invasions.[278] Three European nations—Britain, France, and Italy—asserted their dominance through agreements forged with clan elders along the Somali coast. Concurrently, the Ethiopian empire expanded its influence, claiming a portion of territories inhabited by Somalis in the inland regions.[279] This colonial intrusion marked a significant turning point in Somali history, as external powers sought to carve out and control areas. The impact of these colonial legacies continues to shape the political, social, and economic landscape of the region, underscoring the enduring repercussions of these historical events on the Somali people and their cultural norms.

---

277. Abdullahi, *Revisiting Somali Historiography*, 48.
278. Abdullahi, Abdurahman, *Making Sense of Somali History*, Volume One (Adonis & Abbey, 2017), 59–63.
279. Ibid., 85–89.

THE FORMATIVE PERIOD OF SOMALI POLITICAL CULTURE

The Somali elite political culture unfolds as a complex entity, initially shaped by the fusion of traditional clan systems, Islamic principles, and Italian cultural influences. Subsequently, the imprint of a socialist-oriented military regime and the consequences of civil war further compounded new elements that deteriorated this culture.[280] Grasping this intricate amalgamation is crucial for comprehending Somali politics and the continuous development of its elite political culture. This chapter limits its scope to the dominant political culture until the military coup in October 1969.

The first aspect of Somali political culture is rooted in traditional culture, such as clan solidarity, resource competition, collective leadership, solid Islamic identity, and skepticism toward state authorities.[281] Echoing Emile Durkheim's 'mechanical solidarity,'[282] clannism, akin to nationalism, may generate positive solidarity or oppressive culture, often leading to pride, superiority, and societal fragmentation.[283] Governance involves participatory decision-making, mixing hereditary leadership with elite sub-clan participation. Somali identity strongly aligns with protecting Islam, emphasizing sacrifice for clan culture and Islam. Finally, as noted by Ibn-Khaldun, nomadic authority derives from religious elements, intertwining local customary law with Islamic Sharia and rejecting imposed secular laws.[284]

The second aspect of elite political culture centers around Islam, with three main branches: Ashariyah theology, Shafi jurisprudence, and Sufism.[285] Ashariyah theology, established in response

280. Abdullahi, *Somali Elite Political Culture*, 68–70.

281. Ibid., 58.

282. Lukes, Steven, and Andrew Scull, *Durkheim and the Law*, 2013, 1.

283. Lewis, I.M. "The Politics of the 1969 Somali Coup," The Journal of Modern African Studies 10, no. 3 (1972): 385.

284. Ibn Khaldün, The Muqaddimah, *An Introduction to History - Volume 1*, 2020, 309.

285. Abdullahi, Abdurahman. "The Conception of Islam in Somalia: Consensus and Controversy," Bildhaan: An International Journal of Somali Studies 21

to Mu'tazilah rationalism, emphasizes a balanced interpretation of Allah's attributes. It became the mainstream Sunni theology in Somalia, promoting a middle path and influencing its religious landscape. Shafi jurisprudence, founded by al-Shafi, contributed to the framework for deducing Islamic laws. It is one of the four leading Sunni schools of Jurisprudence. Sufism plays a crucial role in Somali religious identity, mainly through orders like Qadiriyah and Ahmadiyah.[286] This moderate Sufism, rooted in al-Ghazali's teachings, preserves historical heritage through genealogies, educational institutions, and social functions. The period around Somalia's struggle for independence and Adan Abdulle Osman's presidency saw the dominance of traditional Islam, and modern Islamist movements emerged later.

The third element of elite political culture is influenced by Italian political culture. Italian rule during the Fascist era (1922–1941) and the UN trusteeship period (1950–1960) left a lasting impact on Somali political development. During the trusteeship period, Somali political elites adopted a hybrid culture blending Italian and local traditional cultures. In contrast, British cultural influence during its rule was relatively insignificant. Italian political culture, known for fragmentation and instability, emphasizes local identification, low national pride, and a reluctance to make sacrifices when needed.[287] Key elements include localism, akin to clannism in the Somali context, and an "amoral familist" culture marked by greed, corruption, ineptitude, and lack of political direction. Widespread corruption, manifested in bribery and graft, is a prominent feature of the Italian political culture, contributing to Italy's high rank in the party patronage index.[288] Instability and fragmentation are defining

(2021), Article 9. Also, Abdurahman Abdullahi, *The Islamic Movement in Somalia: A Study of the Islah Movement, 1950-2000* (London: Adonis & Abbey, 2015).

286. Abdullahi, *The Conception of Islam*, 48.

287. Ginsborg, Paul. "The Italian Political Culture in Historical Perspective." Modern Italy 1, no. 1 (1995): 3–17.

288. Cavalli, Alessandro. "Reflections on Political Culture and the 'Italian National

features, with over sixty governments attributed to factors like the party system and electoral model since World War II. Italy's politics is characterized by coalition building and power-sharing, aligning with the cultural values of Italian society.

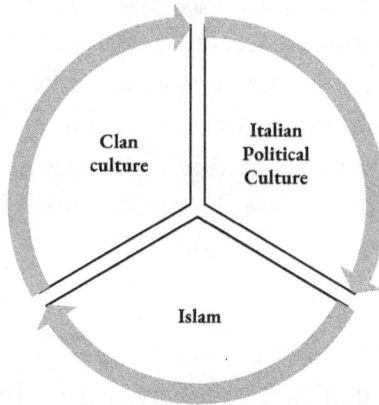

Fig. 13. The three elements that influence Somali political culture.

In summary, key factors influencing Somali political culture include the prevalence of (1) exclusion and prioritization of personal interests realized through clan rhetoric, (2) plundering with resource exploitation lacking strict adherence to rules, (3) disregard for state rules leading to political instability, and (4) decision-making dominated by self-centered behavior, hindering the establishment of inclusive political institutions. Additionally, (5) a strong sense of community interdependence fosters tight-knit bonds but resists external influences. Understanding these factors is crucial for addressing political challenges in Somalia. On the other hand, Italy's historical fragmentation contributes to a dynamic and unstable political landscape marked by frequent changes in government. Socially, familial relationships, networks, affiliations, and economic considerations intersect with political decision-making, shaping policies reflecting diverse sector interests. The Somali political elite has adopted elements of this compounded culture of local and Italian influences. Notably, few Somali leaders, including President Adan Abdulle

---

Character'," Daedalus 130, no. 3 (Summer, 2001): 119–137.

Osman, fully embraced this cultural synthesis, often misused as a hindrance to establishing a stable state in Somalia. Exploring the cultural differences between Adan and his counterparts during his tenure, understanding the contributing factors, and examining the aftermath of his presidency are essential questions that remain unanswered.

ADAN ABDULLE'S UNIQUE POLITICAL CULTURE

Adan Abdulle's leadership exemplifies servant leadership, marked by a deep commitment to serving others and a focus on ethical and moral principles that set him apart from his contemporaries. His leadership style is defined by humility, empathy, and a genuine concern for the well-being of those he leads. Adan Abdulle prioritizes the needs of his constituents and works tirelessly to uplift and empower them rather than seeking personal gain or glory. He leads by example, demonstrating integrity, honesty, and transparency in all his actions and decisions. Analyzing Adan Abdulle's biography reveals a unique political culture distinct from traditional Somali and Italian elite cultures. Unlike the prevalent norms of exclusion, embezzlement, and clannism in Somali politics, Abdulle demonstrated a departure by prioritizing democratic values, ethical governance, and transparency. His approach contrasted with the Italian elite culture, which was marked by greed, corruption, and a lack of coherent political direction. Abdulle aimed to establish a precedent for a more moral and accountable political culture, emphasizing values that stood in contrast to the corrupt practices often found in the political landscapes he navigated. Adan Abdulle was renowned for his principled governance, blending the strengths of traditional Somali and Italian political cultures while avoiding unethical practices. Grounded in Islamic values, he prioritized justice and moral conduct in his leadership. Adan recognized the significance of community ties and inclusive decision-making, deviating from contemporary politicians in five key aspects. His approach aimed at fostering a political environment aligned with principles deeply rooted in Islam, distancing from practices that contradicted ethical standards.

Encouraging Political Inclusivity

Adan consistently advocated against applying a majoritarian government formation in clan-based Somali politics. His unwavering belief in the need for diverse representation led him to suggest to his fellow SYL central committees that smaller parties should be included in the government. However, his suggestion of forming a national unity government faced resistance from the party until 1960. For example, in the aftermath of the first election held in 1956, where the SYL secured 43 out of 60 elected parliament seats, Adan proposed "a multi-party cabinet so that other parties could gain experience in the executive responsibility, but the parry congress voted down his proposal."[289] Further illustrating his commitment to inclusivity, upon being elected as the speaker of the parliament and chairman of the SYL party in 1959, Adan reiterated his proposal for a coalition government. Despite his efforts, the SYL congress rejected the proposal and "passed a motion of favor of a SYL government."[290] Instead, consideration was given to the clan balancing in the government formation.[291] In addition, during the Constitution-making process, the elected legislative assembly of 1959 was tasked with constituting an assembly to frame and approve the Constitution of the independent Somali state. Adan Abdulle proposed including representatives of all political parties in the constituent assembly, which was finally agreed upon with the support of the UN Trusteeship authority. The application of inclusivity of government formation was partially realized in 1960, including members of USP and SNL in the government.[292] The political inclusion was advanced further after Adan was elected the President of Somalia in 1961 and Dr. Abdirashid was reappointed as the premier. Even though SYL was a majority party, the formed coalition government brought together the SYL, SNL, and USP parties.[293] Notably, even individuals who were among the most

---

289. Trunji, *President Adan Abdulle*, 50.
290. Ibid., 63.
291. Abdullahi, *Making Sense of Somali History, vol.1*, 140.
292. Ibid.
293. Trunji, *President Adan Abdulle*, 82.

ardent opposition to President Adan's election, such as Mohamed Ibrahim Igal, Sheikh Ali Jimale, and Abdullahi Isse, were included in the cabinet.[294] This move was a significant gesture of reconciliation and inclusiveness, showcasing Adan's commitment to fostering unity and representation across the political spectrum.

Despising the Culture of Political Clannism

President Adan's second political stance involved rejecting political clannism and self-centered political behavior prevalent among politicians. Political clannism, a crucial instrument for securing parliamentary positions, was the main arena where individuals mobilized their clans to ensure electoral success. Rooted in Somali political history from the 1950s, this culture blended influences from the political system, such as the political party system, electoral laws, and traditional Somali practices. It created an ambivalent political atmosphere tied to clans and personal interests, leading to a constant inclination towards personal greed, often exploiting national resources and seeking external support. President Adan Abdulle, a prominent nationalist, openly rejected all forms of clannism in the public domain. However, clan sensitivities within the SYL party and smaller parties since 1956 posed dangerous trends challenging Somali independence. Despite accusations of abandoning his Hawiye clan during the 1961 election campaign, Adan was known for reconciling differences among various political elites.[295]

Political clannism was prominently evident during various key political crises, such as the SYL leadership dispute in 1959, the conflict between PM Abdullahi Isse and Haji Muse Boqor, the 1959 government formation crisis, and the aftermath of the northern officers' military coup. The first crisis involved a rift between SYL Chairman Haji Mohamed Hussein and the central committee, leading to the resignation of Adan, the deputy chairman. This discord intensified between the Darood and Hawiye clans, causing polarization within the central

---

294. Ibid., 83.
295. Trunji, *President Adan Abdulle*, 82.

committee. The second crisis arose after the government formation in 1959, balancing representation among the Hawiye, Darood, and Digil & Mirifle clans. Parliamentarians, primarily Majeerteen Darood, criticized the government for election rigging and a lack of professionalism, reflecting the influence of clannism.[296] The third crisis unfolded when Interior Minister Muse Boqor unilaterally reopened the offices of GSL and SNU parties, allegedly acting to the Egyptian wishes who supported GSL, previously closed on February 26, 1959, accusing them of inciting violence.[297] Despite reconciliation efforts, Muse Boqor's resignation heightened clan sensitivities, exacerbating the situation. The fourth crisis emerged following the failed northern officers' coup in 1961 and the unification of import taxes in the Somali Republic. The excessive force used in suppressing demonstrations led to casualties, and the clan-related mishandling of the incident by the Ministry of the Interior led to the resignation of Isaq ministers Mohamed Ibrahim Egal and Sheikh Ali Ismail Yaqub, prompting Isaq's MPs to protest by walking out of parliament and subsequently gain support from other MPs. The fifth crisis emerged when eleven Hawiye MPs, led by Sheikh Ali Jimale and Haji Farah, broke away from SYL and, in alliance with SNL, formed the SNC party.[298]

Scorning corruption and vote-paying.

After the election of 1964 and the consultation to appoint a new PM, the central committee of the SYL proposed that Abdirashid Ali Sharmarke be reappointed as the PM. However, the president needed more convincing. He met some members of the central committee of the SYL party and told them (quoted from the Diary of President Adan):

---

296. Ibid., 64.
297   Trunji, *Somalia: The Untold History*, 330–34. Also, Lewis, I.M, *A Modern History of Somalia: Nation and State in the Horn of Africa* (Westview Press, 1965), 160. According to Samatar, GSL was closed as a result of successive incidents in Gardo, Mogadishu, and Jama, in which members of GSL were involved in throwing a bomb and preparing to intimidate the Italians, snubbing the governor of Banadir Ahmed Shuqul. See Samatar, *Africa's First Democrat*, 66.
298. Trunji, *President Adan Abdulle*, 417.

I want to do everything possible to deal with corruption, nepotism, and every other bad habit of the public administration, would help me to try to find a Prime Minister who could hold himself to the level responsibility required.[299]

After the no-confidence vote with the Abdirizak government, President Adan was dismayed by those who were self-centered and interested only in being appointed to a ministerial position. Describing this political culture of MPs, he expressed, "God save Somalis from starving beasts in human form that are supposed "representatives of the people."[300] Moreover, in the July 6, 1967, presidential election, President Adan refused to campaign and make any concessions or promises of government positions in exchange for votes. Groups of MPs flocked to him to promise votes in exchange for positions. Moreover, several businessmen, including Haji Ahmed Abdullahi Hashiish and Haji Naser Ali Hubeishi, promised the president to support him financially for his reelection. However, the president told them: "I told them that I do not need money, for I believe it is not only shameful but unnecessary to do things using corruption."[301] He played the politics of decency, honesty, and fair play, avoiding any actions that may jeopardize democratic culture and values. At the same time, his contenders promised everyone a job and used the oath to convince PMs of their truthfulness.

Refraining from campaigning for a political position.

Adan Abdulle's wide-ranging political career was characterized by a unique and admirable culture in that he never campaigned for any of his positions. This may seem very strange in the modern political culture and environment. Mohamed Trunji described that "he had never run or sought any positions he had served in during his long political career. His sense of the state and his political integrity were the base for his election to all the positions he served in."[302] His

299. Ibid.
300. Samatar, *Africa's First Democrat*, 141.
301. Trunji, *President Adan Abdulle*, 121.
302. Ibid., 72.

election to various roles within the political positions, from being a SYL branch leader to the president of Somalia, was rooted in the trust of his colleagues because of his leadership capacity and his unwavering political integrity. Moreover, Adan Abdulle exemplified a leadership culture devoid of an insatiable hunger for power. His ascent to various positions was not driven by personal ambition but by a genuine dedication to serving the people. This distinctive leadership style, where individuals emerge as the people's choice organically, is a rarity in the annals of history.

In the 1961 presidential election, the central committee of the SYL endorsed President Adan's presidency, but he refused to campaign. Abdirizak Haji Hussein testified that:

> [President Adan] believed that campaigning for himself would convey a feeling that someone who held the office would not want to leave it. It was up to members of the parliament to decide whether, in view of the interest of the country, he was the most qualified candidate.[303]

Moreover, talking to his friend MP Hussein Abdi Abdulle (Farmacia), who was campaigning for him in the 1961 election, Adan wrote the following entry in his diary: "In my life, I have never solicited votes for getting elected, and I see no reason why I should do so now, for it is the undignified thing for a self-respecting person."[304] Moreover, in the 1967 election, President Adan expressed his unwillingness to the second term, saying that he "used all the gas in the tank and that it was "time to go."[305]

Adan Abdulle's commitment to this approach mirrors a cultural ethos reminiscent of the early years of Islam, a time when leadership was characterized by humility, selflessness, and a deep sense of duty to the community. Adan Abdulle embraced the essence of Islamic principles, mainly reflected in the following hadith:

---

303. Ibid., 77
304. Trunji, *President Adan Abdulle*, 78.
305. Ibid., xiv.

"Avoid seeking positions of authority, for if bestowed upon you without solicitation, you will be assisted in managing it; however, if acquired through your pursuit, you will be left to navigate it on your own."[306]

Indeed, striving for leadership motivated by power and self-interest is discouraged, whereas seeking it for valid reasons is commendable and, at times, necessary for individuals with the requisite capabilities. This sentiment finds support in the Quran, where Yusuf (Joseph) seeks responsibility over the state treasury, underscoring his trustworthiness and competence for the broader welfare of society.[307] The difference that emerged in 1957–58 was not only a personal matter between Adan Abdulle and Haji Mohamed, but between Haji Mohamed and his close associates, on the one side, and the SYL party mainstream, the Italian administrator and the Somali government, on the other. Thus, Adan Abdulle withdrew his resignation after resolving contentious issues with the SYL central committees. In the 1967 presidential campaign, President Adan refused to compromise his principle of not campaigning for the position while his opponents did everything to gain the election of their candidate, Abdirashid Ali Sharmarke. Below is what President Adan's writing in his diary:

"I will seek re-election only if it is imposed on me by those who believe that the country still needs me."[308] "If they wanted him as president, he would be willing to serve. If they chose someone else, he would be equally happy." After losing the 1967 election, the resident said, "As far as I am concerned, I consider the results a blessing for me as that lets me return free."[309]

---

306. Sahih Muslim 1652 (book 33, Hadith 15).
307. See the Quranic verse in which Allah says: "Joseph proposed, "Put me in charge of the storehouses of the land, for I am truly reliable and adept." [Quran, 12:55]
308. Trunji, *President Adan Abdulle*, 120.
309. Ibid., 131.

President Adan was a reconciler among political elites.

Aden Abdulle led the moderate members of SYL and always tried to mitigate internal conflicts within the party, in which sectarian individuals and more nationalistic elements were always in continuous conflict. The president wanted more than the large number of ministers in the council of the Abdirashid-led government and the capacity of some individuals. However, as a gesture to avoid internal conflict, President Adan did not oppose it. Even though he was dismayed by many of PM Abdirashid's actions and policies and had the constitutional prerogative to dismiss him, he demonstrated restraint to ensure the stability of the government. President Adan recorded in his diary after the formation of the government in 1961 that:

> With the number of the cabinet ministers and the inclusion of the government of certain individuals, Abdirashid made me swallow a bitter bill for fear of who knows what. He left some good men out. I am sorry, but this is a disappointment and disservice to his honor.[310]

The president expressed that Abdirashid had done the same when he criticized the Abdullahi Isse government in 1959.[311] For example, when Haji Mohamed Hussein, the chairman of the party, undertook a different left-wing policy in contradiction with the official policy of the SYL, Adan Abdulle met him while the party congress was still in session to discuss the issue of Haji Mohamed. Adan, for the sake of clarification and reconciliation, stated:

> The ill-feeling you harbor towards me cannot be interpreted if not in relation to your ambition to become, in the future, president of Republic, and you think that I might be

---

310. Trunji, *President Adan Abdulle*, 3.
311. After the formation of the government of balanced clan power-sharing with SYL, which was implemented in 1959, learning lessons from the formation of the government in 1956. However, a group of parliamentarians, including Abdirashid, Abdirizak, and Mohamed Sheikh Gabyow, criticized the government for rigging elections, forming a large government, and the lack of professional qualifications. Trunji, *President Adan Abdulle*, 65.

among those, if not the only one, who may overshadow you. If this is the case, I swear on what I most value in the life that it had never crossed my mind to compete with you and that I have no obsession or anxious to become president, even I would not mind having such an honor. [312]

Another example of reconciliation is when he talks to Sheikh Ali Jimale, a long-time friend from the same city as Beledweyne, when they contended for the presidential position in 1961. Adan contacted Sheikh Ali Jimale to get assurance of collective work, regardless of who won the election. President Adan recorded in his diary:

I told him that life often plays tricks of the kind we are currently experiencing, putting friends and brothers against each other in competition for a position of responsibility and that the present confusion will be over in a few days' time when one of us wins the election. I said that if he is elected president, I am ready to extend my full collaboration to him, and I expect him to do the same in the event I win the election. Shiekh Ali felt instead that two individuals, divided by serious contrast, could not collaborate. [313]

Another significant reconciliatory event occurred when Speaker Jama Mohamed Galib signed an agreement between Somalia and the USSR during the president's official visit to Italy in October 1963. Upon returning, the president was briefed by Army Commander General Daud. It appears the speaker signed the agreement under pressure from the prime minister, who denied this. Nevertheless, the president resolved the unconstitutional issue by signing the agreement to settle the disagreement among himself, the speaker, and the prime minister. [314] The Western governments, including the USA, Italy, and Germany, offered military assistance that was not satisfactory to Somalia. All Western countries opposed Somalia's "Greater Somalia" project, and signing the military agreement with the USSR strained

---

312. Ibid., 59.
313. Ibid., 78.
314. Ibid., 89–90.

Somali relations with the Western countries. Consequently, Britain retaliated by offering Kenya the Northern Frontier District (NFD), even though a referendum showed that 87 percent of the population preferred to join Somalia. As a result, Somalia severed its diplomatic relations with Britain.[315]

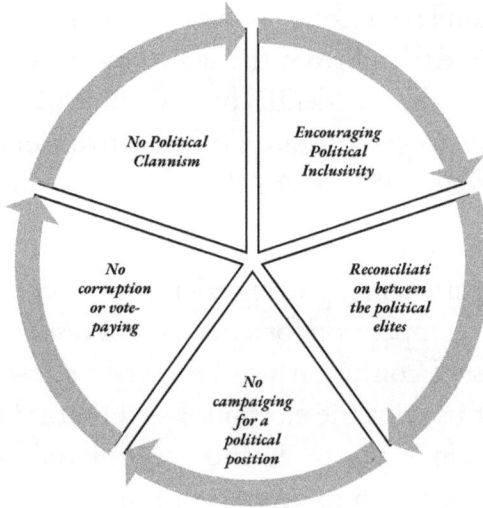

Fig 14. The Major Political Culture of President Adan Abdulle

FACTORS SHAPED ADAN'S POLITICAL CULTURE

Six factors shaped Adan Abdulle's political culture: his growing up as an orphan, his extensive experience working alongside Italians, his belonging to the Udeejeen clan, his marriage to a Majeerteen/Darood wife, his strong connection to his religious roots, and his passion for literacy and reading habits. These six factors shaped Adan Abdulle's unique political culture and leadership approach.

The first factor epitomized his life as an orphan and his self-made personality, eschewing any reliance on or residence with his extended family. The key to his accomplishments was a testament to his un-adulterated self-reliance, sense of personal responsibility, and navigating life pathways independently and free from any external

---

315. Ibid.

support or relatives. His unwavering commitment to self-sufficiency and resolute determination set him apart from most other political elites, becoming defining characteristics that engraved his unique identity. His life journey unfolded as evidence of singular dedication, a narrative written on the image of self-discovery. In every step he took, the resonances of autonomy and resilience reverberated, illustrating a remarkable commitment to shaping his destiny on his terms, unconstrained by conventional familial expectations and support.

The second factor was his childhood years working with many Italian individuals, absorbing the nuances of the European work culture from each of them. This immersive experience provided him with training in the dynamics of European professional practices. This multifaceted training broadened his skill set and allowed him to develop a profound understanding of the cultural particulars that shape European work ethics. From mastering the art of effective communication with the Italian language, each employer contributed a unique example to their professional development. As a result, he emerged from this coaching period as someone who seamlessly integrates a culturally enriched approach to his work.

The third factor was his belonging to the Isse Mudulood (Udeejeen) clan, which was distinguished by not pursuing dominance over other clans and state institutions—a departure from the prevailing trend among other political elites who hailed from ambitious, dominating, and power-seeking clans.[316] Unlike many of his contemporaries, whose political agendas were fueled by the desire for supremacy and domination, his clan adopted a more individualistic approach as citizens of the government. Fortunately, he was unaffected by the baggage of clan pressures that other politicians faced. In contrast to the power-hungry motivations of certain political elites, his clan was not pressuring him for special privileges. This distinctive condition set him apart, positioning him as an advocate for a

---

316. Isse Mudulood is the uncle of Abgal Osman Mudulood, who originally resided in the Hiiraan region. Mudulood settles in Banadir, Hirshabeelle, and the eastern part of Galmudug.

more harmonious and balanced political culture. His clan stood as a testament to an alternative vision emphasizing responsible leadership and a commitment to the common good in a political landscape often marked by intense competition and power struggles.

The fourth factor was his marriage to a wife from the Majeerteen/Darood clan family, thereby forging familial relations that bridged the Hawiye and Darood clan families.[317] In the confines of his household, these two competing clan families found a unique solace and synthesis that echoed his commitment to fostering unity and reconciliation. As he assumed a leadership role within the state, his residence symbolized a harmonious convergence of political influences from the Hawiye and Darood clans. Functioning as a mediator and reconciler, he navigated the dynamics between these two clans. His ability to handle the complicated web of clan politics with impartiality and tact earned him the respect of moderate politicians from the Hawiye and Darood clan families. The unity emanating from his household became a symbol of inclusivity and cooperation, transcending the historical divisions that had often fueled tensions. By cultivating an environment of mutual understanding and shared goals within his familial sphere, he became a beacon of hope for those advocating for a more collaborative and reconciliatory approach to politics.

The fifth factor was deeply entrenched in his religious family with an anti-colonialist background. The Darwish movement, to which his father belonged, represented a political ideology and a profound spiritual and cultural resistance against colonial domination. Raised within the nurturing embrace of a family deeply committed to Islamic values, such as equality, justice, transparency, and anti-corruption, he internalized the principles of anti-colonialism from an early age. As a member of the new anti-colonial movement of SYC,

---

317. Most Darood politicians, particularly Majeerteen, looked to President Adan as a brother-in-law since he was married to a wife from their clan. In Somali culture, the brother-in-law (*Seedi*) enjoys a mutual special respect. They were called Abti (maternal uncle) of the president's children, who are the most respected.

he actively contributed to preserving cultural identity and religious autonomy and rejecting external influences. Through his commitment to the cause, he emerged as a steadfast proponent of anti-colonial sentiments, blending his religious upbringing with a dedication to safeguarding the cultural heritage of Somali society.

The sixth factor was his unwavering passion for delving into vast literary works. Through an extensive exploration of literature, he gained valuable insights into global politics, nationalist movements, state-building processes, and economic development. Moreover, his literary pursuits equipped him with a profound comprehension of the challenges and successes associated with state-building endeavors. The diverse narratives and perspectives embedded in the literature he consumed allowed him to draw parallels between different nations' experiences, contributing to his ability to manage the complexities of governance and political development. In essence, Adan Abdulle's passion for literature was not merely a pastime but a dynamic force that enriched his political culture, providing him with the intellectual tools to deal with the complex environment of state-building and democratic values.

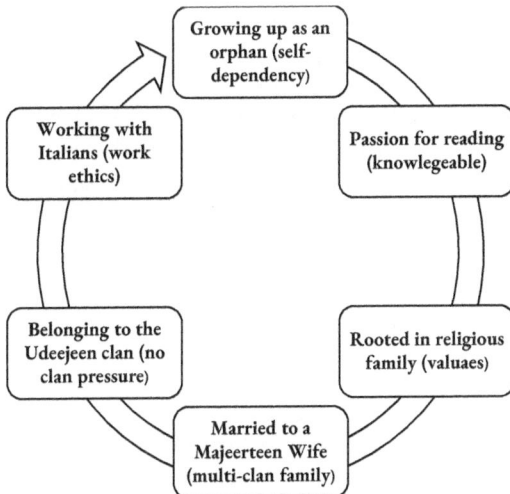

Fig. 15. Six factors that shaped President Adan's political culture.

PRESIDENT ADAN AND HIS OPPOSITION'S CHALLENGES

President Adan faced opposition from diverse groups, each motivated by distinct reasons and agendas. These groups comprised leftist ideologues, some Hawiye politicians, certain politicians from the northern regions of Somalia, and individuals of the deep state and previous members of PM Abdirashid's regime. The convergence of these disparate groups against President Adan reflected the complex dynamics and competing interests within Somali politics. Their collective opposition posed significant challenges to Adan's presidency, culminating in his eventual ousting and Abdirashid's ascension to power.

Opposition from Hawiye Politicians

One of the groups that opposed President Adan Abdulle comprised several Hawiye politicians who had anticipated a different approach from a leader from the Hawiye clan. Their expectations were rooted in the desire of President Adan to align with their clan-centric agenda and actively support their interests in the face of political confrontations with Darood politicians.[318] However, President Adan Abdulle remained steadfast in his commitment to serving as the president of Somalia, rejecting clan competitions and prioritizing national unity over factional interests. The discontent among Hawiye politicians manifested in their opposition to President Adan's leadership, driven by a perceived lack of special consideration for their clan within the broader political landscape. This opposition was particularly evident when these Hawiye politicians actively contested against President Adan in both the Somali Youth League (SYL) leadership in 1959 and the presidential race in 1961.

---

318. Sheikh Ali Jimale expressed the testament of these accusations in the election list of the SYL parliamentary candidates in Beledweyne in 1959, where he placed his name at the top of the list as the chairman of the party and the Speaker of the parliament's second in this list. "Sheik Ali and friends accused Osman and Haji Farah Ali Omar of not favoring their kin groups in the party dispute." Samatar, *Africa's First Democrat*, 66.

In the 1959 SYL leadership contest, Sheikh Mohamud Ahmed "Kutubaxoor," a member of parliament from the Adale district, faced off against President Adan Abdulle. Adan narrowly won the contest with 44 votes, while Kutubaxoor received 42.[319] This internal party competition underscored the growing dissatisfaction within the Hawiye political ranks, which sought a more clan-centric agenda within the SYL. This clan-centric politics was an open exercise of most politicians from other clan families, particularly the Darood politicians. On the other hand, the presidential race in 1961 witnessed another challenge to President Adan's leadership from within his Hawiye clan. Sheikh Ali Jimale, in alliance with Mohamed Ibrahim Egal, an old friend from the same city, Beledwayne, emerged as a contender, further highlighting the division within the Hawiye politicians regarding the direction of Somali politics under President Adan's leadership.[320] The voting was extremely tight. During the first round, the vote ended in a tie at 60-60. In the second round, the vote shifted slightly to 60–61 in favor of Sheikh Ali Jimale. By the third round, the results changed again, with a 62–59 vote in favor of Adan Abdulle. President Adan Abdulle's steadfast commitment to a unified Somalia, free from the influence of clan affiliations, fueled tensions with those Hawiye politicians who sought a more exclusive focus on their interests cloaked with the clan's interests. The political landscape thus became a battleground where competing visions for the nation's future clashed, revealing the complexities and challenges associated with achieving a harmonious and inclusive post-independence political order.

The leftist opposition

During the tumultuous era of the 1950s, amidst the geopolitical tensions of the Cold War, the winds of leftist ideology swept across various liberation movements worldwide, finding fertile ground in Somalia. This ideological current made its way into the nation through a conduit of educated individuals, particularly students who had studied in countries such as Egypt, the USSR, and China. Among

---

319. Trunji, *President Adan Abdulle*, 60.
320. Trunji, *President Adan Abdulle*, 80–81.

these educated elites, one figure stood out prominently: Haji Mohamed Hussein, who emerged as a leading advocate of leftist principles within Somali political circles. Haji Mohamed Hussein's ideological shift was evident during his tenure as the elected chairman of the Somali Youth League (SYL) in 1957, a position he assumed following his education at Al-Azhar University in Egypt. Embracing the tenets of leftist ideology, he swiftly became a vocal critic of what he perceived as the pro-Western leanings of figures like President Adan Abdulle, whom he accused of lacking genuine nationalist passion.

The ideological split between Adan and Haji Mohamed Hussein eventually reached a boiling point, culminating in Hussein's expulsion from the SYL on April 1, 1958.[321] Undeterred, Hussein established the Great Somalia League (GSL). This political entity attracted many prominent leftists and "a segment of Darod tribesmen who resented Hawiye's predominance in the government."[322] The GSL swiftly emerged as a formidable force within Somali politics, positioning itself as a staunch advocate for leftist principles and the unification of Somalia under a progressive, nationalist banner. Central to the GSL's platform was the accusation against the SYL, which accused them of lacking genuine commitment to the cause of Somali unification. This accusation was a rallying cry for the GSL and its supporters, galvanizing widespread discontent and paving the way for a seismic shift in the Somali political landscape.

Discontented Isaaq Politicians

In the aftermath of the Somali Republic's unification, a sense of discontent simmered among politicians from the northern regions, spearheaded by Mohamed Ibrahim Egal. Frustration brewed over what they perceived as Southern dominance in the newly unified nation's corridors of power. Three events showcased Isaaq's discontent: the aborted officer's coup in 1961, the resignation of the ministers Mohamed Ibrahim Egal and Sheikh Ali Ismael from the

---

321. Ibid., 56–60.
322. Trunji, *Somalia: the Told History*, 304.

government in 1963, and the revolt of Isaaq lawmakers.[323] Egal, a shrewd political operator, became the leader of the Somali National Congress (SNC), which is seen as mainly the coalition of Isaaq and Hawiye politicians who supported Sheikh Ali Jumale, forming the "Irir coalition" in 1963.[324] The NSC party gained 22 seats in the 1964 election against 69 for SYL.[325] Egal strategically navigated various political platforms to ascend to the position of Prime Minister of Somalia.[326] His political tactics gained traction as he garnered support from like-minded individuals who shared his dissatisfaction with the prevailing power dynamics. Among those who allied with Egal was a group led by Abdirashid Ali Sharmarke after losing his premiership position in 1964. This coalition of disaffected politicians coalesced around a common goal: challenging the authority of President Adan and Prime Minister Abdirizak. The alliance between Egal's faction and Abdirashid's team marked a significant turning point in Somali politics, as it brought together disparate groups united by their shared grievances and aspirations for political leadership. Together, they formed a formidable opposition front, leveraging their combined influence and resources to mount a concerted challenge against the entrenched leadership of President Adan and Prime Minister Abdirizak.

Former PM Abdirashid A. Sharmarke's Group

The faction led by PM Abdirashid faced a significant setback following the 1964 election when the president declined to endorse his nomination despite the central committee of SYL advocating for it. Consequently, Abdirashid and several ex-cabinet members were thrust into a vehement opposition against the Adan/Abdirizak administration. This marked the genesis of a tumultuous period characterized by intense political discord and strategic maneuver-

---

323. Ibid., 409--13. Trunji, President Adan, 85.
324. I.M. Lewis. A Modern History of Somalia: Nation and State in the Horn of Africa (Westview Press, 1965), 176.
325. Trunji, Somalia: the Told History, 471.
326. Ibid., 417.

ing as Abdirashid and his allies sought to assert their influence and challenge the ruling regime's policies. Abdirashid solidified his alliance with Mohamed Ibrahim Egal and the discontented Isaaq MPs by offering Egal the role of Prime Minister. This strategic move aimed to strengthen their political bond and ensure greater unity and cooperation in their future endeavors.

Elements of Deep State

The civil service reform implemented by the Abdirizak government, famously known as "*Pusta Roso*," led to the dismissal of numerous veteran civil servants. Among them were seasoned individuals who had held high-ranking positions for years. Displaced from their roles, some of these experienced bureaucrats transitioned into politics. This transformation birthed a new opposition force against the Adan/Abdirizak administration, composed of individuals well-versed in the inner workings of government and armed with a wealth of institutional knowledge. Their entry into the political arena added depth and complexity to the landscape as they leveraged their expertise and networks to challenge the policies and decisions of the ruling regime.

Despite their concerted efforts, the combined opposition of leftist ideologues and discontented Hawiye politicians proved unsuccessful in dislodging President Adan Abdulle from power despite refusing to campaign for re-election. However, the political landscape witnessed a significant shift in the presidential election of 1967, when a formidable coalition was formed. This alliance comprised the previously disenfranchised groups, including those rooted in leftist ideology and disgruntled Hawiye politicians, along with individuals of northern politicians and from the deep state aggrieved by Prime Minister Abdirizak's civil service reforms emphasizing capacity and anti-corruption program.[327] This formidable coalition campaigned during the presidential election of 1967 in a collective endeavor to dislodge President Adan Abdulle's presidency. Their approach en-

---

327. Ibid., 495–500.

compassed a multifaceted strategy that exploited various forms of corruption, leveraging covert and overt means to sway the political climate in their support.

The culmination of these efforts resulted in the replacement of President Adan Abdulle with Abdirashid in the presidential election of June 10, 1967. The election marked a turning point in Somali political history, as the collective grievances of leftist ideologues, discontented Hawiye politicians, and northern politicians, and elements of the deep state coalesced to bring about a significant regime change. The success of this coalition highlighted the potency of a unified front against a sitting president, mainly when fuelled by a combination of ideological differences, ethnic affiliations, and internal disputes within the political structure. The events leading up to and following June 10, 1967, underscored the intricate interplay of power dynamics, strategic maneuverings, and the complex socio-political landscape that defined Somalia during this pivotal period. Abdirashid won the presidency in the third ballot of 73, and Adan got 50 votes.[328] The president resigned on June 30 to give the elected president the chance to address the nation on Independence Day, July 1, instead of giving up power on July 6, 1967.

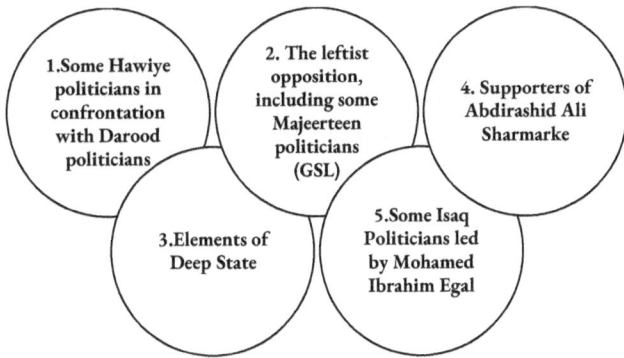

Fig. 16. The five oppositions to the Adan /Abdirizak government

---

328. In the first ballot, Abdirashid received 63 votes and Adan 57. Abdirashid received 67 votes in the second ballot, while Adan received 55. See Trunji, *President Adan*, 129.

The relevant question and essential for our analysis is to answer why Adan Abdulle was elected without campaigning for sixteen years of tenure in many high political positions. Adan Abdulle's consistent rise in Somali politics from 1951 to 1967 is intriguing and extraordinary. His political career began with his election to the first Territorial Council in 1951, where he was also chosen as the council's deputy chairman. His strong leadership quickly led him to become the Somali Youth League (SYL) chairman from 1953 to 1956. In 1956, Adan Abdulle became the first parliament speaker, and his leadership further blossomed when he was re-elected as SYL chairman in 1958. In 1960, he became Somalia's first president and was re-elected in 1961 without ever campaigning, a surprising and unusual modern political culture. There are several reasons for his success. First, Adan Abdulle's advanced education distinguished him from his peers, enabling him to approach governance with insight and wisdom. Second, his reputation for integrity and modesty endeared him to the public and his colleagues. Third, his diplomatic and conciliatory approach to politics earned him the respect and trust of his colleagues in the SYL and Italian administration under the UN trusteeship. Moreover, leadership is a dynamic interaction between leaders and followers and situational influence by the context. Adan's leadership occurred during the nascent state-building period when the political environment had not yet succumbed much to self-serving interests, and the dominance of cultural integrity was high. Despite the potential for political disputes and conflicts within a democratic system and the opposition he faced from prominent SYL figures, Adan Abdulle continued to be elected without campaigning until 1967. Adan Abdulle's sixteen-year tenure in high-ranking positions without campaigning reflects his exceptional education, honest character, diplomatic leadership style, and political contexts in which he operated. His story exemplifies the significance of integrity, humility, and dedication to serving the people.

SOMALIA'S PATH POST-PRESIDENT ADAN ABDULLE

The 1967 leadership transition from President Adan Abdulle and Prime Minister Abdirizak H. Hussein to President Abdirashid Sharmarke and Prime Minister Egal marked a pivotal moment in Somali history. Understanding President Adan's role in promoting democracy, fostering reconciliation among clan-centric politicians, combating corruption, and advocating for good governance requires juxtaposing with the tumultuous political environment of the ruling elites from 1967 to 1969. A lack of commitment to democratic principles characterized the political atmosphere two years after President Adan's term. The prevailing clan-centric politics fostered divisiveness, hindering the nation's progress towards unity and shared national identity. Corruption permeated the political system, with political elites prioritizing personal gain over the country's welfare.[329] Good governance practices were notably absent, contributing to a growing disillusionment among the citizens and educated elites.[330]

The culmination of this era of mismanagement manifested in the 1969 election, which was marred by widespread rigging and irregularities.[331] The strategic plan prepared by President Sharmarke, PM Egal, and his interior minister, Yassin Nur Hassan, was founded on segmenting political parties, which reached about eighty parties and then joining them into a single political party, SYL.[332] This plan was realized, and all newly elected MPs joined SYL, except Abdirizak Haji Hussein. This compromised electoral process not only undermined the nation's democratic history and aspirations, but it also marked a

329. Ibid.

330. Metz, Helen Chapin, ed. *Somalia: A Country Study*, fourth edition (Library of Congress Cataloging-in-Publication Data, 1992), 36.

331. Ingriis, *The Suicidal State in Somalia*, 48.

332. The Interior Minister Yasin Nur was the mastermind of the Abdirashid/Egal reconciliation and formed a coalition against Adan/Abdirizak in the 1967 election. Even though he was one of the early members of SYL, he was famous for his insubordination to party policies. He was expelled from the party three times (1959, 1964, and 1966) and readmitted after clan-based reconciliation. He managed the highly rigged election of 1969. See Trunji, *President Adan Abdulle*, 420–21.

period of terrible governance, ultimately leading to the rigging of the 1969 election and the establishment of a one-party system.[333] Italian historian Angelo Del Boca portrayed Somalia in the late 1960s as plagued by a lack of direction and pervasive despair. Nine years after its independence, by the summer of 1969, Somalia, known as "the darling child of the UN," had no characteristics that made her an example. "The democracy is a mere memory. The multi-party system is a mockery; the neutrality, a faded option, and in the national assembly, confusion reigns."[334] Moreover, Mohamed Trunji lucidly explains the conditions of Somalia by the end of 1969 as follows:

> Fraud in the March 1969 election was not the only fuse that could lead to an explosion at any moment. Another was the rampant corruption in the public administration, which wasted vast amounts of public money, including aid from foreign governments, and fueled anger among the masses of Somalis, who resented economic deprivation and the opulence enjoyed by the political elite. Public unease mounted, faith in the regime waned, and the optimistic mood quickly gave way to cynicism. By 1969, after nearly a decade of independence, Somalia was effectively bankrupt, shackled to foreign aid for survival, and prone to sliding into a dictatorial regime.[335]

This era of political instability reached its nadir with the tragic assassination of President Abdirashid Ali Sharmarke on October 15, 1969. His death further destabilized the political environment, creating a power vacuum that was exploited by the military. The military takeover on October 21, 1969 marked a decisive turning point in the nation's history, replacing civilian rule with military governance. Political elites were detained, including President Adan

---

333. Ibid. Mohamed Sharif related that Saudi Arabia offered 50 million dollars, which seems excessive, and most likely $5 million for the election expenses in support of the Abdirashid/Egal SYL party. See Chapter three, footnote 2, 166. Abdurahman Abdullahi, *The Islamic Movement in Somalia: The Case of the Islah Movement (1950–2000)* (Adonis & Abey, 2015).
334. Trunji, *President Adan Abdulle*, 155.
335. Ibid., 156.

Abdulle, Prime Minister Abdirizak, Prime Minister Mohamed Ibrahim Egal, and Speaker of the Parliament Sheikh Mukhtar.[336]

Military rule emerged from this political upheaval and endured for 21 years. Somalia underwent significant political, social, and economic changes throughout this extended period. Adopting socialism confronted traditional values and aggravated state-society conflict. The one-party system that developed under the dominance of SYL and came to fruition during the Sharmarke/Egal regime was reincarnated by the military government, despite having a different philosophy, socialism. The authoritarian rule of Mohamed Siyad Barre's regime continued until it was toppled by various armed oppositions in 1991. In comparing the events after the 1967 leadership transition with the period of the tenure of President Adan, the variance in the political culture of the leadership becomes very cloudless. In particular, the environment of the assassination of President Abdirashid Sharmarke and the peaceful life of President Adan in his firm as a simple citizen showcase the difference.

CRITIQUE OF PRESIDENT ADAN'S NON-CAMPAIGNING IN THE 1967 ELECTION

Some individuals I have met were highly critical of President Adan's decision not to campaign in the 1967 election, particularly as his competitors vigorously promoted their candidacies. His strategic choice raised significant concerns and drew sharp criticism. Critics argued that his failure to participate in the electoral process actively undermined democratic principles and cast doubt on his commitment to fair political competition. By abstaining from campaigning, Adan appeared to disregard the importance of engaging with his supporters, giving his opponents a considerable advantage. This passive approach was perceived as a dereliction of duty, diminishing the legitimacy of the electoral process. Moreover, some critics suggest that President Adan's re-election in 1967 could have averted the military coup that occurred in 1969. They argue that his continued leader-

---

336. Ibid., 159, and Samatar, *Africa's First Democrat*, 204.

155

ship might have provided the political stability necessary to prevent the military from seizing control, addressing underlying tensions that contributed to the coup. However, this remains speculative, as the complex interplay of political, social, and economic factors leading to the 1969 coup require further examination to draw definitive conclusions.

Addressing critiques of President Adan for non-campaigning in 1967, it is a fact that President Adan established his political ethos in 1951, adhering to the principle of never actively campaigning for political positions. The president wrote in his diary: "During all my life, I have never said please elect me, not I will do it now, because the presidency is a post of trust and requires a great deal of responsibility." This approach was rooted in his belief that leadership should be based on merit and service rather than personal promotion. Critics who fault him for not campaigning in 1967 overlook the consistency and integrity of his political philosophy. Adan's stance can be seen as an effort to save Somalia from the pitfalls of intense political competition and potential manipulation. By not engaging in the often contentious and divisive nature of electoral campaigning, he sought to maintain a higher standard of political conduct and focus on the nation's broader needs rather than personal ambition. Furthermore, his approach can be interpreted as an attempt to protect Somalia's fledgling democracy from destabilization. In this light, Adan's reluctance to campaign was not a sign of disengagement but a strategic choice to uphold the stability and integrity of Somalia's political system during a critical period in its history. Additionally, Adan believed that campaigning often entailed engaging in corrupt practices, such as vote-buying and making unrealistic promises in offering political positions in exchange for support. He steadfastly refused to participate in these activities throughout his political career, maintaining a commitment to integrity and ethical governance. Adan's approach reflected his belief that true leadership should be earned through integrity and service, not through the compromises and corruption often associated with electioneering.

In the complex and highly competitive arena of contemporary politics, the effectiveness of abstaining from campaigning is a topic of much debate. Political campaigns have traditionally been the cornerstone of democratic processes, serving as the primary means for candidates to communicate their messages, connect with voters, and differentiate themselves from their opponents. However, the question arises: can a strategy of abstaining from active campaigning be viable in today's political climate? While abstaining from campaigning might have worked in certain historical contexts, it is generally not a viable strategy in today's political environment. The demands of modern media, voter expectations, and the competitive nature of elections necessitate active engagement and visibility. Candidates must carefully weigh the risks and benefits of their campaign strategies, recognizing that abstention could significantly hinder their electoral prospects.

The second critique posits that Adan's re-election could have averted the military coup of 1969. Military takeovers were a common trend in postcolonial African states. By the end of the 1960s, Africa had witnessed many military coups, with 106 successful coups out of at least 242 globally since 1950, highlighting the continent's historical susceptibility to military interventions in politics. At least 45 of the 54 African nations have experienced at least one coup attempt since 1950.[337] Somalia's strategic location at the crossroads of Africa and the Middle East made it a focal point of superpower rivalry during the Cold War, significantly influencing its political and military dynamics. The Soviet Union played a crucial role in shaping Somalia's military capabilities by providing extensive training and support to its armed forces. Given this context, the likelihood of a military takeover in Somalia, with Soviet support, was very high. The coup's timing, however, depended on creating a conducive environment for such a takeover. Therefore, the notion that Adan's re-election could have averted the military coup is not entirely plausible,

337. By The Numbers: Coups in Africa - VOA Special Reports, accessed August 2, 2024, https://projects.voanews.com/african-coups/.

considering the external influences on Somalia and its internal economic, political, and social challenges. While his re-election might have provided some stability, the broader context of superpower rivalry and internal strife suggests that preventing the coup required addressing these deeper issues.

PRESIDENT ADAN'S EFFORTS TO RESCUE SOMALIA FROM COLLAPSE

President Adan led a serene life as a farmer in his Janale firm, remaining largely uninvolved in politics. This peaceful existence continued until 1990, when a pivotal moment drew him into politics. Witnessing the imminent collapse of the Somali state, Adan assumed a leadership role in the Manifesto Group, a collective dedicated to salvaging the nation from turmoil. The Manifesto Group was a coalition of 114 distinguished Somali figures, including intellectuals, professionals, scholars of Islam, prominent clan elders, and former government officials.[338] United by a common cause, they crafted a comprehensive manifesto addressing the country's escalating crisis. This document directly appealed to both the incumbent government, led by Mohamed Siyad Barre, and the armed opposition factions. The group's manifesto underscored the urgent need for dialogue, reconciliation, and reform to halt the descent into chaos and restore stability to Somalia. Adan's involvement with the Manifesto Group marked a significant turning point. He transitioned from a life of agricultural tranquility to active political engagement, driven by a profound duty to his country.

Unfortunately, the urgent appeal of the Manifesto Group fell on deaf ears. Despite their best efforts, the government and the armed opposition ignored the warnings and recommendations outlined in

---

338. The Manifesto formed a committee of distinguished leaders to prepare for a National Reconciliation and Salvation Conference. See the committee names in Mohamed Ingriis, "The Making of 1990 Manifesto: Somalia's Last Chance for State Survival," Northeast African Studies 12, no. 2 (2012): 63–94.

their manifesto.[339] Consequently, the efforts to avert the collapse of the Somali state were unsuccessful. The government's refusal to heed the group's call for dialogue and reform exacerbated the situation, leading to a rapid deterioration of political stability. Simultaneously, the armed opposition remained stubborn, further fueling the conflict. As a result, the country plunged deeper into chaos, culminating in the eventual disintegration of state structures. The collapse of the Somali state in 1991 led to widespread violence, humanitarian crises, and a prolonged period of lawlessness. The inability to avert this disaster marked a tragic chapter in Somalia's history, highlighting the critical need for responsive and inclusive governance.

Following the collapse of the state, President Adan spearheaded the first reconciliation efforts in Djibouti. Accompanying him in this critical endeavor were former Prime Ministers Abdirizak Haji Hussein and Mohamed Ibrahim Egal, as well as the former Speaker of Parliament, Sheikh Mukhtar Mohamed. Despite their collective experience and dedication, the conference yielded unsuccessful results. The deep-seated divisions and ongoing conflict proved too formidable to resolve then. Dismayed by the conditions of the Somali people and its elite culture, the president was hospitalized in Djibouti; President Adan returned to his farm, where he led a quiet life away from the political spotlight. He remained there until he died on June 8, 2007, at Nairobi Hospital. President Adan was laid to rest in the family cemetery in Mogadishu. His funeral was attended by President Abdullahi Yusuf, Prime Minister Ali Mohamed Geedi, the former presidents of Somalia Ali Mahdi Mohamed and Abdulqasim Salad, and numerous dignitaries, reflecting the high regard in which he was held and his lasting impact on Somalia's history. He was honored by naming the Mogadishu International Airport to Adan Abdulle International Airport.

339.

CONCLUSION

The life and leadership style of President Adan Abdulle stands out as a distinctive departure from the prevalent political culture among most Somali political elites. His approach deserves thorough study and consideration, especially for the emerging generation of Somali leaders aspiring to reconstruct the collapsed Somali state based on good governance. President Adan Abdulle's exceptional political values, characterized by his reluctance to seek positions and refraining from campaigning for political power in his long political career, present a unique culture in the modern era. His life story started as an orphan, working various menial jobs, reaching the top level of education during that time, and joining the first nationalist movement, demonstrating his dedication and commitment to excellence. His biography is a testament to a principled and selfless approach to public service, which reflects a commitment to the nation's well-being, prioritizing the people's interests over personal ambition. For the new generation of Somali elites aspiring to rebuild the Somali state, the lessons from President Adan Abdulle's life are invaluable. Emulating his commitment to good governance, selfless service, and a moral leadership philosophy can contribute to developing a more stable and prosperous Somalia. By prioritizing the needs of the people and eschewing the divisive power struggles that have marred the nation's political history, the new Somali leaders can set a positive trajectory for the future.

Six key factors significantly shaped Adan Abdulle's political culture: the experience of growing up as an orphan instilled in him a profound sense of independence and responsibility; his extensive work with Italians gave him a strong work ethic and familiarity with state institutions; and belonging to a clan known for emphasizing individuality shielded him from familial pressures and expectations of government favors. Furthermore, his marriage to a Majeerteen/Darod wife strategically garnered support from politicians of the competing Hawiye and Darod clans; Adan's deep connection to his religious roots, influenced by his father's role as a Quranic teacher and involvement in the Darwish movement, shaped his commitment to values such as decency, fairness, anti-corruption, and adherence to the rule of law; and lastly, his passion for literacy and reading habits contributed to a profound understanding of statehood, institution-building, and a broader worldview. These factors collectively played a pivotal role in shaping Adan Abdulle's unique political culture.

Two years after President Adan's term, the political atmosphere witnessed a lack of commitment to democratic principles. Clan-centric politics prevailed, fostering divisiveness and hindering progress toward national unity. Corruption had become widespread among political elites, prioritizing personal gain over the country's welfare. The absence of good governance practices contributed to growing disillusionment among citizens and educated elites. President Adan's leadership, in this context, stood out as a stark contrast. His commitment to democratic values, reconciliation efforts, and anti-corruption measures set a new standard for ethical governance. The transition from Adan Abdulle to Abdirashid Sharmarke underscored the challenges faced by the nation and highlighted the crucial role of visionary leaders in shaping Somalia's politics. After handing over power to President Abdirashid, Somalia lost democratic credentials due to bad governance practices and began to slide into authoritarianism. The assassination of President Sharmarke, the military coup, the armed opposition, the collapse of the state in 1991, and the civil war are a testament to the worsening elite political culture, which still strives to restore the functioning Somali state.

4

ABDIRIZAK H. HUSSEIN: THE POLITICAL CULTURE OF A REFORMER

"This chap (Abdirizak) has the making of a statesman; I need to nominate him, Prime Minister, at the next occasion. He is full of energy, and he is honest. His weak point is his obstinacy and tendency to demonize his political adversaries."

— **President Adan Abdulle Osman**, Diary notes in 1963.

"I will make an attempt, and if it goes the way I want, very well; otherwise, I will resign and give back the honour and the responsibility invested in me..."

— **Abdirizak H. Hussein** on the occasion of accepting the Premiership.

"Most of the Somali political class were known to be corrupt, inclined only to keep the status quo and resistant to any reforms and innovations, which they feared might undermine their positions. In a contrary of unabashed kleptocrats, the designated Prime Minister shone like a beacon of probity. His opponents saw him as a threat to their dubious business interests and feared that he might undermine them."

— **Mohamed Isse Trunji**, Somali Jurist and historian.

$\mathcal{L}$eaders can be compared to diamonds due to their mul-
tilayered qualities and characteristics.[340] As such, "Leaders are like
diamonds. They are unique and individual. No two are just alike.
They are rare, very valuable, formed under pressure, and are very
strong."[341] Just as diamonds are formed under immense pressure,
leaders often emerge and grow through challenging situations,
demonstrating resilience and strength. These experiences shape
their decision-making abilities and guide their approach to problem-solving. Furthermore, like diamonds, leaders possess a remarkable strength that enables them to face adversity and inspire others—
their brilliance and unique aspects illuminate paths for those they
guide. Moreover, assuming the role of a leader-reformer in a culturally divided society, fragmented by deep-seated clan affiliations
and lacking exposure to modern governance, poses an even more
monumental leadership challenge.[342] In such an environment, entrenched divisions and longstanding allegiances can impede efforts
to unify and modernize society. Moreover, the political landscape,
characterized by self-serving and corrupt politicians prioritizing their
interests over the public's welfare, further complicates the reformer's

340. James G. Clawson, "General Model of Leadership in Organizations: A
Diamond in the Rough," SSRN Electronic Journal, June 2009, accessed April
26, 2024, https://www.researchgate.net/publication/228144633.
341. Ria Story, "Leaders Are Like Diamonds" (Topstoryleadership.com, 2017).
342. Zamokuhle Mbandlwa, "Challenges of African Leadership after the Independence," Solid State Technology, December 2020, accessed April 26, 2024,
https://www.researchgate.net/publication/346972230.

mission, as they must navigate and overcome resistance from those who benefit from the status quo.

Indeed, the reformer must work to bridge cultural divides, promote inclusivity, and foster trust among various factions while introducing progressive policies and ethical governance practices. This delicate balancing act requires exceptional resilience, diplomatic skills, and a commitment to transparency and accountability to lead society toward a brighter future. Yet, some individuals possess the audacity, integrity, and unwavering resolve to confront these formidable obstacles without succumbing to the fear of jeopardizing their political careers. Delving into the history of these exceptional individuals within Somali society while recognizing their inherent shortcomings as humans susceptible to errors is crucial for our people. We elevate them as role models and extract lessons from their triumphs and setbacks. Genuine moral leadership is a rarity, but those nations fortunate enough to be led by such individuals thrive and uphold their dignity. At the same time, those misled by pseudo-leaders face destruction and decline. Recognizing and commemorating the efforts of these exceptional leaders serves as a beacon of hope and inspiration for our nation's present and future.

The success of principled leaders in realizing their goals and aspirations often hinges upon the complex interplay of internal and external political factors. In some instances, these leaders navigate the turbulent waters of their political environment with skill and determination, ultimately achieving significant reforms and leaving a legacy. However, there are occasions when opposing forces thwart principled leaders with divergent agendas, despite their best efforts. Internal factors such as institutional resistance, entrenched interests, and bureaucratic inertia can pose formidable challenges to implementing reforms. Furthermore, the individual's characteristics and leadership style are crucial to success. While some may ultimately succeed in reshaping their societies for the better, others may be sidelined or derailed by competing interests and opposing forces.

During the crucial period of Somali state-building from 1960 to 1967, the nation was graced with a principled president tasked with integrating Somaliland and southern Somalia's regions into a cohesive nation-state. President Adan Abdulle Osman, Prime Minister Abdirashid A. Sharmarke, and Interior Minister Abdirizak forged a solid national identity and built early institutions with a limited drive for reform.[343] However, Somalia witnessed a period of remarkable reform during Abdirizak Haji Hussein's premiership (1964–1967), who exhibited unwavering resolve in his efforts to root out corruption and instill transparency and accountability in government institutions. President Adan Abdulle Osman and Prime Minister Abdirizak advocated for democratic values, principles, and morality. They championed citizens' rights to participate in the political process freely and fairly, laying the groundwork for a more open and democratic society. The leadership culture's principles and values shared by President Adan and Prime Minister Abdirizak during this period in Somali history are a testament to their principled leadership and steadfastness to good governance.

Writing on the biography of Abdirizak Haji Hussein and the deep dive into his political culture was made possible by a meticulous examination of four works: "Africa's First Democrats" authored by Abdi Samatar, "President Adan's Live and Legacy" and " Somalia: Untold History" penned by Mohamed Trunji, and the Political Memoir of Abdirizak Haji Hussein.[344] These foundational works

---

343. During this period, President Adan Abdulle was unsatisfied with the government's reform drive to curb nepotism, corruption, and democratization. However, Abdirizak undertook tangible reforms in his ministerial portfolio in the interior and public work. See the Diary of Adan, who expressed his displeasure with Abdirashid in dealing with growing clannism and forming a large cabinet without considering capacity. Mohamed Trunji, *President Adan Abdulle: His Life & Legacy* (London: Looh Press, 2023), 83, 87.

344. The four primary references of this paper are Abdi Samatar, *Africa's First Democrats: Somalia's Adan A. Osman and Abdirizak H. Hussein* (Bloomington, IN: Indiana University Press, 2016); Mohamed Trunji, *President Adan Abdulle; Mohamed Isse Trunji, Somalia: The Untold History (1941-1967)* (London: Looh Press, 2015) and Abdirizak Haji Hussein, *My Role in the Foundation of*

provided invaluable insights into Abdirizak's life, political culture, and the broader socio-political landscape of Somalia during his tenure. Moreover, while these four works formed the cornerstone of the research, a myriad of supplementary literature further enriched the exploration. Data from scholarly analyses to historical narratives were consulted to paint a comprehensive picture of Abdirizak's multifaceted persona and enduring impact on Somali politics. This inclusive approach ensured a nuanced understanding of Abdirizak's political culture. Through the synthesis of these various perspectives, the biography not only illuminated the personality of Abdirizak but also offered profound insights into the evolution of Somali political history, democracy, governance structures, and the interplay of nationalistic and clannish approaches to politics.

Abdirizak Haji Hussein, who served as Prime Minister of Somalia from 1964 to 1967, is celebrated for his audacious and moral leadership in reshaping state institutions and promoting ethical governance. He spearheaded sweeping reforms to modernize governmental structures and enhance transparency and accountability. His steadfast devotion to moral values and dedication to the well-being of his people earned him widespread praise as an ethical and moral leader.[345] For example, when he left the premiership, he did not have a house to move to and requested to stay in the same house he lived in since he was a member of the parliament and to pay the rent. However, when PM Egal heard about the situation, he was authorized to remain in the house and to retain his private driver.[346] Moreover, Abdirizak abstained from embarking on a pilgrimage funded by the state, and following the military coup, it came to light that his bank

---

the *Somali Nation-State: A Political Memoir,* ed. *Abdisalam Ise-Salwe* (Trenton, NJ: The Red Sea Press, 2017).

345. Mohamed Ibrahim Egal, his political adversary, testified, "The Italians also don't like Abdirizak because he is not corruptible." Samatar, *Africa's First Democrats,* 192.

346. It is worth mentioning that Abdirizak was a vice-chairman of Banco Credito Somalo, which was opened in 1954 by the Italian Trust Administration. He had all the opportunity to use authority to build a house like many other politicians did, but he refrained from that practice. Ibid., 192.

account held a mere $500.[347] Amid political fluidity and continuous tiffs among politicians, he stood as a beacon of integrity, inspiring trust and confidence while fostering a responsive and inclusive governance framework. Prime Minister Abdirizak's political ethos closely resembled and resonated, in most respects, that of President Adan Abdulle Osman. Their governance approach departed from Somalia's self-centered elite political culture, contributing to courageous institutional reform and demand for good governance.[348]

Prime Minister Abdirizak and President Adan distinguished themselves from the prevailing Somali elite political culture by prioritizing the nation's common good over individualistic interests.[349] Their governance emphasized transparency, accountability, and the rule of law, restoring public trust in institutions. By prioritizing the nation's interests, they laid the foundation for development and national unity. Their legacy is evidence of principled moral leadership and good governance, setting a new standard for Somalia's political culture and inspiring hope for a brighter future.

This research examines the governance principles and practices of Prime Minister Abdirizak Haji Hussein over four distinct periods: his tenure as the Secretary General of SYL in 1956, his shift to opposition against the SYL government in 1959, his ministerial duties from 1960 to 1964, his being a Prime Minister from 1964 to 1967, his subsequent opposition role from 1967 to 1969, and beyond. In a fractured state and a harmful elite culture, Abdirizak stands out as one of the few exemplary leaders within Somalia's civilian government. Through an analysis spanning 13 years (1956–1969), the paper aims to uncover the fundamental principles, values, and practices that shaped Abdirizak's political legacy. Hussein's adeptness in navi-

---

347. Ibid., 194, 195. 207.

348. See the definition of good governance in The United Nations Economic and Social Commission for Asia and the Pacific, accessed March 24, 2024, https://www.unescap.org/sites/default/files/good-governance.pdf.

349. Abdurahman Abdullahi, "Somali Elite Political Culture: Conceptions, Structures, and Historical Evolution," Somali Studies: A Peer-Reviewed Academic Journal for Somali Studies 5 (2020): 30–92.

gating challenges with integrity, resilience, and a commitment to the Somali populace provides valuable lessons for those tasked with the nation's reconstruction.

Additionally, this chapter underscores the urgency of breaking from detrimental patterns of political elite culture that have historically impacted Somali politics, leading to state collapse and hindrances to its restoration. Moreover, it delves into the primary factors that shaped Abdirizak's political ethos. Through critically examining Abdirizak's political ethos and its formative influences, the research aims to highlight alternative paths characterized by transparency, accountability, and a sincere dedication to collective welfare. It emphasizes the transformative power of ethical leadership amidst challenging conditions. Drawing from Hussein's legacy, the research seeks to motivate the current and the next generations of Somali leaders to steer their nation toward a more hopeful and prosperous future. In addition to uncovering Abdirizak's political culture, this research explores the historical trajectory of Somali state-building through Abdirizak's biography. It delves into the arduous struggle for independence and the multifaceted challenges Somali nationalists encounter in establishing viable state institutions and fostering a sustainable democratic framework.

A SHORT BIOGRAPHY OF ABDIRIZAK H. HUSSEIN

Abdirizak's origins can be traced back to the settlements of the Nugal region in Puntland, Somalia, where he was born around 1924/25.[350] His father, Haji Hussein Warsame (alias Attosh), held esteemed status as a respected elder within the Mohamud Sulaiman/ Omar Mohamud sub-clan of Reer Hirsi.[351] Known for his wealth

---

350. The exact date of his birth is not specific as the Gregorian calendar was used in the rural areas of Somalia. His birth date is an estimation. Samatar, *Africa's First Democrats*, 29.

351. When Italy took over the Mujeirtain region in 1927, they proposed Haji Hussein to be one of the salaried chiefs. However, he declined and instead proposed to his cousin Aw-Hersi jama Tigey, designated chief of the sub-clan. See Abdirizak, *A Political Memoir*, 7.

and influence, Haji Hussein had three wives and a large family of 17 sons, four nephews, three grandsons (a total of 24), and 13 daughters.[352] The family's prosperity, evidenced by Haji Hussein's ability to undertake the Hajj pilgrimage, placed them among the affluent traditional elites of the region.[353] Abdirizak, born to Haji Hussein's youngest wife, Ambaro Firdhiye, was the seventh among her ten children. However, Abdirizak experienced significant hardship at a young age with the loss of his mother when he was only six years old.[354]

Despite the adversity of losing his mother at a young age, Abdirizak's upbringing was characterized by the resilience and resourcefulness typical of Somali tradition. During his formative years, he worked as a camel boy, a common occupation in nomadic communities where camels are essential to daily life. This experience instilled in him a sense of responsibility and practical skills that would later shape his character and leadership style. Abdirizak's beginnings as a camel boy highlight his journey from modest origins to becoming a significant figure in Somali politics. He was raised amidst the rough landscapes of Puntland, shaping his values of perseverance, hard work, courage, and an uncorrupted way of life. These early experiences laid the foundation for Abdirizak's future leadership, which is characterized by dedication, resilience, and a commitment to serving his fellow Somalis.

At a young age, Abdirizak began his educational journey by attending a Quranic school in the coastal port of Eil. He devoted three years to his studies there, demonstrating remarkable commitment and diligence, and achieved the milestone of memorizing

---

352. Samatar, *Africa's First Democrats*, 29. Also, See Abdirizak, *A Political Memoir*, 12.
353. Abdirizak's father was an elder and wealthy. See the continuance of the leadership between traditional and modern leaders. Abdurahman Abdullahi, *Tribalism, Nationalism, and Islam: The Crisis of Political Loyalty* (master's thesis, Islamic Institute, McGill University, 1992), 73–76.
354. Samatar, *Africa's First Democrats*, 27.

nearly one-third of the Quran.[355] However, tragedy struck when Abdirizak's father passed away, prompting him to seek support from his extended family. He then moved to Galkayo, where one of his sisters lived, and enrolled in an Islamic school, continuing his spiritual enlightenment for three years. Abdirizak remained steadfast in his commitment to education, recognizing its transformative power in shaping his future and empowering him to navigate life's challenges with resilience and determination. Sheikh Mohamed Isse, Abdirizak's instructor at the Islamic school, was highly knowledgeable and well-versed in Islamic scholarship. He often referred to the teachings of the Lebanese scholar Shakib Arsalan, particularly his seminal work in 1930, which addressed "why Muslims lagged while others progressed." These teachings deeply resonated with Abdirizak, influencing his worldview and shaping his approach to leadership. Throughout his life, Abdirizak echoed Sheikh Esa's teachings, emphasizing the importance of self-reflection, critical inquiry, and the pursuit of knowledge. The insights from Shakib Arsalan's work imbued him with purpose and commitment to addressing Muslim communities' challenges.[356]

In 1939, Abdirizak and his brother traveled to Mogadishu to reunite with their elder brother. However, their plans changed when their brother was sent to Nagele town for the Italian war campaign in Ethiopia. He began his early job as a shopkeeper in 1939 and enrolled in an Italian school in Mogadishu, but it was closed after two years due to the war.[357] Abdirizak and his brother bought an old truck and began carrying goods to Ethiopia, but the British forces appropriated their lorry and were never compensated.[358] When he returned to Mogadishu, Abdirizak got a job as a house boy for the Italian

---

355. Ibid., 30

356   Shakib Arslan, "Li-madha ta'akhkhara al-Muslimun wa-li-madha taqaddama ghairuhum" (Cairo, 1930), in *Why Muslims Lagged, and Others Progressed*, trans. Nadeem M. Qureshi (London: Austin Macauley Publishers, 2012).

357. Abdirizak, *A Political Memoir*, 23. *Samatar*, 30–31.

358. Ibid., 23

lady Miss Ballerina, a secretary to the British Lieutenant Colonel Daniel.[359] Lt. Col. Daniel was transferred to Kenya and secured a radio operator job for Abdirizak. He joined a signal squadron in 1943, significantly shifting his life and career. After six months of intensive military training, Abdirizak was deployed to Beledweyne and subsequently participated in military campaigns across several towns, including Wardheer, Bulo-Manyo, Dollow, and Qallafo.[360] In Qallafo, a defining moment occurred when he challenged the oppressive actions of British officer Captain Fitzpatrick, influenced by his growing anti-colonial sentiments.[361] This confrontation led to Abdirizak's imprisonment and subsequent trial in Mogadishu, where he was eventually acquitted. Afterward, continuing his journey, he traveled to Dire Dawa, where he encountered influential figures, deepened his study of Islam under Sheikh Azhari's mentorship, and joined the SYL branch in 1944.[362] Returning to Mogadishu, Abdirizak resumed his service in the signal job, which was reformed to be a civilian institution before being stationed in Iskushuban. He collaborated with Abdirashid Ali Sharmarke to expand the SYL's influence in the Majeerteen region. In 1947, SYL lost one of its prominent founders Yassin Haji Osma in Jawhar from pneumonia at the age of 32 and was replaced by Abdullahi Isse.[363] Transferred to Baidoa in 1948 as postmaster and supervisor of the telegraph office in Boidoa, Abdirizak further solidified his role in the SYL mobilization efforts and shaping Somalia's political landscape.

In 1948, Abdirizak was among the organizers of the SYL demonstration in Mogadishu, which took place amid the presence of the UN Commission.[364] After Italy's UN trusteeship of Somalia in 1950 and

359. Ibid., 27.
360. Ibid., 28–29.
361. British officer Captain Fitzpatrick was a British commissioner in Galkayo, but the people rejected him, which led to his transfer to Qallafo. Abdirizak, *A Political Memoir*, 30. *Samatar*, 33–35.
362. Europa Publications Limited, *The Middle East and North Africa*, vol. *5-17* (London: Europa Publications, 1961), 909.
363. Abdirizak, *A Political Memoir*, 48.
364. Samatar, *Africa's First Democrats*, 44.

SYL opposition, he faced persecution by Italian authorities with a fascist background and was falsely accused of possessing explosives to incite violence while working in Baidoa. He endured imprisonment and torture before being rescued by police inspector Daud Abdulle Hirsi.[365] He was acquitted in Mogadishu general prison and then worked as a clerk for two months in the Michelin Coutts General Trading Company. Abdirizak decided to eliminate Mr. Benerdelli, director of the political department, who was known for his hardline policy against SYL, but failed. In the face of adversity, he remained committed to political activism, establishing a notary public office in Galkayo and continuing his activism with SYL in Galkayo. In 1953, he was offered an interpreter and public relations position in Mogadishu's UN trusteeship committee office of the Egyptian Ambassador Kamalu Addin Salah and moved to Mogadishu.[366]

His dedication to public service became evident when he assumed the role of Galkayo Councilor in 1954, participating in Somalia's inaugural municipal elections. Abdirizak's influence extended beyond local governance. In June 1955, he was entrusted with representing the SYL at the United Nations, replacing SYL Secretary General Abdullahi Isse, who stayed for four years. During his tenure at the UN, he passionately advocated for Somali interests, presenting a petition on behalf of the SYL party. Recognizing his leadership qualities, Abdirizak was elected as the SYL's chairman shortly after that, replacing Adan Abdulle Osman, who was elected the parliament speaker.[367] Abdirizak resigned in 1957 from the chairmanship of SYL due to internal conflicts between the central committee and the government and growing dissatisfaction among the SYL supporters.[368] In 1959, Abdirizak further solidified his political standing

---

365. Ibid.,53.
366. Ibid., 54. Abdirizak, *A Political Memoir*, 96.
367. Ibid., 60. Also, Trunji, *Somalia: the Untold History*, second edition (Looh Press, 2020), 266. The SYL Congress proposed Adan Abulle be the prime minister, but Adan refused and proposed that Abdullahi Isse be elected as the prime minister. See Abdirizak, *A Political Memoir*, 113.
368. Samatar, *Africa's First Democrats*, 63.

by securing a seat as a member of Parliament representing the Nugal District. This marked a significant milestone in his career, providing him with a platform to enact change at the national level. Concurrently, he held prominent positions within educational institutions, serving as president of the Higher Institute of Law and Economics and the Vice President of Banco Credito.[369] This institute was renamed the University College of Somalia, which later became the Somali National University, officially pronounced in 1969.

Following the 1959 election, Abdirizak and fellow SYL members became vocal critics of the Abdullahi Isse government's perceived deficiencies, including a large, clan-balanced cabinet and allegations of electoral manipulation.[370] Abdirizak led opposition efforts, particularly at the United Nations; nonetheless, he shifted his position and advocated national unity as a spokesperson for all Somali political parties who agreed to speak in one voice.[371] He was expelled from SYL with the other twelve oppositions and later reinstated after traditional reconciliation.[372] With the dawn of independence, Hussein's talents were called upon to serve in Prime Minister Abdirashid Ali Sharmarke's government. From 1960 to 1962, he assumed the crucial role of Minister of Interior, responsible for maintaining internal stability, conducting referendum, and security.[373] Subsequently, from 1962 to 1964, Hussein took on the mantle of Minister of Public Works and Communications at his request, contributing to the development

369. Abdirizak, *A Political Memoir*, 116.
370. The opposition was interpreted as Darood members of SYL against Prime Minister Abdullahi Isse's Hawiye-led government. This was a manifestation of growing clan sensitivities to the Hawiye-Darod rivalry. However, not all rebel MPs were Darood, even though most were. Also, without looking into the clan composition of the MPs, the focus must be the legitimacy of their grievance, particularly the 1959 election, which many political parties boycotted. SYL got 83 seats, the Hizbia party got 5, and the Liberal Party got 2 seats. Trunji, *The Told History*, second edition, 316–25.
371. Abdirizak, *A Political Memoir*, 130.
372. Samatar, *Africa's First Democrats*, 75.
373. Abdirizak, *A Political Memoir*, 153.

of Somalia's infrastructure and communication networks.[374] His tenure in these key ministerial positions underscored his commitment to nation-building and his capacity for effective governance. He became Prime Minister from June 14, 1964, to July 15, 1967. He led a sweeping reform and anti-corruption program that alienated many anti-reform politicians and deep state elements. President Adan strongly supported his drive for reform. He retained the premiership position until July 15, 1967, after the presidential election on June 26 and the appointment of Mohamed Ibrahim Egal to the position of Prime minister, who took over the premiership of Somalia.

Following the 1967 election, Abdirizak faced challenges with the administration led by Abdirashid Ali Shermarke, Mohamed Ibrahim Egal, and Interior Minister Yassin Nur Hassan. He subsequently broke away from the SYL party and established the Democratic Action Party (DAP) in the belief that the SYL party under Mohamed Ibrahim Egal had dishonored its original principles. Regrettably, the March 26, 1969 election was tainted by massive fraud, which Prof. Abdalla Mansur characterized as "Democracy gone mad."[375] SYL won 73 of the 123 seats, and the other 27 parties won seats. After the election, all members of Parliament except Abdirizak joined the SYL, a deliberate agenda of the new regime to establish the one-party ruling system like many African states, destroying the culture of democracy.[376] Abdirizak remained the only voice of opposition in the new parliament, symbolizing his strong leadership qualities.[377] Douglas

---

374. Ibid., 157.

375 Abdulla Mansur, "Contrary to a Nation: The Cancer of Somali State," in *The Invention of Somalia*, ed. Ali Jimale (Lawrenceville, NJ: Red Sea Press, 1995), 114.

376. Most of the members of the parliament belonging to the SYL ascertained that the government was planning to eliminate their candidacy from the SYL party and, therefore, established their parties. Moreover, new parliamentary candidates established their parties. Thus, 64 parties participated in the election of 1969.

377. Abdirizak is remembered for saying, "Allah is one, and I am alone." Footnote 5, Abdurahman Baadiyow, "Abdirizak Haji Hussein: The Audacious and Principled Leader," accessed April 26, 2024, https://www.academia.

MacArthur, an American military leader, praised this quality and is quoted as saying, "A true leader has the confidence to stand alone, the courage to make tough decisions."[378] The election's fraudulent mismanagement triggered a series of events, such as the assassination of President Abdirashid A. Shermarke and a subsequent military coup, plunging Somalia into chaos. General Siad Barre's military regime seized power, detaining political elites, accusing them of corruption and tribalism, and instituting authoritarian rule for the next two decades.[379]

Following the 1969 coup d'état in Somalia that toppled the civilian government, Hussein found himself a political prisoner alongside his friends, including President Adan Abdulle, many parliamentarians, and the ministers of the Egal government.[380] He endured detention from 1969 until April 1973. After he was released, he became a farmer until President Mohamed Siyad Barre repeatedly requested that he work with the government and resisted his offer. Fortunately, however, in 1974, the president offered to become Somalia's ambassador to the United Nations, which he hesitantly accepted after consulting many friends who considered this offer a great opportunity.[381] He held this prestigious role until 1979, when he had difficulty working with the regime at the beginning of the armed opposition.[382] He was given

---

edu/116853719/Abdirizak_Haji_Hussein.

378. Douglas McArthur Quotes accessed April 29, 2024, https://www.goodreads.com/quotes/359193-a-true-leader-has-the-confidence-to-stand-alone-the.

379. Mohamed Haji Ingiriis, *The Suicidal State in Somalia: The Rise and Fall of the Siad Barre Regime, 1969–1991* (Lanham, MD: University Press of America, 2016), 68.

380. Ibid.

381. Most consulted friends recommended accepting the president's offer because they feared I might be imprisoned again if I did not take this deal. Abdirizak, *A Political Memoir*, 327–28.

382. Samatar, *Africa's First Democrat*, 209. This was after the Somali opposition established the SDF after the April 9, 1978, aborted of April 9, 1978. The coup was assigned the Majeerteen coup, to which Ambassador Abdiririzak belongs.

political asylum status and American citizenship. After resigning from the ambassadorial position, his first job was as a security guard in a factory in New York, which he qualified for because of his early military background and with the recommendation of his friend and neighbor who was vacating the position.[383] After a few months, with the help of his medical doctor and old friend Dr. Kevin M. Cahill, he got a job in the New York State Department of Health Management as an assistant to the project manager, and later in the Department of Housing and Community Service.[384] After the collapse of the state in 1991 and throughout the turbulent years of the Somali civil war, Abdirizak was among the elder Somali statesmen led by former President Adan Abdulle to mediate peace and reconciliation in the first Djibouti conference of 1991.[385] Also, Abdirizak was among the civil society groups participating in a warlord-driven, IGAD-sponsored conference masterminded by Ethiopia in Kenya to replace the outcome of the civil society-driven conference in Djibouti in 2000.[386]

In a notable development on May 6, 2001, the Transitional National Government (TNG) sought to establish the National Commission for Reconciliation and Property Settlement (NCRPS), a crucial initiative to foster peace and resolve property disputes. However, the appointment of Abdirizak Haji Hussein as its chief

---

383. Abdirizak, *A Political Memoir*, 334–38.

384. Dr. Cahill was an Irish American, a well-known tropical disease specialist who had been very aware of Somalia since his arrival in 1962. Kate, the wife of Dr. Cavin, suggested that Abdirizak write his memoir and helped him with the initial skeleton framework of this memoir. Abdirizak, *A Political Memoir*, 338–39.

385. The initial effort towards Somali national reconciliation occurred at a Djibouti conference held from June 5 to 11, 1991 (Djibouti I). Four factions participated in the event. Mohamed Osman Omar, *Somalia: A Nation Driven to Despair: A Case of Leadership Failure* (Mogadishu: Somali Publications, 2002), 1.

386. Former Prime Minister Abdirizak participated in the Eldoret Somali conference. He asserted that "the conference is being manipulated by external interests." See International Crisis Group, "Salvaging Somalia's Chance for Peace," December 9, 2002, 6.

faced opposition from the Somalia Reconciliation and Restoration Council (SRRC) and the leadership of Puntland Abdullahi Yusuf.[387] Faced with mounting challenges, he decided to resign from the post on July 25, 2001. Abdirizak was always active in Somali community engagements and conferences in Minnesota, United States, sharing his experiences. Abdirizak H. Hussein died of pneumonia on January 31, 2014 in Minneapolis, Minnesota, after being hospitalized for a week.[388] On February 7, 2014, Somalia bid farewell to a towering figure in its history, Abdirizak Haji Hussein, as he was laid to rest in a solemn memorial service at Mogadishu. His final resting place, beside his friend and former President Aden Abdulle Osman, symbolizes his commitment to national unity and rejection of clan-based divisions. Despite family requests for a clan-focused burial, he chose this site during his life to be remembered as a national figure, making a powerful statement against clannism and reinforcing his dedication to unity and inclusiveness. The funereal occasion brought together dignitaries, politicians, and ordinary citizens to pay their respects to a man whose legacy transcended political divides. Abdirizak's contributions to the nation, spanning decades of service and sacrifice, were commemorated with heartfelt tributes and prayers for his eternal peace.[389]

THE EVOLUTION OF SYL AND ITS GOVERNANCE CULTURE

During the tumultuous aftermath of the collapse of the centralized states of Ajuran and Adal Imamates in the seventeenth century, the Somali people were fragmented across the Horn of Africa, residing

---

387. Report of the Secretary-General on the situation in Somalia, United Nations' S/2001/963, accessed April 29, 2024, Distr.: General 11 October 2001. Also, Hussein Omar, "Somalia: Former Somali Prime Minister Abdirizak Haji Hussein died in the USA," Raxanreeb, accessed April 29, 2024, https://en.wikipedia.org/wiki/Abdirizak_Haji_Hussein.
388. Euan Kerr, "Former Somali Prime Minister Abdirizak Haji Hussein dies," MPR News, February 1, 2014. It is worth observing that Abdirizak died from the same illness, pneumonia, of which Yassin Haji Osman died in 1947.
389. "Former Somali Prime Minister laid to rest in a Mogadishu Cemetery," Horseed Media, accessed April 29, 2024.

within small city-states and clan-based mini-states.[390] This era of internal fragmentation and weakness of the Somali nation coincided with European ascendancy, marked by their expansion and domination.[391] Strategically positioned in the Horn of Africa, Somalia became a target for various foreign powers. It fell under the sway of colonial rule, with Britain, Italy, France, and neighboring Ethiopia all asserting control over different parts of the Somali territory. Scholar of Islam spearheaded the initial resistance against colonial encroachment. However, by 1927, this anti-colonial resistance had been suppressed, plunging Somalia into a leadership vacuum.[392] Somali people suffered fifteen years of disorientation when traditional leaders were suppressed, and new leaders did not emerge. A rejuvenated sense of national identity appeared in 1943, introducing a non-clan, non-religious youth organization with political consciousness. This organization was symbolized by the emergence of the Somali Youth Club (SYC), which marked a critical moment in Somali history. It galvanized people towards a unified cause of unity, freedom, and independence. By April 1947, this movement had evolved into a formal political party, laying the groundwork for a more organized and peaceful resistance against colonial domination.[393]

A pivotal characteristic of SYL lies in the absence of an overarching leader deemed indispensable. For instance, the party's inaugural chairman, Abdulkadir Sakhau Addin, departed from the party's ranks early on. At the same time, its first secretary-general, Yassin Haji Osman Kenidid, passed away in 1947, and his deputy Abdullahi

---

390. Abdurahman Abdullahi, *Making Sense of Somali History*, vol. I (London: Adonis & Abbey, 2017), 119.

391. When Somalia had strong states during the rule of Ajuran Imamate and Adal Sultanate, its people defended themselves from Portuguese and Ethiopian invasions. Ibid., 59.

392. Ibid., 122.

393. Ibid.,123. A. Mohamoud, *State Collapse and Post-Conflict Development in Africa: The Case of Somalia (1960-2001)*, 2002, 71–74, accessed April 29, 2024, https://pure.uva.nl/ws/files/1061731/48811_UBA002000838_10.pdf. Cederic Barnes, "The Somali Youth League, Ethiopian Somalis, and the Greater Somalia Idea, c.1946–48," Journal of Eastern African Studies 1, no. 2 (2007): 277–91.

Isse took the position of the secretary-general of the party. The remaining thirteen founding members continued with the party and did not play any significant role during the struggle for independence or after the establishment of the Somali state.[394] The longest-serving chairman and a founding member, Haji Mohamed Hussein (1947–1951), was expelled from the party when he was accused of violating the party's policy in 1957 by advocating revolutionary ideas and leftist ideology. This led to the creation of a new party under the leadership of Haji Mohamed Hussein named the Great Somali League (GSL) on July 24, 1958.[395] The secretary general of the GSL was Yusuf Osman Samatar (Barda'ad), a well-known indoctrinated by the Italian Communist Party during his study in Italy and linked with the Soviet Union.[396] The GSL enjoyed the support of the Soviet Union, and its members were given privileged scholarships to the Soviet Union universities in preparation for the future leaders of Somalia.[397] Moreover, a significant event in SYL's history occurred in 1959, when thirteen senior members of SYL were expelled from the party due to their opposition to the SYL government.[398] However, a

394. Apart from Haji Mohamed Hussein and Yassin Haji Osman, the remaining eleven founding members of SYC did not significantly contribute to the party's endeavors. See Trunji, *Somalia: The Untold History*, 15–16.
395. The GSL party was split into two factions in November 1960 when Haji Mohamed unliterally declared socialism ideology after returning from China. The party's conservative wing renounced this tendency and was divided. As a political tactician, Haji Mohamed formed a new party, the Somali Democratic Union (SDU), getting elected from Marca in 1946 and losing in 1969. See Mohamed Trunji, *Somalia: the Untold History*, 302–306.
396. Abdirizak, *A Political Memoir*, 125.
397. The policy of offering scholarships to followers of the GSL was evident in the 1960s; about 500 Somali students were studying in the Soviet Union (45 percent) compared to all other scholarships in Western and Arab countries, totaling 645 scholarships. See Abdurahman Abdullahi (Baadiyow), *The Islamic Movement in Somalia: A Study of Islah Movement (1950-2000)* (Adonis and Abbey 2015), 145.
398. Names of the 13 senior members of SYL expelled from the SYL were: Abdirashid Ali Sharmarke, Dahir Nur Igal, Haji Muse Boqor, Haji Muse Samatar, Haji Said Muse Osman, Ibrahim Haji Muse, Yassin Nur Hassan, Mohamed Ossoble Adde, Nour Haji Alas, Sugule Mohamed. Osman Mohamud Adde

spirit of reconciliation and conflict resolution rooted in the Somali culture prevailed, leading to the reinstatement of these members into the party. Despite the regular occurrence of dissent within the SYL and the establishment of alternative political parties, the innate ability of Somali culture to facilitate dialogue and consensus-building was instrumental in fostering unity within the SYL ranks.

The annual SYL congresses since its inception, the central committee's one-year term, and the election of the party's office holders, including the chairman, were evidence of the party's internal democracy. Even though the annual rejuvenation of the central committee looks like a prelude to instability, it unified the party and caused its continuity. These annual congresses offered fresh leadership in the new political environment. This pattern of leadership turnover within SYL underscores its devotion to institutional resilience and collective decision-making rather than relying on singular figures. In the thirteen years since its foundation, from 1947 to 1960, SYL had elected seven chairmen and five secretary generals. Additionally, in 1960, the by-law of SYL was changed, abolishing the chairmanship position, and the secretary general position remained. Four secretary generals were elected over eight years (1960–1968).[399] The absence of a dominant leader allowed for a more dynamic and inclusive political environment where no individual held an irreplaceable position of power. Instead, leadership transitions were navigated through democratic processes and the collective will of the party's members.

July 1, 1960, marks a significant milestone in Somali history. It heralded the birth of the Somali Republic, emerging proudly as the fifth independent state among seventeen African states to gain in-

---

obtained from the voting. See Mohamed Trunji, Somalia: the Untold History, 347, as quoted from the Corriere Della Sera, Agosto 2, 1959. It is interesting to observe that no.13 was used as the incarnation of the image of the early founders of SYL. See Abdirizak, a Political memoir, 127.
399. See appendix I, List of SYL Central Committee, Trunji, President Adan Abdulle, 199-209.

dependence in 1960.[400] This momentous occasion culminated in a nationalist struggle that saw the Somaliland protectorate and Italian Somalia union. With the dawn of independence, the Somali people embraced a new era of self-determination and sovereignty. The unified parliament elected Jama Abdullahi Galib from Somaliland as the speaker.[401] Moreover, former parliament speaker Adan Abdulle was elected unopposed as the interim president of the Somali Republic. The adopted system of governance was a parliamentary system. As such, the president appointed Abdurashid Ali Sharmarke as the Republic's first prime minister on July 12, 1960. Abdirashid Ali Sharmarke played a significant role in the early years of Somalia's independence. He was born on June 16, 1919, in Harardhere, in the central Mudug region of Somalia. He pursued higher education and earned a degree in Political Science from the Sapienza University of Rome. Tragically, Sharmarke's life and presidency were cut short when he was assassinated on October 15, 1969.

The first government that was formed brought forth figures of notable importance. It was a national unity government, which President Adan called for since the first government in 1956 but was rejected by the central committee of the SYL. The new national government included most prominent politicians like Mohamed Ibrahim Egal (former premier of Somaliland), Abdullahi Isse (former PM of the pre-independent administration of Somalia), and Sheikh Ali Jimale, a former minister, and Abdirizak Haji Hussein, former chairman of SYL. The prime minister's slogan was, "I prefer to have

---

400. William Henry Chamberlin, "Africa's Year," January 5, 1960, accessed via ProQuest. Paul Hoffmann, "Bunche says '60 is the Year of Africa," New York Times, February 16, 1960, accessed via ProQuest. Manuel Manrique Gil, "1960–2010: 50 Years of 'African Independences,'" On Africa, January 4, 2010.
401. Jama Mohamed Galib from the SNL party was elected speaker of the unified parliament on July 7, 1960. His election automatically blocked Mohamed Ibrahim Egal from being the prime minister since the speaker was from Somaliland. The two positions could not go to the northerners or even to the same city of Berbera. See Ruth Gordon, "Growing Constitutions," University of Pennsylvania Journal of Constitutional Law 1 (1999): 528-69, accessed April 29, 2024, https://scholarship.law.upenn.edu/jcl/vol1/iss3/3.

a divided government rather than a divided nation."[402] Abdirizak was initially entrusted with the role of Interior Minister from 1960 to 1962 and the portfolio of Minister of Public Works and Communication from 1962 to 64 until the 1964 elections, after which he became the second Prime Minister from 1964 to 1967.

Throughout its history, the Somali Youth League (SYL) witnessed significant shifts in its composition and direction, reflecting the dynamic nature of Somalia's political landscape. As the political environment evolved, senior members of the SYL occasionally found themselves at odds with the party's discipline and core policies, leading to resignations or expulsions. This phenomenon underscored the challenges of maintaining cohesion within the party. One notable instance occurred in 1959 when thirteen SYL stalwarts were expelled from the party and reinstituted again. Moreover, in 1962, when eleven senior members of SYL led by Sheikh Ali Jimale resigned from SYL and established their new party, the Somali National Congress (SNC), mainly allying with the SNL group led by Mohamed Ibrahim Egal.[403] In 1964, during the first Abdirizak government, thirty-three SYL PMs voted against the government, and four abstained, including Secretary General Yassin Nur Hassan. As a result, the Central Committee decided to take disciplinary action against four members and expelled them from the party.[404] Moreover, in 1966, another pivotal moment unfolded when

---

402. Abdirizak, *A Political Memoir*, 149.

403. These MPs were Sheikh Ali Jumale, Salad Elmi Dhurwa, Abdullahi Hussein Major, Mohamed Osoble Adde, Mohamed Abdulle Assir, Haji Abdio Ebrow, Haji Abdisamad Moalim Ali, Osman Ahd Roble, Hassan Ali, Ali Isse Ali, and Abdullahi Amin. This was perceived as an Irir coalition against advocated government domination by the Darood clan families. IRIR consisted of Hawiye and Dir, occasionally used by politicians to challenge Darood politicians. Trunji, *The Told History*, second edition, 417.

404. The four expelled from the SYL were Secretary General Yassin Nur Hassan, Sheikh Mukhtar Mohamed, Abdullahi Mohamed Qablan, and Abdi Hassan Boni. This undertaking was similar to the expulsion of the thirteen senior SYL members from the SYL in 1959. See Trunji, *Untold History*, second edition, 483.

a group of thirteen senior SYL members was expelled for voting against the SYL government-proposed laws in the parliament led by Abdirizak Haji Hussein.[405] Despite their expulsion, they were later reinstated, underscoring the fluid nature of alliances and loyalties within the party. Furthermore, in a significant development, senior members led by Abdirizak Haji Hussein chose to resign from SYL altogether in 1968, forming the Democratic Action Party (DAP). This fragmentation within SYL highlighted underlying tensions and differing visions for Somalia's political culture. Amidst these departures and expulsions, the party's instability became apparent, reflecting a political culture driven by self-interest and personal agendas. To compensate for these losses, SYL routinely admitted new members, some without a history of the party's earlier struggles, reshaping its identity and priorities and diluting the original principles of the SYL.

The experience of the SYL's persistent internal divisions teaches us that when opposition parties are weak, and their challenges to the ruling party are minimal, it often leads to internal strife within the dominant party. Without a solid external challenge to unite against, the party can turn inwards, and competing interests and personal ambitions among its members can lead to fragmentation and disputes. This situation highlights the importance of a vibrant and competitive political landscape for the health of any party. When a ruling party faces little pressure from outside forces, there is less incentive for more cohesion and unity within its ranks. Consequently, factions may emerge, each pursuing its agenda rather than working towards a common goal.

Before the Somali independence in 1960, it was imperative to comprehend and distinguish between two phases of the SYL party's role and attributes: a nationalist movement and a ruling party post-

---

405. These members were Haji Muse Boqor, Haji Muse Samatar, Osman Mohamud Adde, Ismael Dualeh, Ahmed Mohamed "Alora," Awil Haji Abdullahi, Abdullahi Mohmed Qablan, Mohamed Ahmed Haji Salah, Yassin Nur Hassan, Ahmed Gure Mumin, Ahmed Abdi Jibril, Islow Nur Osman, and Ali Aliow Mohamed. Trunji, *The Untold History*, second edition, 497.

1956. As a fervent nationalist movement, the overarching objective is the liberation of the homeland, the unification of its people, and the active engagement of all sectors in the collective struggle for freedom and self-determination. They aimed to mobilize every segment of society, instilling a deep sense of patriotism and solidarity and galvanizing the nation toward a brighter future. However, amidst the movement's noble aspirations during the ruling period, it was confronted with the harsh realities of governance. The dynamics of power politics come to the forefront, overshadowing the pure ideals of nationalism. Interests diverge, factions form, and the temptation to prioritize personal or group gains over the broader national interest can be all too seductive.[406]

During this transition from movement to the ruling party, SYL embarked on democratization characterized by disputes and conflicts, unknown election practices, and institution-building amidst challenges such as limited educational level and prevalent political clannism. Abdirizak emerged as a prominent figure within SYL ranks, characterized by his unwavering commitment to the party's founding principles of meritocracy and the equitable treatment of all citizens. His stubborn adherence to these ideals exemplified his steadfast stance on matters he deemed morally and ethically incorrect, such as his resignation from the chairmanship of SYL in 1957 and opposing the 1959 Abdullahi Isse government for Abdirizak and his opposition group of their romantic view considered in the breach of the SYL principles.[407] His leadership underscored the importance of integrity and adherence to foundational values, steering SYL through periods of change and uncertainty.

The history of SYL can be delineated into three distinct phases: its origins as a nationalist movement (1943–1956), its tenure as a ruling party (1956–1967), and finally, under Prime Minister Mohamed

---

406. Abdirizak, *A Political Memoir*, 114–15.
407. As they claimed, the issues they raised included clan-balancing the members of the council of ministers by offering equal numbers to the three major southern clans: Hawiye, Darood, and Digl & Mirifle.

Ibrahim Egal's leadership, joined the SYL in 1966 for personal pow-er-seeking and pursued the establishment of a one-party author-itarian system akin to many post-independence African states.[408] However, SYL's trajectory was abruptly altered by the assassination of President Abdirashid Ali Sharmarke and the subsequent 1969 military coup, which marked the demise of the nationalist party after twenty-two years of existence. The final demise of the SYL and its failure to transform, even in the Diaspora or as an underground party, demonstrate its fragility. This event symbolized a turning point in Somali politics, reshaping the country's trajectory and leaving a legacy of political turbulence and uncertainty.

Comparing the ideals and challenges the Somali Youth League (SYL) faced with its founders' educational and economic capac-ities and subsequent Somali elites, their achievements can only be described as nothing short of miraculous. The SYL founders operated within an environment of limited resources and education, yet they succeeded in inspiring a movement that fundamentally transformed Somalia. Their vision of "Somaliness" promoted national identity and unity, striving to unify all Somalis under a single banner. The SYL fought tirelessly to unify Somalia's British and Italian territo-ries, ultimately establishing an independent Somali state. Imagining Somalia's history without the emergence of the SYL underscores the profound impact of their efforts. Without their advocacy for Somali unity and independence, the nation might have remained fragment-ed and under foreign control for much longer. The legacy of the SYL highlights the power of determined leadership and collective action in overcoming seemingly insurmountable challenges to achieve national sovereignty and cohesion. Abdirizak H. Hussein describes SYL as "God's gift to the Somali people. Instead of thanking God for the glorious gift, the Somali people had elected a wayward path- like the Israelites in Sinai- and returned to their old ways of clannishness and sectarianism."[409]

---

408. Abdullahi, *Making Sense of Somali History*, 174. Also, Samatar, *Africa's First Democrats*, 200–201.
409. Abdirizak, *A Political Memoir*, 377.

However, it is equally important to critically examine the limitations and shortcomings of the Somali Youth League (SYL) and subsequent leaders. While their achievements were monumental, their governance also had significant flaws that ultimately contributed to the distortion of democratic values and led to the military takeover. Acknowledging these historical limitations allows a more balanced understanding of Somalia's political history. It moves beyond glorifying past achievements and fosters a culture of accountability and continuous improvement. By learning from the past, Somalia can better navigate its current political landscape and work towards a more stable and democratic future.

ABDIRIZAK HAJI HUSSEIN'S POLITICAL CULTURE

Abdirizak's leadership style can be aptly described as transactional and principled, influenced by his military training background, emphasizing exchanges of value and negotiation to achieve desired outcomes. In a transactional leadership approach, leaders focus on the give-and-take aspect of interactions, offering rewards or incentives in exchange for compliance or performance. Abdirizak is known for his pragmatic approach to leadership, prioritizing tangible results and efficiency in decision-making. Abdi Samatar argues that Prime Minister Abdirizak's political leadership and the subsequent evolution of his political culture were deeply influenced by four distinct qualities: "a resolute determination to secure a livelihood, extraordinary self-discipline, hard work, and courage."[410] Samatar highlights how these traits formed the foundation of Hussein's childhood in the colonial service and during the national movement. They guided his governance style, inspiring hope, fostering unity, and driving the nation toward progress. The analysis of Abdirizak H. Hussein's political culture encompasses pivotal moments in his career, starting from his tenure as the Somali Youth League (SYL) chairman in 1956. Moreover, he played an opposition role during the Abdullahi Isse government in 1959. Furthermore, upon his ap-

---

410. Samatar, *Africa's First Democrats*, 29.

pointment as a minister from 1960 to 1964, and subsequently as prime minister from 1964 to 1967, Abdirizak H. Hussein wielded substantial influence in shaping national policies and agendas in critical issues such as clannism, corruption, and mismanagement. Even during his time in opposition within the 1969 parliament, Abdirizak continued to champion his principles and advocate for the interests of the Somali people, demonstrating a dedication to democratic principles and good governance.

The Political Culture of Abdirizak as the Chairman of SYL

During Abdirizak's tenure as chairman of the Somali Youth League (SYL) from 1956 to 1957, several significant issues emerged that shaped the political landscape of the time. Among these challenges was the unresolved border delineation with Ethiopia, the assassination of Kamaludiin Salah, the Egyptian Ambassador with whom Abdirizak worked with him, and Minister Muse Boqor's appointment of his cousin Haji Muse Samatar as the central prison director without the Council's approval.[411] Moreover, allegations of widespread nepotism in the ministries tarnished the SYL's reputation as a nationalist party. Furthermore, reciprocal accusations of nepotism among ministers deepened divisions within the central committee of the SYL and the government.[412] Due to the failure to address these internal rifts by the government and the central committee of the SYL amidst growing discontent among the SYL supporters, Abdirizak took the decisive step of resigning from both the chairmanship of the SYL and the central committee.[413] Abdirizak's resignation from the chairmanship of the SYL ruling party manifests his profound frustration with both the government and the SYL's internal dynamics. He discerned early signs of decay and the gradual erosion of the party's foundational values and principles. At the heart of his concerns lay the troubling emergence of clan-based politics, a phenomenon that ran counter to the lofty ideals

---

411. Ibid., 61.
412. Abdirizak, *A Political Memoir*, 115–16.
413. Ibid., 116.

upon which the party was founded. Abdirizak's actions emphasized a commitment to principle over power and a refusal to compromise on the principles of integrity, unity, and the rule of law.

The Political Culture of Abdirizak as a Member of the Opposition

From 1957 to 1960, the SYL encountered a series of three crises caused by senior party members despite contravention of the established policies and principles. The first crisis stemmed from internal discord among cabinet members between Abdullahi Isse and Haji Muse Boqor, the interior minister. The second crisis emerged within the SYL leadership, leading to the expulsion of the chairman of the party Haji Mohamed Hussein.[414] The third crisis revolved around the contentious issue of electoral deadlines and performance, pitting the SYL against opposition forces in a battle for political legitimacy.[415] The third crisis caused Prime Minister Abdullahi Isse's conflicts with the senior party members on several issues. Abdirizak was among 13 senior members of the SYL who initially expressed dissatisfaction with the new council of ministers. These SYL stalwarts criticized the government on three issues: the mismanagement of the 1959 election and irregularities, the composition of the clan-balanced Council of Ministers, and the number and qualifications of ministers. "The Flaudelent condition under which the election was held caused the UN Advisory Council to challenge both the legality of the electoral procedure and the legitimacy of the electoral results."[416] However, the Italian administrator Marion DeStefano supported the SYL position.

This further fuelled discontent among the senior SYL group, who feared incompetence and nepotism would compromise the government's capacity to address pressing national challenges. The overwhelming majority of this dissident group belonged to the Darood

---

414. Trunji, *The Untold History*, 286.
415. Ibid., 316–26.
416. Okbahazi Yohannes, *The United States and the Horn of Africa: An Analytical Study of Patterns and Process* (Routledge 1997), 24.

clan family, and their opposition was interpreted as opposition related to the Hawiye-Darood political row.[417] Nonetheless, we must not be disillusioned and always remember that clan rhetoric and mobilization are part of Somali elite political culture and are just instruments for political objectives. They have nothing to do with clan interest, which is the interest of all citizens in acquiring equitable public service and security, development, and independent and effective justice. Analyzing this and any other opposition, we should avoid clan interpretation and consider the issues under discussion, not the clan belonging to those who raise the issue. Each side of the political competitors typically accuses the other side of clannism. However, this argument does not mean denying the existence of clan factors in Somali politics.

As tensions within the SYL reached a boiling point, the central committee expelled the 13 senior members from the party, signaling a rupture in party unity and solidarity along clan lines.[418] However, in a remarkable turn of events, the dissenting faction led by Abdirizak changed their minds upon realizing the potential harm their actions could inflict on Somalia's interests.[419] Recognizing the need to prioritize national unity above personal grievances, the delegation led by Abdirizak at the UN trusteeship administration in New York abstained from further critique of the government. Upon their return to Mogadishu, the group was reinstated within the party fold through mediation and dialogue.[420] Abdirizak's prominent role as the opposition's spokesperson before the Trusteeship Council in New York is a testament to his commitment to patriotism and adherence to the SYL's core principles. A steadfast dedication to the SYL principle lies at the heart of his dignified position. By advocat-

---

417. The conflict between PM Abdullahi Isse and Muse Boqor, the interior minister, was resolved through reconciliation within the party apparatus. See Mohamed Trunji, *Somalia: the Untold Story*, second edition, 286–87. Regarding the expulsion of the Haji Mohamed Hussein from the SYL, see Ibid., 300.
418. Abdirizak, *A Political Memoir*, 127.
419. Trunji, *President Adan Abdulle*, 66.
420. Ibid., 347–48.

ing for a governance model based on meritocracy and inclusivity rather than clan affiliation, he sought to chart a course toward a more equitable and harmonious society.

The Political Culture of Abdirizak as a Minister (1960–1964)

Abdirizak's appointment to the executive position of the Ministry of the Interior of the newly unified government of the Somali Republic offered him an opportunity to exercise his governance culture. The president and the prime minister gave him their trust, knowing his audacity, sincerity, and commitment to the ideals of national unity. Under this ministry comes the police force, governors, and district commissioners. Thus, he was entrusted with internal security and administration of regions and districts. However, the ministry faced multiple challenges, such as harmonizing two disparate administrative systems (British and Italian) into a cohesive whole. Bridging the divide between divergent approaches and practices of the two systems (the Italian and British) incorporated demanded prudence and audacity. Moreover, Abdirizak administered a critical juncture in the nation's history by implementing the referendum on the Constitution held in Somalia on June 20, 1961 and dealing with security issues during and after this great event.[421] Furthermore, the ministry dealt with security after the officers' aborted coup in Hargeisa, which casts uncertainty over the nation's stability and unity.[422] Compounding these challenges was the security crisis in Hiiran following the dismissal of Sheikh Ali Jimale from the ministry on November 30, 1962.[423] Abdirizak personally confronted these crises, implementing measures to restore order and bolster confidence in the government's ability to uphold security. Abdirizak exhibited steadfast leadership during his visit to the northern regions and dedication to the nation's

---

421. The total number of votes cast during the referendum was 1,948,343, of which 1,756 216 voted yes and 183,000 voted no. While the spoiled ballots were 9,132. Trunji, *The Untold History*, 389.

422. Trunji, *President Adan Abdulle*, 83–84.

423. Abdirizak, *A Political Memoir*,141–43. Also, Samatar, *Africa's First Democrats*, 109.

welfare throughout his tenure.[424] His vision for a united and secure Somalia drove him to confront adversity with resilience and resolve, leaving an unforgettable mark on the fabric of the nation's history.

The dynamic and intriguing nature of Somali political culture was revealed strikingly through the actions of certain government members. Notably, figures such as Mohamed Ibrahim Egal, the Minister of Defense, and Sheikh Ali Jimale, holding the portfolio of Health and Labor, found themselves at the forefront of the opposition during the constitutional referendum. Despite their official roles within the government, Egal and Jimale boldly opposed the proposed Constitution.[425] The referendum was hailed as a beacon of democracy, with most Somali citizens exercising their right to vote fairly and freely. However, the picture could have been more rosy, as reports of irregularities in a few districts, most notably Adan Yabal and Wanlawayn in the South, surfaced.[426] These isolated incidents marred an otherwise commendable display of civic engagement. Despite the support for the constitution, pockets of resistance emerged, notably in regions such as Hiiran and the central area of Somaliland. The influence wielded by Sheikh Ali Jimale and Mohamed Ibrahim Egal and their supporters proved formidable in their constituencies. Indeed, Egal's and Jimale's motivations were clear: to undermine the government's authority and discredit its leadership, all in preparation for the forthcoming presidential election on July 6, 1961, in which Sheikh Ali Jimale intended to be a presidential candidate. Abdirizak's strict measures to ensure that governors and employees of the ministry should play a neutral and non-political role during and after the referendum were acknowledged and praised.

Following his tenure at the Ministry of the Interior, Abdirizak was entrusted with the Ministry of Public Works in 1962 following a reshuffling of the Council of Ministers. Armed with the experience garnered during his two-year stewardship in the interior ministry, he

---

424. Ibid., 132 and 109.
425. Abdirizak, *A Political Memoir*, 141–44.
426. Ibid., 143.

began revitalizing the Somali Republic's infrastructure. Abdirizak spent little time initiating a comprehensive overhaul of the ministry and addressing rampant corruption within the public works sector. Moreover, he renegotiated projects with the USSR, forging mutually beneficial agreements that bolstered bilateral relations and optimized resource allocation for national development priorities.[427] Furthermore, Abdirizak recognized the strategic importance of a robust transportation network in driving economic growth and facilitating social cohesion. In pursuit of this vision, he spearheaded the establishment of Somali Airlines, the nation's flagship carrier.[428] By providing reliable air connectivity across domestic and international routes, Somali Airlines not only enhanced accessibility but also showcased the country's commitment to modernization and progress on the global stage.

Abdirizak confronted a disheartening reality at the Ministry of Public Works: a culture of lax discipline and rampant corruption. Employees came and went as they pleased, breaking any semblance of accountability or work ethic. The scourge of corruption loomed large, with reports of theft and illicit sale of construction materials by warehouse keepers tarnishing the ministry's reputation. Compounding these challenges were the numerous development projects administered by the ministry, primarily funded by the USSR. Despite the support extended by their Soviet partners, complaints regarding the Somali counterparts' low capacity and inefficiency reverberated through diplomatic channels. It was clear that decisive action was needed to salvage the ministry's credibility and restore confidence in its ability to deliver on its mandates. Minister Abdirizak embarked on a mission to instil a culture of discipline and ethical work habits in the ministry. Recognizing that meaningful change required a top-down approach, he led by example, setting stringent standards for employee conduct and performance. Those lacking in loyalty to

---

427. Ibid., 161–65.
428. Ibid., 165–69. Samatar, *Africa's First Democrats*, 133–35.

the ministry's objectives were swiftly transferred, ensuring that only individuals dedicated to the cause remained within the ministry.

Furthermore, Abdirizak implemented comprehensive reforms to bolster transparency and accountability across all facets of ministry operations. Robust oversight mechanisms were put in place to prevent the misappropriation of resources and ensure that development projects proceeded with utmost integrity and efficiency. By fostering a culture of ethical conduct and stewardship, he sought to rebuild trust internally among staff and externally with key stakeholders, including the USSR. Through his unwavering determination and decisive leadership, Abdirizak succeeded in effecting a remarkable transformation within the ministry. Gone were the days of impunity and disregard for the rule of law, replaced instead by a renewed sense of purpose and dedication to serving the interests of the Somali people. Under his guidance, the ministry emerged stronger and more resilient, poised to fulfill its mandate of driving sustainable development and progress across the nation.

Abdirizak's commitment to meritocracy shone brightly through his ambitious initiative to establish Somali Airlines. When the USA generously offered three Dakota planes, he saw an opportunity to propel his vision forward. However, the offer came with a caveat— the technical staff and pilots' training were withheld. Undeterred, Abdirizak sought assistance from West Germany, which agreed to provide the necessary training and set stringent participation criteria. West Germany's conditions were clear: prospective candidates had to possess secondary school certificates and have a proficient command of English. This posed a significant challenge, particularly in a nation divided linguistically. In the North, where English was the medium of education, candidates fared well in meeting these criteria. Conversely, in the South, where Italians held official status, the pool of eligible candidates was limited.

The outcome of the selection process highlighted the stark divide: most successful candidates hail from the Northern region. This was not due to favoritism but rather a reflection of the educational landscape. Abdirizak's adherence to meritocracy and avoidance of clan-balancing were blatant throughout this endeavor, as he remained steadfast in upholding fairness and equal opportunity principles. This initiative resonated deeply with many, serving as a testament to Abdirizak's integrity and dedication to his ideals. It underscored the importance of merit-based systems in fostering progress and inclusivity within society.

Abdirizak's health began to deteriorate, leading to a period of significant illness and exhaustion. This decline in his well-being necessitated a critical medical operation in the United States. From March to October 1963, Abdirizak spent seven months in the US and Europe recovering from the surgery. Recognizing the strain his health placed on his ability to fulfill his duties, he resigned from his ministerial position. However, his attempt to step down was met with resistance. Prime Minister Abdirashid, valuing Abdirizak's contributions and leadership, rejected his resignation.

The Political Culture of Abdirizak as a Prime Minister (1964–1967)

Abdirizak's journey from a humble camel boy in his formative years to a self-made individual was remarkable. However, his ascent was marked by a reputation for hostility towards rivals and a notable inflexibility in his approach. The president penned his nuanced thoughts on Abdirizak's character in his diary. Quoted by Mr. Trunji, the president reflected, "I have always admired and liked Abdirizak Haji Hussein, even if I know he is resentful and vengeful towards those he thinks are his enemies."[429] Delving deeper into his assessment, the president's diary entry from November 1963 revealed a more elaborate understanding of Abdirizak's capabilities. "This chap (Abdirizak) has the making of a statesman; I need to nominate him, Prime Minister, at the next occasion. He is full of energy, and he is honest. His weak point is his obstinacy and tendency to demonize

---

429. Trunji, *President Adan Abdulle*, 100.

his political adversaries."[430] In these candid reflections, the president grappled with Abdirizak's complexities, recognizing his potential for leadership and the challenges inherent in his character.

Mohamed Trunji, a prominent Somali historian and eyewitness of this period, poses a perplexing question: why did President Adan nominate Abdirizak, fully aware of his myriad shortcomings? He gave the following long and sufficient answer:

> He was chosen because of his personality and his approach to the administration of state affairs, which distinguished him from his predecessors, who were often accused of condoning, or at the very least not being tough enough on corruption on the top level, widespread maladministration. He was chosen because he represented corruption drive [as] the centrepiece of his term in the office. In fact, his first action was to request the members of his government to sign an understanding not to engage in any professional, commercial, industrial, or financial activities during their time in office. Most of the Somali political class were known to be corrupt, inclined only to keep the status quo and resistant to any reforms and innovations, which they feared might undermine their positions. In a contrary of unabashed kleptocrats, the designated Prime Minister shone like a beacon of probity. His opponents saw him as a threat to their dubious business interests and feared that he might undermine them. [431]

On the other hand, Abdi Samatar, answering why President Adan chose Abdirizak for the position of Prime Minister, focuses on the performance of Abdirizak during his term as a Minister of Interior and Public Works. He lucidly writes:

> Hussein belonged to a different breed of politicians. His resolute self-monitoring in the honeymoon period of the

---

430. Ibid.
431. Trunji, *President Adan Abdulle*, 101.

new state, when unlawful seduction was abundant; his scrupulousness towards the office and morals of his staff; and his admiration as well as concrete support for competent senior civil servants, many from the North, testified to his developing national reputation as a one of a kind. Hussein's perspective captured, and preceded by nearly three decades, what is now proffered as the only solution to Africa's troubles: good governance.[432]

The president's decision to nominate Abdirizak instead of Abdirashid, whom the SYL's central committee had recommended, reverberated like a political earthquake within the heart of the establishment. It sent shockwaves through the corridors of power and stirred a whirlwind of speculation and debate among politicians and citizens alike. Many questioned the motives behind such a bold and unexpected move, while others grappled with its implications for the nation's future direction. The political environment of his nomination was best captured in the African Report:

> [Hussein} character as a tough-minded, fair, and enlightened leader was noted by many. His friends say he is firm. His enemies say that he has the making of a tyrant. Nobody disputes his courage, nor the drive to work 18 hours a day, to the detriment of his health, even after a serious operation at Walter Reed Hospital in Washington DC.[433]

Abdirizak assembled a technocratic government, prioritizing expertise over clan-based considerations. However, during the crucial vote of confidence, the government faced defeat by a single vote, compounded by the absence of two ministerial members of parliament.[434] In response, visibly disappointed, the President defiantly reinstated Abdirizak, daring the parliament to challenge his decision. This standoff underscored a deeper rift within Somali politics, pitting reform-minded individuals against those driven by personal ambition

432. Samatar, *Africa's First Democrats*, 136.
433. Samatar, *Africa's First Democrats*, 137.
434. Ibid., 141.

and the pursuit of power, often exploiting clan affiliations to further their agendas. With tensions escalating, the president contemplated the drastic measure of dissolving the parliament, which instilled fear among its members. Ultimately, after intense negotiations and deliberations, the government secured approval, marking a critical moment of reconciliation. However, the underlying divisions and power struggles within the political landscape remained, reminding us of the challenges inherent in directing Somalia's complex socio-political terrain.

The government's cornerstone program encompassed a multifaceted approach to shaping domestic and foreign policy. It committed to non-alignment in foreign affairs, fortification of democratic institutions, moralization of public administration, campaigning against corruption and immorality within governmental ranks, and promotion and propagation of Islamic principles, emphasizing observance, respect, and dissemination of Islamic values. Dubbed the "competent and ethical government" (*Karti iyo Hufnan*), this epithet encapsulated the administration's reputation for efficiency, integrity, and moral rectitude.[435]

Following enacting legal and procedural frameworks, the inaugural reform initiative, as an example of Abdirizaks' governance culture, targeted restructuring 450 senior and mid-level civil service positions. Abdirizak's civil service reform left a lasting impact, notably by introducing the renowned *"Pusta Rosa,"* colloquially known as the pink slip policy.[436] This initiative aimed to streamline and modernize the civil service by evaluating personnel performance rigorously. Under this policy, civil servants were assessed with the assistance of a United Nations committee, ensuring a fair and transparent evaluation process. The *"Pusta Rosa"* became synonymous with the reform efforts championed by Abdirizak, symbolizing the necessity and the challenge of restructuring Somalia's bureaucratic framework.

---

435. Ibid.,145. Abdirizak, *A Political Memoir*, 201.
436. Ibid., 204.

Spearheaded by the prime minister, this decisive move aimed to inject efficiency and meritocracy into the civil service. However, while lauded for his audacity and decisiveness, the reform stirred an angry opposition reaction. Undeterred by the mounting criticism, the prime minister remained resolute in his conviction, prioritizing fairness and righteousness over placating detractors. His steadfast devotion to meritocracy and integrity rendered him impervious to accusations of nepotism and corruption. Indeed, Abdirizak's dedication to ethical governance and equitable practices set him apart in the political elite culture marred by patronage and graft. His refusal to compromise on principles in pursuit of political expediency earned him respect and hatred in equal measure. Yet, this unyielding adherence to his moral compass solidified his reputation as a statesman of unimpeachable integrity. Abdirizak was not afraid to lose his position and acted as President Adan recorded in his diary: "Steadfastness can only be obtained by those who are not afraid to lose their positions."[437]

Three episodes showcase a testament to the political culture of Abdirizak that he was not power hungry. To glean insights into his motivations, one need only examine his response when President Adan offered him the role of prime minister, his recommendation of Egal to join SYL if he is interested in being the prime minister after the end of the term, and his resignation after the parliament rejected two of his government bills. Rather than seizing the opportunity for personal advancement with unchecked ambition, Abdirizak's response to the president's proposal was measured and reflective. Abdirizak, when called to be appointed prime minister, didn't shy away from confronting the president with the realities of his health conditions and the bad reputation he garnered during his tenure as minister of the interior. Despite his reservations, Abdirizak urged the president to reconsider Abdirashid as prime minister. Grateful for the offer, Abdirizak respectfully declined the position, citing his concerns and perhaps sensing the weighty challenges ahead. Yet, the

---

437. Samatar, *Africa's First Democrats*, 168.

president persisted in his pursuit, indicating a steadfast belief in Abdirizak's ability to lead. General Mohamed Abshir, likely dispatched by the president to sway Abdirizak's decision, convinced Abdirizak to accept the nomination.

The second episode is another poignant illustration of Abdirizak's disinterest in pursuing power for its own sake, which unfolded during a significant political juncture. Following Egal's defeat in his bid for the parliament speaker position, Abdirizak extended an unexpected invitation for dinner. Throughout their meal, Abdirizak made his stance unequivocally clear: he harbored no aspirations for the role of Prime Minister after the conclusion of his term. Instead, he offered sage advice to Egal, suggesting that aligning with the Somali Youth League (SYL) might serve his interests if he harbored political ambitions. Egal, recognizing the wisdom in Abdirizak's counsel, accepted the invitation to join SYL, a decision facilitated by Abdirizak's recommendation. This gesture underscored Abdirizak's humility and lack of personal ambition and highlighted his propensity for fostering political alliances based on shared values and objectives. This could also demonstrate his recognition of the grievances among Northern politicians and his intent to strengthen the unity by advocating for the next prime minister to hail from the Northern constituency.

The third episode was another compelling testament to Abdirizak's aversion to power for its own sake, which surfaced when he resigned from the prime ministership. This bold move came in response to the parliament's rejection of two seemingly minor government bills, a decision that underscored Abdirizak's dedication to principles over political expediency.[438] Among the bills in question were foundational pieces of legislation, including the civil code, civil procedural code, health code, navigation code, labor integration code, criminal procedure code, and traffic code. Despite their significance, the parliament's dismissal of two bills prompted Abdirizak to take decisive action. In a display of unity and solidarity, the president

---

438. Trunji, *President Adan Abdulle*, 112

implored Abdirizak to reconsider his resignation, recognizing that his departure would only exacerbate the political turbulence. Together, they reached a consensus: Abdirizak would instead seek a vote of confidence from the parliament, reaffirming the government's legitimacy and resolve. The ensuing vote of confidence proved pivotal, underscoring the government's resilience in adversity.[439] Despite facing dissent from within its ranks, with thirteen members of SYL voting against their government, the administration ultimately emerged victorious, securing the confidence of the parliament and reaffirming its mandate to govern.

> *Three episodes that show Abdirizak was not power-hungry*
> • *Advising Egal to join SYL and telling him that he was not interested in continuing as prime minister after this term.*
> • *Resigning when the parliament rejected two bills and later seeking a vote of confidence on the advice of President Adan.*
> • *Reluctance to accept the premiership and recommending Abdirashid instead.*

Fig 17. Three episodes that show Abdirizak was not power-hungry

Political Culture of Abdirizak as an Opposition After the 1967 Election

Following the peaceful transition of power to the newly elected president, Abdirashid, and the appointment of Mohamed Ibrahim Egal as Prime Minister, with Abdirizak serving as the Secretary General of the ruling SYL party, marked a significant shift in political strategy. Rather than prioritizing national unity and accommodating Abdirizak, the new regime's leaders devised a plan to remove him as the secretary general of the SYL party and overhaul his anti-corruption policy. As part of this strategy, PM Mohamed Ibrahim Egal, eager to consolidate power, proposed an initiative: opening up the SYL party to any parliament member willing to join in paving the way for a one-party system (the party MPs reached a total of 103 out of 123). Initially hesitant, Abdirizak recognized the plan behind Egal's proposal, particularly considering the capricious nature of SYL's

---

439. Ibid., 116.

central committee members. Despite his reservations, Abdirizak acquiesced to Egal's plan. President Adan, acknowledging Abdirizak's cautious approach, commended his foresight and discretion in navigating this delicate political development. In his private diary, the President reflected on Abdirizak's judiciousness, recognizing the situation's complexity and the necessity of adapting to ensure stability and unity within the government. "For whatever reason, he did it, I raise my had to Abdirizak who showed himself to be ever greater. It's a pity that so few have recognized his qualities."[440]

Mohamed Ibrahim Egal presented his government and its program to the parliament, enjoying substantial support from members of the SYL party. Despite this overwhelming backing, the government faced a notable dissenting voice: Abdirizak H. Hussein, the secretary general of SYL. While most MPs approved Egal's administration, Abdirizak stood as a solitary figure in opposition.[441] His decision to withhold support sparked speculation within political circles, prompting questions about the motivations behind his dissent. Some viewed it as principled, reflecting Abdirizak's commitment to accountability and transparency. Others speculated about underlying tensions or differences within the ruling elite. Abdirizak's refusal to endorse the government underscored the complexity of internal dynamics within SYL and hinted at potential rifts within its leadership.

In their strategic maneuverings to gain control of the SYL party, President Abdirashid, PM Egal, and Interior Minister Yassin planned how to remove Abdirizak as its Secretary General of SYL. Despite their discomfort with his continued role, they faced legal constraints preventing his immediate removal until the party's upcoming congress. Frustrated by this obstacle, they resorted to attempts to tarnish Abdirizak's reputation, yet their efforts yielded little success. For Abdirizak, the realization dawned gradually that the party to which he had dedicated his loyalty throughout his life was now

---

440. Samatar, *Africa's First Democrats*, 189.
441. Abdirizak, *A Political Memoir*, 289.

imperiled under the emerging regime. Faced with this stark reality, he resigned from the party after two months of wrangling with the new government's leaders. The resignation marked a significant turning point for Abdirizak, offering him a reprieve from the relentless political battles that had consumed him. Seizing the opportunity for reflection and rejuvenation, he embarked on a pilgrimage to Hajj through Sudan before venturing to destinations such as Lebanon, Cairo, and Rome. He reunited with President Adan in Rome, and together, they forged plans for a tour across Europe. They toured Belgium, Holland, Denmark, Norway, and Sweden.[442]

Abdirizak established a new political party, the Democratic Action Party (DAP), rallying support from trusted allies and friends. The birth of DAP heralded a formidable opposition force poised to challenge the status quo with its commitment to transparency and accountability. Central to DAP's strategy were its weekly programs, meticulously designed to scrutinize and critique government policies, serving as a platform to amplify Abdirizak's impassioned speeches that resonated with the masses. These electrifying addresses galvanized public sentiment, igniting a genuine desire for change and reform. However, as the government fortified its grip on power, it spared no effort in ensuring its continued dominance, even at the expense of democratic principles. Utilizing legal procedures and policies to its advantage, the regime orchestrated a systematic campaign to rig the upcoming 1969 election, leaving little room for dissent. In March 1969, over 1,000 candidates from 64 parties (mostly clan-based) competed for the 123 seats in the National Assembly. Following these disorderly elections, all but one deputy joined the SYL, which became more authoritarian. Despite the formidable obstacles arrayed against them, DAP secured three seats in the new parliament. While most elected MPs succumbed to the allure of the ruling SYL party, Abdirizak remained steadfast in his allegiance to the principles of the opposition, standing resolute as the sole dissenting voice in a sea of conformity.

---

442. Ibid., 267–70.

> *Abdirizak's political culture could be summarized by the following eight points:*
>
> 1. *A profound sense of self-discipline guided him with unwavering resolve.*
> 2. *A diligent dedication to work ethics, consistently striving for excellence.*
> 3. *Bravery in facing humiliation, fearlessly pursuing justice and equity.*
> 4. *A commitment to principles, values, and moral integrity over power.*
> 5. *A dedication to realizing meritocracy, transparency, and accountability.*
> 6. *A staunch opponent of corruption as a societal cancer that erodes trust.*
> 7. *A devotion to Islam and exercising fairness, justice, and moral values.*
> 8. *A staunch opposition to clannism and nepotism in the public affairs.*

Fig. 18. Summary of Abdirizak's political culture

FACTORS THAT SHAPED POLITICAL CULTURE OF ABDIRIZAK

After illuminating Abdirizak's political culture, it becomes imperative to analyze factors that have influenced the development of this political culture. Such an analysis necessitates exploring his formative years and subsequent efforts in the political sphere. Examining Abdirizak's political culture requires a thorough investigation into the factors contributing to its formation. Five key influences stand out as pivotal in shaping his personality and ethos. These include his family background, characterized by its significance in shaping his worldview. His devout Islamic belief and adherence to its values have also profoundly guided his principles and actions. Abdirizak's vigorous opposition to colonialism and his unwavering nationalist fervor have been driving forces behind his political endeavors. Furthermore, his military training has imbued him with strategic thinking and a sense of discipline crucial to his leadership. Lastly, his passion for literature and avid reading habits have enriched his understanding of the world and informed his political perspectives. These factors offer insight into the intricate tapestry of influences that have shaped Abdirizak's political culture.

The first factor that shaped Abdirizak's political culture is deeply rooted in his family background and upbringing, shaped by the rich traditions and values passed down through generations. Born into a large family with a revered father who held the esteemed position of elder within his sub-clan, Abdirizak was surrounded by a supportive network of relatives. In his political memoir, Abdirizak wrote, "Two main events influenced my later life: the first was my nomadic environment and the second my family background."[443] Despite facing the loss of both parents at a young age, the bonds of kinship remained unyielding, providing him with resilience and strength in the face of adversity. Hailing from the rugged Mudug region, known for its conflicts over resources, Abdirizak embodies the enduring spirit of the nomadic people. His upbringing instilled in him a profound sense of pride and determination derived from the virtues of his ancestors. Steeped in the nomadic tradition, he values stead-fastness and truth-telling. His nomadic heritage has instilled in him a profound appreciation for resilience and integrity, essential qualities for surviving and thriving in ever-changing environments. Integrity and honesty are integral to his character, reflecting his unwavering commitment to his heritage and principles. Abdirizak's political culture is thus shaped by the resilience, dignity, and honesty instilled in him through his family upbringing and nomadic heritage. These values guide his political endeavors, grounding his commitment to truth and integrity.

The second factor that shaped Abdirizak's culture is his deep-root-ed Islamic beliefs and unwavering commitment to its values, which significantly influenced his cultural identity. Raised in a devout family, he immersed himself in Islamic teachings early, attending Quranic schools, and memorizing a substantial portion of the Quran.[444] His thirst for knowledge led him to study under esteemed scholars like Sheikh Mohamed Isse and Sheikh Azhari, whose wisdom profoundly impacted his worldview. Inspired by why Muslims lagged behind in progress, Abdirizak delved into Islamic thought and Arabic language studies, further enriching his understanding.[445]

---

443. Abdirizak Haji Hussein, *My Role in the Foundation of a Nation-State: A Political Memoir*, ed. Abdislan Issa-Salwe (African World Press, 2017), 1.
444. The Quranic teacher of Abdirizak was Moallim Abdille Mohamed Ahmed (Dhalawayne) from Haradheere town. Abdirizak, *A Political Memoir*, 13. Also, Samatar, *Africa's First Democrats*, 30
445. Samatar, *Africa's First Democrats*, 30.

During his time in Dire Dawa, he deepened his knowledge under the tutelage of Sheikh Azhari, expanding his grasp of Islamic principles and Arabic language intricacies.[446] This proficiency opened doors for him, leading to significant roles working with the Egyptian Ambassador, Kamalu Addin Salah, in Mogadishu. Abdirizak's commitment to Islam was not merely theoretical but a guiding force in his life, shaping his character and actions.[447] Values such as courage, truth, justice, and disdain for corruption became integral to his daily existence. This dedication was notably reflected in his parliamentary initiatives in 1964, where he emphasized "observance, respect, and spread of the principles of Islam" and "moralization of public administration" as critical objectives.[448] Overall, Abdirizak's profound devotion to Islam permeated every aspect of his being, shaping his cultural identity and guiding his interactions with society.

The third factor is Abdirizak's hate of colonialism and his nationalistic zeal—the following two episodes of Abdirizak's persistent commitment to defy humiliation and defend his dignity. Abdirizak staunchly opposed the racial prejudice displayed by the colonial officers he encountered during his service, refusing to tolerate their sense of superiority. He fearlessly confronted them, often resorting to direct challenges and sometimes contemplating violent retaliation. The first episode of Abdirizak's confrontations unfolds in Qalaafo, where he served alongside British Captain Fitzpatrick in the mission's signal squadron. Despite Fitzpatrick's attempts to demean and corrupt him, Abdirizak stood his ground, leading to imprisonment for twenty years. His unwavering spirit endured, though he sacrificed his job to defend his principles and dignity.[449] In the second episode, while working at a post office in Baidoa, Abdirizak faced harassment and discrimination from Italian officials instructed to eliminate SYL

446. Ibid., 36

447. Ibid., 54.

448. See the summary of Abdirizak's government program, which consists of ten main points. See Samatar, *Africa's First Democrats*, 144.

449. Abdirizak, *A Political Memoir*, 31–46. Also, Samatar, *Africa's First Democrats*, 33–35.

supporters. Despite the Italian authorities' attempts to undermine him, Abdirizak confronted the injustices and refused to succumb to intimidation tactics. Framed with false accusations, he endured imprisonment and torture, his health deteriorating until Somali police Inspector Daud Abdulle Hirsi's intervention led him to medical treatment. After nine agonizing months, Abdirizak emerged as a symbol of resilience and unwavering commitment to justice.[450]

The fourth factor concerns his military training. Abdirizak underwent six months of rigorous military training, immersing himself in a culture that epitomized values such as loyalty, duty, respect, selfless service, honor, integrity, and personal courage.[451] These principles formed the bedrock of military ethos, instilling in him a sense of purpose and responsibility that transcended mere training. The military environment provided Abdirizak with a unique personal and professional development. Moreover, the ethos of selfless service and personal courage cultivated within the military sphere undoubtedly left an indelible mark on Abdirizak's character. These values instilled a sense of duty not only to his fellow soldiers but also to his community and nation, shaping his outlook and guiding his actions long after his training concluded. Furthermore, Abdirizak's interactions with British officers during his military service likely exposed him to a different work culture influenced by the traditions and practices of the British military. This exposure would have provided him with valuable insights into alternative leadership. Overall, Abdirizak's military training served as a crucible for developing his work ethic and discipline, laying the foundation for his future endeavors and instilling the values of service, integrity, and courage that would define his path forward.

The fifth factor was his unwavering passion for delving into vast literary works. Abdirizak was profoundly committed to self-education, cultivating a rich intellectual landscape through the voracious reading of books and journals covering global affairs. This dedica-

---

450. Samatar, *Africa's First Democrats*, 52–53.
451. Abdirizak, *A Political Memoir*, 28.

tion facilitated his mastery of multiple languages, including Arabic, English, and Italian, broadening his understanding of geopolitics in the Horn of Africa and beyond.[452] Delving into the intricacies of non-aligned nations and dissecting Western neocolonial agendas, Abdirizak's intellectual pursuits made him keenly aware of international dynamics. Amidst his scholarly pursuits, Abdirizak found resonance with the ideals of Arab nationalism, drawing inspiration from the struggles of leaders who spearheaded the liberation of their nations. This influence served as a guiding light for Abdirizak as he navigated the political landscape of Somalia, imbuing his leadership with a sense of purpose rooted in the quest for sovereignty and self-determination. Thus, Abdirizak's intellectual curiosity underscored his role as a moral leader, driven by a genuine commitment to emancipate his nation from external influences and chart a course toward self-reliance and empowerment.

The following five factors have shaped Abdirizak's political culture:

1. *His family background and upbringing as a camel boy and an orphan taught him self-reliance.*
2. *Deep-seated Islamic beliefs instilled in him a commitment to its values.*
3. *His strong hatred of colonialism and fervent nationalistic zeal.*
4. *Military training equipped him with skills, discipline, and perseverance.*
5. *His passionate reading habits and dedication to continuous self-education.*

Fig. 19. The five factors have shaped Abdirizak's political culture.

CONCLUSION

The enduring political legacy of Abdirizak Haji Hussein is rooted in a lifetime of unwavering dedication to Somalia's liberation and nationalist movement. His consistent engagement in political affairs spans pivotal roles within the Somali Youth League (SYL). He served as Chairman of the SYL in 1956, where he played a role in shaping the party's agenda, and resigned when he could not tolerate the internal party divisions along clan lines. During the following years,

---

452. Abdirizak was self-educated and fluent in Arabic, English, Italian, and his native Somali language. He enjoyed reading books while in the Tuberculosis Hospital in Mogadishu. See Abdirizak, *A Political memoir*, 93.

Abdirizak demonstrated a steadfast commitment to his principles, even when challenging the status quo from within the SYL party. As internal opposition within the SYL in 1959 after forming a sizeable clan-balanced government, accused of lacking professionalism, he fearlessly opposed the government. His ascent to ministerial positions from 1960 to 1964 further solidified his standing as a critical figure in Somali politics, providing him the platform to introduce meaning-ful reform in his ministries, fight corruption, promote meritocracy, and disdain clannism. Culminating in his tenure as Prime Minister from 1964 to 1967, Abdirizak wielded significant influence, steering the nation's course with a steady hand and unwavering determina-tion for good governance and reforming the poisonous culture of politicians. President Adan strongly supported him, seeing him as an audacious reformer who needed to promote democracy, develop-ment, and social cohesion in the nation.

Yet, despite his deep-seated loyalty to the SYL, he ultimately reached the intersection after being convinced that new leaders who emerged after the 1967 election were uncomfortable with him and compelled him to make a difficult decision. In a momentous act of defiance, Abdirizak resigned from the party he had devoted his life to, recognizing that the vehicle for Somalia's liberation had veered off course. He continued his defiance by establishing his new party, DAP, to challenge the regime. His departure symbolized a profound shift in the political landscape, underscoring his unwavering com-mitment to principle above party allegiance. Through his tireless advocacy and principled leadership, Abdirizak left an indelible mark on Somali politics, inspiring future generations to uphold the values of integrity, resilience, and unwavering dedication to pursuing a better future for Somalia.

Abdirizak endured imprisonment on three separate occasions throughout his life. The first instance occurred under the British military administration while he was working in Qalafo, where he was detained under the orders of a British Military Administration. His second imprisonment occurred in Baidoa during the Trusteeship period, under the new Italian administration poised to diminish the role of the SYL. The third and final imprisonment happened under the military regime that took power in Somalia. Despite all these challenges, Abdirizak remained a steadfast and resilient figure in Somali politics, demonstrating his unwavering commitment to nationalistic beliefs. Abdirizak Haji Hussein went on to serve his country as the Somali ambassador to the United Nations in 1974. This diplomatic role allowed him to contribute significantly to international discussions and represent Somalia globally. Resigning from this work as ambassador in 1979, Hussein remained actively involved in efforts to promote Somali reconciliation and awareness. His dedication to peace and unity in Somalia continued until he died in 2014, marking him as a critical figure in the nation's history and a respected advocate for his people's well-being.

The biography of Abdirizak Haji Hussein serves as a beacon for new generations of Somalis, highlighting the values of integrity, resilience, and dedication to public service. Abdirizak is regarded as one of the exceptional leaders in Somalia's history, symbolizing morality and ethical governance. His life and career offer invaluable lessons in leadership and the importance of maintaining strong moral principles in government, inspiring future leaders to uphold these ideals in their endeavors.

5

THE CORE OBSTACLE IN STATE-BUILDING: THE SOMALI ELITE POLITICAL CULTURE

*A*fter gaining Somali independence in 1960, the Somali civilian government witnessed a few exceptional leaders who stood out against the backdrop of the dominant political elite culture. We concentrated on three top national political leaders: President Adan, Prime Minister Abdirizak, and Prime Minister Abdullahi Isse. We traced their biographies and political culture in chapters two, three, and four. These unique cases demonstrated a departure from the dominant elite political culture, characterized by entrenched self-interest and clan-based power struggles. Understanding the evolution of this elite political culture is crucial, as it has progressively deteriorated over the decades, ultimately leading to the collapse of the state in 1991. This negative culture perpetuated corrupt and exclusionary practices among the ruling elites. Moreover, this entrenched elite culture has made it challenging to restore effective governance and reestablish the state's legitimacy since the collapse.

Somalia recently celebrated sixty-four years of independence while continuing to recover from a long period of state collapse and protracted civil conflict. Since gaining independence in 1960 until its collapse in 1991, the country has experienced two distinct governance systems, each with challenges and impact on the nation. During these two governance systems, the ruling political elites mainly "remained aloof from society"[453] and evolved later during the

---

453. Terrence Lyons and Ahmed Samatar, *Somalia: State Collapse, Multilateral Intervention, and Strategies for Political Reconstruction* (Brookings Occasional Papers, 1995), 8.

military regime as "a government at war with its own people."[454] The first phase of governance was an era of liberal democracy from 1960 to 1969. During this time, Somalia attempted to establish democratic institutions and foster political participation. However, the fledgling government faced limited resources, the Cold War superpower rivalry, and conflict with its neighbors. Despite its initial promise, the era of democracy was ultimately disrupted by rigging elections and establishing the one-party system, leading to the assassination of President Abdirashid A. Sharmarke on October 15, 1969.[455] The immediate military coup on October 21 ended the democratic era and ushered in a military dictatorship until 1991. Under the rule of General Mohamed Siad Barre, the state became increasingly authoritarian. Adopting socialism, the army regime consolidated power and suppressed dissent. Human rights abuses, censorship, and the suppression of opposition groups marked this period. The regime suppressed societal tradition, Islam, and the clan system, leading to the growing disconnection and conflict between the ruling elites and society.[456] This undertaking was evident in the harsh measures used to maintain control, including the use of force against civilians and the suppression of regional and clan-based armed opposition movements.

Over three decades, multiple complex factors combined contributed to the collapse of the Somali state. These factors included escalating tensions between the state and society. This disconnect was further exacerbated by ongoing conflicts with neighboring Ethiopia, leading to geopolitical instability and the diversion of resources away from national development.[457] The authoritarian dictatorship, which

---

454. African watch committee, *Somalia: A Government at war with its own people* (Human Rights Watch; first edition (June 1, 1990).
455. Mohamed H. Ingriis, "Who Assassinated the Somali President in 1969? The Cold War, the Clan Connection, or the Coup d'Etat." African Security, 10(2), 2017, 131–54.
456. An example of this rift is the adopted secular family law, contrary to Islamic law. Moreover, the regime attempted to eliminate the role of clan elders and offered new titles such as "*Nabadoon*," among others.
457. Abdurahman Abdullahi, *Making Sense of Somali History, Volume One*

spanned from 1969 to 1991, intensified these issues. The regime's repressive measures, such as censorship and crackdowns on dissent, alienated large segments of the population and stifled civil liberties. The centralized control of power further deepened the divide between the government and the country's diverse regional and clan-based groups. Economic underdevelopment also played a significant role in the state's collapse. The regime's mismanagement and neglect of vital economic sectors, such as agriculture and industry, hindered growth and created widespread poverty. Fragmentation within the political elite further undermined the state's stability. Competing interests and infighting among different factions led to a lack of cohesive governance and an inability to effectively address the country's challenges. This fragmentation weakened the state's ability to respond to crises and maintain control over its territory. The convergence of these issues led to a descent into chaos and a severe civil war. The breakdown of law and order created an environment ripe for the emergence and rise of militant traditions.[458] These groups capitalized on the power vacuum and lack of effective governance, further destabilizing the country and prolonging the conflict.

Following the collapse of the state in 1991, the political landscape in Somalia was dominated by warlords and their allies. These groups filled the power vacuum left by the downfall of the centralized regime, exerting control over different regions and territories. As a result, Somalia experienced a period of intense fragmentation and instability, with warlords often vying for power and resources. These ruling political elites encountered significant challenges in reaching meaningful agreements during twelve reconciliation conferences.[459] The negotiations were marked by deep-seated mistrust and competition

---

(Adonis & Abbey, 2017), 196.

458. Somali tradition has two components: clan and Islam. Both elements have been used to mobilize the population for war and peace.

459. Interpeace, "History of Mediation in Somalia since 1988." Research for Peace Program. https://www.interpeace.org/wp-content/uploads/2009/05/2009_Som_Interpeace_A_History_Of_Mediation_In_Somalila_Since_1988_EN.pdf (accessed on May 27, 2020), 10.

between the various factions, each seeking to secure its interests and retain power. The persistent inability to achieve consensus further prolonged the chaos and division within the country. In response to this ongoing instability, the Somali Peace and Reconciliation Conference (SPRC) was held in Djibouti in 2000. The conference aimed to establish a path toward peace and stability by introducing a third governance model to empower civil society and include marginalized armed factions in the political process. This approach recognized the importance of broadening participation and incorporating diverse voices in state-building.

One of the measures adopted at the SPRC was implementing the 4.5 clan power-sharing formula.[460] This formula aimed to ensure the representation of the clans in the governing bodies. It was envisioned as a temporary transitional solution to stabilize the political environment and pave the way for the eventual restoration of a democratic system. Although the 4.5 power-sharing formula could foster inclusivity and cooperation, its effectiveness was limited by the deep-seated divisions and historical grievances between the clans. Moreover, the model faced criticism for perpetuating clan-based politics and entrenching the influence of the same political elites who had contributed to the country's instability. Despite these challenges, introducing the third governance model marked a crucial step toward establishing a more inclusive and representative political framework.

Although the 4.5 clan power-sharing model was initially intended as a temporary solution to promote stability in the wake of the state collapse, it remained in place for twenty-five years, spanning five consecutive regimes. The model's reliance on clan-based representation entrenched the influence of political elites aligned with the dominant clans. As a result, this approach did not deliver on its promise of

---

460. 4.5 clan power-sharing was adopted in the Somali National Peace and Reconciliation Conference held in Djibouti in 2000. This formula allocated parliamentary seats equally to four major clans and half of the seats to collections of other smaller clans.

fostering inclusive governance and long-term stability.[461] One of the shortcomings of the clan-centric model was its failure to establish a functional and legitimate government with control over Somalia's territory. Instead, the model often reinforced existing divisions and perpetuated power struggles among different clans and factions. This division weakened the central government's authority and limited its ability to effectively govern or provide essential services to its citizens. Moreover, the concentration of wealth and power within the ruling political elites who thrived under the clan-centric system hindered progress toward democratic reforms. These elites frequently resisted efforts to move away from the power-sharing formula, as it threatened their established interests and influence. This resistance created significant barriers to democratization and a more inclusive political system.

The prolonged use of the clan-centric model also contributed to corruption and inefficiency within the government. Political appointments and resource allocations were often determined by clan affiliations rather than merit, leading to patronage networks and a lack of accountability. This environment further undermined public trust in the government and hindered efforts to combat corruption. Despite these challenges, there have been some positive steps toward reform in recent years, such as holding more inclusive elections and gradually strengthening state institutions. These developments signal a potential shift away from the clan-centric model and towards a more democratic and representative system of governance. Ultimately, achieving lasting stability and progress in Somalia will require continued efforts to address the root causes of division and promote national unity. Building inclusive institutions, fostering political pluralism, and strengthening the rule of law are essential steps toward establishing a more functional and accountable government capable of meeting the needs of its diverse population.

---

461. All milestones of state-building are not achieved, such as completing the constitution, security arrangement, and democratic election.

The collapse of the Somali state within thirty years, followed by more than another thirty years of insufficient achievements, presents a complex puzzle. This trajectory challenges the predictions of early modernization scholars who believed Somalia was better equipped for state-building than many other African countries.[462] Indeed, Somalia remains "in search of a state"—a phrase borrowed from Samatar and Laitin's book title—as it has experienced three different governance systems throughout its history.[463] The first was a unitary parliamentary system that upheld liberal democracy under post-colonial civilian governments. However, this system gradually eroded due to its inability to provide essential public services and maintain social cohesion. In the aftermath, a new system of governance emerged under the military regime. The regime adopted a socialist ideology, including a presidential system, authoritarian rule, aggressive nationalist programs, and a one-party system. These policies widened the divide between the state (representing modernity) and society (representing tradition), exacerbating existing tensions. The regime's aggressive stance towards neighboring Ethiopia and armed opposition groups further fueled internal conflicts and ultimately led to the regime's collapse in 1991.[464]

In 2000, the Somali Peace and Reconciliation Conference (SPRC) in Djibouti introduced the third system of governance, which sought to integrate traditional elites as partners in state-building. This clan-centric approach empowered clan elders as key political figures, granting them the authority to select members of parliament from their respective sub-clans. Although this approach aimed to bring stability, state institutions have continued to falter under all

---

462. These scholars considered Somalia a nation that can quickly build a state because of the homogeneous nature of its people. See Neil Joseph Smelser, *Toward a Theory of Modernization* (New York: Basic Books, 1964), 268–74, Marion Levy, *Social Patterns and Problems of Modernization* (Englewood Cliffs, New Jersey: Prentice-Hall, 1967), 189–207.
463. The title of the book *Somalia: Nation in Search of a State* by David Laitin and Said Samatar expresses this phenomenon very well.
464. Mohamed H. Ingriis. *The Suicidal State: The Rise and Fall of Siad Barre Regime, 1969-1991* (UPA, 2016).

three governance systems. Over the past sixty-four years, the recurring failure to establish a stable and functioning Somali state, despite changes in political elites and governance systems, suggests that the fundamental issues lie within the prevailing political culture.[465] A thorough re-examination of this culture is necessary to understand and address Somalia's persistent challenges. A greater emphasis on inclusive governance, transparency, and accountability may offer a way to build a more resilient and cohesive state.

In this research, the author delves into the reasons behind the Somali government's repeated failures and the obstacles hindering its recovery. Central to this analysis is the ruling political elites' role in constructing and dismantling the state. It emphasizes the critical role of the ruling political elites, particularly in the formative stages of state-building. This perspective aligns with Montesquieu's assertion that "at the birth of societies, it is the leaders of the commonwealth who create the institutions; afterward, it is the institutions that shape the leaders."[466] The premise is that the prevailing political culture among the ruling elite has been instrumental in causing the collapse of the Somali state and hindering its recovery. This entrenched culture permeates all levels of "the governing elites," to borrow the term coined by Italian sociologist Wilfredo Pareto. Despite the significance of the ruling elites' political culture, there is a notable scarcity of academic research in Somali studies. Many researchers focus on the clannization of politics, adhering to modernization theory, which tends to oversimplify Somali politics by reducing it to clan dynamics.[467] This perspective often leads scholars and poli-

---

465. Many works of literature have been produced about elite failure in Africa. Most of these studies were tailored to "extraversion" and elite dependence on former colonial powers. See Samir Amin, *Accumulation on a World Scale: A Critique of the Theory of Underdevelopment* (New York and London: Monthly Review Press, 1974), Also, Jean-François Bayart and Stephen Ellis, "Africa in the World: A History of Extraversion." African Affairs, Vol. 99, No. 395, 2000, 217–67.

466. Quoted in Danwart A. Rustow, *A World of Nations* (Washington, DC: Brookings, 1967), 135.

467. Abdurahman Abdullahi, "Revisiting Somali Historiography: Critique and

ticians to attribute the challenges in political development primarily to the societal structure and cultural traditions. Besides, ruling political elites considered clans and the associated sense of clannism as incurable cancer that requires elimination.[468] Furthermore, ruling political elites have often portrayed clans and clannism as obstacles to progress, justifying their leadership failures by blaming society and its cultural norms.[469] This narrative overlooks the potential impact of European governance systems and ideologies, such as liberal democracy and socialism, which have fluctuated throughout Somalia's history. A critical assessment of these imported governance models and ideologies is essential for understanding Somalia's current predicament. This approach resonates with Chinua Achebe's assessment of Nigeria's issues, which he attributed to "a failure of leadership."[470] This chapter examines the influence of the ruling political elites and their culture to illuminate the underlying causes of Somalia's struggles and provide insights for a more effective path to recovery.

In this research, the author explores why the ruling political elites in Somalia have consistently failed over the past sixty-four years despite employing various political systems. The Chapter posits that the ruling elite's intertwined political culture has played a central role in the state's collapse and the obstacles to its recovery. However, the author also acknowledges the need to consider other significant factors that shape this political culture, such as institutional and systemic influences. The Chapter begins by establishing a clear conceptual framework, defining key terms such as culture, politics,

---

Idea of Comprehensive Perspective." Journal of Somali Studies, Volume 5, 1–2, 2018, 31–59. Also, Tobias Hogman, "Stabilization, Extraversion, and Political Settlement in Somalia." The Rift Valley Institute, 2016.

468. Abdalla Omar Mansur, "Contrary to a Nation: The Cancer of the Somali State," in *The Invention of Somalia,* ed. Ali Jumale (The Red Sea Press, 1995), 107–16.

469. See Thomas Hodgkin, *Nationalism in Colonial Africa* (London: Frederick Muller, 1956).

470. Chinua Achebe, *The Trouble with Nigeria* (Fourth Dimension Publishing Co, 2000), 1.

elite culture, and political culture. This provides a foundation for understanding the context in which Somalia's political elite operates and how their culture intersects with broader societal dynamics. Following this conceptual groundwork, the author examines the formation and structure of the primary elite groups in Somalia. This includes exploring the historical and socio-political context in which these elites emerged and how they have shaped and been shaped by their environments.

The research then traces the historical evolution of the dominant political culture among the ruling elite class, exploring how this blended culture contributed to the state's collapse and continues to hinder its recovery. The analysis considers the interplay between tradition and modernity, examining how the ruling elites' reliance on clan-based power structures and imported governance systems has influenced the political landscape. Rather than providing a detailed analysis of each phase of political development, the Chapter presents a sequential narrative of the main elements of the ruling elite's political culture and their connections. This approach highlights the continuity and changes within the political elite class, shedding light on the Somali state's persistent challenges. Ultimately, the Chapter seeks to offer insights into the complex web of factors that have contributed to Somalia's political instability and provide a nuanced understanding of how the ruling elite's political culture continues to impact the country's journey toward stability and recovery.

CONCEPTUALIZATION OF THE BASIC TERMINOLOGIES

Exploring the notion of ruling elite political culture has long captivated the minds of early political philosophers and modern theorists alike.[471] Among the luminaries delving into this domain, scholars such as C. Wright Mills, Floyd Hunter, G. William Domhoff, and

---

471. These scholars include Plato, Aristotle, St. Thomas Aquinas, Machiavelli, Montesquieu, Rousseau, Max Weber, Foucault, and Marcuse. Italian scholars like Vilfredo Pareto, Gaetano Mosca, and Robert Michels greatly influenced the elite theory in the Western tradition.

Thomas Ferguson stand prominent, each contributing nuanced perspectives to our understanding. At its core, the concept of ruling elite political culture emerges from the fusion of three fundamental pillars: culture, politics, and the elite. Yet, the interpretations of these pillars are as varied as the disciplines from which they draw. The author selects diverse definitions from these fields within this discourse, crafting the essence of ruling elite political culture. Through this synthesis, the author seeks to shed light on the intricate interplay between cultural norms, political structures, and the privileged echelons of society, offering a comprehensive exploration that transcends disciplinary boundaries.

What is Culture?

Culture, a term whose roots stretch deep into antiquity, has undergone a transformative meaning over the centuries. Originating from the Latin term *Cultura Animi*, coined by Marcus Cicero, culture was initially conceptualized as the cultivation of the soul. In Middle English, the term took on the guise of "place tilled," evoking images of inhabited and cared-for land. This evolution laid the groundwork for culture to morph into a vast umbrella, encompassing human society's rich social behaviors and norms.[472] Yet, within the realm of social science, culture remains a multifaceted enigma, subject to a plethora of interpretations and debates. Orlando Patterson captures this complexity succinctly: "Leaders and activists, as well as scholars, challenge each other, not only on the interpretation of their cultures but also on the very definition and meaning of culture itself."[473] One of its definitions is "a set [of] perspectives shared by a group of people and reflected by their actions, relationships, communities, and artifacts."[474] These perspectives span a spectrum of perceptions,

---

472. Edward Tylor, *Primitive Culture, Vol 1* (New York: J.P. Putnam's Son, 1871).

473. Orlando Patterson, "Making Sense of Culture." The Annual Review of Sociology 2014. Available from https://scholar.harvard.edu/files/patterson/files/making_sense_of_culture.pdf (accessed on Jan.15, 2020).

474. Andrew Riemann, *Introduction to Culture Studies: Introductory activities for exploring and comparing cultures* (Intergraphica Press, 2013), 5.

beliefs, values, and attitudes, weaving together the intricate fabric of societal identity. To grasp the essence of culture is akin to navigating the allegorical narratives of blind individuals touching different parts of an elephant, each perceiving their fragment as the entirety of reality. Indeed, culture defies singular categorization, encompassing many dimensions such as codes of manners, dress, language, religion, rituals, art, norms, behaviors, and systems of belief that bind specific communities together. Indeed, culture could be signified simply as a broad set of relationships that include "codes of manners, dress, language, religion, rituals, art, norms, behavior, and a system of belief that binds a specific community."[475]

Culture is a cornerstone of anthropology and sociology, embodying the intricacy of human existence and societal dynamics. Rooted in the seminal definition by E.B. Tylor, culture is conceived as "that complex whole which includes knowledge, belief, art, morals, law, custom, and any other capabilities and habits acquired by man as a member of society."[476] Culture reveals itself through expressive, material, and immaterial dimensions in its manifold manifestations. Expressive culture "refers to the intentional use of the human body to engage in performances of group identity."[477] Expressive culture embodies the intentional use of the human body to enact performances of group identity, encompassing diverse forms such as dance, rituals, arts, sports, fashion, oratory, song, body language, and religious ceremonies. These intentional expressions serve as potent vehicles for transmitting and reinforcing communal identity and values. Conversely, material culture encompasses the tangible artifacts and inventions crafted by human ingenuity, ranging from

475. Carol Frieze, Lenore Blum, Orit Hazzan and M. Bernardine Dias, "Culture and Environment as Determinants of Women's Participation in Computing: Revealing the 'Women-CS Fit'." Available from https://www.cs.cmu.edu/~cfrieze/women@scs/SIGCSE_06_final.pdf (accessed on 15 January 2020).
476. Tylor, *Primitive Culture.*
477. Kawan J. Allen, "Expressive Culture," *The Department of Cultural References*, accessed January 16, 2020, http://tammysgordon.org/DCR/items/show/55 (accessed on October 12, 2020).

everyday objects like cars, airplanes, and tools to grand structures such as buildings, cities, and factories. These physical manifestations serve practical functions as symbols and markers of cultural identity, shaping societal behaviors and perceptions. Moreover, the immaterial realm of culture delves into the intangible ideas, beliefs, values, rules, norms, morals, language, organizations, and institutions that underpin societal frameworks. These abstract constructs form the backbone of social cohesion and governance, providing the guiding principles that govern interpersonal interactions and collective behaviors.

In the sociological domain, culture further delineates non-material and material manifestations, encapsulating the cognitive frameworks and tangible artifacts that define a people's way of life. "When considering non-material culture, sociologists refer to several processes that a culture uses to shape its members' thoughts, feelings, and behaviors. Four of the most important non-material elements of culture are symbols, language, values, and norms."[478] A cultural symbol is a physical manifestation that signifies the ideology of a particular culture or that merely has meaning within a culture.[479] Non-material culture encompasses symbols, language, values, and norms, which are the bedrock of social organization and cohesion. For example, Islam has the symbol of the crescent moon and star, Christianity has the cross, and Judaism has the Star of David. Moreover, all countries, organizations, and companies have symbols, such as flags and emblems. The other common cultural symbols are the language in which the letters of an alphabet symbolize the sounds of a specific spoken language of a social group. Furthermore, norms and values are necessary pillars for social survival. It is the agreed expectations and rules by which a culture guides the behavior of its members in any given situation. These shared norms and values serve

---

478. See https://www.cliffsnotes.com/study-guides/sociology/culture-and-societies/material-and-nonmaterial-culture (accessed on January 16, 2020)
479. https://study.com/academy/lesson/cultural-symbol-definition-examples.html (accessed on 14 July 2020).

as the moral compass guiding societal interactions and shaping the fabric of collective identity.

Four distinct societal norms operate at varying levels: folkways, mores, taboos, and laws. Folkways represent learned behaviors shared by social groups, often called customs, which, while not morally significant, hold importance for social acceptance. Mores, conversely, encompass norms of morality, delineating concepts of right and wrong; transgressions against mores are generally deemed offensive to the majority within a culture.[480] Taboos extend even further, constituting highly negative norms whose violation can evoke strong societal condemnation, potentially leading to exclusion from the group or society. The severity and nature of taboos are typically rooted in mores. Laws, meanwhile, represent social norms that have been formally codified at the state or federal level, carrying with them the weight of formal punishment for violations, ranging from fines to incarceration or, in extreme cases, even capital punishment.

Every individual is born into a specific societal culture characterized by prevailing values and norms that influence and mold their way of life. This process of cultural acquisition occurs through mechanisms such as enculturation, socialization, and acculturation.[481] Furthermore, according to the theory of continuity and change, societal cultures exhibit dynamism over time, evolving in response to historical shifts and societal dynamics.[482] Moreover, culture can be conceptualized through covert and overt levels, akin to an iceberg, of which the majority remains unseen beneath the surface. Surface culture encompasses observable human actions such as language, art,

---

480. William Graham Sumner, *Folkways: A Study of Mores, Manners, Customs, and Morals (Cosimo Classics, 2007)*.

481. Enculturation is learning how to use the accepted patterns of cultural behavior that one's culture prescribes. Conversely, acculturation is the learning process where knowledge is transferred from one culture to another, usually a more powerful one. For example, colonialism, modernization, and globalization created intense acculturation of the people in the former colonies of the South.

482. B. Howitt, And R. Julian, *Society and Culture* (Heinemann, Second Edition, Sydney, 2009).

food, traditions, customs, rituals, and institutions. In contrast, deep culture delves into human cognition and emotion, encompassing norms, roles, ideologies, philosophies, beliefs, values, tastes, desires, assumptions, and expectations.

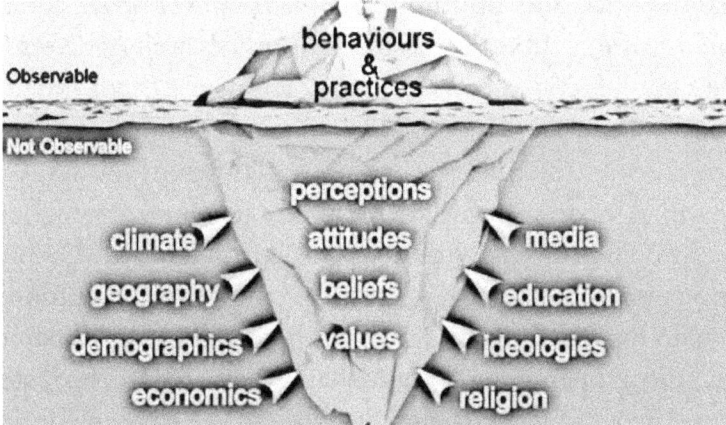

Fig 20. Culture is covert and overt levels akin to an iceberg

However, it's crucial to recognize that not all human behavior can be solely attributed to culture. Universal values and behaviors, alongside unique individual traits, exist independently of cultural influences. In this context, we adopt the definition of culture proposed by David Matsumoto and Linda Juang, which conceptualizes culture as a "unique meaning and information system, shared by a group and transmitted across generations, enabling the group to fulfill basic survival needs, pursue happiness and well-being, and find meaning in life."[483]

Every nation invariably encompasses a dominant societal culture and a sub-culture from diverse sub-nationalities, ethnicities, or tribes. The discourse on culture often employs overarching labels such as Western, Eastern, Islamic, and African cultures, among others. Western culture, influenced mainly by Judeo-Christian and Greco-Roman traditions originating from Europe, has proliferated across continents through migrations and colonial expansions.

---

483. David Matsumoto and Linda Juang, *Culture and psychology* (Jon-David Hague publisher, 2013), 15.

Its geographical boundaries are fluid, although it predominates in regions spanning North and South America, Europe, and Australia. In contrast, Eastern Culture encompasses many cultural groups and belief systems primarily situated in the Asian continent. Among these are Islam, Hinduism, Buddhism, Jainism, and Taoism adherents. Muslim culture, a subset of Eastern culture, exhibits a diverse array of beliefs and practices shaped by the teachings of Islam and infused with local societal norms. While Islam is significant in Eastern and Western cultures, its practices vary across different locales. On the other hand, African cultures emerge from a fusion of colonial legacies and traditional customs within diverse ethnic groups. Despite the vast diversity within African cultures, they share commonalities and distinctive characteristics that set them apart from Western and Eastern cultural paradigms. These shared traits reflect the historical, social, and geographical dynamics unique to the African continent.

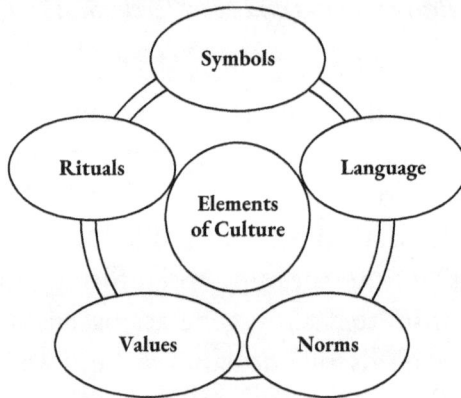

Fig, 21. Elements of Culture

Defining Politics

The term "politics" traces its roots back to the Greek word "polis," meaning a city and initially confined to studying the state. It is linked with power, defined as "the ability to exercise one's will over others."[484] Within politics, two fundamental concepts emerge: legiti-

---

484. Max Weber, *Economy, and Society: An Outline of Interpretive Sociology*

macy and authority. Legitimacy denotes "a value whereby something or someone is recognized and accepted as right and proper."[485] German sociologist Max Weber delineated three types of political legitimacy: traditional, charismatic, and rational-legal.[486] Traditional legitimacy emanates from societal customs and historical traditions, emphasizing the authority vested in tradition. Charismatic legitimacy, conversely, derives from the captivating ideas and persona of a leader whose charismatic appeal psychologically influences and dominates society. Rational-legal legitimacy hinges on institutional procedures, wherein government institutions establish and enforce laws and order. Conversely, "authority is the legitimate power which one person or group possesses and practices over another."[487]

In contemporary discourse, politics permeates daily discussions among the masses, who engage with political issues spanning local, national, and international affairs through various media platforms such as radio, television, newspapers, and social media. However, popular perceptions of politics "is usually thought of as a 'dirty' word: it conjures up images of trouble, disruption, and even violence on the one hand, and deceit, manipulation, and lies on the other."[488] Isaac Disraeli encapsulated this sentiment, describing politics as "the art of governing mankind by deceiving them."[489] Within the field of political science, diverse definitions of politics abound. Harold Lasswell characterized politics as "who gets what, when, and how,"

(Berkley, CA: U. California Press, 1922).

485. Chen, Jing (2016). *Useful Complaints: How Petitions Assist Decentralized Authoritarianism in China* (New York: Lexington Books, 2016), 165.

486. Patrick H. O'Neil, *Essentials of Comparative Politics* (New York: W.W. Norton & Company, 2010), 35–38.

487. Frank Bealey, *The Blackwell Dictionary of Political Science: A User's Guide to Its Terms, 1999)*, 22–23.

488. "What is politics?" Available from https://www.macmillanihe.com/resources/sample-chapters/9780230363373_sample.pdf (accessed on January 15, 2020).

489. Quoted by Bernard Crick, *In Defence of Politics* (London: Pelican Books, 1964), 16.

highlighting its essence in allocating societal resources and power.[490] David Easton defined politics as "the authoritative allocation of values for a society," emphasizing its role in shaping societal norms and priorities.[491] Vladimir Lenin provided a Marxist perspective, viewing "politics as the most concentrated expression of economics."[492] Bernard Crick proposed a nuanced definition, portraying "politics as a distinctive form of rue, whereby people act together through institutionalized procedures to resolve differences, to conciliate diverse interests and values, and to make public policies in the pursuit of common purpose."[493]

Hence, politics encompasses various contexts, allowing political science students to explore its manifestations across various social landscapes beyond governmental structures and official institutions. Politics permeates every facet of life, from domestic settings and workplaces to commercial arenas, legislative bodies, corporate entities, and educational institutions. Thus, while one might define politics narrowly as the realm of governance, politicians, and political parties, it also embraces a broader perspective, encompassing the dynamics between individuals, societal regulations, institutional frameworks, and behaviors across all spheres of human interaction.

Defining Political Culture

The concept of political culture intertwines the realms of culture and politics, effectively rendering politics a reflection of public culture. This term encompasses various definitions, offering insight into a society's collective mindset regarding its political system. Larry Diamond characterizes political culture as "a people's predominant beliefs, attitudes, values, ideals, sentiments, and evaluations about the political system of its country and the role of the self in

---

490. Harold Lasswell, *Politics: Who Gets What, When, and How?* (Meridian Books, 1951), 13.
491. David Easton, *The political system: an inquiry into the state of political science* (University of Chicago Press, 1981).
492. Lenin, V. I., *Collected Works. September 1903 – December 1904*, 1965.
493. Crick, *In Defence of Politics*, 16.

that system."[494] Lucian Pye adds that "political culture is the set of attitudes, beliefs, and sentiments, which give order and meaning to a political process and which provide underlying assumptions and rules that govern behavior in the political system."[495] Consequently, political cultures vary across nations due to each society's unique cultural fabric. Political culture significantly influences political behavior, "defined as any action regarding authority in general and government in particular."[496]

Political behavior encompasses a broad spectrum of activities, from voting and protesting to engaging in civil disobedience. It epitomizes the manifestation of underlying beliefs and values within political systems, shaping how individuals participate in the political landscape. The adage succinctly captures the intricate relationship between political culture and behavior; one could say, "By their political behavior (their deeds), we can know their political culture (their beliefs)."[497] Numerous factors influence political behavior, including ideology, ethnic background, and anticipated consequences. Political behavior is inherently linked to political attitudes, which Eagly and Chaiken define as "a psychological tendency that is expressed by evaluating a particular entity with some degree of favour or disfavour."[498] These attitudes reflect individuals' thoughts, emotions, and behavioral inclinations towards various entities, whether people or concepts. Furthermore, attitudes typically precede actions, with rational individuals demonstrating consistency between their attitudes and behaviors, a phenomenon termed "cognitive resonance." However, inconsistencies between attitude and behavior create cognitive dissonance, generating internal tension.

---

494. Larry Diamond, *Political Culture and Democracy in Developing Countries* (Lynne Rienner Publisher, 1994), 7.
495. Leonardo Morlino, Dirk Berg-Schlosser, Bertrand Badie, *Political Science: a global perspective* (Sage Publications, 2017), 64–74.
496. Trevor Munroe, *An Introduction to Politics: Lectures for first-year students* (Jamaica: Canoe Press, 2002), 3.
497. Ibid, 8.
498. Alice H. Eagly and Shelly Chaiken, *The Psychology of Attitudes* (Belmont USA: Wadsworth, 1993), 1.

Political culture necessitates individuals to grasp four key attitudinal dimensions. Firstly, political attitudes and values encompass orientations towards political matters, often influenced by contextual factors and evolving circumstances. These attitudes are intertwined with more profound political beliefs. Political attitudes and values are "the opinions and values individuals hold about political issues, events, and personalities."[499] Embracing democratic principles, advocating for freedom and justice, or opposing authoritarian regimes are examples of political attitudes. Conversely, negative attitudes may manifest in beliefs supporting racial supremacy, authoritarianism, or anarchy. The second dimension pertains to attitudes towards political and national institutions, encompassing diverse entities such as media outlets, religious institutions, civil society organizations, and governmental bodies. Trust, respect, and legitimacy issues emerge, shaping individuals' perceptions and interactions with these institutions.

The third dimension revolves around attitudes toward political identity, which correlates with an individual's primary sense of self. Identity is the narrative we construct for ourselves and convey to others, encompassing our past, present, and future selves. For instance, individuals of Somali descent may delineate their identity based on various factors, including geographic location (such as district or regional state), national affiliation (Somali), religious adherence (Muslim), and other relevant aspects. Moving to the fourth dimension, we delve into leadership attitudes, where leadership is understood simply as the capacity of an individual or group to inspire action or consensus around a specific agenda. Leadership can generally be categorized into three archetypes: charismatic (embodied by a visionary figure), paternalistic (exemplified by authoritative guidance akin to a parental figure demanding obedience), and managerial (characterized by a pragmatic approach akin to that of an institutional manager).

---

499. Attitudes, Political. https://www.encyclopedia.com/social-sciences/applied-and-social-sciences-magazines/attitudes-political (accessed on May 13, 2020).

Defining Elite Political Culture

In any given society, two primary groups can be distinguished: the "elite" and the "masses." The elite refers to a select and often small cohort of individuals or organizations wielding significant power within the societal framework. Typically, the elite is "somebody who enjoys the best social, economic, political, as well as cultural levels."[500] Elite theory is grounded in two foundational assumptions. Firstly, it acknowledges the inherent inequality in the distribution of political power within any society.[501] Secondly, it recognizes that specific individuals or groups wield more power within any system than others. These power differentials encompass various spheres, including economic, political, and religious domains. These individuals, whether singular figures such as political leaders or cohesive groups like the elite exert considerable influence over societal dynamics. The concept of the elite primarily analyzes those groups occupying or controlling the upper echelons of society. The notion of the elite traces back to Plato's Republic, wherein he delineated societal classes into gold, silver, iron, and copper categories.

> You who are the people of this city. You are all brothers, but among you, there are those who deserve to rule the others. God has molded their nature on the gold. Hence, they are considered as the most valuable and desirable individuals. However, God has used silver for molding the guards' nature and has utilized iron and copper for molding the farmers' and artisans, nature.[502]

As John Higley articulates, "Elites may [be] defined as persons who, by virtue of their strategic locations in large or otherwise

---

500. A.R. Khajeh-Sarvi, *Political Competition and Political Stability in Iran* (Tehran: Revolution Documents Center Publications, 2003), 339.
501. Asaf Hussain, *Political Perspective on the Muslim World* (New York: Praeger, 1981).
502. Plato. *The Republic* (Tehran: Cultural and Scientific Publications, 1995), 202.

pivotal organizations and movements, are able to affect political outcomes regularly and substantially."[503] In the Qur'an, the term for elite, *al-Mala*, conveys notions of greatness, leadership, nobility, and authority.[504] However, despite their privileged status, the Qur'an portrays these elites as staunchly resistant to prophets' messages, which advocate for profound ideological shifts and socio-economic reforms within societies. Class theory contends that political elites derive power from economic wealth and other resources, facilitating access to and consolidation of political influence. These resources encompass various social factors such as gender, education, ethnicity, religious affiliation, and political party allegiance.[505] Critical analysis of elites emphasizes the shared backgrounds among political elites, leading to similarities in political socialization, attitude formation, and interest alignment.[506] Ultimately, the elite concept encapsulates individuals esteemed within the community who enjoy the highest social, economic, political, and cultural status.[507] Robert Putman says, "elite political culture may be defined as the set of politically relevant beliefs, values, and habits of the most highly involved and in-fluential participants in a political system."[508] From an elitist perspective, elites are perceived as irreplaceable, suggesting that governance inevitably rests with a minority ruling over a majority. Analyzing elite political culture poses significant challenges, particularly in non-Western societies, where external influences intersect with indigenous

503. John Higley, *Elite theory in political sociology* (the University of Texas at Austin, 2008), 3.

504. See the meaning of *al-Mala* in the Qur'anic translations of Pickthall, Yusuf Ali, Shakir, Arberry, and others.

505. Weber M. *The theory of social and economic organization* (New York: Oxford University Press 1943).

506. Prewitt K, Stone A. "The ruling elite." In Olsen ME, Marger MN, Eds. *Power in modern societies. Boulder* (Westview Press 1993).

507. A. R. Khajeh-Sarvi, *Political Competition and Political Stability in Iran* (Tehran: Revolution Documents Center Publications, 2003), 339.

508. Robert Putman, "Studying Elite Political Culture." Available from https://www.cambridge.org/core/journals/american-political-science-review/article/studying-elite-political-culture-the-case-of-ideology/2EE8F3FE3 (accessed on September 17, 2020).

cultural norms. In post-colonial nations like Somalia, elite political culture represents a blend of externally imposed political norms and local clan traditions. The subsequent section will delineate the structures and formations of fundamental Somali elites, categorized into traditional and modern paradigms.

FORMATION AND STRUCTURE OF THE BASIC SOMALI ELITES

Segmented, clan-based mini-states emerged in various territories after the fall of medieval Somali states in the seventeenth century.[509] During the colonial partition of Africa, different colonial powers, including Britain, France, Italy, and Ethiopia, took control of various Somali territories. This period led to the formation of Somali elites, blending top-down, authoritarian colonial governance with local systems of authority. This fusion is evident in the rise of modern elites, political parties, electoral and legal systems, state institutions, and governance methods.[510] Simultaneously, local culture is rooted in deep Islamic faith blended with traditional clan ethos. Modern elites see the modern state and traditional society as dichotomous and mutually exclusive, drawing on modernization theory, which emphasizes tradition's inevitable demise and modernity's dominance.[511] This approach led to a perceived conflict between modernity and tradition, culminating in the military regime's policies that ultimately precipitated the collapse of the state in 1991. However, the combination of these two cultures gave rise to four distinct types of elites in Somalia: two traditional types and two modern types.[512]

---

509. The strongest medieval Somali states were Ajuran Imamate in the South and Adal in Northern Somalia. See Abdullahi, *Making Sense of Somali History, volume one,* 59–62.
510. Endalcachew Bayeh, "The Political and Economic Legacy of Colonialism in the Post-independent African States." *International Journal of Commerce, IT, and Social Sciences, Volume 2, Issue* 2 (February 2015). Available from https://www.researchgate.net/publication/273577309 (accessed on January 22, 2020).
511. Samuel Huntington, *The Change to Change: Modernization, development and politics* (New York: Free Press, 1976), 58–60.
512. Other elites, such as economic, civil society, and professional elites, are

The traditional elites consist of clan elders and scholars of Islam, particularly from Sufi orders. The modern elites, however, include Islamists and non-Islamists, with differing ideological stances.[513] Among these modern elites are political elites with diverse viewpoints. The four primary types of elites can be categorized as traditional and modern. Traditional elites tend to be amicable and cooperative, while modern elites often conflict due to opposing perspectives on the state's nature and legal structure. The ruling non-Islamist elites, mainly modern descendants of traditional elites, view traditional elites as outdated for establishing a modern state. In contrast, Islamists see them as hindrances to a proper understanding of Islam.[514] Nonetheless, both modern groups agree on the marginalization of traditional elites.

The ruling non-Islamist elites inherited the post-colonial state and aimed to maintain its quasi-secular nature. At the same time, political Islamists strongly support incorporating Islamic principles and values into the state and society.[515] Initially, political Islamists, influenced by the Salafia school, had strained relationships with traditional Islamic scholars of the Sufi order.[516] However, as the political Islamists matured, their relationship with the Sufi orders improved significantly. Additionally, the adversarial dynamic between political

---

crosscurrent.

513. See definitions of Islamist and non-Islamist in Abdullahi, Abdurahman. "Theorizing Islam and Islamists in Somalia: Critical Conception and Cultural Challenges." In *Theorizing Somalia Society: Hope, Transformation, and Development*, edited by Abdulkadir Osman Farah and Mohamed A. Eno, 122-159. Author's Press, 2022.

514. See the diagram of the basic elites and their relations from Abdurahman Abdullahi, "Tribalism, Nationalism, and Islam: The Crisis of the Political Loyalties in Somalia," master's thesis, Islamic Institute, McGill University, 1992, 93.

515. The author developed a diagram of the Somali elite formation and its relations. See Abdullahi, Abdurahman, "Tribalism, Nationalism, and Islam: The Crisis of the Political Loyalties in Somalia," master's thesis, Islamic Institute, McGill University, 1992, 92-101.

516. Salafia school is an ardent enemy of Sufi orders and considers them creators of innovations (*bid'a*) prohibited by Islam. Ibid, 96–97.

Islamists and ruling non-Islamists has eased since the adoption of the Islamic-compliant Transitional National Charter (TNC) in 2000.[517] These two political groups have also worked in regimes led by the Union of the Islamic Courts (Presidents Sheikh Sharif and Hassan Sheikh) and beyond. The current trend suggests an all-encompassing reconciliation between all Somali elites.

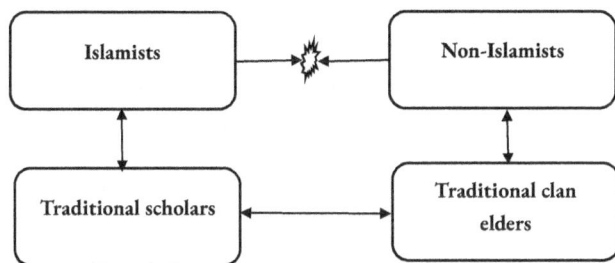

Fig. 22. The Four Main Elite Groups in Somalia

Formation of Traditional Clan Elders

Before the late nineteenth-century colonial incursion into Somalia, two types of traditional elites jointly governed the fragmented Somali society: clan elders and traditional scholars of Islam. These two groups harmonized their authority, with clan elders managing worldly affairs and scholars of Islam overseeing religious matters.[518] Clan elders primarily exercised their power through customary laws (Xeer), which incorporate aspects of Islamic sharia and local traditions. The structure includes various levels, from small Diya-paying units to large "clan families," as described by I.M. Lewis.[519] In

---

517. See National Transitional Charter, "The Islamic Sharia shall be the basic source for national legislation and any law contradicting Islamic Sharia shall be void and null," article 4: 4.

518. Lee Cassanelli, *The Shaping of Somali Society: Reconstructing the history of a Pastoral People, 1960–1900* (University of Pennsylvania Press, 1982), 112.

519. Diya-paying unit is derived from the Arabic language of Diya; Somali, mag. I.M. Lewis, "Force, and Fission in Northern Somali Lineage Structure." American Anthropologist, Available from https://anthrosource.onlinelibrary.wiley.com/doi/pdfdirect/10.1525/aa.1961.63.1.02a00060 (accessed September 20, 2020).

pastoral areas, Diya-paying units are based on blood relations, while in agricultural and urban areas, they are formed through naturalization and alliances. They constitute "4 to 8 generations of span, whose members are bound not only by their close agnatic ties but also by an explicit treaty or contract."[520] It is estimated that Diya-paying units range from hundreds to thousands. At higher clan levels, multiple Diya-paying units merge to form larger clan lineages, with elders assuming titles such as Imam, Ugas, Islan, Boqor, Wabar, Malaaq, Grad, Sultan, etc. These lineages form clan families, including four major families—Darood, Dir, Digl & Mirifle, and Hawiye—and several minority clans. Minority clans include Banadiri, Barawani, Bajuni, Jareer-Wayne,[521] Yahar, Meheri, and Reer Aw-Hassan. These groups were not related by blood or shared territory but were amalgamated in 2000 for political purposes. Consequently, political power in Somalia is divided according to a 4.5 power-sharing formula.[522]

Each Diya-paying unit operates autonomously, with its territory, clan wells, customary laws, and clan elders recognized by neighboring clans. Clan elders are primarily responsible for maintaining security, resolving conflicts, overseeing the Diya system, and managing inter- and intra-clan relations. Thus, Diya-paying units function similarly to small states with modern state-like features.[523] Decisions are made through participatory deliberations among adult male members until a consensus is reached, a process I.M. Lewis described as "Pastoral Democracy" in his study of Northern Somalis.[524] Clans are not dis-

---

520. Ibid, 97.
521. Jareer-Wayne is not a numerical minority, but a sociological minority. One of the major clans in Somalia, most live at the banks of the rivers of Shabelle and Juba and exercise agriculture. They constitute original settlers and remnants of the slave trade era. Ethnically, they are linked to the Bantu race, and were marginalized educationally and economically.
522. The 4.5 power-sharing formula was adopted in the Somali Peace and Reconciliation Conference held in Djibouti in 2000. It was founded to offer the main clan families equal shares in the parliament and to give amalgamation of the minority clans half of the share.
523. Abdullahi, *Tribalism, Nationalism and Islam*, 37–39.
524. I.M. Lewis, *Pastoral Democracy: A Study of Pastoralism and Politics among*

organized groups wandering; they follow customary laws and procedures that guide their inter- and intra-clan relationships. These laws
are unwritten but memorized and passed down through generations
by clan elders.

Before colonial rule, traditional elders led their clans as supreme
leaders. However, after signing various agreements, colonial powers
recognized them as local partners, incorporating them into the
colonial governance system as salaried employees. As reported by
Lewis, "In the late 1950s, there were 950 recognized Diya-paying
groups in Italian Somaliland and 361 in British Somaliland."[525]
These elders often utilized the state's coercive power to manage their
clans. Over time, many clan elders moved to urban areas, establishing permanent homes and gaining early access to modern education
and state employment for their descendants.[526] Colonial policies that
offered educational opportunities to traditional leaders' offspring to
ensure continuity in leadership encouraged this shift. The formation
of the Territorial Council in the UN Trust Territory under the Italian
Administration highlighted the dominance of traditional elites.[527] In
British Somaliland, the first Legislative Council was formed in 1957,
and twenty-four Advisory Council members representing major
clans were appointed.[528]

In contrast, Somali nationalists viewed clan elders as a threat to
their goals and reframed colonial integration policies as marginalization strategies. Traditional institutions were seen as opposing and
undermining nationalist ambitions. Thus, nationalists worked to
diminish the influence of clan elders and promote nationalism. After
the state collapsed in 1991, the role of clan elders evolved. In addition

Northern Somali of the Horn of Africa (LIT Verlag, 1999).
525. I.M. Lewis, *A Modern History of Somalia: Nation and State in the Horn of Africa* (Longman, 1980), 166–67. Also, Abdullahi, *Tribalism, Nationalism, and Islam*, 36–37.
526. Sylvia Pankhurst, *Ex-Italian Somaliland* (London: Watts & Co., 1951), 214.
527. Abdullahi, *Making Sense of Somali History, Volume two*, 145.
528. Lewis, *Modern History of Somalia*, 152.

to their traditional functions, they actively rebuilt local and national institutions.

Formation of Traditional Scholars of Islam

Traditional scholars of Islam play a central role in communities by overseeing religious functions. Their responsibilities include providing Islamic education, guiding and overseeing events such as teaching the Qur'an and other Islamic disciplines, conducting marriage contracts and managing inheritance, and leading prayers, fasting, and celebrating Islamic holidays, among other duties. Due to their religious authority, these scholars hold high respect and reverence within the community. During the broader Islamization period of the thirteenth century, scholars of Islam established a sustainable educational system using effective teaching methods. This Islamic education was "community-centered and locally administered."[529] Schooling began with memorizing the Qur'an in early childhood, facilitated by a creative method for learning the Arabic alphabet invented by Somali scholar Sheikh Yuusuf al-Kawnayn. Sheikh Yusuf al-Kawnayn (Aw-Barkhadle) is one of the oldest known scholars of Islam, propagating Islam in Somalia around the thirteenth century. Little is known about his biography. He introduced the notation system for Arabic alphabets in the Somali language, known as *Higaad*.[530] Memorizing the Qur'an represents the first stage of Islamic education, which has remained a sustainable practice for centuries. Talented graduates from this primary level often become Qur'anic teachers and open Qur'anic schools.

The second level of Islamic education commences when ambitious students pursue advanced Islamic learning, supported by the community through scholarships and other forms of en-

529. Abdinoor Abdullahi, "*Constructing Education in the Stateless Society: The Case of Somalia,*" Ph.D. thesis submitted to the University of Ohio, 2007, 25.
530. I.M. Lewis reconstructed some insights from oral traditions and findings of Cerulli in Harrar. His tomb is located at Dagor, about 20 km from Hargeysa. See I.M. Lewis, *Saints, and Somalis: Popular Islam in Clan-based Society (The Red Sea Press, 1998)*, 89–98.

couragement. This scholarship package encompasses free education offered by the learned scholars and free accommodation provided by the community members. This system is called *Jilidda Xer-cilmiga* (feeding seekers of knowledge), in which dwellers of cities provided food for the rural students of Islamic studies. After completing their studies, some scholars return to their home areas to establish Islamic education centers. They contribute to establishing new villages that promote the settlement and urbanization of pastoral populations. Their mentors often send the most accomplished graduates as emissaries to their home territories to spread Islam, which aligns with the Qur'an's teachings. This proceeding accords with the Quranic verse, "and it is not proper for the believers to go out to fight (Jihad), all together. Of every troop of them, a party only should go forth, that they may get instructions in the Islamic religion, and that they may warn their people when they return to them, so that they may beware (of evil)" (9:122).

The third level of Islamic education focuses on Sufism, taught by masters of Sufi orders who are also mainly prominent scholars of Islam. Sufism emphasizes spiritual purification under the guidance of a spiritual master, fostering a closer personal relationship with Allah through special disciplines and spiritual practices. Sufi orders have played a significant role in reviving Islam among the masses through innovative mobilization methods that promote collective identity, belonging, and mutual support. These techniques help reduce clan polarization and segmentation by establishing trans-clan networks within society. Sufi orders are active across Somalia and enjoy broad popular support. There are two primary Sufi orders in Somalia: Qaadiriyah and Ahmadiyah.[531] These orders have local offshoots, such as Zayli'iyah and Uweysiyah for Qadiriyah, and

---

531. Most scholars fail to distinguish between the original Sufi order and its later derivatives. Sometimes, these Sufi orders are said to be three, making Salihiyah a separate order from Ahmadiyah and neglecting the existence of the Rufaiyah order. See David Laitin and Said Samatar, *Somalia: Nation in Search of a State* (Westview, 1987), 45.

Rahmaniyah, Salihiyah, and Dandarawiyah for Ahmadiyah.[532] The influence of modern education has led to a process of reformation among followers of Sufi orders.

Formation of Non-Islamist Elites

Non-Islamists are the elites who may or may not be devoted to Islam. They share the common characteristic of not advocating for the application of Islam in society and state. They are not synonymous with secularists. Indeed, Islamists and secularists are minorities among Muslims in all countries, though they are more organized and vocal. The early development of non-Islamist elites was associated with the descendants of traditional elites because of the colonial policy of creating a continuation of the loyal line of the traditional elites. The children of traditional elites who dwelled in the cities received early education opportunities. Thus, non-Islamist elites were developed with the proliferation of modern schools and during the state-building process. In general, the development of modern education in Somalia was sluggish for many reasons. The reasons include insufficient budgetary allocation of colonial rulers, religious sensitivities, socio-political unrest, volatile security, and the lack of vested interests. "With such a slow process, the formation of the Somali elite was sluggish, deficient, and divergent, mired within the Cold War atmosphere and Muslim-Christian tensions."[533]

Modern education was taught in colonial languages, and colonial curricula were adopted to promote a Western outlook. Thus, Italian and English became the official languages of education, while Arabic (the official language of the early educated elites) was kept an insignificant part of the curricula. Unluckily, the Somali language was not committed to writing until 1972. Moreover, non-state modern education, which appeared mainly in the 1950s, embodied a hodgepodge of different schools and curricula, such as Christian Mission

---

532. Abdurahman Abdullahi, *The Islamic Movement in Somalia: A Study of Islah Movement, 1950-2000* (Adonis & Abbey, 2015), 39-42.
533. Abdurahman Abdullahi, *Making Sense of Somali History, Volume one* (Adonis & Abbey, 2017), 101.

schools, Egyptian Arabic schools, and Italian schools.[534] In the past, the Italian Fascist regime that took power in 1923 prohibited formal education in all Italian colonies. It allowed cultural schools to bequeathed to the Roman Christian Church. The objective of that education was to provide qualified workers for jobs unsuitable for the "superior race" of Italians.[535] Moreover, it was unfair that cultural schools were reserved only for the sons of obedient notables and those expected to succeed their fathers in serving colonial masters as interpreters, clerks, and office boys.[536] Nevertheless, this policy changed after the defeat of Italy in World War II in 1941 and the establishment of the British Military Administration (BMA). Since then, modern education has begun "without a ceiling."[537] Therefore, the Somalis took great interest in modern education through the local initiatives of civil society groups and political parties. Remarkably, emerging political parties competed by investing in education to attract public support. The SYL party took a pioneering role in this race by making the advancement of education one of its major programs.[538] Other political parties also followed suit and conducted similar education programs. By 1947, a total of 19 state-funded elementary schools were taught in Arabic with English as the second language. This trend was spreading horizontally, and by 1950, there

---

534. Moḥamed Sharif Moḥamūd, "*Abdirizāq Hāji Hussein, Rais Wasāra al-Somāli (1964-1967)*, 2009," available from http://arabic.alshahid.net/columnists/6110 (accessed on April 21, 2010).

535. Italy was ruled by a fascist regime from 1922 to 1943, a far-right ideology based on racism and authoritarianism.

536. Abdurahman Abdullahi, *Tribalism, Nationalism, and Islam*, 63.

537. Salah Mohamed's terminology means freedom to establish schools and even local organizations were granted. During fascist rule, these activities were prohibited. See Salah Mohamed Ali, *Hudur and the History of Southern Somalia* (Cairo: Nahda Book Publisher, 2005), 358.

538. The party had opened many adult night classes with the generous contributions of its members, and by 1948, 65 percent percent of its classes were taught in English compared with 35 percent percent in Arabic. The Somali Youth League (SYL) was the first political party in Somalia. It was founded as a youth organization in 1943 and became a political party in 1947. Being the major nationalist party, it became the ruling party (1956–1969).

were 29 schools with an enrolment of 1,600 students employing 45 teachers.[539]

When the UN Trusteeship mandated Italy in 1950 to prepare Somalia for independence within 10 years, the objective of education was radically changed.[540] A five-year development program was launched in 1952 in collaboration with UNESCO. According to this plan, modern schools, technical institutes, and teacher training programs were established. As reported by I.M. Lewis, "By 1957, some 31,000 children and adults of both sexes were enrolled in primary schools, 246 in junior secondary schools, 336 in technical institutes, and a few hundred more in higher educational institutions."[541] The above data shows a notable advance in modern education compared with the conditions before the 1950s, when fewer than 2,000 students were receiving education. Moreover, specialized schools, such as the School of Politics and Administration, were established in Mogadishu in the 1950s. Some of the graduates of this institute were offered scholarships for further studies at Perugia University in Italy. Others were employed during the speedy Somalization program in the government administration after 1956.

During this period, 4,380 Somalis (88 percent of the labor force) were employed in government institutions. This was a large number compared with the British Administration in Somaliland during the same period, where only 300 were employed in the state administration, with only 30 (10 percent) being Somali.[542] Other institutes were

---

539. Lee Cassanelli and Farah Sheikh Abdulkadir, "*Somali Education in Transition*" (Bildhan, vol. 7, 2007), 91–125. There is a discrepancy in the statistical data on student enrolment numbers. This paper gives 1,600, while Tripodi gives 2,850. See Paolo Tripodi, *The Colonial Legacy in Somalia: Rome and Mogadishu: From Colonial Administration to Operation Restore Hope* (Palgrave Macmillan, 1999), 59.
540. Tripodi, Ibid, 59.
541. Lewis, *A History of Somalia*, 140.
542. Somalization of administration was a program that gave Somalis the responsibility of administering the country through training and coaching by Italian administrators. The significant difference in administrative style and nur-

also opened in 1954, the most important of which was the Higher Institute of Law and Economics, which later became Somalia's University College. It subsequently developed into the Somali National University in 1972.[543] Moreover, scholarships, seminars, and official visits to Italy were provided to the emerging Somali elites to familiarize them with the Italian language and culture. Gradually, new Somali elites emerged through better modern education and improved employment privileges imbued with Italian culture. These elites became leaders of the political parties, senior administrators, district councilors, and provincial governors. They were also employed in the state's security apparatus. The role of the new elites grew even more rapidly in 1956. They emerged as the ruling elite when they replaced Italians in all senior administrative positions to prepare Somalia for independence in 1960. Nonetheless, there was not much development to boast in the higher echelons of education. "According to [the] UN report on Somalia, three years before independence, there was not a single Somali medical doctor, professional pharmacist, engineer, or high school teacher in Somalia."[544] However, 37 Somali students attended Italian universities in 1957–58, of whom 27 were expected to graduate in 1960.[545]

In British Somaliland, all attempts to introduce modern education were delayed because of the expulsion of the Christian Mission in 1910, the subsequent atmosphere of public worries about introducing Christianity, and the impact of the Jihad of Sayid Mohamed

---

turing of the new elites is evident in the two colonies of the British and Italians under the UN trusteeship. See Tripodi, *The Colonial Legacy,* 75.

543. Lewis, *A History of Somalia,* 141.

544. Abdirahman Ahmed Noor, "Arabic Language and Script in Somalia: History, attitudes and prospects." PhD diss., Georgetown University, 1999, 52.

545. "In 1960, the year of independence, only 27 seven Somalis would receive university degrees in Italy; one in medicine, six in political science, one in social science, nine in economics and business administration, one in journalism, three in veterinary medicine, two in agronomy, one in natural science, one in pharmacy, and one in linguistics." See Mohamed Osman Omar, *The Road to Zero: Somalia's Self-destruction* (HAAN associates, 1992), 45.

Abdulle Hasan.[546] Moreover, a combination of the Somali resistance to taxation and the insufficiency of colonial financial allocations contributed to the postponement of modern education in British Somaliland. In 1950, the first two intermediate schools were opened and expanded gradually afterward. According to the public records, the total number of students in Somaliland had increased from 623 in 1948 to 6,209 in 1959.[547]

With the Somali independence in 1960 and the unification of British Somaliland and UN Trust territory of Somalia under Italy, the non-Islamist elites became the national leaders of the Somali state. Somali students received scholarships to many countries under the Cold War competition between the West and the East. For instance, incomplete statistical data shows the following trends: in the 1960s, about 500 civilian students were studying in the Soviet Union, 272 in Italy, 152 in Saudi Arabia, 86 in the USA, 40 in Sudan, 34 in the UK, 32 in France, and 29 in India.[548] This indicates that the total number of scholarships awarded by Western countries was less than that of the Soviet Union alone. Looking into the military sector, this trend is even more evident. After Somalia grew dissatisfied with the small amount of Western assistance for military purposes, in 1963, the Soviets agreed to help Somalia build a strong army as part of a Cold War strategy to balance the US presence in Ethiopia. According to Laitin and Samatar, "a joint Western countries' proposal for the military assistance to Somalia was $10 million for an army of 5,000 persons. However, the Soviet offer was a loan of $52 million and an army of 14,000 persons. Thus, the Soviets succeeded in taking over the training of the Somali army."[549] As a result, Somali military

---

546. Saadia Touval, *Somali Nationalism: International Politics and the Drive for Unity in the Horn of Africa* (Cambridge: Cambridge University Press, 1963), 64.

547. Ahmed Samatar, *Socialist Somalia: Rhetoric and Reality* (London: Zed Press, 1988), 47.

548. Luigi Pastaloza, *The Somali Revolution* (Bari: Edition Afrique Asie Amerique Latine, 1973), 350.

549. Laitin and Samatar, *Somalia: Nation,* 78.

officers trained in the Soviet Union alone were estimated at more than 500 by 1969. Thus, most non-Islamist elites were indoctrinated with the socialist ideology.[550] Elites trained in the socialist countries added to a far-left drift to the growing Westernization, and the ramifications of this phenomenon were experienced during the military regime in 1969.

Formation of Islamist Elites

Islamists signify devoted individuals or organized groups (movements) who assertively promote Islamic teachings and values in society and advocate for applying Islamic principles at the state level. Islamists are not monolithic and range from moderate reformists to extremist revolutionaries and state collaborators.[551] They differ in their objectives, approaches, understanding of Islam, and relations with non-Muslims. Islamist elites were developed through two processes. The first was formal education in Arabic/Islamic schools, where some graduates had an opportunity to further their studies at Arab higher education institutions in Egypt, Syria, Iraq, and Saudi Arabia. This does not mean that these students were automatically subjected to an Islamic agenda since most Arab institutions of higher learning had also been secularized during the colonial period and in the subsequent Arab nationalist movements. Nevertheless, students of Arabic schools were imbued with Islamic/Arabic culture, and some of them, either through direct contact or by reading published literature, became aware of the new Islamist trends in the Muslim world. The second process was through those who, after becoming traditional scholars of Islam in Somalia, traveled abroad and joined Islamic higher learning institutions. These scholars contacted other Islamic scholars and students from many Muslim countries with strong Islamist activism. These scholars could be called "transition-

---

550. Samatar, *Socialist Somalia*, 78.
551. Abdurahman Abdullahi, "Theorizing Somalia: Islam and Islamists in state-building." A paper submitted to the Conference on Somalia: Continuity and Change in Somali Society, Politics, and Economy in the Longue Durée. Maxis Planck Institute for Social Anthropology, 20–22 June 2018.

al scholars of Islam" since they bridged traditional and modern ed-ucational systems.[552] Indeed, these scholars pioneered the modern Islamist movements in Somalia.

In the process of state-building, Islamist elites were marginalized, initially through unequal job opportunities. For instance, graduates of Arabic high schools and universities could not compete for local jobs with graduates from government schools or other non-state schools because of language barriers. The language of the adminis-tration in Somalia remained either Italian or English until the Somali language was committed to writing in 1972. Therefore, the only jobs available for graduates from Arabic schools and universities were low-paying jobs for teachers of Arabic and Islamic subjects in schools, judges, or joining the national army. This structural inequal-ity through diversified curricula and languages created a bifurcation of the elites. Discrimination against the elites educated in Arabic forced many of them to explore alternatives.

Students educated in the Arabic language realized that the only equal opportunity for them was to join the national army or explore scholarships in socialist countries such as the Soviet Union, East Germany, or China. All Somalis had equal opportunities in these countries since new languages had to be learned. Exceptions were a small number of civilian scholarships, and cadet officers sent to Italy who had to be graduates from Italian schools. Similarly, civilian scholarships and cadet officers sent to Arab countries such as Egypt, Syria, and Iraq had to converse in Arabic. The trend of sending young Somalis to Eastern and Western countries with either Socialist or capitalist ideologies eventually brought a cultural and ideological schism orchestrated through the Cold War fever. Regarding Islamist scholars, with their meager resources and capacity, they were initially

---

552. The most notable Islamist scholars were Sheikh Ali Sufi, Sayid Ahmad Sheikh Muse, Sheikh Abdulqani Sheikh Ahmad, Sheikh Nur Ali Olow, Sheikh Mahamad Ahmad Nuur (Garyare), Sheikh Mohamad Moallim Hasan, Ab-dullahi Moallim and Sheikh Abdirahman Hussein Samatar, Sheikh Ali Ismael, Sheikh Ibrahim Hashi, Sharif Mohamud, and others.

advocating the revival of the Islamic culture and promotion of the Arabic language.

The Islamic revivalism was the culmination of the rising consciousness of Islam in Somalia as part of a broader awakening that was taking place in the Muslim world. It began in the 1950s and gradually spread in the 1960s, with the founding of the organizations Nahdah, Ahal, and Wahdah, which actively preached the Muslim Brotherhood approach to preaching Islam. Even though early Islamist movements were short-lived, their impact was significant and lasting. Nahdah operated for only three years, although its members remained prominent in Islamic activism for an extended period. Ahal ceased to exist in 1977 after about eight years of active work, and its members were divided into different new Islamic organizations. In 1983, Wahdah ceased to exist officially after it was united with Jama Islamiyah and became part of Al-Itihad.[553] It is essential, however, to characterize the Islamist awakening in this period as immature and with a high emotional attachment to Islam, low organizational capacity, meager economic resources, and a romantic approach to social and political realities.

The establishment of the Islamist movements was linked to a global trend that had taken root in Somalia since 1978. For instance, Islah was established in 1978 as a Muslim Brotherhood branch of Somalia. Jama Islamiyah was formed in 1979 as a neo-Salafia movement, which later transformed into Al-Ittihad in 1983. Moreover, other smaller organizations, such as al-Takfir and al-Ikhwan, were also operating. The collective work of these organizations created a wave of spreading modern ideas of the Islamist movements among Somali ethnic communities in the Horn of Africa. Acquiring higher education like the ordinary Somalis, the formation of Islamist elites took great strides

---

553. This unification did not last long, and many members of Wahdah quit Al-Ittihad and reorganized themselves. This group made a great effort to work with SNM during the difficult period of the civil war. They focused their work on the refugee camps and later influenced the Somaliland Constitution and flag. The author interviewed Ismail Abdi Hurre on August 14, 2009, in Hargeisa, Somaliland.

by the 1990s. After the collapse of the state in 1991, Al-Islah and Al-Ittihad emerged as strong organizations, adopting two different approaches to the civil war: moderation and militancy.[554]

The Islamist movement's political impact appeared strongly during the SPRC in Djibouti in 2000. Their influence is evident from the adopted Transitional National Charter (TNC), which makes Islam the ultimate reference of all laws. Moreover, many Islamists became members of the parliament and cabinet ministers. The political role of Islamists grew exponentially after the emergence of the Islamic Courts Union in 2006. Since then, various persuasions of Islamists participated actively in Somali politics and even took a leadership role in the two regimes (2009–2016).[555] The impact of Somali Islamist movements is ubiquitous in all sectors encompassing politics, economics, and society. Thus, Islamist political elites are growing and occupying more spaces.

Concluding this section, the Somali elite formation went through stages and transformed gradually. Its new trends indicate the rapprochement of all elites since the SPRC in 2000. Traditional and modern elites accepted each other during this conference, and the state and society were reconciled in the adopted TNC. Further, modern elites abandoned eschewing traditional elites after their empowerment to select members of the parliament in the clan power-sharing formula of 4.5. Moreover, Islam was adopted as the ultimate reference of laws in the TNC, and Islamists and non-Islamists had equal opportunities to be selected by their clans. This trend has been growing in the last twenty years, and the biased view based on ideology has dwindled. Moreover, many traditional elites

---

554. Abdurahman Abdullahi, "The Islah Movement in Somalia: Islamic Moderation in War-torn Somalia," available from https://www.hiiraan.com/oct2008/ISLAH.pdf (accessed on October 4, 2020). Also, see Andrew McGregor, "The Muslim Brotherhood in Somalia: An Interview with Islah's Abdurahman M. Abdullahi (Baadiyow)," Terrorism Monitor, volume 9, issue 30, July 29, 2011.
555. The regimes of Sheikh Sharif and Hassan Sheikh (2009–2017) were considered to belong to the Islamic persuasions.

transformed, whereas many others became highly educated individuals who inherited their fathers' leadership. Furthermore, the distinction between Islamists and non-Islamists has become cloudy and increasingly narrow because of pervasive Islamism. Nonetheless, in the elite political culture, Islamic values remain shallow, while performing essential Islamic practical obligations is ubiquitous.[556] The new trend shows the early stage of reconciling tradition and modernity, and Islamists and non-Islamists.

HISTORICAL EVOLUTION OF ELITE POLITICAL CULTURE

The elite political culture and the impact of the institutions of the society are the two variables that must be understood regarding the failure of the Somali state. These two variables are mutually interdependent and co-evolve in a complementary way.[557] Culture may change in different ways depending on the nature of institutions, and institutions may perform differently in various cultures. This section examines the Somali elite political culture, which is very complex, with multiple factors shaping its development. The first factor is the local political culture of clannish society, a fusion of the universal Islamic culture and particularistic Somali clan culture. The second culture is the Italian political culture imposed/acquired as part of elite acculturation during the 70 years of Italian rule. Relatively, the British indirect rule of Somaliland and its cultural influence was ephemeral. The first manifestation of modern elite political culture appeared in Somalia under UN trusteeship with the establishment of the first local administration in 1956. This culture was formed as a hybrid of the asymmetrical mixture of the top-down, authoritarian, and bureaucratic Italian colonial rule and local societal elite culture. The hybrid culture of local and Italian continued to be dominant until 1969. The second phase was introduced during the military rule that espoused socialism (1969–1991). The twenty-one-year rule of the dictatorial regime left behind an enduring impact on the

556. See Abdullahi, *Theorizing Somalia: Islam and Islamists.*
557. Alberto Alesina; Poala Giuliano. *"Culture and Institutions,"* IZA Discussion Papers, No. 9246, Institute for the Study of Labor (IZA), Bonn, 2015.

elite political culture of the subsequent generations. The third phase was during the civil war and the dominance of the warlords (1991–2000). The culture of warlordism had the characteristics of anarchy, lawlessness, marginalization of the minority clans, and strong foreign patronage. The fourth phase was acquired in 2000 through clan-power sharing. As a result, Somali nationalism has been weakened, and sub-nationalism has been consolidated by adopting the federal system. To understand the chemistry of the complex fusion of these multiple elite cultures, the following section provides an overview of the major trends of each phase. Then, through synthesis, the section describes the resultant elite political culture currently discernible in Somalia.

The Formative Period of Elite Political Culture (1956–1969)

In the pre-colonial era, clans were the only existing socio-political units that functioned in small geographical areas. In general, the type of political culture in this clannish society is termed a parochial-localism culture. The fundamental unit of the Somali clan system is called the Diya-paying unit, which provides two essential functions. First, it provides the basic human need for affection, belonging, and identity; second, it offers solidarity among its members to provide social welfare and collective security. According to Harold Lasswell's broad definition, politics takes place everywhere. Thus, this paper considers the Diya-paying unit as a sovereign mini-state. The following list describes the main elements of the political culture of clannish society.

Clan Solidarity: The main cultural characteristic of the clans is strong solidarity among its members, which generates the ideology of clannism. This solidarity is called 'mechanical solidarity' compared to 'organic solidarity' as theorized by the French sociologist Emile Durkheim (1858–1917).[558] Although this solidarity is necessary for

---

558. According to French sociologist, Emile Durkheim, mechanical solidarity refers to connection, cohesion, and integration born from homogeneity, or similar work, education, religiosity, and lifestyle. On the other hand, organic solidarity is born from the interdependence of individuals in more advanced societies.

the survival of the pastoral communities, it is not always positive and often discriminates against and excludes those not a member of their clan. Clannism is like nationalism in many aspects, with the only differences between them being the levels of solidarity. Clannism is located at the micro level, while nationalism is at the macro level. Both clannism and nationalism may be positively used as factors of solidarity or negatively as factors of oppression and intolerance to others. Clannism generates dominant sentiments such as the fame and glory of an individual derive from "the fame and the glory of his ancestor."[559] Accordingly, clan members glorify their clans and ancestors and express solidarity with their political elites. This behavior generates vanity and an attitude of superiority among clans. This cultural pattern produces the exclusion of other clans and the fragmentation of society. Clan solidarity in Somalia is more robust in the pastoral areas and among their extended families in the urban centers.

Rivalry over Resources: The other political culture concerns rivalry over scarce resources. This rivalry instigates continuous fighting between neighboring clans over posture and water wells. These clans have a high rate of intermarriages that often mitigate their conflicts because of their blood relations through their mothers. Nonetheless, continuous conflicts over scarce resources and fighting are cyclical and part of nomadic life. The recurring conflicts have produced a culture of looting the properties of the defeated clans, particularly their camels. However, this culture is dominant in the nomadic pastoral societies. In urban and agro-pastoral societies, peaceful and cooperative cultural trends have developed. This cultural attitude generates violent behavior among the nomadic population.

Collective Leadership: Somalis are traditionally independent and egalitarian people, and as I.M. Lewis described them, "all men are

---

For more details, see Emile Durkheim, *The Division of Labour in Society*. Trans. W.D. Halls (New York: Free Press, 1997).

559. Ignaz Goldziher, *Muslim Studies,* vol. 1. (London: George Allen & Unwin Ltd., 1910), 22.

councilors, all men are politicians."[560] Generally, there is no dictatorship culture in the local Somali culture. Governance is founded on participatory consultation among all male members of the clan and a consensus decision-making process. In some areas, hereditary hierarchical leadership had developed but maintained a high level of participation by the elites of sub-clans. In general, Somalis are independent-minded, excessively freedom-loving people who sometimes reach a chaotic level of anarchy.

Strong Islamic Identity: Somalia is located at the periphery of the Muslim world, where Muslims and Christians interact with each other. It is a frontier state that defends the heartland of Islam from external invasions and extends its frontiers through various means. On the other hand, Somalia is the place where the Islamic identity took prominence, and the Christian-Muslim borders are drawn. It is also a source of inspiration for the Muslim population in the Horn of Africa region. The depth of the Somali identity is expressed by the maxim that "Somalis, for the most part, do not by and large apply Islamic values, but they always protect Islam and guard it against abuses of others." Moreover, the Somali wisdom that "two are inviolable in Somalia: clan culture and Islam" conveys the same message, meaning that most Somalis are ready to sacrifice their lives to defend these inviolable ideals.[561]

Disregarding State Authority: According to Michael Bauman, "all laws, regardless of their content or their intent, arise from a system of values, from a belief that some things are right and others wrong, that some things are good and others bad, that some things are better and others worse."[562] Moreover, Ibn-Khaldun wrote, "Arabs [nomads] can obtain royal authority only making use of some religious coloring such as prophecy, or sainthood, or some

---

560. Quoted in David Laitin, *Politics, Language and Thought: The Somali Experience* (The University of Chicago Press, 1977), 26.

561. Abdurahman Abdullahi, *Recovering the Somali State: The Role of Islam, Islamism and Transitional Justice* (Adonis & Abbey, 2017), 67.

562. Michael Bauman, "Law and Morality," available from http://www.equip.org/article/law-andmorality/ (accessed on October 4, 2020).

great religious event in general."[563] Accordingly, Somali people respect local customary laws and accept Islamic Sharia founded on their values. However, they "disregard secular laws derived from the inherited colonial laws [and] imposed on the Somali society."[564]

The Impact of Italian Political Culture

Having the above-stated characteristics of the local political culture in general, Italy and Britain occupied Somali territories in the nineteenth century, as did France and Ethiopia. The Italian rule was effective in two periods: the Fascist rule (1922–1941) and the UN trusteeship period under the Italian Administration (1950–1960). In between, Somalia was under BMA (1941–1950). Somali political development occurred during the UN trusteeship period, during which Somali political elites were trained, and socio-economic programs were implemented. Thus, Italian political culture was introduced in Somalia. The emerging political elites adopted the Italian political culture mixed with local political clannish culture, which created a cultural dynamism that "once established, these orientations [the hybrid culture] have a momentum of their own, and may act as an autonomous influence on politics and economics long after the events that gave rise to them."[565] Comparatively, the cultural impact of Britain's indirect rule in Somaliland and its 10-year rule under BMA in most Somali territories was insignificant. We will briefly address Italian political culture to better comprehend the new hybrid culture.

Italian politics are founded on a parliamentary system of governance and a multi-party system. This system has a reputation for political fragmentation and government instability. Indeed, the predominant narrative of Italian political culture was characterized as "static, backward, 'immobile,' and impermeable to change,

---

563. Ibn-Khaldun, *The Muqaddimah: An Introduction to History* (Princeton University Press, 1980), 305.
564. Abdullahi, *Recovering the Somali State*, 81.
565. Ronald Inglehart, *Culture Shift in Advanced Industrial Society* (Princeton University Press, 1990), 17.

as described in the early 1950s."[566] Moreover, the Italian political culture was summarized during the 1950s as "familistic-parochial-localistic."[567] The familistic-parochial culture is "the prevalence of local sources of identifications, low pride for the country, and unwillingness to make sacrifices if required."[568] The main elements of this political culture could be summarized as follows:

Localism: Localism is identification with a group to which each Italian refers when he thinks of himself as part of the body politic. It is like clannism, based on agentic affiliation or territorial alliance in the Somali context. When studying Italian political culture, Edward Benfield coined the term "amoral familist" to describe a person who behaves according to the following rule: "maximize the material, short-run advantage of the nuclear family; assume that all others will do likewise."[569] In this political culture, individuals are greedy and busy amassing wealth for personal gain, which is characterized by a high level of corruption, ineptitude, and lack of political direction. Early scholars defined familism as a strong identification with family characterized by loyalty, reciprocity, and solidarity among family members.

Widespread Corruption: Another characteristic of Italian political culture is widespread corruption. Diego Gambetta explained Italian corruption culture: "The level of corruption is on a par with or worse than that of much less developed countries while being far above the level of similarly developed countries."[570] Empirical evidence demon-

---

566. Pierangelo Isernia and Danilo Di Mauro, "The Bumble-Bee is Still Flying: Italian Political Culture at 50." Available from https://en.idi.org.il/media/6383/bythepeople_iserniadimauro.pdf (accessed on September 30, 2020).
567. Ibid.
568. Ibid, 150.
569. Edward Banfield, *The Moral Basis of a Backward Society* (Free Press, 1958), 83.
570. Diego Gambetta, "Why is Italy Disproportionally Corrupt? A Conjecture." In *Institutions, Governance, and the Control of Corruption*, eds. Kaushik Basu and Tito Gardella (Palgrave McMillan, 2018, 133).

strates that bribery, extortion, and graft are often the outgrowths of the deeper Italian culture of "corruption."[571]

Political Patronage: This culture allowed groups of citizens linked directly to politicians to reap high rewards through special laws (legging) or political appointments. The internal patronage that produced rewards and appointments was not aimed at enhancing efficiency or recruiting professional expertise. The interaction between politicians, bureaucracy, and groups of citizens directly linked to politicians was a characteristic of the Italian political system. Political patronage is a worldwide phenomenon; however, Italy ranks high in the index of party patronage.[572]

Political Fragmentation and Instability: One of the main features of the Italian political culture is instability and fragmentation. This culture often leads to short-lived coalition governments and unlimited political parties. "Political instability and fragmentation have been constants of the Italian scene through most of the post-war period. Until recently, governments changed with bewildering frequency. Italy has had over 60 governments since the end of World War II."[573] The instability of the political system is associated with the political party system, the structures of two houses of representatives, the electoral model, and so on.

Democratic Culture: Democratic countries choose one of two models of democracy: consensual or competitive (majoritarian). Consensus democracy is founded on the culture of consensus de-

---

571. Corruption costs Italy 60 billion euros or 4 percent of its GDP annually. Italy ranks equally corrupt as Senegal, Montenegro, and South Africa. See https://www.thelocal.it/20160127/italy-is-still-one-of-europes-most-corrupt-countries (accessed on September 8, 2020).
572. Research Note: Party patronage in contemporary democracies: Results from an expert survey in 22 countries from five regions. European Journal of Political Research. Available from https://openaccess.leidenuniv.nl/bitstream/handle/1887/46621/a23ff93a9bbc5d48e219e1c585e186485c48477b7ba1e-29101ce134b907b5e2b.pdf?sequence=1 (accessed on September 8, 2020).
573. Michael Calingaert, "Italy's Choice: Reform or Stagnation." Current History, March 2008, 105–111.

cision-making, which involves coalition building and a broad range of opinions. On the other hand, the majoritarian system considers only the decision-making of the majority party, and minority parties and voices are ignored.[574] The adopted type of democracy depends on the culture of that society, and each type has advantages and limitations. Italian democracy belongs to the consensus system, which is characterized by a broad coalition of power-sharing, the executive and legislative balance of power, a multi-party system, a proportional representation election model, a federal and decentralized system, strong bi-cameralism, and so on.[575]

Countries	Somali Traditional Political Culture	Italian Political Culture
Political Culture	1. *Clan solidarity* 2. *Fighting over resources (violence)* 3. *Collective leadership and participatory decision making* 4. *Strong Islamic identity* 5. *Disregarding state authorities*	1. *Localistic culture* 2. *Political patronage* 3. *Widespread corruption* 4. *Political fragmentation and instability* 5. *Democratic culture*

Table 1. Comparative analysis of Italy and Somalia.

It is noticeable from the above comparative cultures that Somali political elites adopted the Italian political culture, while some elements of their traditional culture were assimilated or disregarded. The disregarded elements of local Somali culture include the culture of collective leadership and consensus decision-making process. Moreover, strong Islamic identity and adherence to Islamic values were substantially weakened. Furthermore, political clannism,

---

574. Arend Lijphart, *Democracies: Patterns of majoritarian and consensus government in twenty-one countries.* (New Haven, CT: Yale University Press, 1984).
575. Matthijis Bogaards, *Comparative Political Regimes: Consensus and Majoritarian Democracy* (Oxford Research Encyclopaedia and Oxford University Press, USA, 2016). Online Publication Date: Mar 2017, 4.

which was similar to the Italian culture of localism, was assimilated. The manifestation of such localism or political clannism was the unlimited clan-based political parties established in Somalia. Thus, the resultant political culture of Somali elites includes political patronage (internal and external), political clannism, widespread corruption, political instability, and a volatile democratic culture.

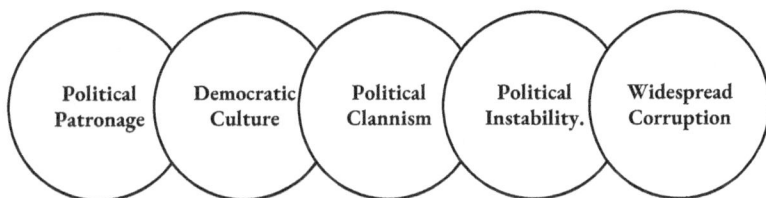

Fig.23. Somali Elite Political Culture (1956–1969)

This political culture developed in the formative period of Somali state-building and persisted for fourteen years (1956–1969). However, the system corroded gradually, and new political elites emerged with different ideological persuasions. Many new elites were educated in socialist countries (USSR, Germany, and China, and others) and Arab military regimes (Egypt, Iraq, and Syria).[576] The fragile democratic culture in the Somali Republic's early years has deteriorated since 1967.[577] As such, the corruption level and rigging of elections reached an unprecedented level in the election of 1969. This malicious practice caused the assassination of the second President of the Republic, Abdirashid Ali Sharmarke, on October 15, 1969.[578] As a consequence, the Somali army took overpower in a bloodless coup on October 21, 1969. On the other hand, as a reaction to West-

---

576. Ibid, 145.
577. The early culture of democracy abysmally deteriorated during the Sharmarke-Igal regime (1967-1969). The country was transformed into a one-party system, the SYL, under the leadership of Premier Mohamed Ibrahim Igal in 1969. After the election, all members of Parliament joined SYL, except former Premier Abdirisaz Haji Hussein.
578. Mohamed H. Ingiris, "Who Assassinated the Somali President in October 1969? The Cold War, the Clan Connection or Coup d'état." African Security Journal, Volume 10, 2017.

ernized elite behavior, a new generation of Islamists emerged in the 1960s to advocate for the observance of Islamic tenets and manners. The new period of Somali history began with millinery rule, socialist orientation, dictatorship, and a growing Islamist awakening.

THE EVOLUTION OF ELITE POLITICAL CULTURE (1969–1991)

The evolution of elite political culture began with the military coup in 1969. The military regime had added new elements to the political culture of the elites and illuminated others. The military regime abrogated the constitution, disbanded the parliament, and imprisoned leaders of the government. The regime adopted socialism in 1970 and implemented anti-societal policies.[579] The new regime's socialist policies included suppressing Islamic activism, rigorous programs that diminished the role of traditional elders, the elimination of democratic tradition, and a transformation of the whole society into subjects. This means that relations between the military leadership and citizens were patron-follower relations. The role of the military and the National Security Service (NSS) was oriented to suppress any plausible opposition. Included in the militaristic policy was the forming of "*Guulwadayaal*," a militia designated as a para-military force to act as a watchful eye over the communities.

The military regime's rule could be divided into two phases. The first phase (1969–1978) was a socialist transformation, national mobilization, and rebuilding of institutions. The main characteristics of this phase were the formation of new socialist elites, which began with committing the Somali language into writing in 1972 and opening hundreds of schools in every village with a new socialist curriculum. Included in this program was an illiteracy campaign conducted in 1974 to educate the rural population. Moreover, Somali National University was opened in 1971 to produce socialist indoctrinated elites. In the university's curriculum, studies of socialist ideologies were made compulsory. Besides that, specialized political faculty

---

579. The anti-societal policies included diminishing the role of clan elders, introducing forced secularism, and suppressing Islamic activism.

to train socialist party cadres were opened. Other cultural manifestations were established, such as the National Academy of Arts, Sciences, and Culture, the National Theatre, and the National Museum. Moreover, the rich Somali poetry was excessively instrumentalized to propagate the new ideology of socialism and to praise the supreme leader of the military regime, General Mohamed Siyad Barre. The regime empowered women, and girls' enrolment in the schools increased extensively. Also, many women were promoted to higher bureaucratic positions, diplomatic corps, and cabinet ministers. As part of women's empowerment, secular family law was issued in 1975, which encountered great societal opposition. As a result, ten Islamic scholars were executed by the regime who publicly opposed the law on the pretext that it contravenes the Qur'an.[580] This event energized embryonic Islamist activism and the regime was then branded as anti-Islamic and Godless Atheists. To further promote the socialist transformation, the Somali Revolutionary Socialist Party (SRSP) was formed in 1976, the only party in the country. However, the defining moment of this phase is the Somali-Ethiopian war of 1977/78 in which the Somali military was humiliated and defeated.[581]

The second phase of the military regime begins after the military defeat of Somalia in 1978. In this phase, the early impetus of national mobilization, along with the socialist ideology, was exhausted and faltering. The second wave of military officers' coup d'état, launched on April 9, 1978, was nevertheless aborted.[582] Since then, the national army disintegrated along clan-lines and clannish armed oppositions

---

580. The first attempted coup d'état emanated within the military junta. As a result, General Gavere, General Ainanshe, and Colonel Abdulakdir Dheel were executed. See Abdurahman Abdullahi, "Women, Islamists and Military Regime in Somalia: The New Family Law and its Implications," in ed, Markus Hoehne and Virginia Luling, *Milk and Peace, Drought and War: Somali Culture, Society, and Politics* (London: Hurst & Company, 2010), 137–60.
581. Abdullahi, *Making Sense, volume one*, 152. Also, Gebru Tareke. "The Ethiopia Somalia War Revisited." International Journal of African Historical Studies 33, no. 3, 2000, 615–34.
582. Abdullahi, ibid.

emerged one after another.[583] The opposition of the regime was growing and included diplomatic corps, former ministers, high-ranking military officers, and Islamist movements. Failing to resolve internal conflicts through democratization and peaceful dialogue, the regime opted for a militaristic policy and the use of unrestrained force. The process of armed conflict between the regime and the armed oppositions continued until the total collapse of the regime and the state in 1991. Indeed, three elite political cultures continued from the previous civilian government during the military regime: political patronage, political clannism, and widespread corruption. Moreover, the military regime introduced dictatorship/violence and related behavior, which thus led to the elimination of the democratic culture and the interconnected political instability.

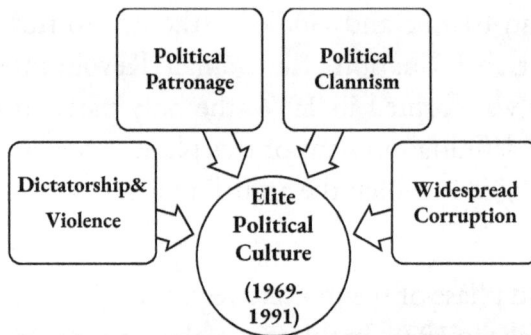

Fig.24.The Ruling Elite Political Culture (1969–1991)

After the collapse of the state, the ruling elite political culture of the previous regime continued in the context of the radicalized clans, and warlordism resulted in excessive violence. The pre-state culture of clannish society based on relentless fighting became rampant. Moreover, extremism in the name of Islam emerged and intensified. The former Somaliland unilaterally declared succession on May 18, 1991. In southern Somalia, after ten years of continuous

---

583. Four armed opposition movements were established in the 1980s. These are the Somali Democratic Salvation Front (SSDF), the Somali National Movement (SNM), the United Somali Congress (USC), and the Somali Patriotic Movement (SPM).

conflict and the failure of twelve warlord-reconciliation conferences, the direction of reconciliation shifted to a civil society-driven course. In this process, the clan-power sharing 4.5 formula was institutionalized, and the Islamic-compliant constitution was adopted during the SPRC in Djibouti in 2000. Since then, reconstructing the Somali state has been sluggish and revolved around clan-power sharing and the vicious recycling of dysfunctional national institutions. The elite political culture accumulated elements of the previous phases following continuity and change theory. Since 2000, the following elite political culture has persisted: political patronage, institutionalization of political clannism, the ubiquity of corruption, and political violence. The culture of violence, which is a continuation of the mentality of dictatorship and warlordism, has continued to some extent. Political instability and quasi-democratic culture have also been revived.[584] Moreover, foreign political patronage intensified, and internal patronage became more insidious.

In conclusion, the ruling elite political culture since 2000 was a collection of pieces of all elements of culture acquired in 1956. Some elements were weakened and faded, while others persisted and augmented. The main resultant political culture is as follows:

Institutionalization of Political Clannism: Although this culture persisted during all the phases of Somali state-building, it was nonetheless institutionalized at the SPRC in Djibouti in 2000. The adopted 4.5 clan power-sharing formula marked a complete shift in the elite political culture, previously based on demeaning clannism. The electoral system promoted and encouraged the culture of political clannism, permitting unrestricted political parties introduced by the Italians in 1954. However, political clannism grew and was finally institutionalized after the SPRC.

Ubiquity of Political Corruption: This culture existed since the beginning of elections in Somalia in 1954; however, it has been

---

584. Since SPRC in Djibouti in 2000, a quasi-democratic transfer of power has been occurring and members of parliaments were selected by their clans. However, there was no direct election so far.

growing in magnitude gradually. Corruption has many phases, but the most prominent one in Somalia is open vote-buying. It reached the level of commercialization of politics, having all the characteristics of commercial goods in buying and selling votes publicly to the highest bidder. This means that to become a member of the parliament, individuals should buy the seat from the clan elders and associates and then sell it to the presidential candidates. As reported, the highest cost of one of the seats in the 2016 election reached approximately one million dollars, while the average cost to buy the vote of an MP on the night before the presidential election was estimated at around $50,000.[585] Over the last ten years, Somalia has ranked first in the corruption perceptions of the International Transparent index.[586] This culture enabled foreign countries to invest in empowering their proxies for the highest public offices and presidential candidates.[587]

Political Violence: This culture was developed since the early years of the election in the 1950s as part of traditional clan culture and the disability of Italian administration to register voters and conduct a census. For instance, "the planned census, to be completed in 1957, failed miserably in three of the total six administrative regions: Majeerteen, Mudug, and Lower Juba, while it was successful in Banadir, Upper Juba, and Hiiran. As a result of the shortcoming of AFIS to accomplish a reliable census, the early unfair represen-

---

585. Marsai Viktor, "Somali Elections 2016-2017: Business as usual or new hope?" National University of public service, July 2017. This paper quotes from the Somali Auditor General, Nur Jimale Farah that "Some votes were bought with $5,000, some with $10,000, and some with $20,000 or $30,000. The Auditor General told reporters that two seats cost their respective winners $1.3 million each." Available from file:///C:/Users/user/Downloads/CSDS_Analyses_2017_14_Somalielectionsin2016-2017_MarsaiV..pdf (accessed on October 10, 2020). The average cost paid by President Hassan Sheikh to MPs on the night before the election was estimated to be $50,000.
586. Somalia is ranked the lowest in the corruption perceptions index ranking 180 (9/100). See https://www.transparency.org/en/cpi/2019 (accessed on 10 October 2020).
587. It is speculated that money to buy votes of the MPs were received from the rich Gulf countries, in particular, UAE, and Qatar.

tation of the seats in parliament began, which also led to the early culture of rigging elections.'[588] Thus, unfair allocation of seats of the parliament and the rigging of elections by the authorities in power became a norm. For instance, in the early period of 1956–1969, the SYL ruling party was accused of rigging elections.[589] The same phenomenon recurred since 2000, and rigging elections and violence were even more evident afterward.[590]

Strong Foreign Patronage: The culture of foreign patronage started during the UN trusteeship period. This period was the height of the Cold War, and competition between the East and West to dominate the strategic Horn of Africa was at a high pace. Western countries supported moderate leaders of the ruling party of SYL and contributed to suppressing other ideologically oriented parties towards the Eastern bloc.[591] The major countries that influenced Somali foreign policies during this period were Italy, Egypt, and the USA. However, the USSR's role gradually grew, particularly since 1963, in its assistance in building the Somali National Army. The USSR became the major country that patronized Somali political

---

588. Abdullahi, *Making Sense, volume one,* 137.

589. SYL corruption is well documented since the election of 1959. However, the biggest corruption was witnessed in the election of 1969. See ibid, 147.

590. Election violence in the South-West state of Somalia was reported. See Amnesty International, Somalia: Use of Lethal Force to Quell Protests is Unjustifiable. Available from https://www.amnesty.org/en/latest/news/2018/12/somalia-use-of-lethal-force-to-quell-protests-in-baidoa-unjustifiable/ (accessed on 10 October 2020). Moreover, as a result of Galmudug election of 2019, violence erupted between soldiers loyal to Ahlu-Sunna Wa-Al-Jama and the newly established administration. See https://www.somaliaffairs.com/news/close-to-10-killed-as-government-forces-ahlu-sunnah-fight-in-galmudug/ (accessed on 10 October 2020). Furthermore, the Jubaland conflict continued from the outset of its establishment, having many faces.

591. The USA and Italy orchestrated a policy of keeping Somalia aligned with the West. Their approach was to cultivate pro-Western orientation in the dominant SYL party. Reciprocally, this had warranted the SYL the support of the West to overshadow other parties in 1956. See, Okbazghi Yohannes, *The United States and the Horn of Africa: An Analytical Study of Pattern and Process* (Westview Press, 1997), 204-212.

elites after the military takeover in 1969. Subsequently, Somalia also received US and Italian patronage after its relations with the USSR deteriorated in 1977. With the collapse of the state, Ethiopia was the major country that provided patronage to the warlords. Finally, after the Gulf crisis, the role of the rich Arab countries' patronage increased substantially, particularly the UAE, Qatar, and Saudi Arabia. Local political patronage in the form of clientelism and nepotism also continued.

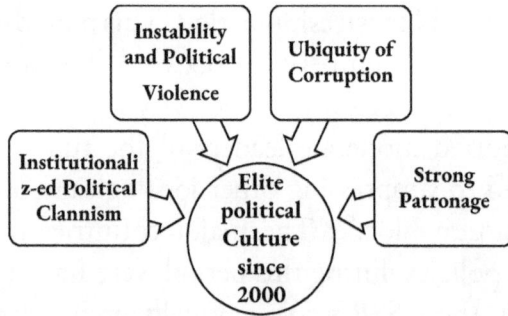

Fig.25. Somali Elite Political Culture Since 2000

CONCLUSION

This Chapter explores what has made the Somali government fail repetitively and frustrate its recovery for the last sixty four years. The hypothesis is founded on the basis that the elite political culture is the main contributing factor in building and breaking the state. Other contributing factors to the failure of the Somali state are considered the socio-political and economic environment in which political elites navigate to succeed or fail. However, this is not to negate that this environment necessarily shapes the culture of political elites in a complex process of reciprocal relations. There are limited studies on elite political culture and placing the responsibility for state failure on the governing elites. Instead, most literature concurs, blaming the Somali clan structure and related clannism as an impediment to state-building.

The Chapter's first section provides a theoretical backdrop to elite political culture by defining its components (e.g., culture, politics, and elitism) and combining them to constitute the conception of elite political culture. It posits various conceptions of culture and its expression as expressive, material, and immaterial forms. It is evident that every individual is born into a specific societal culture, but culture can be learned through enculturation, socialization, and acculturation. Moreover, culture can be divided into covert and overt levels, like the iceberg. On the other hand, politics could be narrowly defined as activities of governments, politicians, and political parties or so broadly that it includes the interrelationships between people and their rules and norms, institutions, and actions in all social spheres. Combining these two words gives the term political culture, which is different in each country producing political behavior. In post-colonial countries like Somalia, elite political culture is a mixture of elements of the colonial elite political culture blended with local clan culture.

The second section traces the formation and structure of the basic components of the Somali elites, dividing them into traditional and modern. Traditional elites mean clan authorities comprising clan elders and traditional scholars of Islam, who collectively manage the affairs of the clans. It was evident that relations between traditional authorities were cordial and cooperative, while modern elites consisting of Islamists and non-Islamists were conflictual. However, after the collapse of the state, the role of traditional elites had grown from a purely managing clan affair to selecting members of the parliament and, in some regions, as part of decision-making institutions.

The third section explores the historical evolution of elite political culture since 1956. It is evident from the historical analysis that the Somali elite political culture was formed in stages. Initially, it was formed as a hybrid of the asymmetrical mixture of the top-down, authoritarian, and bureaucratic Italian colonial rule and local participatory and collective leadership elite culture. The formative political elite culture produced a shaky democracy plagued with corruption while maintaining clannism and internal and external political patronage. Then, the military rule introduced the ideology of socialism, dictatorship, and the violence that followed until its collapse in 1991. After the collapse of the state, the previous culture continued by the warlords during the civil war can be characterized by anarchy, lawlessness, and strong foreign patronage. The final stage of the historical evolution of the ruling elite political culture was acquired in 2000 through clan-power sharing. Hence, the resultant culture has accumulated all the above cultures since 1956. However, its main elements are the clannization of politics, pervasive commercialization of politics, violence, rigging elections, and strong foreign and local patronage. Having acquired this culture, politicians swing between instrumentalizing clannism, Islamism, and nationalism to serve their self-centric interests. Finally, recovering the Somali state depends primarily on transforming the above-stated ruling elite political culture and breaking the vicious cycle of state failure. The question of how to break from the existing political culture to reform a viable Somali state and its institutions requires further comprehensive academic study.

6

A NEW COURSE ON SOMALI STATE- BUILDING: A COMPREHENSIVE APPROACH

*H*aving seen the challenges faced by the leadership and political culture of three exceptional Somali leaders and the concern about the drift of the Somali elite political culture in the wrong direction, it is evident that the Somali state has lost its compass. In light of these issues, exploring an ideological and practical solution to the Somali debacle is crucial. To remedy this situation, a comprehensive approach is needed. This approach must encompass ideological foundations and practical measures to realign the political culture and restore the state's trajectory. Ideologically, the Somali people need to foster a sense of national unity through proper reorganizing and prioritizing its three ideological components: Islam, clan, and nationalism. Implementing effective governance structures, anti-corruption measures, and capacity-building initiatives is essential. Strengthening institutions, enhancing transparency, and ensuring accountability will create a more stable and resilient political environment. Further, investing in education and economic development will empower citizens and reduce reliance on a flawed political elite. Moreover, strengthening the civil society, both modern and traditional, leads to the stability of the state-building framework. Addressing the Somali crisis's ideological and practical aspects makes it possible to chart a new course for the nation. This dual approach can help to overcome the current challenges and set Somalia on a path toward lasting peace, stability, and prosperity.

This comprehensive approach necessitates revisiting and critically examining the dominant theories within Somali studies that have perpetuated and ingrained erroneous concepts. These prevailing theories have often shaped the understanding and policies surrounding Somalia, contributing to the ongoing challenges faced by the nation. Firstly, it is crucial to identify and deconstruct the flawed assumptions embedded within these dominant theories. These theories have frequently oversimplified the complexities of Somali society, politics, and culture, leading to misguided interpretations and ineffective solutions. By scrutinizing these assumptions, we can uncover the biases and misconceptions that have influenced academic discourse and policymaking. In addition to theoretical and methodological revisions, addressing the practical implications of these erroneous concepts is essential. Policies and interventions based on flawed theories have often exacerbated the issues they sought to resolve. We can develop effective and sustainable strategies by aligning research and practice with a more accurate and contextually informed understanding of Somalia. Ultimately, this comprehensive approach aims to transform the field of Somali studies and, by extension, the policies and practices that impact the nation. By challenging and refining the dominant theories, we can pave the way for a more informed, equitable, and resilient path forward for Somalia.

Somali studies are a multi-disciplinary academic term for studying Somali people in the Horn of Africa, their diasporic communities, and their interactions with other peoples worldwide. The main fields used in Somali studies are social science, humanities, and fine arts. Somali studies analyze the historical, social, economic, and political aspects and their interaction with local culture. Rooted in the ancient history of the Horn of Africa, Somali studies draw from the chronicles and literature written by Greek, Jewish, Chinese, and Arab/Muslim geographers and explorers in the Middle Ages.[592] It is also embedded in the works of scholars of Islam, who focused mainly on Islamic studies, memorized poetic literature, and travelogues of the European explorers of the nineteenth century.[593] Moreover,

---

592. The Chinese explorers were Tuan Chéng-Sbib, Chou Ju-Hua, Zheng. The Arab explorers and geographers were Ibnu Said al-Magribi, Mohammad al-Idrisi, and Ibn Battuta. In addition, there was a Jewish traveller Benjamin of Tudela.
593. European explorers of Somalia were mainly Italians, such as Luigi Robec-

Somali studies hinge on colonial literature, archives, and scholarly work produced by researchers and published books.[594] Furthermore, since Somali people bridge Africa and the Middle East, Somali studies are influenced by African and Middle Eastern studies.[595] The term Somali studies was coined in 1978 with the establishment of the Somali Studies International Association, emulating other country studies that were booming during that period.[596]

Somali studies have grown considerably since adopting a Latin orthography as the official national alphabet of the Somali language in 1972, founding various state institutions to promote arts, theater, and culture.[597] Somali studies were booming with the growing trend of publishing books in Somali, English, Arabic, and other languages. Annual book fairs started throughout Somalia's big cities, and publishing houses and translation services have boomed. Moreover, several specialized journals on Somali studies are being published.[598] Additionally, the annual conferences of Somali Studies are

chi-Bricchetti, Vittorio Bottego, and Prince Luigi Amedeo, Duke of the Abruzzi. They focused their trips on southern Somalia. On the other hand, Richard Burton was a British explorer who visited northern Somalia like Luigi Robecchi-Bricchetti, Vittorio Bottego, and Prince Luigi Amedeo, Duke of the Abruzzi. They focused their trips on southern Somalia. On the other hand, the British explorer who visited northern Somalia was Richard Burton.

594. Most notable books on Somali Studies developed from the Ph.D. thesis were authored by Lee Cassanelli, Saadia Touval, Ahmed Samatar, Abdi Samatar, Said Samatar, Abdi Sheikh Abdi, Afyare Abdi Elmi, Robert Hees, Virginia Lulling, Mohamed Nuh, Abdirahman Ahmed Noor, Scott Rees, Mary Hope Schwoebel, Abdurahman Baadiyow, Abdislam Salwe, and others.

595. Abdurahman Abdullahi, "Revisiting Somali historiography: critique and idea of comprehensive perspective." Journal of Somali Studies: Research on Somalia and the Greater Horn of African Countries Vol. 5, No. 1–2, 2018, 31-59,32.

596. Lee Cassanelli, "The Somali Studies International Association: A Brief History." Bildhaan, vol. 1, 2001, 1–10.

597. These institutions include establishing the Somali Academy of Arts and Sciences in 1973, the national theater opened in 1967, and the National Museum in 1933.

598. See "Somaliland Standard," retrieved April 26, 2023. Also, see Mogadishu Book Fair. Https://qz.com/africa/740313/somalias-new-love-affair-with-books-

conducted at many universities and Institutes, such as Mogadishu, JigJiga, SIMAD, Banadir universities, and East African Association for Research and Development (DAD) and Heritage Institute.[599]

However, despite such progress in Somali studies, the fundamental question as to why the Somali state collapsed and how to re-institute it remains disputed. Even worse, the military regimes' elite political culture and policies are recuperated in the new state-building processes.[600] Studies explaining the Somali state collapse and its causes could be summarized into three main categories. To simplify, let us compare the Somali state collapse to a crumbled building and the possible factors that could cause its collapse. The first factor may be external, such as a tsunami, artillery shells, or missiles hitting the building. The second factor may be the quality of the material that was incapable of bearing the burden of the structure. Hence, the building scramble because of engineering miscalculations or the poor quality of the building materials. The third factor may be the defective engineering of the building that, over time, collapses by itself.

Comparing the collapsed Somali state to the collapsed building, we can assert that the causes of the breakdown of the Somali state were multiple external factors (colonial legacy, war with Ethiopia, Cold War, etc.), defective engineering of state-building, and the low capacity of the political leadership. The flawed engineering is like a state's inimical relation with its societal roots: Islam and the clan system. The poor quality of construction materials is comparable to the political elites' low capacity and the society's poor cohesion. Figure 26 demonstrates the concept of state-society relations in which Islam and the clan system are the basis and the modern state is the superstructure. The state-society conflict is like a foolish person

---

ramps-up-as-safety-returns-to-the-country (accessed on April 27, 2023).
599. The most famous specialized journals on Somali studies are Bildhan, Journal of Somali Studies, and Somali Studies: A Peer-reviewed Academic Journal.
600. Abdurahman Abdullahi, "The Somali Elite Political Culture: Conceptions, Structures, and Historical Evolution." Available from https://mu.edu.so/somali-elite-political-culture/ (accessed on April 26, 2013).

representing the state's political elite, which cuts the root of the tree on which they are sitting. Is there any doubt as to whether this person will fall?

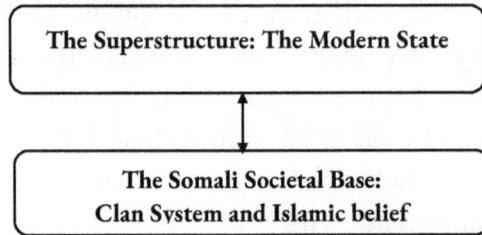

Fig. 26. The Somali Societal Base and Superstructure

Fig. 27. A political elite cutting the roots of Somali society: Islam and the clan system

This paper utilizes two theoretical frameworks: the theory of state-society relations and the elite theory. These two frameworks focus on the relationship between the state and society, which cuts across aspects of the theoretical borderlines and explores how governance and society interact and influence one another. Scholars in state-society relations agree that society provides crucial support for a state to be effective and that a state is critical to collective action in society.[601] The UK *Department for International Development* (DFID) defined state-society relations as 'interactions between state institutions and societal groups to negotiate how public authority is exercised and how people can influence it. They are focused on issues such as defining the mutual rights and obligations of the state and society, negotiating how public resources should be allocated, and establishing different modes of representation and accountability."[602] On the other hand, the elite theory seeks to describe power relationships in contemporary society, positing that a small minority holds the most power, the central premise being that "no societies are governed by the people, by a majority; all societies, including societies called democratic, are ruled by a minority."[603] Even when entire groups are supposedly entirely excluded from the state's traditional power networks, elite theory recognizes that "counter-elites" frequently develop within such excluded groups. The elitist method permits the integration of the two levels of analysis: micro-systems studies by anthropology and macro-systems that fall in the domain of political science.[604]

In the post-colonial Somali state, state-society relations were confrontational because of the secular view of the inherited state that disdained the culture and norms of the clan-based Muslim society.

601. Atul Kohli, "State, Society, and Development," in Katznelson, Ira and Helen Milner (eds.), *Political Science: The State of the Discipline* (New York: Norton, 2002), 84–117; Joel Migdal, *State in Society: Studying How States and Societies Transform and Constitute Each Other* (New York: Cambridge University Press, 2001); Peter Evans, *Embedded Autonomy* (Princeton: Princeton University Press, 1995); Stephen Haggard, *Pathways from the Periphery* (Ithaca, NY: Cornell University Press, 1990).
602. "Building Peaceful States and Societies," A DFID Practice Paper. London: Department for International Development, 2010, 15.
603. James Burnham, "The Machiavellians: Defenders of Freedom," The John Day Company, 1943, 165.
604. Abdurahman Abdullahi. "Tribalism, Nationalism, and Islam: The Crisis of Political Loyalties in Somalia," master's thesis submitted to the Islamic Institute, McGill University, 1992, 6.

Moreover, the modern elites trained in Western schools retained the political ideology and culture inherited from the colonial rulers. As a result, the confrontation between the state and society worsened considerably under military rule (1969–1991), which adopted the ideology of socialism. This essay briefly describes the critical challenges of Somali state-building that expound the root cause of the current crisis and proceeds to provide an overview of the various perspectives of Somali Studies as a background for developing the Comprehensive Perspective (CP). After exploring and categorizing the main Somali conflicts, this essay suggests the Inclusive Reconciliation Framework (IRF), which could be developed into the Stability Model (SM) for Somali state-building.

THE KEY CHALLENGES OF SOMALI STATE-BUILDING

The main challenges regarding Somali state-building are its strategic geographic location, the division of the Somali territory among multiple colonial powers, the Somali aspiration to unite them (Great Somalia), and the Westernized state model in conflict with its society. The geography of Somalia connects Asia, Europe, and Africa, which attracted competition among the various colonial powers to dominate Somalia. Also, adjacent to the Suez Canal and the oil-rich Gulf region, Somalia was drawn into the Cold War theater by the 1950s and the politics of the Nile River between Egypt and Ethiopia.[605] Furthermore, Somalia became a place where the double identity of Arabness and Africanness compete and conflict,[606] with global terrorism now designating Somalia as a suitable location to wage what they called global Jihad to restore the Islamic Caliphate. Finally, the renewed superpower rivalry between the USA and China

---

605. Osman Abdullahi, "The Role of Egypt, Ethiopia the Blue Nile in the Failure of the Somali Conflict Resolutions: A Zero-Sum Game" (paper presented at the annual meeting of the International Studies Association, Hilton Hawaiian Village, Honolulu, Hawaii, March 2005).
606. See Ibrahim Farah, "Foreign Policy and Conflict in Somalia, 1960-1990," Ph.D. diss., University of Nairobi, 2009, 187.

and rising regional powers like Turkey, Gulf states, and neighboring countries pose new challenges to Somali state-building.

The second challenge required the division of the Somali cultural nation into five parts shared between multiple colonial powers, which resulted in Somali nationalists struggling to unify all Somali territories. This venture positioned Somalia on a collision course with international conventions on the inviolability of the colonially inherited borders.[607] Moreover, it also embroiled Somalia in continuous conflict with its neighbors. Gradually, Somali nationalism began to decline with the defeat of Somalia in the war with Ethiopia in 1977/78 and the proclamation of the independent Republic of Djibouti in 1977. What is more, the repressive policy of the military regime and the armed opposition movements organized on a clan basis further weakened Somali nationalism.[608] Therefore, the centrifugal forces of Somali clannish particularism overwhelmed the centripetal forces of nationalism that were substantially weakened during long years of dictatorship (1969–1991), and the Somali state collapsed in 1991. Since then, Somalia has remained the emblem of the longest-collapsed state in modern history. Indeed, Somali nationalism never dies because it is organic and alive among all Somalis but requires a new vision and interpretations which draws lessons from past experiences.

The third challenge concerned the postcolonial state built on the Westernized model, which failed to accommodate Somali traditions: Islam and the clan system, resulting in pervasive state penetration in society ineptly colliding with a strong society based on the clan system and Islam. As a reaction, Somali society kindled a defense

---

607. Somalia did not endorse the declaration of the Organization of African Unity on the sanctity of the borders in Cairo, 1964; Saadia Touval, "The Organization of African Unity and Borders," International Organization 21, no. 1 (1967): 102–27.
608. The Armed opposition movements established with the support of Ethiopia were Somali Salvation Democratic Front (SSDF), Somali National Movement (SNM), United Somali Congress (USC), and Somali Patriotic Movement (SPM).

mechanism provoking rebellious confrontations, thus straining state-society relations instigated the emergence of three competing ideologies: clannism, Islamism, and nationalism, even though these ideologies are dynamic, crosscurrent, and often overlap.[609] However, without a reconciliatory arrangement, the notion of their mutual exclusion prevailed. Indeed, the polarization of the society started manifestly with the enforced secular reforms of the military regime, which provoked the emergence of insurgencies under the banners of Islam and clan. Therefore, it is arguable that Somali society has been systematically radicalized since 1969.[610]

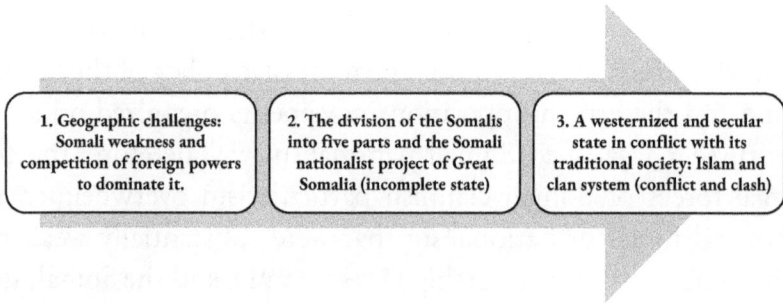

1. Geographic challenges: Somali weakness and competition of foreign powers to dominate it.	2. The division of the Somalis into five parts and the Somali nationalist project of Great Somalia (incomplete state)	3. A westernized and secular state in conflict with its traditional society: Islam and clan system (conflict and clash)

Fig.28. The three Key Successive Challenges of Somali State-building

The two challenges related to the strategic location that attracts foreign powers' competition and the division of Somalia into five parts are political realities that compel pragmatic handling. Dealing with foreign competition requires a prudent foreign policy safeguarding Somali national interests and mitigating foreign influence. Regarding Great Somalia, reinterpreting its vision and adopting a new strategy based on regional integration resolves this case. The third challenge of state-society conflict is that Somali scholars are required to critically analyze the past and develop a stable system of governance for Somalia. The failure of the Somali state resulted from

609. Abdurahman Abdullahi, *Tribalism, Nationalism, and Islam.*
610. Exceptions are Somaliland and Puntland, which had developed a consensus-based administration after the collapse of the state. In particular, Somaliland has shown a culture of tolerance and political development toward democracy. However, that culture is being challenged now with the popular uprising and war in Laas-Anood seeking to reunite with the Somali Federal Republic.

bankrupt ideas invented by foreign and Somali intellectuals and implemented by Somali politicians. The following section examines these ideas that, after being internalized by the Somali politicians, caused the state's breakdown within three decades and still place obstacles in its reinstitution.

OVERVIEW OF THE PERSPECTIVES OF SOMALI STUDIES

Somali studies were dominated by narratives rooted in sociocultural anthropology, which focuses on kinships and social organizations, religion, myth, symbols, values, and the relationship between traditional and modern structures. Some scholars argue that anthropology originated and developed as the study of "other cultures," both in terms of time (ancient times) and space (non-Western societies).[611] These scholars' viewpoints consider anthropology as a colonial intellectual tool developed for understanding colonized populations, which enables them to conquer, dominate, and administer.[612] In addition, colonial scholars imbued with racial superiority produced debasing images and distorted descriptions of the colonized nations. These images permeated the various educational means and research methodologies in postcolonial knowledge production. For example, there is a persistent repetition of the clannish image of the Somali people in most academic literature representing Somalis as exceptional and clannistic while dooming them to be fractious forever and incapable of building a viable state.[613] Scholars of anthropology make their assumptions on "the modernization metanarrative, which focuses on the transition from tradition to modernity. This theory is founded on the belief that traditional societies can be developed with

611. Prem Poddar and David Johnson, ed., *A Historical Companion to Post-colonial Thought in English* (Colombia University Press, 2007;) Also, David Johnson, ed., *A Historical Companion to Postcolonial Literatures – Continental Europe and its Empires* (Edinburgh University Press, 2008).
612. Maxwell Owusu, *Colonial and Postcolonial Anthropology of Africa: Scholarship or Sentiment?* (De Gruyter Mouton, 1979).
613. Ahmed Samatar. "The Curse of Allah: Civic Disembowelment and the Collapse of the State in Somalia," in *The Somali Challenge: From Catastrophe to Renewal?* ed., Ahmed Samatar (Boulder, CO: Lynne Rienner, 1994), 110.

the assistance of the developed countries along the same path taken by the more developed Western countries."[614] This theory draws from the ideas of Max Weber (1864–1920) on the role of rationality and irrationality in the transition from traditional to modern society, popularized later by Talcott Parsons (1902–1979). Many modernization theorists often saw traditions as obstacles to economic growth and related democracy with modernization, taking national states as the unit of analysis.[615]

The above concept was ingrained in the minds of the Somali political elites. As a result, they espoused the idea of peripheralizing traditional identities: Islam and the clan system. In doing so, they aspired to be modern and developed. The conception of modernity against tradition was the core ideology of Somali nationalism and the state that gained independence in 1960. The damaging impact of this perspective was very high in creating a rift between the national state and its societal base. In the first nine years of civilian rule (1960–69), the state-society conflict was mild and manageable; however, during the military regime (1969–1991), the ideological gap between the state and society had widened due to the adoption of socialism and ruthless modernization programs of the totalitarian military regime.

The military regime followed, to a certain degree, the footsteps of Kemal Attaturk in adopting his principles such as secularism, nationalism, statism, populism, and revolutionary.[616] However, these principles were camouflaged with the rhetoric of socialism and expressed in the secularization of the family law, abolishing the Diya system, the execution of scholars of Islam, forming the one-party system, and the persecution of the political opposition.[617] Somali studies

---

614. Abdullahi, *Revisiting Somali Historiography*, 36.

615. Dean Tipps, "Modernization Theory and Comparative Study of the Societies: A Critical Perspective." Comparative Study of Society and History, Vol. 15, No.2, 1973,199–226.

616. Seyfettin Aslan, "Historical Background and Principles of Kemalism," NWSA-SOCIAL SCIENCES, 2013.

617. Ozlem Demirtas Bagdons, "A Poststructuralist Approach to Ideology and Foreign Policy: Kemalism in the Turkish Foreign Policy Discourse," a Ph.D.

reacted to the military regimes' policies and adoption of socialism with the emergence of the Marxist perspective. This perspective is founded on class analysis and historical materialism.[618] The Marxist analysis of the Somali studies criticized anthropological and modernization theories. Nonetheless, the military regime had been hybridizing the concepts of sociocultural anthropology and the ideology of socialism. Both perspectives shared a secular worldview and enmity toward the traditions of the societies. The oppressive nature of the military regime and its harsh policies against traditional values were confronted with the radicalization of clans and the emergence of armed oppositions by the end of the 1970s. Moreover, the phenomenon of Islamism that appeared in the 1960s as part of the global rise of Islamist movements became more structured, and various organizations were instituted.[619] Indeed, during this period, the seeds of extremism in the name of Islam surfaced in reaction to the execution of the Ulama in 1975, who opposed secular family law.[620]

The negative impact of the marginalized Somali traditions paved the way for extreme state-society conflict, which gradually triggered a total breakdown of the state in 1991. With the end of the Cold War, the demise of the Soviet Union, and the collapse of the Somali state, the Marxist perspective reached a dead end, even though the theory of class analysis was sustained. Thus, proponents of the Marxist perspective reverted to accepting the need to reconcile modernity

---

thesis submitted to the Central European University, Hungary, 2008, 26–29. Available from file:///C:/Users/Dr. percent20Baadiyow/Downloads/iphdeo01. pdf (accessed on April 25, 2023).

618. Erik Wright. *Approaches to Class Analysis* (Cambridge: Cambridge University Press, 2005).

619. Abdurahman Abdullahi, *The Islamic Movement in Somalia: A Case Study of Islah Movement (1950-2000)* (London: Adonis & Abbey, 2015), 141–70.

620. Abdurahman Abdullahi, "Women, Islamists and Military Regime in Somalia: The New Family Law and Its Implications," in *Milk and Peace, Drought, and War: Somali Culture and Politics*, ed. M.V. Hoehne, and V. Luling (London: Hurst, 2010), 137–60. The first radical reaction was Takfir group that emerged at the end of the 1970s, and the current al-Shabaab and Daish are rooted in the same ideology but reformed to adopt a violent approach.

and traditions. This transformation was more evident in the thesis of Ahmed Samatar, who proposed the synthesis of modernity and tradition [clan (tol), customary law (Xeer), and Islamic law (Qanoon)].[621] However, the practical integration of modernity and tradition remains the most significant unsolved challenge in Somalia and all Muslim states.

The collapsed state of Somalia in 1991 posed an unprecedented challenge to state-building. As professor Hassan Kaynan expresses, "Somalia has not been the only country that has experienced state failure; but the scale, magnitude, duration, and consequences of state disintegration have earned it the infamy of being the first and most enduring failed state."[622] During this long and traumatic period, a perspective of revisionism emerged strongly, expressing the historical marginalization of southern semi-pastoral regions versus northern and central nomadic areas of Somalia in "a more epistemologically holistic and pluralistic way of articulating Somali society."[623] Proponents of the revisionist perspective criticized the two other perspectives cited above for accepting the constructed myths and utilizing the official narratives that contributed to the conceptualization of Somalia.

Scholars who adopted this new perspective demystified the conventional image of Somaliness as one constructed by idealistic Somali nationalists, colonial historiographers, and post-colonial political hegemonic clannists. Moreover, these scholars criticized history as chauvinistic, focusing on northern pastoralists and excluding the southern agrarian population. The revisionists have re-examined conventional national symbols and myths such as racial homogeneity, linguistic unity, and shared historical experience. They advocated

---

621. Ahmed Samatar, "The Curse of Allah: Civic Disembowelment and the Collapse of the State in Somalia," 95–133, 138.
622. Notes of Professor Hassan Kaynan on the Concept Note of the Workshop on the Somali Equation Framework to be held in June 2023.
623. Abdullahi, Revisiting Somali Historiography, 42. Interview with Professor Abdi Kusow, one of the prominent scholars from the revisionist perspective, in 2018.

for comprehensive Somali Studies that do not exclude sociological minorities and marginalized communities. However, the revisionist perspective does not disagree with anthropological and Marxist perspectives on the secular view. Indeed, their difference is confined to criticizing the marriage of power and knowledge that nomadic-rooted and camel culture national leaders promoted.[624] The objectives of the revisionist scholars have been partially achieved in the development of the constitutional provisions, which recognized linguistic diversity and minority rights, and the adoption of a federal system demanded by the Hizbia Dastur Mustaqil al-Somalia (HDMS) party, which represented the South/Western clans of Digil and Mirifle, before the Somali independence in 1960.[625]

The three above-stated perspectives are just two sides of the same coin regarding their belonging to secular philosophy and overlapping understanding of Somali society and its relationship with the modern state. Indeed, the ideology of the postcolonial Somali state in its two phases, civilian and military, was founded on the hybridization of anthropological, liberalism, and Marxist perspectives, which suffered failure as an intellectual framework for Somali state-building. The three above-stated perspectives are just two sides of the same coin and belong to secular philosophy. Nevertheless, they have an overlapping understanding of Somali society and its relationship with the modern state. Indeed, the ideology of the postcolonial Somali state

---

624. It is noteworthy that all presidents and Prime Ministers of Somalia since the independence in 1960 were rooted in the pastoral nomadic regions. As a result, the nomadic culture became dominant in Somali studies, educational curricula, and mass media.

625. The Digil & Mirifle clan family is one of Somalia's prominent four clan families, which were given an equal quota with Hawiye, Darood, and Dir in the 4.5 clan power-sharing. This clan family is concentrated in the South/Western state of Somalia. See Somali Provisional Constitution, Article (31:3), which states, "The state shall promote the cultural practices and local dialects of minorities." Also, see Elmi. Afyare. "Decentralization options for Somalia: Paper for the Heritage Institute for Policy Studies," 2014. http://www.heritage-institute.org/wp-content/uploads/2014/01/Decentralization_Options_for_Somalia-ENGLISH.pdf (accessed on May 10, 2023)

in its two phases, civilian and military, was founded on the hybridization of anthropological, liberalism, and Marxist perspectives, which suffered abysmal failure as an intellectual framework for Somali state-building. On the other hand, the revisionist perspective contributed to addressing internal grievances among Somalis and criticizing the propensity of Somali studies to specific regions. Therefore, their central thesis was confined to demanding an inclusive approach to Somali studies. As a result, these three perspectives were criticized by this author, who proposed the "Comprehensive Perspective" (CP) of Somali studies.

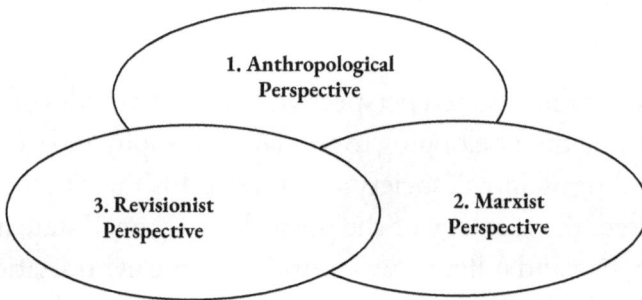

Fig.29. The three perspectives with overlapping Secular views

THE COMPREHENSIVE PERSPECTIVE

The Comprehensive Critical Perspective (CP) was founded to explore Somali studies from its origins in ancient history to the present day, discovering periods of strength and weakness, the impact of Islam in framing societal culture and building states, the colonial intrusion, and Somali reaction, the introduction of the modern state system, the rise and fall of the Somali state, the civil war and reconciliations, recovering the Somali state in 2000 and occurrences from then on. This perspective refutes four prevalent features of Somali studies: secularism, patriarchism, exceptionalism, and clannism. Historically, this author developed the initial idea of the CP as a critical approach in 1989 while he was a graduate student at the Islamic Institute, McGill University, and it has been gradually expanded since then.[626] It offers an alternative perspective and scholarly foundation for revisiting and reconstructing Somali studies.

The first premise of the CP is criticizing the other three perspectives in their adoption of the secular view in their analysis. In the Somali context, a secular view means that despite accepting Islam as the state religion, the colonially inherited legal system and elite political culture tend to separate religion from state affairs. The Somali state acquired a mixed legal system in which familial and financial disputes were adjugated in Sharia legal frameworks while, in other matters, secular laws took precedence. During military rule, even the family laws were secularized, which provoked societal uproar and the execution of opposing Ulama.[627] Indeed, these three perspectives share these attributes in following methodologies that divorce Islam in their research or rarely mention the Sufi orders as part of society's presupposed declining traditional culture.[628] Con-

---

626. The initial idea was expressed in the master's thesis submitted to the Islamic Institute, McGill University, titled "Tribalism, Nationalism, and Islam: The Crisis of Political Loyalties in Somalia." Since then, this author has published four books and several papers and articles in the spirit of this perspective. See https://mogadishuuniversity.academia.edu/AbdurahmanAbdullahibaadiyow (accessed on 16 May 20123)

627. On January 23, 1975, ten leading scholars of Islam were executed because they opposed secularized family law. See Abdurahman Abdullahi, *Women, Islamists and Military Regime in Somalia*.

628. The academic literature on Islam in English mainly focuses on Sufi Orders. They include Mohamed Mukhtar, "Islam in the Somali History: Fact and Fiction," in *The Invention of Somalia*, ed. Ali Jumale (Red Sed Sea Press, 1995), 1–29. Mohamed M. Kassim, "Aspects of Banadir Cultural History: The Case of Baravan Ulama," in *The Invention of Somalia*, ed. Ali Jumale (Red Sed Sea Press, 1995), 29-43. Christine Choi Ahmed, *God, Anti-Colonialism and Drums: Sheikh Uways and the Uwaysiyya*; B.G. Martin, *Shaykh Uways Bin Mouhammad Al-Barawi. A Traditional Somali Sufi*; Scott Rees, *Urban Woes and Pious Remedies: Sufism in Nineteenth Century Banaadir (Somalia)* (Indiana: Indiana University Press, 1999); Said Samatar, "Sheikh Uways Muhammad of Baraawe, 1847-1909: Mystic and Reformer in East Africa," in *The Shadows of Conquest: Islam in Colonial Northeast Africa*, ed. Said S. Samatar (Trenton, NJ: The Red Sea Press), 1992, 48–74. After 9/11, western academia began to study modern Islamic movements as part of security studies. Currently, there is an overflow of

versely, CP calls for including the role of Islam, Islamism, and Sufi orders in Somali studies as part of the Somali equation.

The second premise of the CP is to include women in historical research and not to confine the analysis to the patriarchal segment of society. This means that besides reaffirming the early marginalization of women in the decision-making of the pastoral/nomadic communities, contemporary Somali studies should not peripheralize women's crucial societal role and give attention to their rich cultural contributions.[629] Moreover, women's social, political, and economic roles should be revised and restored. To do so, women should be liberated from the traditional clan bonds and extreme interpretation of Islam by ultra-conservative groups. Instead, women must be given the role articulated by the moderate scholars of Islam.[630]

The third premise of this critique is to avoid the exceptionalization of Somalia and to explore its shared features with African and Middle Eastern studies. Professor Cassanelli rightly expressed "that Somali Studies, as a collective enterprise, has been too insular, too unwilling to view Somalia as a variant of other societies."[631] He further observed that the sense of "Somali exceptionalism" prevents seeing Somalia as resembling other African and Muslim societies.[632] Moreover, it must be seen through its similarities with African and

---

literature on al-Shabaab.

629. Literature on Somali women and their role in politics, economics, and civil society are growing. There are several publications authored by Dr. Hamdi Sheikh Mohamed, a book chapter by Christine Choi Ahmed, Judith Gardner, and Judy El Bushra, and many others.

630. See Yusuf al-Qaradawi, "The Status of Women in Islam," available from https://www.centuryassociation.org/download/marriage_2016/books/The_Status_of_Women_in_Islam__by_Yusuf_al_Qaradawi.pdf (accessed on May 17, 2023); Hiam Salah EI-din Ali eI-Gousi, "Women's Rights in Islam and Contemporary Ulama: Limitations and Constraints. (Egypt as Case Study)," Ph.D. thesis submitted to The University of Leeds, 2010. Available from https://etheses.whiterose.ac.uk/15221/1/535101.pdf (accessed on May 15, 2023), 91–103.

631. Lee Cassanelli, "The Somali Studies International Association: A Brief History," *Bildhaan: An International Journal of Somali Studies* 1 (2008), 8.

632. Ibid.

Middle Eastern Studies. Thus, Somalis share geography, culture, colonial legacy, religion, and postcolonial challenges with African people. African Studies began as part of the colonial project to understand the colonial subjects. On the other hand, Middle Eastern Studies includes Islamic Studies extensively due to the preponderance of the Muslims in the region. Somalia, being a member of the League of Arab States, shares many things with countries in the Middle East, including cultural traits, political culture, and the Islamic faith. Thus, Middle Eastern Studies have influenced Somali Studies, and many of their conclusions may apply to the Somali context.

The fourth premise is the clannization of Somali studies, which leads to the clannization of the Somali conflict, the prevailing narrative of academic circles, and public perception. Clannization of the conflict was intended to divert individual responsibilities to the collective responsibility of the clans for crimes committed during the civil war and to offer impunity to the perpetrators of heinous crimes. This premise affirms the political elite's responsibility for the Somali conundrum, state failure, and collapse due to their inability to deal with state-building challenges. This failure resulted from the elite conflict between Islamists and non-Islamists on the nature of the state on the one hand and the conflict among non-Islamist elites on power and prestige on the other.[633] The clannization of the conflict led to failed reconciliations and conflict resolution processes and methods during the first ten years of the state collapse. Moreover, even power-sharing of the political elites based on clan affiliation in 2000 failed to produce a functioning Somali state. Although the clan factor could not be utterly disregarded, its precarious practices must be managed and tamed through policies that confine it in its indispensable societal role.

Thus, understanding the dynamics of the four factors: secularism, patriarchism, exceptionalism, and clannism of Somali studies

---

633. Due to elite conflict for power, specific clans were mobilized to support the regime, while others supported their opposition political elites. In the process, Somali society was polarized in line with clan belonging.

is crucial to deciphering Somali chronic state failure. Moreover, it enables us to develop new perspectives that offer a microscopic view of the root conflicts and fault lines underlying state-society relations, elite political conflict, the politicization of clan structures, the radicalization of national politics, and the misuse of Islam as a vehicle of violent extremism. Finally, the CP is not just a theoretical framework but suggests a comprehensive reconciliation framework.

To simplify, the explanation of the CP's basic premises will refer to the theory of mind in psychology, which refers to understanding thoughts in people's minds (mental states).[634] I will analyze the state of mind of Somali individuals by illustrating the six possible scenarios of the state of mind represented in the following six circles that show hierarchies of loyalties to clan, Islam, and nationalism. Let us imagine dissecting the minds of the various Somali individuals horizontally to understand their belief system and the hierarchies of their loyalties to the Somali equation: clan system, Islam, and modern state. Eventually, we will see the reconfiguration of the individual's state of mind in one of the following six figures (Diagram. 31)

Fig.1 shows the map of the mind of extreme clannists, in which Islam comes the lowest in the hierarchy of loyalties while nationalism becomes second after clannism. Fig. 2 shows the map of a traditionalist where clan comes first, the traditional conception of Islam (Sufism) comes second, and nationalism acquires the smallest loyalty. This type of mind is prevalent in most Somali populations who practice general Islamic obligations but are mainly apolitical. Fig.3 demonstrates the mind of an extreme secular nationalist who gives his loyalty to nationalism first, followed by clan comes, while Islam is the smallest in his hierarchy of loyalties. This form of mind tolerates clannism but opposes and oppresses activists aspiring to apply sharia. It is the mind of the secular absolutists experienced in Somalia during the military rule. Fig.4 demonstrates the mind of moderate nation-

---

634. Ian A. Apperly and Butterfill, Stephen A. "Do humans have two systems to track beliefs and belief-like states?" Psychological Review, 116 (4), 2009, 953–70.

alists, where the hierarchy of loyalty to nationalism comes first, and Islam gets the next rank, while clannism is the lowest. Fig. 5 shows the properly organized mind of a Muslim individual in whom loyalty to Islam comes first, nationalism second, with clannism taking the lowest rank. However, the realization of this model based on inclusivity and prioritization of three elements of the Somali equation is yet to be developed. This form of mind belongs to the moderate Islamists who aspire to transform their society through peaceful and democratic means while advocating Islamic principles and values in the state and society.[635] Fig. 6 shows the mind of an extreme Islamist who does not recognize the modern state system and nationalism. Instead, he aspires to realize international order based on the historical Muslim state (Caliphate) through violence.[636] This mind hardly swings to another ideology like the other five mindsets. This extremism in the name of Islam is apparent in al-Shabab, Daish, and similar organizations. These six types of minds among Somali individuals are extreme clannists, moderate clannists, extreme secular nationalists, moderate nationalists, moderate Islamists, and extreme Islamists. The three extreme loyalties do not tolerate each other and believe in the total exclusion of the others: a zero-sum game. On the other hand, moderates are tolerant of each other and open to mutual interactions, dialogue, and peaceful conflict resolutions. Indeed, the biggest challenge in Somali cosmology is fluctuating the hierarchy of loyalties to the Somali equation and the delusions of each element. Accordingly, it is common to see an individual offering his loyalty to Islam in one circumstance, his clan on another occasion, and his nation in another period. It is all circumstantial, and even concur-

---

635. Organized moderate Islamists generally belong to the Muslim Brotherhood persuasions organizationally or ideologically. In Somalia, the Muslim Brotherhood persuasion includes Islah Movement, Aala-Sheikh, and other smaller entities.

636. Dan Josef and Harun Maruf, *Inside al-Shabaab: The Secret History of al-Qaida's Most Powerful Ally* (Indiana University Press, 2021). Also, Abdi Said M.A, "The Al-Shabaab Al-Mujahidiin: A Profile of the First Somali Terrorist Organisation," available from https://www.files.ethz.ch/isn/55851/AlShabaab.pdf (accessed on April 25 2023), 3.

rent loyalties may occur occasionally. Fluctuating loyalties poses the biggest obstacle to developing a strategy to deal with the crisis of loyalties and creating an environment of reconciliation and could be likened to a civil war taking place in the minds of every individual, where various loyalties contest each other for dominance. Unquestionably, this continuous contestation of loyalties generates traumatic syndrome, identity crises, and disordered thinking and delusions.

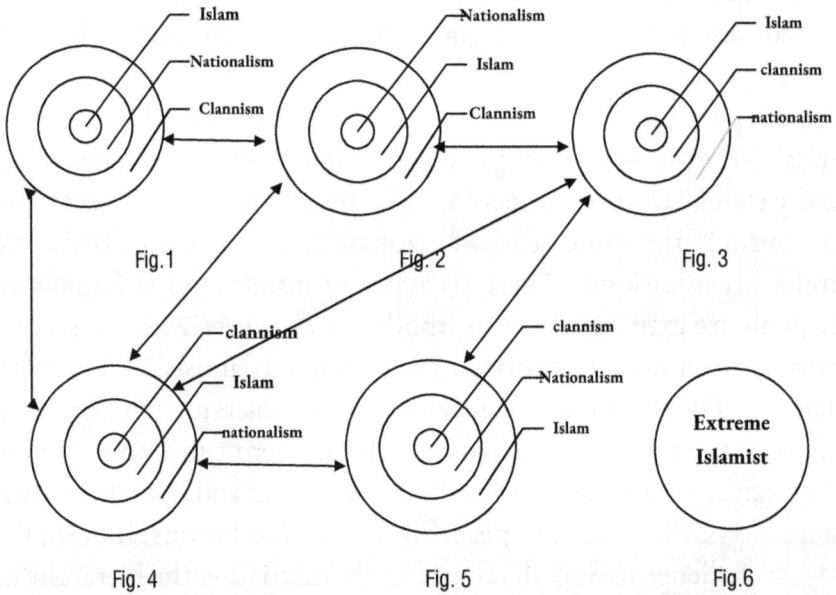

Fig.31. Six Types of Minds Showing The Fluctuation Process.

The second illustration depicting the basic premise of the CP requires examining the reconfiguration of the Somali elite structure and relations. It is an appropriate tool for analyzing state-society relations. The elitist analysis method is applicable in the political analysis of Muslim countries where the impact of kinship in politics is still dominant. Diagram 5 shows the four main categories of the Somali elites, divided into traditional elites (traditional *Ulama* and traditional clan elders) belonging to the micro-level analysis and modern elites (Islamists and non-Islamists) belonging to the macro-level analysis.[637] We use the term non-Islamist to represent a Muslim who practices Islam and does not deny its principles but does not advocate its application as an Islamist does. It is to this category that most people belong. These four elite categories are illustrated in diagram no.2.

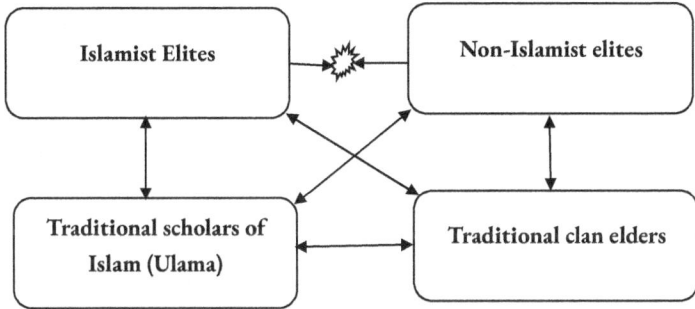

Fig. 32. The Somali Elite Structure and Their Relations

Here, we will examine these four elite categories' horizontal and vertical relations. The relationship between clan elders and traditional ulama is complementary because their community authorities are well divided. Clan elders have the power to manage the day-to-day affairs of the clan and make peace and war. At the same time, the role of Ulama is mainly confined to religious activities and reconciliation.[638] Their relations generally are courteous and friendly, creating an environment of stability and solidarity in their community.[639] Often, they became relatives through family marriages, which even solidified their affinities and cooperation. Contrary to the traditional elites, relations between the modern elites are confrontational because of their different political views and agenda. They disagree on the nature and ideology of the state. Whereas moderate Islamists aspire to transform the modern state into one that applies Islamic laws and follows principles and values, non-Islamist elites cling to the

---

637. This model was developed in 1991 during my MA program at the Islamic Institute, McGill University. See Abdullahi, Tribalism, *Nationalism and Islam*, 92.

638. Abdurahman Abdullahi, *The Islamic Movement in Somalia*.

639. Ibid.

form of state inherited from the colonial powers. The postcolonial state was generally secular in its legal, economic, and cultural values.

On the other hand, the relations between traditional Ulama and modern Islamists are somehow suspicious because Islamists aspire to political agenda while most traditional Ulama are apolitical. Moreover, modern Islamists compete with traditional Ulama on the religious authority in society. Indeed, different groups of modern Islamists deal with traditional Ulama differently. For example, Salafia groups' relations with traditional Ulama in more intolerant than the Muslim Brotherhood's persuasions.[640] Moreover, the relationship between traditional clan elders and non-Islamist elites is courteous and primarily rooted in next-of-kin empathy. In addition, traditional clan elders and modern elites are, to a certain degree, linked to each other through relative networks. Indeed, the role of clan elders changed significantly after the adoption of clan-power sharing in 2000 and since their empowerment to select members of the parliament. In this circumstance, all politicians must cultivate closer relations with their clan elders. Finally, the relations between Islamists and traditional clan elders and between non-Islamists and Traditional Ulama are generally courteous and based on respect.

THE INCLUSIVE RECONCILIATION FRAMEWORK (IRF)

The Comprehensive Critical Perspective aims to explore and offer a new interpretation for Somali studies and suggest a framework for resolving the Somali crisis. Having seen the configuration of the Somali mind and elite structure and their relations, we understood the nature and hierarchies of the Somali conflicts. As such, this perspective calls the Inclusive Reconciliation Framework (IRF), which aims to set a new direction in resolving the four levels of Somali conflicts: the modern state and traditional Somali society,

---

640. Abdurahman Abdullahi, "The Conception of Islam in Somalia: Consensus and Controversy," Bildhaan Vol. 21, 2023, 79–98, 87-90. Available from https://digitalcommons.macalester.edu/cgi/viewcontent.cgi?article=1240&context=bildhaan (accessed on April 25, 2023).

the elite political conflict for power; the politicized and clannized armed conflict; and internal conflicts among traditional elites and conflicts in the name of Islam. These conflicts exclude traditional clan conflicts for posture, land, water, and other factors, which are quickly resolved through traditional conflict resolution mechanisms. See these four levels of conflicts in Diagram No. 6 below.

Having grasped the four levels of conflict, let us begin addressing their reconciliation. The first level of the IRF is the state-society conflict which is the root cause and the father and mother of all other conflicts. However, before proceeding further, we must grasp historical approaches to state-building and its relationship with the traditional system. There were two models of Somali state-building with divergent state-society relations. The first approach was exercised during the two phases of the state-building approaches, the democratic system (1960–69) and the military dictatorship (1969–91).

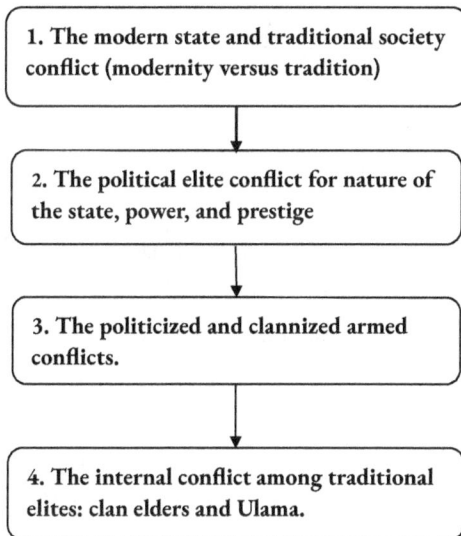

1. The modern state and traditional society conflict (modernity versus tradition)

2. The political elite conflict for nature of the state, power, and prestige

3. The politicized and clannized armed conflicts.

4. The internal conflict among traditional elites: clan elders and Ulama.

Fig. 33. The four layers of Somali conflicts

In this approach, the state-building process was based on Westernization, secularization, and despising traditions. Its concept was based on moving society to the Western system of governance by indoctrinating society to accept and adopt this system. However, this system failed to sustain itself because of suppressing traditions on which oppositions organized their armed supporters and toppled the regime and the state in 1991. To exemplify this process, let us consider the state as a house building where people compete to enter because their livelihood depends on that. However, the design of the house does not fit and accommodate these people's features and way of life. The people were overcrowded outside of the house and forcefully rushed at once to enter the house. There were no guides or supervisory bodies that showed the people the systematic way that each of them had a chance to enter the house. There was no culture of line up and who comes first is served first. Through this process, the house falls apart, and the people are either killed or injured, and some of them save their lives by had escaped the scrupling house. This phenomenon is precisely what happened in Somalia in 1991.

The second approach was developed during the Somali Peace and Reconciliation Conference in Djibouti in 2000, which was based on indigenization while keeping features of the Western structure of the state.[641] The indigenization concerned the power-sharing based on clan quotas of 4.5 and the giving clan elders the authority to select and nominate members of the parliament from their clans. In addition, Islam was accepted as the ultimate reference of all laws, and since then, this provision has been included in the Provisional Constitution. On the other hand, the established state system kept the features of the Western system of governance, like the design of governance inherited from the colonial powers in 1960.[642] Moreover, the Somali state adopted a federal system of governance in 2004. Both clan power-sharing and federalism were necessary decisions to recover the state. Nonetheless, these new approaches were abused by the

---

641. The system was built on clan power-sharing and the clan elders' selection of members of the parliament. However, the outcome of the process was the structure of the modern state system constituting a legislative assembly, executive branch, judiciary branch, and the presidency.

642. The system was a parliamentarian who was alike to the Somali governance system of 1960.

political elites who were infused with toxic elite political culture.[643] Nevertheless, this approach failed to produce a functioning Somali state for over two decades. This approach was founded on moving the state to the society and building the state on the traditional structure. Both approaches were extremes in employing either Westernization or indigenization. Therefore, the IRF suggests moving the state and society towards each other in the middle ground where the state and society's main features are preserved. Of course, this requires re-engineering the system of governance in Somalia and reorganizing the design of traditional authority damaged during the civil war.

Westernized system of governance

Developing an effective system of Reconciling state and society

Indigenization mixed with some features of Westernization.

Fig. 34. The process of reconciling state and society in Somalia.

The second level of the IRF is elite political reconciliation. There are two approaches to realizing this phase. The first one is reconciliation between Islamists and non-Islamists on the nature of the state. This phase was realized through the Transitional Charter of 2000 and subsequent constitutional provisions. For instance, the Somali Provisional Constitution stipulates that Islam is the ultimate reference of all state laws. Article (3.1) states, "The Constitution of the Federal Republic of Somalia is based on the foundations of the Holy Quran and the Sunna of our prophet Mohamed (PBUH) and protects the higher objectives of sharia and social justice." Further,

643. Abdurahman Abdullahi, "The Somali Elite Political Culture: Conceptions, Structures, and Historical Evolution." Somali Studies: A Peer-Reviewed Academic Journal for Somali Studies, Volume 5, 2020, 30–92.

Article 2:3 states, "No law can be enacted that is not compliant with the general principles and objectives of Sharia." This phase of the IRF was achieved generally. The second approach of elite reconciliation entails creating an inclusive political system that is not only democratic but also sensitive enough to accommodate all segments of society, including women and minorities. The inclusion of women is well articulated in the Somali Provisional Constitution. As Article 3:5 states, "Women must be included, effectively, in all national institutions, in particular all elected and appointed positions across the three branches of government and in independent national commissions." In traditional societies, political processes based on winners and losers or majoritarian system breeds sectarianism, exclusions, and conflict. Therefore, developing an appropriate political system, election model, and effective public institutions are necessary preconditions to a successful elite reconciliation. The best example of creating consensus and cohesion in a clannish society was the story of the Black Stone when the Quraish sub-clans disputed who would position the Black Stone in its place after reconstructing the Ka'ba. They agreed to accept the judgment of the first person who entered the house of Ka'ba, and the person was young Muhammad (the Prophet). He placed the Black stone on a sheet and requested all the leaders of the tribes to hold the sheet and lift the stone together to the Ka'ba. This story shows that clan prestige is critical; therefore, creating collective leadership and a sense of shared ownership is vital for the stability of the state.[644]

The third level of IRF deals with the politicized and clannized conflict. This entails addressing past grievances and gross human rights violations by adopting transitional justice mechanisms that suit Somali culture and religion. Islam and traditional culture have tools for resolving prolonged human rights violations after the civil war. For example, the practical transitional justice approach and tool in Islam could be derived from the conquering of Mecca by the

644. Muhammad Husayn Haykal, "Life of Muhammad," trans. Isma'il Al-Faruqi. Available from https://muqith.files.wordpress.com/2010/10/muhammadbyhaykal.pdf (accessed on 17 May 2023),128.

Muslims after eight years of their forced migration to Medina and thirteen years of subjugation in Mecca.[645] On the other hand, some grievances of the politicized clan conflict could be resolved through traditional means. Clannization of the Somali conflict deflects individual responsibility for the committed crimes and depicts it as the collective culpability of a clan. Transitional justice in Somalia is a neglected field that CRF strongly recommends.[646]

The fourth level of IRF calls for reorganizing traditional authorities, which have been corrupted and lost their authoritative powers. Traditional institutions of clan elders and the Ulama religious authority have drastically deteriorated. Therefore, it is necessary to revise the structures of the clan elders who have been chaotically divided and ruined inter-clan cohesion and hierarchy of their authorities.[647] The fragmentation of clan elders took a high stake since the collapse of the state in 1991, during the civil war, and the empowerment of clan elders as custodians of authority to select members of the parliament. The politicization of the clan elders ruined the cohesion and stability between clans. On the other hand, IRF advocates for establishing a unified system of meaning of Islam agreed upon by the prominent Ulama and officially accepted by the state. This approach creates an environment of minimizing conflicts on the issues of Islam. Currently, the Ulama are highly fragmented, and various groups adhere to their different interpretations. Establishing a commission of Ulama belonging to the multiple persuasions should be the first step towards the practical unification of understanding Islam in

---

645. Abdurahman Abdullahi, *Recovering the Somali state: The Role of Islam, Islamism, and Transitional Justice* (Adonis and Abbey Publishers, 2017), 123.
646. Abdurahman Abdullahi, "Conceptions of Transitional Justice in Somalia: Findings of Field Research in Mogadishu." North African Studies, Michigan State University Press, Vol. 14, no.2,2014, 7-43.
647. Abdurahman Abdullahi and Ibrahim Farah, "Reconciling the State, and Society: Reordering the Islamic work and Clan System." Available from https://www.scribd.com/document/15327358/Reconciling-the-State-and-Society-in-Somalia# (accessed on April 26, 2023)

Somali society. The following figure depicts the reconciled modern political elite and properly reorganized traditional elders and Ulama.

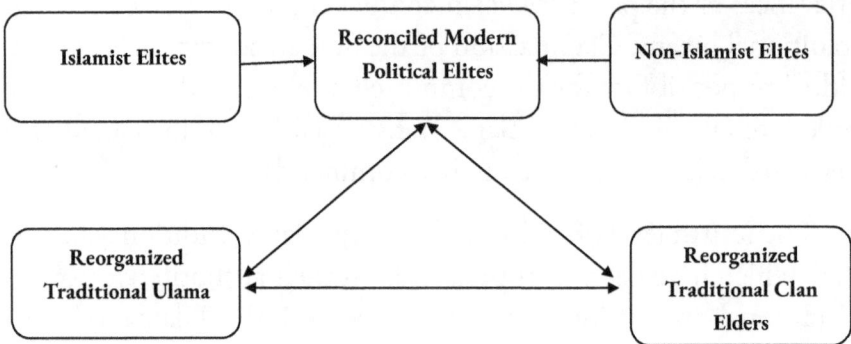

Fig. 35. Triangle of Comprehensive Reconciliation Framework.

STABILITY MODEL OF THE SOMALI STATE

Adopting the IRF triangle is enough to create a stable environment in Somalia. Since the collapse of the state, Somali civil society (CS) successfully emerged, with the traditional elders, Ulama, and modern civil society organizations filling the vacuum of the state. These organizations were engaged in public service provision in education, the health sector, charities, peace, and reconciliation, and they networked with international organizations. CS organizations are networked nationally and are becoming more organized. In addition, the business community is also robust and plays an essential role in all development sectors. Business personalities play a crucial role in making peace and war among clans. The stability of the state necessarily entails cooperating with non-state actors, including the CS and business communities.

There are six scenarios regarding civil society/state relations that all involve CS, apart from the state (mosque committees, sports clubs), which politicized CS in opposition to the state (civil society toppling dictatorial regimes through peaceful means) and CS in continuous dialogue with the state (criticizing when the state deviates from the public good and support when they do good); CS in support of the state (supports civil society and promotes its ideals),

CS in a partnership or substitute to the state (in case the state is weak like Somalia, civil society substitutes the state); and CS beyond the state as a global phenomenon (international NGOs advocating for the global issues).[648]

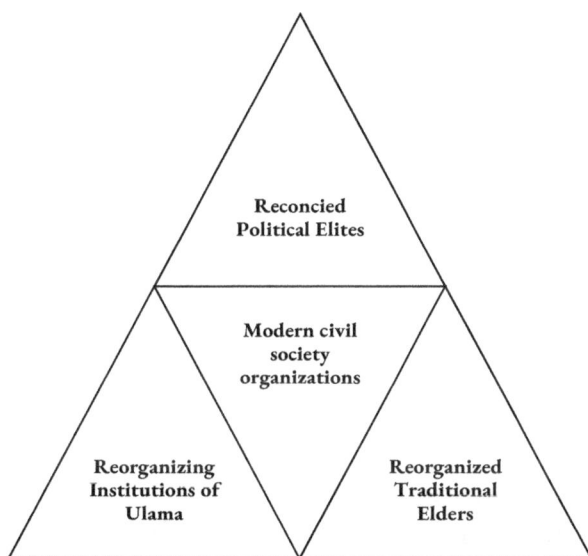

Fig.36. Stability Model of Somali State-building

The role of the Somali CS in rebuilding the state must be to engage in continuous dialogue with the state and avoid its politicization. Hence, they must criticize and dialogue with the state when it deviates from the constitution and undertakes policies not in the public's interest. They also have to support policies and programs of the state when the state is doing beneficial programs such as promoting public education, improving human rights, fighting al-Shabaab, and so on. This concept agrees with the Islamic notion of rejecting the mischievous (*Munkar*) and supporting the virtuous (*Macruuf*).[649] The organized nationwide civil society, including all

648. See Abdurahman Abdullahi, *Making Sense of Somali History*, vol.2 (Adonis & Abbey, 2018), 67–70.
649. See "Let there arise out of you a group of people inviting to all that is good, enjoying al-Ma'roof and forbidding al-Munkar." (aal-Imran, 3:104). Also, see the verse, "You are the best of peoples ever raised up for mankind; you enjoin al-Ma'roof and forbid Al-Munkar, and you believe in Allah (Aal Imran, 3:110).

sectors, is the agent of state stability and an element of a new re-engineering of Somalia's stability model.

CONCLUSION

This Chapter has produced the challenges toward Somali state-building and depicted that modern state relations with the traditional Somali society is one of the main challenges researchers of Somali studies have thus far failed to address. After criticizing three main perspectives—anthropological, Marxist, and Revisionist—this author suggested an alternative perspective named the "comprehensive critical perspective," which refutes Somali studies' exceptionalization, clannization, secularization, and patriarchization, and instead offers an inclusive approach that factors all elements of the Somali equation into Somali studies. The six scenarios of the Somali mind were illustrated to simplify the concept of the comprehensive critical perspective. The fluctuation of individual loyalties exhibits the significant challenges confronting Somali state-building. Moreover, the classification of the Somali elites into traditional and modern and their relations were also produced and examined. The study showed the need to develop a new frame of analysis called the Comprehensive Reconciliation Framework.

The Comprehensive Reconciliation Framework is based on the four levels of Somali conflicts: the state-society conflict, elite political conflict, clannized political conflict, internal conflicts within traditional elites, and conflicts in the name of Islam. It also hinges on understanding the two previously used approaches to state-society relations. The first approach was Westernization, which was based on moving the people to accept the inherited state model from the colonial powers. The second approach was indigenization, founded on moving the state model to the people through clan power-sharing. Thus, the first IRF reconciles the state and society by moving them to a middle space that recognizes the separate spaces and roles of the state and society. The second IRF concerns the reconciliation of the political elites on the nature of the state and practicing democratic values sensitive to the Somali culture and belief system. The third IRF calls to address the human rights violation of the clannized political conflict during the civil war through transitional justice mechanisms rooted in Somali culture and Islam. Finally, the fourth IRF is to reorganize the fragmented traditional institutions during the civil war and the politicization of the clans.

Finally, reconciling state and society entails reconciling political elites, reorganizing traditional institutions, addressing previous grievances, and laying the foundation for a shared future is the only way to institute a viable Somali state. Reorganizing and reconciling Somali society should be expressed through constitutional provisions and legal frameworks. Moreover, non-state actors, like civil society organizations and business communities, must be given cooperative roles in the Somali state-building to bolster this new structure. Assigning a role to the non-state actors offers the final design that produces the "stability model for Somali state-building."

REFERENCES

Abdinoor, Abdullahi. *Constructing Education in the Stateless Society: The Case of Somalia*. Ph.D. thesis, University of Ohio, 2007.

Abdi, Sheik Abdi. *Divine Madness: Mohammed Abdulle Hassan (1856–1920)*. London: Zed Books Ltd., 1993.

Abdullahi, Abdurahman. "Revisiting Somali Historiography: Critique and Idea of Comprehensive Perspective." *Journal of Somali Studies: Research on Somalia and the Greater Horn of African Countries* 5, no. 1-2 (2018): 30–48.

Abdullahi, Abdurahman. "Somali Elite Political Culture: Conceptions, Structures, and Historical Evolution." *Institute of Somali Studies: A Peer-Reviewed Academic Journal for Somali Studies* 5 (2020): 30–92.

Abdullahi, Abdurahman. "The Application of Sharia in Somalia." Accessed April 17, 2024. https://www.scribd.com/document/15419600/The-application-of-Sharia-in-Somalia.

Abdullahi, Abdurahman. "Theorizing Islam and Islamists: Critical Conceptions and Cultural Challenges." In *Theorizing Somali Society: Hope, Transformation, and Development, Vol. 1*, edited by Abdulkadir Osman Farah and Mohamed A. Eno, 122-150. London: Authors Press, 2022.

Abdullahi, Abdurahman. "Theorizing Stability of the Somali State: In the Light of the Comprehensive Perspective of Somali Studies." *Institute of Somali Studies: A Peer-Reviewed Academic Journal for Somali Studies* 8 (2023): 11–55.

Abdullahi, Abdurahman. *Making Sense of Somali History, Vol. 1*. London: Adonis & Abey, 2017.

Abdullahi, Abdurahman. *Making Sense of Somali History, Vol. 2*. London: Adonis & Abey, 2018.

Abdullahi, Abdurahman. *Recovering the Somali State: The Role of Islam, Islamism, and Transitional Justice*. London: Adonis & Abey, 2018.

Abdullahi, Abdurahman. *Reflections on Somalia's Political Deadlock: The Need for a New Political Deal*. Accessed June 1, 2024. https://www.academia.edu/88431391/Reflections_on_Somalias_Political_Deadlock_The_Need_for_a_New_Political_Deal.

Abdullahi, Abdurahman. *The Death of Arta Political Deal*. Available from https://www.academia.edu/87581583/The_death_of_Arta_Political_deal_pdf?uc-sb-sw=34087464. Accessed June 1, 2024.

Abdullahi, Abdurahman. "Women, Islamists, and the Military Regime in Somalia: The New Family Law and Its Implications." In *Milk and Peace, Drought and War: Somali Culture, Society and Politics*, edited by Markus Hoehne and Virginia Luling, 137–160. London: Hurst, 2010.

Abdullahi, Abdurahman (Baadiyow). *The Islamic Movement in Somalia: A Study of Islah Movement (1950-2000)*. London: Adonis & Abbey, 2015.

Abdullahi, Abdurahman. *Tribalism, Nationalism, and Islam: The Crisis of Political Loyalty in Somalia*. Master's thesis, Islamic Institute, McGill University, 1992.

Abdullahi, Abdurahman. *Conceptions of Transitional Justice in Somalia: Findings of Field Research in Mogadishu*. North African Studies, Michigan State University Press, Vol. 14, no.2, 2014.

Abdullahi, Abdurahman. *The Conception of Islam in Somalia: Consensus and Controversy. Bildhaan* Vol. 21, 2023.

Abdullahi, Abdurahman. "The Islah Movement in Somalia: Islamic Moderation in War-torn Somalia." Available from https://www.hiiraan.com/oct2008/ISLAH.pdf. Accessed October 4, 2020.

Abdullahi, Abdurahman and Ibrahim Farah. *Reconciling the State and Society: Reordering the Islamic Work and Clan System*. Available from https://www.scribd.com/document/15327358/Reconciling-the-State-and-Society-in-Somalia. Accessed April 26, 2023.

Abdullahi, Abdurahman. *Conceptions of Transitional Justice in Somalia: Findings of Field Research in Mogadishu. North African Studies*, Michigan State University Press, Vol. 14, no.2, 2014.

Abdullahi, Abdurahman. "The Conception of Islam in Somalia: Consensus and Controversy." *Bildhaan* Vol. 21, 2023.

Abdullahi, Osman and Issaka K. Souare, eds. *Somalia at the Crossroads: Challenges and Perspectives in Reconstituting a Failed State.* London: Adonis & Abbey, 2007.

Abdullahi, Osman. "The Role of Egypt, Ethiopia the Blue Nile in the Failure of the Somali Conflict Resolutions: A Zero-Sum Game." A paper presented at the annual meeting of the International Studies Association, Hilton Hawaiian Village, Honolulu, Hawaii, March 2005.

Achebe, Chinua. *The Trouble with Nigeria*. Fourth Dimension Publishing Co., 2000.

Adan, Hussein M. "Somalia: A Terrible Beauty Being Born?" In *Collapsed States: The Disintegration and Restoration of Legitimate Authority*, edited by I. William Zartman, 69–89. London: Lynne Reinne, 1995.

Adan, Hussein M. "Somalia: Militarism, Warlordism or Democracy?" *Review of African Political Economy* 54 (1992): 11-26.

Ahmed, Christine Choi. "God, Anti-Colonialism, and Drums: Sheikh Uways and the Uwaysiyya." Ufahamu 17, no. 2 (Spring 1989): 96–117.

African Watch Committee. 'Somalia: A Government at War with Its Own People'. Human Rights Watch; 1st ed Edition, 1990.

Afyare, Elmi. "Decentralization Options for Somalia: Paper for the Heritage Institute for Policy Studies," 2014. Accessed May 10, 2023. http://www.heritageinstitute.org/wp-content/uploads/2014/01/Decentralization_Options_for_Somalia-ENGLISH.pdf.

Al-Ghamdi, Hassna. "Muslim World League: A Historical Look at Establishment, Goals and Projects." *International Journal of Humanities and Social Science* Vol. 11, No. 1, January 2021.

Alesina, Alesina, and Giuliano, Poala. "Culture and Institutions." IZA Discussion Papers, No. 9246, Institute for the Study of Labor (IZA), Bonn, 2015.

Ali, Salah Mohamed Ali. *Hudur and the History of Southern Somalia.* Cairo: Nahda Book Publisher, 2005.

Allen, Kawan J. "Expressive Culture," *The Department of Cultural References*. Available from http://tammysgordon.org/DCR/items/show/55 (accessed on 10 October 2020).

Al-Qaradawi, Yusuf. *The Status of Women in Islam*. Available from https://www.centuryassociation.org/download/marriage_2016/books/The_Status_of_Women_in_Islam__by_Yusuf_al_Qaradawi.pdf (accessed on 17 May 2023).

Al-Gousi, Hiam Salah EI-din Ali. "Women's Rights in Islam and Contemporary Ulama: Limitations and Constraints." (Egypt as Case Study). A Ph.D. thesis submitted to The University of Leeds, 2010. Available from https://etheses.whiterose.ac.uk/15221/1/535101.pdf (accessed on 15 May 2023), 91-103.

Ali, Salah Mohamed. Huddur & the History of Southern Somalia. Nahda Bookshop Publisher, 2005.

Amghar, Abderrahim. "Revisiting the Contingency Theories of Leadership: Key Features, Meanings, and Lessons." 2022.

Amin, Samir. *Accumulation on a World Scale: A Critique of the Theory of Underdevelopment.* New York and London: Monthly Review Press, 1974.

Amnesty International. "Somalia: Use of Lethal Force to Quell Protests is Unjustifiable." Available from https://www.amnesty.org/en/latest/news/2018/12/somalia-use-of-lethal-force-to-quell-protests-in-baidoa-unjustifiable/.

Apperly, Ian A. and Butterfill, Stephen A. "Do Humans Have Two Systems to Track Beliefs and Belief-Like States?". *Psychological Review*. 116 (4), 2009, 953–970.

Aslan, Seyfettin. "Historical Background and Principles of Kemalism." *NWSA-SOCIAL SCIENCES*, 2013.

Ayman, Roya, Martin M. Chemers, and Fred Fiedler. "The Contingency Model of Leadership Effectiveness: Its Levels of Analysis." *The Leadership Quarterly* 6, no. 2 (1995): 147–167.

Ayoob, Mohammed. "The Horn of Africa: Regional Conflict and Super-power Involvement." *Canberra Papers on Strategy and Defence*, No. 18, 1978. Accessed April 15, 2024.

Az, Mehmet Ata. "European Values and Islam." In *The Idea and Values of Europe: From Antigone to the Charter of Fundamental Rights*, edited by Angelo Santagostino, 41–64. Newcastle upon Tyne: Cambridge Scholars Publishing, 2020.

Baadiyow, Abdurahman. "Abdirizak Haji Hussein: The Audacious and Principled Leader." Available from https://www.academia.edu/116853719/Abdirizak_Haji_Hussein.

Bacik, Gokhan. "The Genesis, History, and Functioning of the Organization of Islamic Cooperation (OIC): A Formal-Institutional Analysis." Journal of Muslim Minority Affairs 31, no. 4 (December 2011).

Badie, Bertrand. The Imported State: The Westernization of the Political Order. Stanford, CA: Stanford University Press, 2000.

Bagdons, Ozlem Demirtas. "A Poststructuralist Approach to Ideology and Foreign Policy: Kemalism in the Turkish Foreign Policy Discourse." PhD diss., Central European University, Hungary, 2008.

Banfield, Edward. The Moral Basis of a Backward Society. Free Press, 1958.

Barnes, Cedric. "The Somali Youth League, Ethiopian Somalis, and the Greater Somalia Idea, c.1946–48." Journal of Eastern African Studies 1, no. 2 (July 2007).

Barnes, Cedric, and Harun Hassan. "The Rise and Fall of Mogadishu's Islamic Courts." Journal of Eastern African Studies 1, no. 2 (2007): 151-160.

Bauman, Michael. "Law and Morality." Available from http://www.equip.org/article/law-andmorality/ (accessed October 4, 2020).

Bayart, Jean-François, and Stephen Ellis. "Africa in the World: A History of Extraversion." African Affairs 99, no. 395 (2000): 217-267.

Bayeh, Endalcachew. "The Political and Economic Legacy of Colonialism in the Post-independent African States." International Journal of Commerce, IT and Social Sciences 2, no. 2 (February 2015).

Bealey, Frank. The Blackwell Dictionary of Political Science: A User's Guide to Its Terms. Blackwell, 1999.

Behan, Tom. The Italian Resistance: Fascists, Guerrillas, and the Allies. London: Pluto Press, 2009.

Bogaards, Matthijs. "Comparative Political Regimes: Consensus and Majoritarian Democracy." Oxford Research Encyclopaedia and Oxford University Press, USA, March 2017. Online Publication Date.

Brymer, Emma, and Tom Gray. "Effective Leadership: Transformational or Transactional?" Journal of Outdoor and Environmental Education 10 (2006): 13–19.

Building Peaceful States and Societies: A DFID Practice Paper. London: Department for International Development, 2010.

Burnham, James. The Machiavellians: Defenders of Freedom. The John Day Company, 1943.

Burns, J. M. Leadership. New York: Harper & Row, 1978.

Calingaert, Michael. "Italy's Choice: Reform or Stagnation." Current History, March 2008, 105-111.

Cardenas, Manuel Andres Sanchez. "Ethnic and Cultural Homogeneity: An Obstacle for Development?" Northeastern University, Fall 2019.

Cassanelli, Lee. The Shaping of Somali Society: Reconstructing the History of a Pastoral People, 1960-1900.

Cassanelli, Lee, and Farah Sheikh Abdulkadir. "Somali Education in Transition." Bildhan 7 (2007): 91-125.

Cassanelli, Lee. "The Somali Studies International Association: A Brief History." Bildhaan: An International Journal of Somali Studies 1 (2008), Article 5.

Cavalli, Alessandro. "Reflections on Political Culture and the 'Italian National Character'." Daedalus 130, no. 3 (Summer 2001): 119-137.

Chamberlin, William Henry. "Africa's Year," January 5, 1960. Accessed via ProQuest.

Chaudhry, R. Quest for Exceptional Leadership: Mirage to Reality. New Delhi: Response Books, 2011.

Cheeseman, Nic, and Jonathan Fisher. Authoritarian Africa: Repression, Resistance, and the Power of Ideas. Oxford: Oxford University Press, 2021.

Cherry, Kendra. "Leadership Styles." Accessed April 16, 2024. http://psychology.about.com/od/leadership/.

Cherry, Kendra. "Situational Leadership Theory." Available from Verywell Mind. Accessed April 16, 2024.

Chery, Kendra. "The Major Leadership Theories: The Eight Major Theories of Leadership." Available from Reaching New Heights Foundation. Accessed April 13, 2024.

Chomsky, Noam. "The Responsibility of Intellectuals." In The Essential Chomsky. New York: The New Press, 2017.

Clarke, Walter S., and Robert Gosende. "Somalia: Can a Collapsed State Reconstitute Itself?" In State Failure and State Weakness in a Time of Terror, edited by Robert I. Rotberg, 129-158. Washington: Brookings Institution Press, 2003.

Clawson, James G. "General Model of Leadership in Organizations: A Diamond in the Rough." SSRN Electronic Journal, June 2009. https://www.researchgate.net/publication/228144633 (accessed April 26, 2024).

Constitution of Medina, article 16. Available from https://static1.squarespace.com/static/5097fe39e4b0c49016e4c58b/t/5c8153ee-ec212d7117477f8f/1551979503244/Constitution-Medina.pdf. Accessed April 19, 2024.

Contini, Paolo. The Somali Republic: An Experiment in Legal Integration. London: F. Cass & Company, 1969.

Crick, Bernard. In Defence of Politics. University of Chicago Press, 1972.

Cunliffe, Ann L., and Matthew Eriksen. "Relational Leadership." Human Relations 64, no. 11 (2011): 1426–1449.

Chen, Jing. Useful Complaints: How Petitions Assist Decentralized Authoritarianism in China. New York: Lexington Books, 2016.

Dasgupta, Rajashree. "Main Features of a Traditional Society." Available from https://www.govtgirlsekbalpur.com/Study_Materials/Geography/GEOG_PART_II_HONS_Main_Features_of_a_Traditional_Society.pdf.

De Oliveira, Márcio S. B. S. "Modernity and Modernization." Available from Modernità%20S.%20Eisenstadt%20Modernity%20and%20Modernization%20(1).pdf.

Del Boca, Angelo. "The Myths, Suppressions, Denials, and Defaults of Italian Colonialism." In A Place in the Sun: Africa in Italian Colonial Culture from Post-Unification to the Present, edited by Patrizia Palumbo, 17–37. Berkeley: University of California Press, 2003.

Diamond, Larry. Political Culture and Democracy in Developing Countries. Lynne Rienner Publisher, 1994.

Durkheim, Emile. The Division of Labour in Society. Translated by W. D. Halls. New York: Free Press, 1997.

Easton, David. The Political System: An Inquiry into the State of Political Science. Chicago: University of Chicago Press, 1981.

Eagly, Alice H., and Shelly Chaiken. The Psychology of Attitudes. Belmont, USA: Wadsworth, 1993.

Eisenstadt, S. N. "Multiple Modernities." Daedalus 129, no. 1 (2000). http://www.jstor.org/stable/20027613. Accessed February 18, 2024.

Europa Publications Limited. The Middle East and North Africa. Volumes 5-17. London: Europa Publications, 1961, 909.

Evans, Peter. Embedded Autonomy: States and Industrial Transformation. Princeton: Princeton University Press, 1995.

Farah, Ibrahim. "Foreign Policy and Conflict in Somalia, 1960-1990." PhD diss., University of Nairobi, 2009.

Fishel, John T. Civil Military Operations in the New World. Westport, CT: Praeger, 1997.

Fleenor, John W. "Trait Approach to Leadership." In Encyclopedia of Industrial and Organizational Psychology, 830–832. Thousand Oaks, CA: Sage Publications, 2006.

Fox, M. J. The Roots of Somali Political Culture. Boulder, CO: Lynne Rienner Publishers, 2015.

Freeman, C. "Colonialism is No Longer an Excuse for Africa's Failure." Sunday View, June 20, 2010. Accessed July 20, 2010. http://www.zimbabwesituation.com/june20_2010.html.

Ghalib, Jama Mohamed. The Cost of Dictatorship: The Somali Experience. L. Barber Press, 1995.

Gambetta, Diego. "Why is Italy Disproportionately Corrupt? A Conjecture." In Institutions, Governance, and the Control of Corruption, edited by Kaushik Basu and Tito Gordella. London: Palgrave Macmillan, 2018.

Gil, Manuel Manrique. "1960–2010: 50 Years of 'African Independences.'" On Africa, January 4, 2010.

Ginsborg, Paul. "The Italian Political Culture in Historical Perspective." Modern Italy 1, no. 1 (1995).

Goldziher, Ignaz. Muslim Studies, vol. 1. London: George Allen & Unwin Ltd., 1910.

Gordon, Ruth. "Growing Constitutions." University of Pennsylvania Journal of Constitutional Law 1 (1999): 528-569. Accessed April 29, 2024. https://scholarship.law.upenn.edu/jcl/vol1/iss3/3.

Greenleaf, Robert K. On Becoming a Servant-Leader. San Francisco: Jossey-Bass Publishers, 1996.

Greenleaf, Robert K. Servant Leadership: A Journey into the Nature of Legitimate Power and Greatness. New York: Paulist Press, 1977.

Grew, R. "Modernization and Its Discontents." Accessed April 15, 2024. https://deepblue.lib.umich.edu/bitstream/handle/2027.42/6702 2/10.1177_000276427702100208.pdf;sequence=2.

Hansen, Stig Jarle. Al-Shabaab in Somalia: The History and Ideology of a Militant Islamist Group. London: Hurst and Company, 2016.

Haggard, Stephen. Pathways from the Periphery. Ithaca, NY: Cornell University Press, 1990.

Hamish Ion and Elizabeth Jane Errington, eds. Great Powers and Little Wars: The Limits of Power. London: Bloomsbury Academic, 1993.

Harney, Barbara. "Contingency Theory." In Encyclopedia of Human Resource Management, edited by Steven Johnstone and Adrian Wilkinson, 470. Cheltenham, UK: Edward Elgar, 2023.

Harrison, Catherine. Leadership Theory and Research. Cham: Palgrave Macmillan, 2018.

Harold D. Nelson. Somalia: A Country Study. Washington: U.S. Government Printing Office, 1982.

Helen Chapin Metz, ed. Somalia: A Country Study. Washington: GPO for the Library of Congress, 1992.

Hess, Robert L. Italian Colonialism in Somalia. Chicago: University of Chicago Press, 1966.

Higley, John. Elite Theory in Political Sociology. Austin, TX: The University of Texas at Austin, 2008.

Hofmann, Murad Wilfried. "On the Role of Muslim Intellectuals." Accessed April 16, 2024. file:///C/ojsadmin,+AJISS+14-3-2+Reflections.pdf.

Hoffmann, Paul. "Bunche says '60 is the Year of Africa." New York Times, February 16, 1960. Accessed via ProQuest.

Hodgkin, Thomas. Nationalism in Colonial Africa. London: Frederick Muller, 1956.

Hogman, Tobias. "Stabilization, Extraversion, and Political Settlement in Somalia." The Rift Valley Institute, 2016.

Howitt, B., and R. Julian. Society and Culture. 2nd ed. Sydney: Heinemann, 2009.

Humaans. "Participative Leadership: Meaning and Best Practices." Accessed April 13, 2024. Retrieved from Humaans.io.

Huntington, Samuel. The Change to Change: Modernization, Development, and Politics. New York: Free Press, 1976.

Hussein, Abdirizak Haji. My Role in the Foundation of the Somali Nation-State: A Political

Memoir. Edited by Abdisalam Ise-Salwe. Trenton, NJ: The Red Sea Press, 2017.

Hussein, Asaf. Political Perspective on the Muslim World. New York: Praeger, 1981.

Ibn Khaldun. The Muqaddimah: An Introduction to History. Princeton: Princeton University Press, 1980.

Ingiriis, Mohamed Haji. The Suicidal State in Somalia: The Rise and Fall of the Siad Barre Regime, 1969-1991. Lanham, MD: University Press of America, 2016.

Ingiriis, Mohamed Haji. "The Making of the 1990 Manifesto: Somalia's Last Chance for State Survival." Northeast African Studies 12, no. 2 (2012).

Ingiriis, Mohamed Haji. "Who Assassinated the Somali President in October 1969? The Cold War, the Clan Connection or Coup d'État." African Security 10, no. 2 (2017): 131–154.

Interpeace. History of Mediation in Somalia Since 1988. Research for Peace Program.

IMSA Leadership Education and Development. "Great Man Theory." Accessed April 13, 2024. Available from IMSA.

Inglehart, Ronald. Culture Shift in Advanced Industrial Society. Princeton: Princeton University Press, 1990.

Isernia, Pierangelo, and Danilo Di Mauro. "The Bumble-Bee is Still Flying: Italian Political Culture at 50." Accessed April 13, 2024. https://en.idi.org.il/media/6383/bythepeople_iserniadimauro.pdf.

Jaafar, Syaiful Baharee, Noraihan Mamat Zambi, and Nor Fathimah Fathil. "Leadership Style: Is it Autocratic, Democratic, or Laissez-Faire?" ASEAN Journal of Management and Business Studies 3, no. 1 (2021): 1–7.

Jackson, R. H., and C. G. Rosberg. "Sovereignty and Underdevelopment: Juridical Statehood in the African Crisis." The Journal of Modern African Studies 24, no. 1 (1986): 1–31.

Jaqua, Emily E. "Transactional Leadership." American Journal of Biomedical Science & Research 14, no. 5 (2021): 399–400.

Johnson, David (dit). A Historical Companion to Postcolonial Literatures – Continental Europe and Its Empires. Edinburgh: Edinburgh University Press, 2008.

Johnson, Hannah. "Authentic Leadership Theory: The State of Science on Honest Leaders." Technology and Management 5, no. 12 (2016). Available from IJSTM. Accessed April 12, 2024.

Josef, Dan, and Harun Maruf. Inside al-Shabaab: The Secret History of al-Qaida's Most Powerful Ally. Bloomington, IN: Indiana University Press, 2021.

Kaly, Kieth George, and Ida Rousseau Mukenge. Zones of Conflict in Africa: Theories and Cases. Westport, CT: Praeger, 2002.

Kamrava, Mehran. Understanding Comparative Politics: A Framework for Analysis. London: Routledge, 1996.

Kanodia, Rekha, and Arun Sacher. "Trait Theories of Leadership." International Journal of Science.

Karpova, Anna Yu. "The Political Role of Intellectuals." June 2016. Accessed April 15, 2024. https://www.researchgate.net/.

Kassim, Mohamed M. "Aspects of Banadir Cultural History: The Case of Baravan Ulama." In The Invention of Somalia, edited by Ali Jumale. Red Sea Press, 1995.

Khajeh-Sarvi, A. R. Political Competition and Political Stability in Iran. Tehran: Revolution Documents Center Publications, 2003.

Khayre, Ahmed Ali M. "Somalia: An Overview of the Historical and Current Situation." Social Science Research Network, 2016. Accessed April 30, 2024. https://www.academia.edu/24800571/.

Kerr, Euan. "Former Somali Prime Minister Abdirizak Haji Hussein Dies." MPR News, St. Paul, Minn., February 1, 2014.

Kohli, Atul. "State, Society, and Development." In Political Science: The State of the Discipline, edited by Ira Katznelson and Helen Milner, 84–117. New York: W. W. Norton, 2002.

Kouzes, James, and Barry Posner. The Leadership Challenge: How to Make Extraordinary Things Happen in Organizations. 6th ed. Hoboken, NJ: John Wiley & Sons, 2017.

Laitin, David D. "The Political Economy of Military Rule in Somalia." The Journal of Modern African Studies 14, no. 3 (1976): 449–468.

Laitin, David. Politics, Language, and Thought: The Somali Experience. Chicago: The University of Chicago Press, 1977.

Laitin, David, and Said Samatar. Somalia: Nation in Search of a State. Boulder, CO: Westview Press, 1987.

Lasswell, Harold. Politics: Who Gets What, When, and How? Chicago: Meridian Books, 1951.

Lenin, V. I. Collected Works. September 1903 – December 1904. Moscow: Progress Publishers, 1965.

Levy, Marion. Social Patterns and Problems of Modernization. Englewood Cliffs, NJ: Prentice-Hall, 1967.

Lewis, I. M. A Modern History of Somalia: Nation and State in the Horn of Africa. Rev. ed. Boulder, CO: Westview Press, 1988.

Lewis, I. M. A Modern History of the Somali: Revised, Updated & Expanded. 4th ed. Athens, OH: Ohio University Press, 2002.

Lewis, I. M. A Pastoral Democracy: A Study of Pastoralism and Politics Among the Northern Somali of the Horn of Africa. Münster: LIT Verlag, 1999.

Lewis, I. M. Blood and Bone: The Call of Kinship in Somali Society. Lawrenceville, NJ: Red Sea Press, 1994.

Lewis, I. M. Saints, and Somalis: Popular Islam in Clan-based Society. Lawrenceville, NJ: The Red Sea Press, 1998.

Lewis, I. M. "Force and Fission in Northern Somali Lineage Structure." American Anthropologist.

Lewis, I. M. "The Politics of 1969 Somali Coup." The Journal of Modern African Studies. 10: 3(1972).

Lerner, Daniel. The Passing of Traditional Society: Modernizing the Middle East. Glencoe, IL: Free Press, 1958.

Lijphart, Arend. Democracies: Patterns of Majoritarian and Consensus Government in Twenty-One Countries. New Haven, CT: Yale University Press, 1984.

Lyons, Terrence, and Ahmed Samatar. Somalia: State Collapse, Multilateral Intervention, and Strategies for Political Reconstruction. Washington, DC: The Brookings Institution, 1995.

Luthra, Suresh. "Effective Leadership is All About Communicating Effectively: Connecting Leadership and Communication." International Journal of Education and Research 5, no. 3 (2015): 43–48.

Mansur, Abdulla. "Contrary to a Nation: The Cancer of Somali State." In The Invention of Somalia, edited by Ali Jimale, 114. Lawrenceville, NJ: Red Sea Press, 1995.

Mandangu, E. T. C. "Leadership Can Build or Destroy a State." Social Sciences, Leadership, Nationalism, and State Building. Accessed April 14, 2024. https://www.academia.edu/9854728/Leadership_can_build_or_destroy_a_state.

Mansur, Abdalla Omar. "Contrary to a Nation: The Cancer of the Somali State." In The Invention of Somalia, edited by Ali Jumale, 107–116. Red Sea Press, 1995.

Macionis, John J., and Linda Marie Gerber. Sociology. Toronto: Pearson Prentice Hall, 2011.

Mapuva, Jephias, and Freeman Chari. "Colonialism No Longer an Excuse for Africa's Failure." Journal of Sustainable Development in Africa 12, no. 5 (2010).

Marsai, Victor. Somali Elections 2016-2017: Business as Usual or New Hope? National University of Public Service, July 2017.

Martin, B.G. Shaykh Uways Bin Mouhammad Al-Barawi: A Traditional Somali Sufi. Indiana: Indiana University Press, 1999.

Martin, Roger. "Relationship as a Core of Effective Leadership." Low Intensity Conflict & Law Enforcement 13, no. 1 (2013): 76.

Mazrui, Ali A. "Crisis in Somalia: From Tyranny to Anarchy." In Mending Rips in the Sky: Options for Somali Communities in the 21st Century, Adam and Ford edited 5–12. Lawrenceville: The Red Sea Press, 1997.

Mazuri, A. A. "From Social Darwinism to Current Theories of Modernization: A Tradition of Analysis." World Politics 21, no. 1 (October 1968): 69–83.

Mbandlwa, Zamokuhle. "Challenges of African Leadership after the Independence." Solid State Technology, December 2020. Accessed April 26, 2024. https://www.researchgate.net/publication/346972230.

McArthur, Douglas. Quotes. Accessed April 3, 2024. https://www.goodreads.com/quotes/359193-a-true-leader-has-the-confidence-to-stand-alone-the.

McGregor, Andrew. "The Muslim Brotherhood in Somalia: An Interview with Islah Movement's Abdurahman M. Abdullahi (Baadiyow)." Terrorism Monitor 9, no. 30 (July 29, 2011).

Meier, Dirk. "Situational Leadership Theory as a Foundation for a Blended Learning Framework." Journal of Education and Practice 7, no. 10 (2016). Accessed April 12, 2024. Available from IISTE.

Menkhaus, Ken. "US Foreign Assistance Somalia: Phoenix from the Ashes?" Middle Eastern Policy 5 (1997): 126.

Menkhaus, Ken, and John Prendergast. "Governance and Economic Survival in Post-intervention Somalia." CSIS Africa Note, no. 172 (May 1995).

Metz, Helen Chapin, ed. Somalia: A Country Study. 4th ed. Washington, DC: Library of Congress Cataloging-in-Publication Data, 1992.

Migdal, Joel S. Strong Societies and Weak States: State-Society Relations and State Capabilities in the Third World. Princeton: Princeton University Press, 1988.

Migdal, Joel S. State in Society: Studying How States and Societies Transform and Constitute Each Other. New York: Cambridge University Press, 2001.

Mire, Hassan A. "On Providing for the Future." In The Somali Challenge: From Catastrophe to Renewal, edited by Ahmed Samatar, 23. Boulder, CO: Lynne Rienner Publisher, 1994.

Mohamoud, A. State Collapse and Post-Conflict Development in Africa: The Case of Somalia (1960-2001). 2002. Accessed April 29, 2024. https://pure.uva.nl/ws/files/1061731/48811_UBA002000838_10.pdf.

Mohamud, Mohamed Sharif. "Abdirizaq Haji Hussein, Rais Wasara al-Somali (1964-1967)." 2009.

Morlino, Leonardo, Dirk Berg-Schlosser, and Bertrand Badie. Political Science: A Global Perspective. Sage Publications, 2017.

Muhammad Husayn Haykal. Life of Muhammad. Translated by Isma'il Al-Faruqi. Accessed May 17, 2023. https://muqith.files.wordpress.com/2010/10/muhammadbyhaykal.pdf.

Mukhtar, Mohamed. Historical Dictionary of Somalia: African Historical Dictionary Series, No. 87. New Edition. Lanham, MD: The Scarecrow Press, 2003.

Mukhtar, Mohamed. "Islam in the Somali History: Fact and Fiction." In The Invention of Somalia, edited by Ali Jumale. Red Sea Press, 1995.

Munroe, Trevor. An Introduction to Politics: Lectures for First-Year Students. Jamaica: Canoe Press, 2002.

Noor, Abdirahman Ahmed. "Arabic Language and Script in Somalia: History, Attitudes, and Prospects." Ph.D. diss., Georgetown University, 1999.

Northouse, Peter G. Leadership: Theory and Practice. 3rd ed. London: Sage, 2004.

Okbazghi, Yohannes. The United States and the Horn of Africa: An Analytical Study of Pattern and Process. Westview Press, 1997.

Olatunbosun, T. O. "The Characteristics of Exceptional Leaders." Accessed April 15, 2024. https://www.academia.edu/9381172/The_Characteristic_of_Exceptional_Leaders.

Omar, Mohamed Omar. The Road to Zero: Somalia's Self-Destruction. London: Haan Associates, 1993.

Omar, Mohamed Osman. Somalia: A Nation Driven to Despair: A Case of Leadership Failure. Mogadishu: Somali Publications, 2002.

Omar, Mohamed Osman. The Scramble in the Horn of Africa: History of Somalia (1827-1977). Mogadishu: Somali Publications, 1980.

Omar, Hussein. "Somalia: Former Somali Prime Minister Abdirizak Haji Hussein Died in the USA." Raxanreeb. Accessed April 29, 2024. https://en.wikipedia.org/wiki/Abdirizak_Haji_Hussein.

O'Neil, Patrick H. Essentials of Comparative Politics. New York: W.W. Norton & Company, 2010.

Owusu, Maxwell. Colonial and Postcolonial Anthropology of Africa: Scholarship or Sentiment? Published by De Gruyter Mouton, 1979.

Palumbo, Patrizia, ed. A Place in the Sun: Africa in Italian Colonial Culture from Post-Unification to the Present. Berkeley: University of California Press, 2003.

Pankhurst, Sylvia. Ex-Italian Somaliland. London: Watts & Co., 1951.

Pastaloza, Luigi. The Somali Revolution. Bari: Edition Afrique Asie Amerique Latine, 1973.

Patterson, Orlando. "Making Sense of Culture." The Annual Review of Sociology 40 (2014): 1–21.

Pietro Pastorelli. "Italy's Accession to the United Nations Organization." Accessed July 1, 2024. https://www.diplomatie.gouv.fr/IMG/pdf/ONU_pietro_pastorelli.pdf.

Plato. The Republic. Tehran: Cultural and Scientific Publications, 1995.

Poddar, Prem, and David Johnson, eds. A Historical Companion to Postcolonial Thought in English. Columbia University Press, 2007.

Posusney, Marsha Pripstein, and Michele Penner Angrist, eds. Authoritarianism in the Middle East: Regimes and Resistance. London: Lynne Rienner Publishers, 2005.

Pratt, Nicola. Democracy and Authoritarianism in the Arab World. London: Lynne Rienner Publishers, 2006.

Prewitt, K., and A. Stone. "The Ruling Elite." In Power in Modern Societies, edited by M.E. Olsen and M.N. Marger, 143–168. Boulder: Westview Press, 1993.

Purohit, Raveen. "Review on Study of Behavioral Approach to Leadership." International Journal of Scientific and Research Publications 11, no. 1 (January 2021).

Putnam, Robert. "Studying Elite Political Culture: The Case of 'Ideology.'" The American Political Science Review 65, no. 3 (September 1971): 651–681.

Rawson, David. "Dealing with Disintegration: US Assistance and Somali State." In The Somali Challenge: From Catastrophe to Renewal?, edited by Ahmed Samatar, 147–178. London: Lynne Rienner Publishers, 1994.

Rehman, Scheherazade S., and Hossein Askari. "How Islamic are Islamic Countries?" Global Economy Journal 10, no. 2 (2010): 1–40. Islamicity Index. Accessed April 12, 2024.

Report of the Secretary-General on the Situation in Somalia. United Nations S/2001/963. Available from Distr.: General, October 11, 2001. Accessed April 29, 2024.

Reviglio della Veneria, M. "The United Nations, Italy and Somalia: A 'Sui Generis' Relation 1948-1969." MA thesis, Utrecht Universiteit, 2014.

Ria Story. Leaders Are Like Diamonds. Topstoryleadership.com, 2017.

Riemann, Andrew. Introduction to Culture Studies: Introductory Activities for Exploring and Comparing Cultures. Intergraphica Press, 2013.

Robert, Jackson, and C.G. Rosberg. Personal Rule in Black Africa. University of California Press, 1982.

Rotberg, Robert I. The Failure and Collapse of Nation-States: Breakdown, Prevention, and Repair. Accessed February 16, 2024. https://assets.press.princeton.edu/chapters/s7666.pdf.

Rotberg, Robert I. Nation-State Failure: A Recurrence Phenomenon? Washington, DC: Brookings Institution Press, 2003.

Rotberg, Robert I. State Failure and State Weakness in a Time of Terror. Washington, DC: Brookings Institution Press, 2003.

Rotberg, Robert I. "Failed States, Collapsed States, Weak States: Causes and Indicators." Accessed April 5, 2024. https://www.brookings.edu/wp-content/uploads/2016/07/statefailureandstateweaknessinatimeofterror_chapter.pdf.

Rustow, Dankwart A. A World of Nations. Washington, DC: Brookings Institution, 1967.

"Former Somali Prime Minister Laid to Rest in a Mogadishu Cemetery." Horseed Media. Accessed April 29, 2024.

Salwe, Abdisalam. "The Failure of The Daraawiish State, The Clash Between Somali Clanship and State System." Paper presented at the 5th International Congress of Somali Studies, December 1993.

Samatar, Abdi. Africa's First Democrats: Somalia's Adan A. Osman and Abdirizak H. Hussein. Bloomington: Indiana University Press, 2016.

Samatar, Ahmed. Socialist Somalia: Rhetoric and Reality. London: Zed Press, 1988.

Samatar, Ahmed. "The Curse of Allah: Civic Disembowelment and the Collapse of the State in Somalia." In The Somali Challenge: From Catastrophe to Renewal?, edited by Ahmed Samatar, 117. Boulder, CO: Lynne Rienner Publishers, 1994.

Samatar, Said. "Sheikh Uways Muhammad of Baraawe, 1847–1909: Mystic and Reformer in East Africa." In Shadows of Conquest: Islam in Colonial Northeast Africa, edited by Said S. Samatar, 199–224. Trenton, NJ: The Red Sea Press, 1992.

Samatar, Said. "Unhappy Masses and the Challenges of Political Islam in the Horn of Africa." Accessed February 2, 2017. www.wardheer-news.com/March_05/05.

Sanchez Cardenas, Manuel Andres. "Ethnic and Cultural Homogeneity: An Obstacle for Development?" Northeastern University, Fall 2019.

Sesay, Amadu. The African Union: Forward March or About Face-Turn? Uppsala: Universitetstryckeriet, 2008

Shahin, Amany I. "Powerful Insights of Authentic Leadership." International Review of Management and Business Research 9, no. 1 (March 2020).

Sheikh, Mohamed Aden. Back to Mogadishu: Memoirs of a Somali Herder. Barkin Publishing, 2021.

Shonhiwa, D. C. "An Examination of the Situational Leadership Approach: Strengths and Weaknesses." Crosscurrents: International Peer-Reviewed Journal on Humanities & Social Sciences 2, no. 2 (2016): 35–40.

Sinno, Niam. "A Behavioral Approach to Understanding Leadership Effectiveness." Master's thesis, Harvard Extension School, 2018.

Smelser, Neil Joseph. Toward a Theory of Modernization. New York: Basic Books, 1964, 268–274.

Smith Hempstone. The New Africa. London: Faber and Faber, 1961.

Soroush, Abdolkarim. "The Responsibilities of the Muslim Intellectual in the 21st Century." January 30, 2005. Accessed April 15, 2024. https://nawaat.org/2005/01/30/the-responsibilities-of-the-muslim-intellectual-in-the-21st-century/.

Sumner, William Graham. Folkways: A Study of Mores, Manners, Customs, and Morals. Cosimo Classics, 2007.

The United Nations Economic and Social Commission for Asia and the Pacific. "Good Governance." Accessed March 24, 2024. https://www.unescap.org/sites/default/files/good-governance.pdf.

"The Majeerteen Sultanates." Accessed July 1, 2024. http://www.mudugonline.com/MajertainSaltanates/Sultanate.htm.

Tipps, Dean C. "Modernization Theory and the Comparative Study of Societies: A Critical Perspective." Comparative Studies in Society and History 15, no. 2 (March 1973): 199–266.

Touval, Saadia. Somali Nationalism: International Politics and the Drive for Unity in the Horn of Africa. Cambridge: Cambridge University Press, 1963.

Touval, Saadia. "The Organization of African Unity and Borders." International Organization 21, no. 1 (1967).

Tripodi, Paola. "Back to the Horn: Italian Administration and Somalia's Troubled Independence." The International Journal of African Historical Studies 32, no. 2–3 (1999): 359–380.

Tripodi, Paolo. The Colonial Legacy in Somalia: Rome and Mogadishu: From Colonial Administration to Operation Restore Hope. Palgrave Macmillan, 1999.

Trunji, Mohamed Isse. Somalia: The Untold History (1941–1969). Looh Press, 2015.

Trunji, Mohamed Isse. President Adan Abdulla: His Life & Legacy. Looh Press, 2023.

Trunji, Mohamed. "A Haitian Diplomat Who Openly Defied His Government to Support the Somali Cause at the UN." November 23, 2022. Accessed April 3, 2024. https://www.hiiraan.com/op4/2022/nov/188832/haitian_diplomat_who_openly_defied_his_government_to_support_the_somali_cause_at_the_un.aspx.

Tylor, Edward. Primitive Culture. Vol. 1. New York: J.P. Putnam's Sons, 1871.

Tareke, Gebru. "The Ethiopia-Somalia War Revisited." International Journal of African Historical Studies 33, no. 3 (2000): 615–34.

United Nations. Draft Trusteeship Agreement for the Territory of Somaliland under Italian Administration: Special Report of the Trusteeship Council. General Assembly Official Records: Fifth Session, Supplement No. 10 (A/1294). Lake Success, New York, 1950.

United Nations Economic and Social Commission for Asia and the Pacific. "What is Good Governance?" Accessed April 16, 2024. https://www.unescap.org/sites/default/files/good-governance.pdf.

Vroom, Victor H., and Arthur G. Jago. "The Role of the Situation in Leadership." The American Psychologist 62, no. 1 (2007): 17–24.

Ware, Gilbert. "Somalia: From Trust Territory to Nation, 1950-1960." Phylon 26, no. 2 (2nd Quarter, 1965): 173–185.

Watsumoto, David, and Linda Juang. Culture and Psychology. Jon-David Hague Publisher, 2013.

Weber, Max. Economy and Society: An Outline of Interpretive Sociology. Berkeley, CA: University of California Press, 1922.

Weber, Max. The Theory of Social and Economic Organization. New York: Oxford University Press, 1943.

Webersik, Christian. "Mogadishu: An Economy without a State." Third World Quarterly 27, no. 8 (November 2006): 1463–1480.

Wright, Erik. Approaches to Class Analysis. Cambridge: Cambridge University Press, 2005.

Yihdego, Zeray W. "Ethiopia's Military Action against the Union of Islamic Courts and Others in Somalia: Some Legal Implications." The International and Comparative Law Quarterly 56, no. 3 (July 2007): 666–676.

Zhang, Yang. "Rethinking Trait Theory Analysis of the Impacts of Trait Level on Leadership." In Advances in Economics, Business, and Management Research 231, edited by H. Mallick et al., 852–857. Atlantis Press, 2023.

Zarate, Rodrigo A. "What Followers Want from Their Leaders: An Analytical Perspective." December 2009. Accessed April 16, 2024. https://www.researchgate.net/publication/262431070_What_Followers_Want_from_Their_Leaders_An_Analytical_Perspective.

INDEX

www.ingramcontent.com/pod-product-compliance
Lightning Source LLC
Chambersburg PA
CBHW031115020426
42333CB00012B/98